OVERHAUL

OVERHAUL

AN INSIDER'S ACCOUNT OF THE
OBAMA ADMINISTRATION'S
EMERGENCY RESCUE
OF THE AUTO INDUSTRY

Steven Rattner

HOUGHTON MIFFLIN HARCOURT
BOSTON   NEW YORK
2010

www.hmhbooks.com

Library of Congress Cataloging-in-Publication Data
Rattner, Steven.
Overhaul : an insider's account of the Obama administration's emergency
rescue of the auto industry / Steven Rattner.
p. cm.
Includes index.
ISBN 978-0-547-44321-8
1. Automobile industry and trade — Government policy — United States.
2. Bankruptcy — Government policy — United States. 3. Industrial policy —
United States. 4. United States — Economic policy — 2009- I. Title.
HD9710.U52R38 2010
338.4'76292220973 — dc22   2010033188

Book design by Melissa Lotfy

Printed in the United States of America

DOC 10 9 8 7 6 5 4 3 2 1

FOR MAUREEN

Contents

Cast of Characters

TEAM AUTO (*U.S. Treasury, unless otherwise noted*)
RON A. BLOOM
CLAY CALHOON
BRIAN DEESE (National Economic Council)
DIANA FARRELL (National Economic Council)
MATTHEW FELDMAN
ROBERT FRASER
SADIQ MALIK
DAVID MARKOWITZ
PAUL NATHANSON
BRIAN OSIAS
STEVEN RATTNER
BRIAN STERN
HALEY STEVENS
HARRY WILSON

ADVISERS TO AND STAKEHOLDERS IN CHRYSLER

ALFREDO ALTAVILLA, in charge of Fiat power-train technologies
STEPHEN FEINBERG, managing partner of Cerberus Capital Management
(owner of Chrysler)
ANDREW HORROCKS, former managing director of UBS (adviser to Fiat)
THOMAS LAURIA, partner of White & Case (counsel to certain Chrysler
senior lenders)
JAMES "JIMMY" LEE JR., vice chairman of JPMorgan Chase (Chrysler
senior lender)

Robert Manzo, executive director of Capstone Advisory Group (adviser to Chrysler)

Sergio Marchionne, CEO of Fiat; later appointed CEO of Chrysler (since June 2009)

ADVISERS TO TEAM AUTO

Xavier Mosquet, senior partner of Boston Consulting Group

John Rapisardi, partner of Cadwalader, Wickersham & Taft (counsel)

Todd Snyder, managing director of Rothschild

John "Jack" Welch Jr., former chairman and CEO of General Electric

BUSH PERIOD

Joshua Bolten, White House chief of staff

Carlos Gutierrez, secretary of Commerce

Keith Hennessey, director of the National Economic Council

Dan Jester, Treasury contractor

Joel Kaplan, White House deputy chief of staff for policy

Henry "Hank" Paulson, secretary of the Treasury

Joshua Steiner, Obama transition adviser

CANADA

Paul Boothe, senior associate deputy minister of Industry Canada

CHRYSLER

Robert Kidder, chairman (since June 2009)

Ronald Kolka, CFO

Thomas LaSorda, copresident

Robert Nardelli, chairman and CEO

James Press, co-president

CONGRESS

Sen. Robert Corker (R-Tennessee)

Sen. Christopher Dodd (D-Connecticut)

Rep. Barney Frank (D-Massachusetts)

Rep. Steny Hoyer (D-Maryland), House majority leader
Sen. Mitchell McConnell (R-Kentucky), Senate minority leader
Rep. Nancy Pelosi (D-California), Speaker of the House
Sen. Harry Reid (D-Nevada) Senate majority leader
Sen. Charles Schumer (D-New York)

FINANCIAL REGULATORS

Scott Alvarez, general counsel of the Federal Reserve Board
Sheila Bair, chairman of the Federal Deposit Insurance Corporation
Ben Bernanke, chairman of the Federal Reserve Board
Roberta McInerney, deputy general counsel of the Federal Deposit
    Insurance Corporation
Christopher Spoth, senior deputy director for supervisory examina-
    tions at the Federal Deposit Insurance Corporation

FORD

Lewis Booth, CFO
William "Bill" Ford Jr., executive chairman
Alan Mulally, CEO
Ziad Ojakli, group vice president of government and community relations

GENERAL MOTORS

Daniel Akerson, CEO (as of September 2010)
David Bonderman, director
Troy Clarke, president of GM North America
Kenneth Cole, vice president of global public policy and government
    relations
Gary Cowger, group vice president of global manufacturing and labor
    relations
Nicholas Cyprus, controller and chief accounting officer
George Fisher, lead director (until July 2009)
Stephen Girsky, director; later appointed vice chairman of corporate
    strategy and business development
Frederick "Fritz" Henderson, COO; later appointed CEO
    (March–December 2009)

KENT KRESA, director and interim chairman (March–July 2009)

MARK LANEVE, vice president of sales and marketing of GM North America

PHILIP LASKAWY, director

CHRISTOPHER LIDDELL, CFO (since January 2010)

ROBERT LUTZ, vice chairman and responsible for global product development

KATHRYN MARINELLO, director

PATRICIA RUSSO, lead director

JOHN SMITH, group vice president of corporate planning and alliances

CAROL STEPHENSON, director

G. RICHARD WAGONER, chairman and CEO (until March 2009)

EDWARD WHITACRE, chairman (July 2009 to December 2010) and CEO (December 2009 to September 2010)

RAY YOUNG, CFO; later appointed vice president of GM International Operations

MICHIGAN POLITICIANS

DAVID BING (D), mayor of the city of Detroit

REP. JOHN DINGELL (D)

GOV. JENNIFER GRANHOLM (D)

SEN. CARL LEVIN (D)

REP. SANDER LEVIN (D)

SEN. DEBORAH STABENOW (D)

OTHERS

ALVARO "AL" DE MOLINA, CEO of GMAC

CARLOS GHOSN, CEO of Renault-Nissan

JOHN MCELENEY, chairman of National Automobile Dealers Association

TREASURY DEPARTMENT

STEPHANIE CUTTER, chief spokesperson

JENNI ENGEBRETSEN LECOMPTE, spokesperson

KENNETH FEINBERG, special master for TARP executive compensation

TIMOTHY GEITHNER, secretary of the Treasury

ALAN KRUEGER, assistant secretary for economic policy

MARK PATTERSON, chief of staff

GENE SPERLING, counselor to the secretary of the Treasury

UNITED AUTO WORKERS

RON GETTELFINGER, president

GENERAL HOLIEFIELD, vice president and director of Chrysler department

BOB KING, vice president and director of Ford department; later elected president

CAL RAPSON, vice president and director of General Motors department

ANDREW YEARLEY, managing director of Lazard (UAW's financial adviser)

U.S. BANKRUPTCY COURT, SOUTHERN DISTRICT OF NEW YORK

JUDGE ROBERT GERBER, oversaw the bankruptcy proceedings of General Motors

JUDGE ARTHUR GONZALEZ, oversaw the bankruptcy proceedings of Chrysler

WHITE HOUSE

DAVID AXELROD, senior adviser to the President

RAHM EMANUEL, chief of staff

ROBERT GIBBS, press secretary

AUSTAN GOOLSBEE, member of the Council of Economic Advisers

CHRISTINA ROMER, chair of the Council of Economic Advisers

LAWRENCE SUMMERS, director of the National Economic Council

OVERHAUL

PROLOGUE

THE OVAL OFFICE has no proper waiting room, only a small anteroom in which President Obama's "body person," Reggie Love, and his secretary, Katie Johnson, are usually seated. Against the wall is a small TV, normally used to monitor news channels. But on this Sunday evening near the end of March 2009, it was tuned to the Arnold Palmer Invitational golf tournament, where Tiger Woods (then still heroic) was making a long-awaited return from knee surgery.

A few minutes before 7:30 a handful of us from the President's auto industry task force had followed chief economic adviser Larry Summers down a narrow flight of red-carpeted stairs and along a short corridor to this room. We'd spent the past hour in the rabbit warren of offices on the second floor of the West Wing, reviewing once more the key documents for a nationally televised announcement President Obama was to make the next day, the seventieth of his presidency. For Obama, this would be among his first major public actions; for our little task force, it was the point of no return.

Since the task force's hasty formation in February, we had been meeting with General Motors and Chrysler, both of which were being fed intravenously with taxpayers' cash. Dozens of consultants, investment bankers, and other outside experts had presented their views, and the question of what the government should do with the struggling automakers had been debated extensively up the administration chain of command. Finally, in tense meetings at the White House a few days before, the President had made his decisions. Those decisions had remained secret until now; tonight he would call the Michigan lawmakers to alert them to what he was planning to say the next day.

The President hadn't come downstairs from his living quarters yet, giving us a few minutes to root for Tiger's comeback—for me, a welcome distraction from worrying about whether our plans for the largest government intervention in industrial America since World War II could work. We had had only five frenzied weeks to prepare for this moment. One more time I mentally reviewed those plans, which included additional billions in taxpayer funding for General Motors and Chrysler and several other controversial and risky measures. What could go wrong? I'd asked myself over and over. As a prime mixer of the strong medicine that the President was about to administer, I was sure that if disaster ensued, all eyes would be on me.

In particular, I worried about the much-discussed prospect of putting the automakers into "controlled bankruptcy," a radical approach that defied conventional wisdom. While the President's speech the next day would leave open the possibility that bankruptcies might be avoided, I knew that the mere mention of it—let alone actually taking the step—risked imploding the auto companies, crippling thousands of related businesses, vaporizing millions of jobs, and intensifying what was already a deep recession across the Midwest. With America in the midst of the worst financial crisis since the Great Depression, this was no hyperbole: the failure of the auto companies could endanger the economy in ways that were almost too frightening to contemplate.

The President arrived a few minutes late (Tiger was playing a particularly crucial hole), dressed in khakis and a black zippered jacket. I was not surprised that he was wearing casual clothes—I had on khakis myself. Since President Obama's arrival in the White House, shirtsleeves had become the Oval Office norm, and on weekends almost anything went—even T-shirts and jeans worn by unshaven, sockless men.

While his dress was informal, the President's mood was resolute. He had the air of a man in the business of calmly executing his decisions, not second-guessing them. After he'd chatted briefly with Reggie about the golf match, we followed him into the Oval Office, where he sat behind his desk, bare but for a folder of talking points for his calls.

Katie dialed him first into a conference line on which four lawmakers awaited: Michigan's two senators and two of its congressmen. Delegations from our task force had been meeting regularly with them—tense, often testy sessions in which we were lectured about the importance of helping this critical industry.

We clustered around a phone across the room from the President's desk, by the armchair in front of the fireplace where he sat during meetings. Katie had activated the phone's speaker so we would all be able to listen in, but it barely functioned — probably installed by a "well-connected government contractor," the President joked.

He worked through his talking points, fluidly detailing the next day's announcements. Then he paused to let the legislators speak. John Dingell, the longest-serving member of the House of Representatives in history, was gracious and statesmanlike. The others were audibly on edge, although considerably more polite and restrained in conversation with the President than they had been in their meetings with us.

Congressman Sander Levin seemed to interpret the President's allusions to bankruptcy for GM and Chrysler as just a negotiating tactic. "I understand that you have to refer to bankruptcy to get people to the table," he began.

The President interrupted in a measured tone: "I don't want you to leave with that impression. I'm telling you that because it's a real possibility."

At this, a chorus of anxious voices crackled through the speaker. Senator Debbie Stabenow urged that if the President was going to send such a tough message, he ought to couple it with a strong statement of support for the auto industry. Senator Levin beseeched him not to use a broad brush in criticizing the companies and to acknowledge the progress that they had made.

The President listened carefully. When he brought the call to a close after about thirty minutes, he asked Larry to take another look at the speech. By the following morning we'd responded by sanding down the criticism of the companies and adding the "Cash for Clunkers" program to bolster car sales.

The next call was to Governor Jennifer Granholm of Michigan. I'd gotten to know her as an energetic, dynamic candidate during her 2006 campaign, but Michigan was suffering the nation's highest unemployment rate, and in our more recent conversations she'd seemed beaten down and demoralized. Now, as she listened to the President outline his plans, her spirits seemed to fall further and her voice barely rose above a whisper.

"I hope you know what you're doing," she said softly.

During the final call, Ron Gettelfinger, head of the United Auto Workers, who had been defiant the previous autumn when Detroit first asked for federal help, was low-key and respectful now. This augured well for the tough discussions we knew we needed to have with him.

When his calls were completed, the President walked out of the Oval Office and back to the small TV, to learn that Tiger had hit a birdie putt on the eighteenth hole to win. Tiger's day may have ended, but for the task force, a night of work was just beginning.

1

DEAD MAN'S CURVE

FOUR MONTHS EARLIER, on the day before Thanksgiving, I was about to leave my office to take one of my sons to a matinee of *Speed-the-Plow* on Broadway when the phone rang. It was Larry Summers, who'd just been named chief economic adviser to Barack Obama, the President-elect. "I'm calling with a hypothetical question," Larry said. "If you were asked to take on a six- to twelve-month assignment for the administration, would that be something that could work for you?" I replied that such an arrangement would be complicated, but all the same, it was something I'd be happy to consider.

For most of my career, I had majored in Wall Street and minored in Washington. I'd built a career in investment banking and private equity, limiting my involvement in politics to fundraising, serving on a few think-tank boards, and writing the occasional op-ed. While I'd flirted with government service in the past, the beginning of this new administration seemed like a compelling moment to step up. Our country was facing the greatest financial and economic crisis since the Great Depression; when would the skills of a finance guy like me possibly be more useful? If I hung back this time, what would I be saving myself for?

I hadn't worked in D.C. since the days of Jimmy Carter, and then not as a government official but as a reporter for the *New York Times*. I'd fallen into the job in 1974, starting as a news clerk for the *Times*'s legendary columnist James "Scotty" Reston. Arriving in the capital two months before Richard Nixon's resignation was a dizzying experience for a twenty-one-year-old college graduate. A few years later I was a full-fledged Washington correspondent, responsible for covering what in the face of OPEC and stagflation were the two most important domestic issues facing the Carter administration: energy and the economy.

Then came the election of Ronald Reagan. Some of the stories I wrote were deeply skeptical of supply-side economics, to the point where I found myself attacked on the *Wall Street Journal* editorial page. My superiors decided that this would be an excellent moment for me to move to London to cover European economics.

Neither London nor journalism outside Washington was particularly satisfying, however. I grew restless. Although I had leaped at the opportunity to work with Scotty Reston, I had never set out to be a journalist. I'd been raised in the New York suburbs in a nonpolitical, business-oriented family. My father, who had seen his family's fur business go bankrupt during the Depression and now ran our family's paint-manufacturing company in Queens, had urged me toward a professional education. I'd even applied and been accepted to business school and law school, both of which I'd deferred to stay at the *Times*. Now I felt the journalistic frustration of peering through the glass instead of running something or building something in the real world.

I could have tried returning to Washington as a public servant. But the private sector was a more realistic option in those days of Republican ascendance. Several friends I'd known in Washington had shifted to investment banking. That industry had nowhere near the glitz or notoriety it would gain within a few years, but listening to those who had entered the fray, it sounded like an exciting, challenging way to marry some of the variety and competitiveness of journalism with a chance to do more than report.

Money wasn't my main motivation—I was single and earning more than $60,000 a year, with both a cost-of-living allowance and a generous expense account—and it took me a while to realize how weird I sounded saying that on Wall Street. When asked in job interviews why I wanted to become an investment banker, I would speak somewhat airily about doing something different from journalism. My prospective employers would look at me quizzically. The more forthcoming ones told me that this was too tough a profession to take on unless I had a real drive to get rich. So I learned to play up a passion for money-making and to mention the limitations of living on only a five-figure income.

"I understand completely," said one of my last interviewers. "I don't know how anyone can live on sixty thousand dollars a year." At that time, someone making that much ranked in the top 10 percent of all earners.

In my early years on Wall Street, I had no time for politics or policy. I devoted my waking hours to work and tried to be a good family man. The best thing that had come out of my time in London was meeting my wife, Maureen White, another American expat. When we decided we wanted children, we somehow managed to have four in four years' time (one set of twins).

Not until the mid-1990s, after I'd risen to a senior post at the investment bank Lazard Frères, was I able to focus again on Washington. I began to write op-eds. I became involved with several think tanks and started donating to candidates I liked.

Maureen and I had met the Clintons on Martha's Vineyard in the early years of Bill Clinton's presidency. Our relationship was cemented in 1995 when Vernon and Ann Jordan arranged for us to stay over in the Lincoln Bedroom, on the second floor of the White House. We were so naive about fundraising that we took the Jordans at their word when they said that the Clintons wanted to "meet a few new interesting people."

That year, we dove into Clinton's reelection effort — raising money, courting business support, and attending events. After the election, Maureen became the U.S. representative to UNICEF. I had conversations with Treasury Secretary Bob Rubin and his then-deputy Larry Summers, but their needs and my availability never coincided.

Maureen and I worked hard for our friend Al Gore in 2000, and then again for John Kerry in 2004, because we could not bear George W. Bush's policies. At the time, I wasn't thinking of a Washington job; I had made a commitment to the three partners with whom I started a private investment firm, the Quadrangle Group, in 2000, promising that I would not leave for at least five years. And I was enjoying helping our little firm grow and thrive.

When Hillary Clinton ran for President in 2008, the decision to support her was easy. I admired her enormously and thought that she was the best qualified to be President. But as the campaign unfolded, it became clear that on substantive policy grounds, she and Obama were almost indistinguishable. So while I was proud to be a Clinton supporter, I always felt that Obama would also be fine. In August 2007, I ran into him at a Martha's Vineyard golf club and mentioned that if he became the nominee, I'd be pleased to help in any way I could. (At that moment, I suspect neither of us thought that outcome was likely.)

We stayed with Hillary to the bitter end; I've always believed that the girl you bring to the dance is the girl you stay with. But when she dropped out in early June 2008, Maureen and I were happy to support Barack. As always, we tried to keep a low profile and help where we could, mainly in fundraising, business outreach, and cultivating other potential supporters, particularly those who had been for Hillary.

Election night 2008 was a celebratory moment for us. Of course, almost immediately the jockeying and speculating over appointments began. I wanted to serve and felt that now the timing was right: my kids were nearly grown, and Quadrangle was coming up on its ninth anniversary and I had capable partners. But I knew from observing previous transitions that Obama would pick his most senior advisers first. Any potential role for me would be a notch down.

I had not concealed my interest in Washington, so I didn't think I needed to do much to advance myself. I'd seen would-be officeholders put themselves forward shamelessly — and futilely. Any job I would want would be decided on merit, another reason for not trying too hard. My prospects were helped by my relationships with people involved in the transition, including its overall head, John Podesta, a former chief of staff to President Clinton. In charge of the personnel process was Mike Froman, a former Treasury chief of staff, a law school classmate of Obama's, and a good friend of mine. My partner from Quadrangle Josh Steiner, himself a former Treasury chief of staff who had been caught up in the Whitewater scandal, had been asked to help with the economic-policy portion of transition planning. One of the few people I talked to openly during this period, Josh urged me not to be passive. "Very few people get drafted for these jobs," he said. So I visited briefly with Podesta and Froman to register my interest in serving in the new administration.

On the Monday before Thanksgiving, Obama announced the key members of his economic team. Timothy Geithner's appointment as Treasury secretary made him my most likely new boss, so I sent him a congratulatory e-mail noting my willingness to serve. The cryptic phone call from Larry Summers as I was leaving to see *Speed-the-Plow* came the next day. After that, I sat back to wait. While Josh was discreet, I knew he would alert me if there was some action he thought I should take.

Tim was still president of the New York Federal Reserve Bank — a more-than-full-time job as the financial crisis accelerated. I could not imagine how he could manage it and prepare to run the Treasury at the same time. So I was excited to get an e-mail from his assistant, asking me to meet with him on December 18 at 8:30 A.M.

Having allowed plenty of time in case of rush-hour delays, I arrived early at the gray, fortresslike Federal Reserve building on Liberty Street in downtown Manhattan. Ushered into a small sitting room, I waited until Tim, in his customary blue suit and white shirt, rushed in, dropped his BlackBerry and phone on a side table, and began my first job interview in years.

Speaking in his usual concise, focused fashion, Tim explained that Treasury's traditional organization was unsuited to the current economic problems: there were more crises than there were formal jobs. And yet, he explained, it was hard to create new senior positions without congressional approval. So Tim was thinking in terms of tasks rather than positions, implying that he'd get to the specifics of positions and titles later. He mentioned four issues that might be appropriate for me to work on: housing, the immediate banking problems, longer-term financial policy, and autos.

I said that I was open to discussing any of the possibilities and didn't want to make his impossible life more difficult by being finicky. Less than fifteen minutes into our scheduled forty-five-minute meeting, an assistant came to summon him to another meeting, and Tim stood to leave.

"Do you have any questions for me?" I asked, disconcerted by this abrupt turn in my job interview.

"No," he replied and was gone.

Later, it struck me that the jobs Geithner had listed were like a four-point checklist of the financial and economic calamities facing the new President. With the collapse of the subprime mortgage market and the unprecedented fall in property values, homeownership had gone from the American dream to a debt nightmare for millions of families. The nation's biggest banks and investment houses were mostly crippled, threatening to paralyze the entire economy. Financial policy had clearly failed to guard against this, and once the emergencies were resolved, the question would be how to fix the system. And the auto industry, the once proud symbol of America's industrial might and still the employer of millions, was near ruin. If any one of these missions became mine, I thought ruefully, I certainly would not have to worry about being stuck in some purely honorary job.

Like most Wall Street denizens, I had watched closely as these crises cascaded through the financial markets and undermined the broader economy. Our private equity investments were mainly in media and communications, sectors somewhat removed from the financial industry collapse. Nor did we engage in derivatives or subprime or risky lending in our other principal business: serving as the investment arm for Mayor Michael Bloomberg's personal and philanthropic wealth. So we did not feel the same sense of imminent peril that many of my friends experienced. At first the crisis was simply unnerving — also fascinating in a morbid sort of way.

I followed the daily developments closely. As a private equity investor and mergers and acquisitions veteran, I was only vaguely familiar with the new lingo of Wall Street — special investment vehicles, collateralized loan obligations, super senior tranches, conduits and securitizations. Now I did my best to learn, often entreating friends who were closer to the action to explain to me the new alphabet soup of CLOs, SIVs, MBSs, and so on. Writing helped me collect and focus my thoughts. In 2007, I warned in the *Wall Street Journal* of a "coming credit meltdown." As the crisis developed, I contributed op-eds on housing, on the likely emergence of better-capitalized banks, on what to do with Fannie Mae and Freddie Mac, on the future of private equity, and on the state of the economy (about which I was way too optimistic).

For many months, Wall Street was in a muddle about what it wanted Washington to do. In March 2008, when the Fed saved Bear Stearns, many in the financial community were dismayed. "Moral hazard!" they cried. "Poorly run institutions must be allowed to fail!" For the next few months, markets continued to erode only gradually, with the acute pain confined to those in the subprime mortgage arena. But then came the crisis of September 2008. "The Street" wanted the government to let Lehman go—a notch in the moral-hazard belt—and the Federal Reserve and the Bush administration obliged. But from that horrible Monday morning when we awoke to Lehman's bankruptcy—the firm at which I enjoyed beginning my Wall Street career and at which I still had many friends—it was clear that things would never be the same.

I had experienced market crises, but nothing like this. The 1987 stock market crash—unnerving as it was on another Black Monday, October 19—had proved short-lived. The Asian crisis in 1998 had been messier and protracted, but Asia was on the other side of the globe. This meltdown was right here in Manhattan, where we saw friends lose their jobs and much of their net worth. Financial markets began to seize up. Being a private equity guy was no longer a sheltered cove; we had portfolio companies that needed financing and none was available. Meanwhile, the recession that we now know officially began in December 2007 started to affect some of our companies' results, particularly those with substantial advertising revenues. We plunged into intensive reviews of each company, intent on cutting expenses and stretching liquidity as far as possible. The Bloomberg portfolio, conservatively invested, performed better than most of its peers, but the declines still stung. Above all, the sense that no one knew where the bottom was created more widespread terror than I had ever experienced in my Wall Street career. (As determined investors, we tried to find exciting opportunities amid the carnage, but it was hard to summon the courage to run into a burning building.)

I wasn't shocked—maybe I should have been—that Tim would have mentioned four very diverse jobs. For one thing, government has always placed more confidence in the transferability of skills than the private sector. Perhaps more importantly, all four issues had finance at their core, and all would benefit from a fresh look by people who were not wedded to past models and outmoded approaches. Even solving the auto crisis, I understood, would not be a management assignment like running a corporation; it would be a combination of restructuring exercise (cleaning up the mess) and private equity task (investing new capital). While the Wall Street community includes many who are more expert at both tasks than I, after twenty-six years in finance I felt that my "major" and my "minor" had converged.

Josh hinted a few days later that I was likely to be offered autos. My first reaction was to think, "But I live in New York!"—as a Manhattan-ite, I neither knew nor cared much about cars. (I'm a pilot, more interested in planes.) But Josh encouraged me, arguing that I could help prevent the devastation of this iconic industry. Among his many roles, he'd been named the transition team's senior auto adviser and had been scrambling to get up to speed on the ills of Detroit.

The same week as my job interview with Geithner, the Bush administration committed $17 billion of federal funds to General Motors and Chrysler, putting them on financial life support. The money came with a hodgepodge of conditions, including a mid-February deadline, when the automakers had to submit "viability plans," and another at the end of March, when the new Obama administration would revisit the whole issue. By then the automakers would again be almost out of cash.

Josh described this state of affairs as "challenging and interesting," perhaps in part because he was eager to hand it off. Another close friend, Senator Chuck Schumer, gave me a different take when we talked at dinner not long after I'd met with Tim. "Autos is a no-win," the senator bluntly declared. "The situation is probably unsalvageable. You'll run up against the unions and get eviscerated by your own party. Work on housing—it's a big, important issue, it affects everybody, it has to get resolved, and the politics are easier."

A week went by and the holidays came. On December 26, I took my family to Spain for a week of sightseeing ("history trips," our kids called these annual expeditions). But Tim's office interrupted our vacation on the thirtieth, asking to schedule a call for the following day. When my cell phone rang on New Year's Eve, Tim offered me the auto assignment, reporting to both him and Larry. I was very positively inclined, I said, but needed to discuss it with Maureen and a few others. Other than his telling me I would be a counselor to the Treasury secretary, there was no talk of terms or responsibilities, and the call ended in less than five minutes.

A few hours later, as we were about to go to dinner, the phone rang again; this time it was Larry, calling from vacation in Jamaica. "I know you talked to Tim," he began. "It would be great if you did this." He was surprised to discover I was in Barcelona and said, "It's a good thing I didn't call much later." Never one to stay up late, even on New Year's

Eve, I replied, "My phone would have been off." I gave him the same response I had given Tim and went to join my family.

I lay awake for a while that night as 2009 began, sensing I was on the verge of the experience of a lifetime. I was being given a chance to play a central role in the largest industrial restructuring in history from within the most powerful institution in the world — the United States government. I would come to the job thinking I knew a lot about business and a reasonable amount about Washington. I didn't realize that my eyes would be opened to harsh new perspectives on both worlds. I would learn of both the devastation across our manufacturing sector — in part, collateral damage from our sound commitment to free trade and NAFTA — and the intimidating challenge of reversing the trend or even just halting the decline. I would discover that the struggles of GM and Chrysler were as much a failure of management as a consequence of globalization, oil prices, and organized labor. I certainly understood the importance of management to the small companies in which my firm invested; what would astound me was how important one or two individuals could be to the fortunes of businesses that were among the largest on the planet. And I would witness the dysfunction of Congress, its inability to rise above deep partisan divides and narrow parochial interests and produce legislative action to address in a thoughtful manner the many challenges that we face. I would conclude that if sunshine is indeed the best disinfectant, as Justice Brandeis once said, we need to find the most powerful lenses available to focus the sun's rays on the U.S. Congress and, particularly, the Senate.

In the end, the auto rescue would prove to be not just the story of two iconic automakers. It would exemplify many of the challenges that confront Americans in the twenty-first century — from our struggling manufacturing base to our declining middle class — and illustrate how difficult it is in the hothouse of Washington, so deeply divided along partisan lines, to take the desperately needed swift actions. I believe firmly in President Obama's efforts to restore our economy, yet because of such obstacles, the auto rescue remains one of the few actions taken by the administration that, at least in my opinion, can be pronounced an unambiguous success. Detroit should count itself lucky.

• • •

It had taken America's automakers my entire lifetime to come to the crisis they were in. I grew up during Detroit's heyday, the fifties and sixties, when the Big Three were just that. General Motors, Ford, and Chrysler controlled 90 percent of the U.S. car market, by far the world's largest. GM sold half the vehicles purchased annually in America, coming in year after year in the number one spot on the Fortune 500 list of America's largest industrial companies. Driveways and garages up and down the street in my parents' affluent Long Island suburb were filled with Ford Country Squires, Lincolns, Cadillacs, and the like.

In those upbeat days, Detroit's offerings echoed the optimism of the space age, drowning in chrome and sporting glamorous-sounding names like Galaxie, Starliner, Thunderbird, and Barracuda. My best friend in high school got a Camaro convertible as a graduation present from his parents, and we all thought it was about the coolest thing around. It was perhaps a precursor of things to come when in 1966 my mother abandoned our family's preference for Fords and bought herself a small Mercedes, and our family became among the first I knew to own a foreign car.

I was a college junior when gasoline prices first soared to shocking levels, which ended Detroit's hegemony and opened the floodgates for small, inexpensive, fuel-efficient Japanese imports. Competition, high gas prices, and stagflation squeezed the U.S. carmakers hard in the 1970s, ending with Chrysler nearly bankrupt and Ford and GM deep in red ink. At the *New York Times* I helped cover Chrysler's pleas for a government bailout. In one story I described the debate as a "first-rank political and economic controversy over whether it is obligatory, or even desirable, for the Federal Government to come to the rescue of a large, ailing corporation." That question, it turned out, would trail me.

On highways and streets, imports — Corollas, Civics, Datsuns, and Volkswagens — became as popular as American cars. I'd shared the use of a Ford Pinto in college (one of the worst cars ever built), but when I got to pick my own car, I chose a sporty Datsun 260Z. Volvos competed with U.S. station wagons, and Mercedes and BMWs displaced Cadillacs and Lincolns at the luxury end. In 1982 came the first successful "transplant" — a Honda factory opened in Marysville, Ohio, where non-union American workers turned out Accords just as efficiently as workers in Japan. Such plants enabled Detroit's rivals to avoid import restrictions and lessened the effects of currency swings, increasing the pressure on the Big Three.

That is not to say Detroit didn't have successes. After its first bailout, Chrysler, fired up by Lee Iacocca as its CEO and TV pitchman, invented the minivan and changed the world of driving for suburban moms. Ford launched the Taurus, a radically curvaceous full-size car that critics first ridiculed as a "flying potato," then hailed as a design breakthrough. Consumers made it the best-selling car in America, displacing the Honda Accord. These late-eighties successes drove Ford and Chrysler to record-breaking profits and lit up their stocks. Ford's stock price rose 1,500 percent between 1981 and 1987.

But beneath it all was an undertow. U.S. automakers' market share was eroding as the Germans and Japanese developed a better bead on what buyers wanted. Confronted with lagging demand, Detroit was always a lap behind in cutting capacity, raising productivity, and renegotiating with labor. The financial pages chronicled the Big Three's woes: a steady stream of reports about plant closures, layoffs, concessions to unions, and struggles with regulators and consumer watchdog groups.

GM, in particular, seemed incapable of effective change. Starting in the 1980s, top management gambled at least $90 billion on computers and factory robots and a sweeping remake of GM's 800,000-employee organization—all in hopes of leapfrogging the competition into the twenty-first century. Instead, the reorganization stalled and a newly engineered generation of Buick Regals and Oldsmobile Cutlasses fizzled in the marketplace.

In 1989, the once mighty GM became the butt of national ridicule when *Roger & Me,* the most successful documentary ever at the time of its release, skewered the company for exporting jobs to Mexico and impoverishing Flint, Michigan, one of the many seemingly doomed all-American factory towns. Detroit's ingrown management culture looked more arrogant than ever onscreen. How timely the film was: after the recession of 1990–1991 forced more layoffs and plant closures, GM earned the grim distinction of recording the largest one-year loss in American corporate history, $23.5 billion in 1992.

Less prosperity brought more challenges as the Big Three felt the effects of years of concessions to the UAW, including comprehensive

health care for an ever-expanding number of retirees and their families. (The UAW was so central that when crunch time finally came in
2008 and Congress called the Big Three to testify about bailout needs,
there were four chief executives at the table: the CEOs of GM, Ford,
and Chrysler, and Ron Gettelfinger, head of the UAW.) It is not an ex-
aggeration to say that the industry could have crumbled before the
twenty-first century began had not a revolutionary development — the
sport-utility vehicle — hit the streets. Consumers were in love again,
not with American cars exactly, but rather with American light-trucks-
turned-passenger-vehicles. SUVs enabled automakers to exploit cheap
gasoline (the price of which, adjusted for inflation, had fallen to near
pre-OPEC levels) and skirt clean-air regulations. Clinton's economic
boom was on, and these high-riding, road-hogging, gas-guzzling mon-
sters were the hallmark of the era. As foreign automakers initially dismissed the SUV as a craze, Detroit's profits and stocks went up once
more. Detroit was on such a roll that in 1999 the *Wall Street Journal*
predicted a new golden age for GM, Ford, and their top competitors
(Chrysler by then had been bought by Daimler). In 2000, GM stock hit
its all-time high of $93.63 a share.

Yet the reality was that SUVs slowed, but did not reverse, the ero-
sion of Detroit's market share. By 2005, it would be easy to see all the
wrong turns, including the diversion of billions of dollars of capital to
acquisitions (Ford bought Jaguar and Volvo; GM picked up Hummer
and Saab). None of these deals paid off. To juice up sales, the companies became addicted to incentives — cash-back offers and heavy discounts that sustained production but sacrificed profits. (Incentives
weren't as stupid as they seemed: labor contracts guaranteed wages
whether workers made cars or not.)

Detroit's ultimate implosion, begun long before the 2008 housing
market collapse and financial panic, was triggered by the resurgence
of oil prices. In 2004, gasoline, edging up at the pump for a couple of
years, jumped to more than $2 a gallon. Suddenly, filling the tank of a
large SUV cost $60 or more. Dealers had little to offer as consumer de-
mand swerved back toward small, fuel-efficient sedans. The Big Three
had never controlled expenses, especially labor costs, enough to be
able to make money on such cars. In 2006, Ford lost $12.6 billion on
$160 billion in sales.

Each Detroit giant responded in its own way. Chrysler's owner, Daimler, decided to bail — in essence giving away an 80 percent stake in the business, for which it had paid $38 billion nine years before, to the private equity firm Cerberus. Ford, by contrast, strapped in, raising $23.5 billion by taking loans on its factories, real estate, patents, and even the rights to its distinctive blue-oval trademark. GM unloaded assets, including a majority stake in its huge finance company, GMAC.

By 2006 GM's domestic market share had fallen to less than half of its historic peak. Industry watchers began to speculate about whether Toyota might usurp GM as number one in the U.S., once unthinkable in a country where World War II vets had insisted on American-made cars. (Toyota was on the brink of displacing GM worldwide, which it did the following spring.) It was a classic business saga, not unlike those of companies in many other industries that saw a once dominant market share challenged by new competitors. For the U.S. steel giants, it was imports. For the three broadcast TV networks, it was cable. As for Detroit, years of mismanagement had allowed structural problems such as labor costs to become intractable.

These decades of decline had left Detroit frighteningly vulnerable to the mounting calamities of 2008. That summer, when gas prices topped $4 a gallon, car dealers suffered double-digit decreases in sales. As the decline in housing prices gathered speed and the intensifying recession dried up credit, consumers could no longer get car loans and dealers couldn't finance their inventories. Sales plunged and cash began draining from the automakers' treasuries at a dramatic rate.

Increasingly desperate, the companies went into panic mode. Chrysler explored mergers with Fiat and Renault-Nissan. Ford, after experiencing the worst quarterly loss in its 105-year history — $8.7 billion in the second quarter of 2009 — announced a radical shift in its product lines. GM's second-quarter loss was nearly double the size of Ford's — $15.5 billion. Amid other restructuring steps, the company said it would slash production capacity by 300,000 vehicles.

For the president of GM, Fritz Henderson, the months leading up to the company's one hundredth anniversary, in September 2008, were the hardest in his lifelong GM career. A stocky, energetic pragmatist, Henderson began worrying seriously about his company's survival as soon as sales began to ebb in the first quarter. In June, after successfully negotiating the end of an ugly, months-long UAW strike that had crippled production of SUVs, he saw an alarming statistic: GM had more days' supply of unsold trucks at the end of the strike than at the start. Consumers had stopped buying. "We should have let the strike run another sixty days," he grimly joked to the company's North American chief.

At first, the sales collapse was purely domestic — Europe was still strong, as were Asia and the emerging markets. But with oil at $140 a barrel, Henderson knew the malaise would spread and tried to prepare. Money in the capital markets was evaporating; it was becoming as hard for GM to finance operations as it was for consumers to get car loans. Henderson was soon elbow-deep in implementing what General Motors CEO Rick Wagoner and the board of directors called GM's self-help plan — taking production down, slashing jobs and orders with suppliers, cutting inventory and working capital. With Wagoner's acquiescence, he explored even more radical steps.

By late summer, teams of GMers sequestered in a hotel near Detroit were secretly analyzing a merger with Chrysler. The number three Detroit automaker had approached GM after its courtships with Fiat and Renault-Nissan failed. Henderson and his task force made a case to a skeptical Wagoner that by absorbing its smaller rival, GM might attract new investment and bolster its chances of survival, even if demand continued to fall.

The financial panic on Wall Street in September crushed that hope. At a very subdued hundredth anniversary gala two nights after Lehman Brothers went bankrupt, Henderson sat thinking how much he hated birthdays. He wondered if GM would even make it to 101.

The automakers by now had begun quietly asking Washington for help, focusing at first on diverting money from a $25 billion incentive program set up by Congress to speed production of electric cars and other "advanced technology" vehicles. Henderson was sure that GM had no alternative to federal aid. But it filled him with foreboding. In early October he shared his concerns with Wagoner in an e-mail. He believed the government would help — he couldn't envision George W. Bush letting the automakers fail in the last three months of his presidency. Yet if it accepted help, GM would jeopardize its autonomy, and its leaders risked losing their jobs. "Once you open this door, you don't know where it's going to go," Henderson told Wagoner. "You just need to understand that. Because when you ask for support from the taxpayer, things could change."

2

THE BRIDGE TO OBAMA

COLUMBUS DAY IS A holiday for government workers, but on Monday, October 13, 2008, the Treasury Department was frenetic. CEOs from nine of America's largest banks had been summoned by George Bush's Treasury secretary, Hank Paulson, for an afternoon meeting. Together they would be told that to preserve the financial system, each would be required to accept a multibillion-dollar infusion of public money from the Troubled Asset Relief Program (TARP). This intervention in the banks' business — the single most important step in the government's rescue of the financial industry — dominated the news.

Unknown to the world, another summit had taken place at Treasury that morning. General Motors, the second-largest industrial company of the largest economy on earth, was on the verge of bankruptcy and had come to the government, hat in hand. Had this become public knowledge, it would have grabbed more than a few headlines from the banks.

At 8:30 A.M., GM's CEO Rick Wagoner arrived at Paulson's office, accompanied by his chief financial officer and two carefully chosen members of the GM board, Erskine Bowles and John Bryan, both courtly southerners. Bowles had been chief of staff to President Clinton and was expert in the ways of Washington. Bryan, who had brokered the meeting, was Paulson's longtime friend.

What brought the GM team was money: the giant automaker was hemorrhaging cash. In the first quarter of 2008, $3.5 billion had drained away. In the second quarter, the outflow was $2.8 billion. Results for the third quarter, which had ended only two weeks before, were still unannounced — and horrendous. GM had burned through almost $9 billion.

Time had run out on the last of Wagoner's many efforts at a turnaround. The program of selling assets to raise cash had almost reached the end. To try to conserve cash, there had been white-collar headcount reductions, elimination of health care for older white-collar retirees, elimination of executive bonuses, and suspension of the dividend. Privately Wagoner had weighed the merger with Chrysler — an opportunity for significant cost savings — but scuttled it as GM's crisis became too urgent for the benefits of a merger to have time to kick in. "I was trying to reduce brands. Why add Chrysler's?" he later explained to me.

Then, on October 3, GM recognized a potential godsend when Congress created the TARP at President Bush's behest. The program established a $700 billion war chest for the Treasury to use in preventing a financial and economic collapse, of which fully half, $350 billion, was at the immediate disposal of Paulson and his staff.

Understandably, Paulson this morning was focused on banks, not cars. Compared with the upheavals on Wall Street, the woes of General Motors seemed small beer. Paulson, a sixty-two-year-old former Eagle Scout from the Midwest, had survived twenty-seven remarkable months at Treasury, where he had arrived in the sixth year of an unpopular administration obsessed with global terrorism. No one had expected him to be able to accomplish much. Then, in 2007, the housing bubble burst. As the impact spread through the U.S. economy and the world financial system, Paulson became, inarguably, the most important member of the Bush administration.

Indefatigable and relentless, the former Goldman Sachs CEO juggled crises and crammed in cell-phone calls while striding between high-pressure meetings. He had little patience for ceremony or bureaucracy. When some of his former Goldman colleagues materialized at Treasury as "special advisers," there were bruised feelings among the career staff. But Paulson made no apologies and, as the problems worsened, seemed to become ever more blunt. In September he'd caused a furor with a curt three-page pitch to Congress requesting not only a staggering $700 billion for TARP but also the authority to deploy it without review.

Still Wagoner, who had called twice in the past ten days, appeared convinced that his emergency deserved attention too. So Paulson had shoehorned the automaker in before Federal Reserve Board Chairman Ben Bernanke, who was due at 10 A.M. to prepare for the meeting with the bankers. But the Treasury secretary had taken preemptive steps to keep the automakers off his department's crushing caseload. The White House, sympathetic to Paulson's burdens, had agreed to have Commerce Secretary Carlos Gutierrez greet the visitors with Paulson and serve as the administration's point man on GM.

In the back of Paulson's mind, snagging his attention at every turn, was a frightening scenario. He feared that the $350 billion appropriated for TARP would be insufficient to shore up the financial system. The last thing he wanted was to divert rescue money to car companies. With liquidity short throughout the economy, he also worried that bailing out Detroit would entice other strapped companies to try to get on the federal dole too.

At 8:30 A.M., the GM delegation was ushered into Paulson's "small conference room," a modest, nondescript space less ornate and much smaller than the secretary's "large conference room," where the bank CEOs would gather later that day. As the GM visitors — outnumbered by Paulson, Gutierrez, and a half-dozen aides — took their places, John Bryan kicked things off with introductions. Then came Wagoner.

Leaning forward in his seat, the tall, stolid CEO explained matter-of-factly that without help, GM was likely to go bankrupt. That, he said, would almost certainly lead to the company's immediate liquidation, clearly an economic catastrophe. If GM factories locked their gates, suppliers and dealers all over America would fail in a terrible domino effect.

To explain the mess, Wagoner invoked the automakers' familiar litany of forces over which they had no control, specifically the rise in oil prices and the collapse of consumer confidence after the crises in housing and finance. He added a new reason for urgency, declaring that the end for GM might come as soon as Monday, November 3 — the day before the presidential election — when GM was scheduled to announce its grim third-quarter results. Also due on that date was a multibillion-dollar payment to suppliers that threatened to drain GM's cash below the minimum reserves needed to run the business. The company's precarious state, if revealed, would not only spook Wall Street, but also, he warned, trigger "a run on the trade" by suppliers. Like panicked bank customers stampeding to withdraw their savings, the suppliers would cancel their credit and demand cash on delivery — money that GM simply wouldn't be able to pay.

The implied threat was clear: Did the administration want voters waking up on Election Day to news that the nation's largest manufacturer had gone bust? His alternative was $10 billion of TARP money, a loan, for which GM would be willing to pay a generous interest rate and give the Treasury a 19.9 percent ownership stake.

Ray Young, GM's chief financial officer, handed out a PowerPoint presentation to buttress the company's case. (I would later learn that nothing at GM happens without PowerPoint.) To the practiced eyes of the two cabinet secretaries, the recovery plan supposedly justifying the $10 billion loan was long on rosy predictions but short on facts and analysis. GM wanted to gamble taxpayer money on a vast, rapid rebound in auto sales as well as on gains in market share. Asked how he could be confident of such forecasts, Wagoner waxed eloquent about the new Chevy Malibu and GM's gains in J. D. Power quality studies.

Gutierrez broke in to ask about bankruptcy. "Companies in your situation tend to pursue some form of reorganization," he said. "Isn't that something that could make sense here?"

No way, said Wagoner, shaking his head; bankruptcy would sink the business by scaring off customers. "You can't sell cars to people under those circumstances," he argued, holding firm when Gutierrez pushed a little more. Bankruptcy was not on the table.

After that, the federal officials remained largely silent, in part because Paulson had made it clear that he wanted the meeting kept short. Bryan, who hadn't quite picked up the mood, jumped back in to emphasize, "This isn't really a bailout, it's a bridge loan and, as you can see, this company can pay it back." Wagoner called attention to an appendix in the handout showing the importance of auto manufacturing, particularly in Ohio, Michigan, and Indiana. Across the United States, carmakers and their suppliers accounted for millions of jobs, 775,000 pensioners, and two million health care participants. A GM collapse would damage millions of lives.

Then Paulson spoke up, reminding the visitors that TARP was intended to stabilize the financial system, not bail out industrial companies. "You're not going to be able to use it," he said with certainty. "You will probably need to go to Congress." Finally he circled back to soften the message. "The White House cares greatly about this. Carlos is going to be working with you on the President's behalf."

A brief silence following the visitors' departure was broken by Paulson, who declared, "This is complete bullshit!" From long experience as an investment banker, he knew a scare story when he heard one. Yet it was unclear whether this alarm was entirely false — GM was offering only the most superficial analysis, with no detailed support for its assertions.

Studying the page about the Midwest, Ken Wilson, one of Paulson's advisers from Goldman Sachs, mused, "If these companies go down, you could have riots in the streets." And Paulson remembered the terrifying speed with which Lehman Brothers had collapsed weeks before, after the government refused to intervene. With that in mind, he took his undersecretary for domestic finance, Tony Ryan, aside. "I want this kept quiet and secret," he told Ryan, "but come up with a plan in case we find out at five o'clock some afternoon that General Motors is going to file the next day. The President needs the option to prevent a very messy bankruptcy. So find out what's the smallest amount of money we could give GM to get them to the next administration and what would we get for that. Would 19.9 percent of the equity be right, or what?"

As a further precaution, Paulson also asked Joel Kaplan, a deputy chief of staff to President Bush whom Paulson viewed as one of the few sensible people in the White House, to alert the President to the work soon to commence on the secret backup plan.

The Columbus Day meeting set the tone for two months of struggle and confusion. Within the week, Chrysler signaled that it, too, was desperate for cash. Ford, having prudently borrowed billions early in the downturn, was in better shape, although its CEO, Alan Mulally, began calling administration officials to try to ensure that the company wouldn't be put at a competitive disadvantage if its Detroit rivals got help.

For Washington, Detroit's emergency was in some ways more vexing than the cataclysm on Wall Street. The Treasury and other federal entities were rich in expertise for dealing with a banking crisis. But thanks to a long-standing and appropriate aversion to industrial policy, the government had no comparable resources to bring to bear on imploding automobile giants. In fall 2008, this traditional distance from nitty-gritty business was compounded by the complete focus of the economic team on the financial crisis. So now, in response to Detroit's threatened collapse, the administration and Congress were going to have to start from scratch.

On the ride back to the Commerce Department after the secret meeting with Paulson and Wagoner, Carlos Gutierrez was puzzled. If GM really was in danger, was there any way to keep it afloat without having to involve Congress and without TARP? Gutierrez was a seasoned businessman whose career, begun behind the wheel of a Kellogg's delivery truck, had led him to the top of the $10-billion-a-year cereal company. After several uneventful years as commerce secretary, he was open to a challenge. Back at the office, he shifted into CEO mode. "We need facts," he told his lieutenants.

That afternoon, in Gutierrez's private conference room, Ray Young and a group of Treasury and Commerce staffers reviewed a chart of GM's cash position, from the PowerPoint presentation. It showed, week by week, steep decline until, right around Election Day, GM would hit $11 billion of cash on hand. "That's the minimum we need to operate," Young replied when asked about the significance of that figure. To Gutierrez, this in itself was a red flag. A well-managed business, even on GM's vast scale, should never need that much cash.

After two frustrating hours, Young left. "He's the CFO of General Motors and he can't answer a single question," complained Phillip Swagel, a high-level economist, as the team regrouped. Others would also find the forty-six-year-old Young, who had been GM's chief financial officer for only seven months, less than impressive.

During the next several weeks, the Commerce staff scrutinized two possible sources of emergency cash for GM: the Department of Energy's Advanced Technology Vehicles Manufacturing Loan Program and the abandoned plan to merge with Chrysler. GM did its best to cooperate, with Young and his staff scrambling day and night to satisfy requests for data. But Fritz Henderson, for one, despaired of getting help from the Bush administration the minute he heard that the Commerce Department was involved. "Commerce never actually accomplishes anything," he pointed out. "They're good people, but they don't do stuff . . . Treasury gets things done, because that's what they do."

Nor was Wagoner reassured. GM had come to Washington hoping for a quick response — it was, after all, General Motors. Instead it got a paper chase. As the collapse in demand for new vehicles spread around the world, Wagoner concluded that neither of the solutions under study would work. The Department of Energy had yet to publish its rules for tapping the $25 billion in advanced-vehicle incentives, but it was pretty plain that as the law was written, the money was meant for retooling plants and couldn't be used for a bailout. As for resurrecting the merger with Chrysler, Wagoner decided he had to put a stop to the idea. On the day before Halloween he told Gutierrez flatly that the merger was a nonstarter — it would not address the liquidity crisis and would only compound GM's problems. By now it was clear to Wagoner that Paulson had been right; if GM wanted help, it would have to go to Capitol Hill.

Election Day 2008 came and went without General Motors running out of money. But the Commerce Department's studies confirmed that GM's emergency was real and getting worse: before the year was out, the coffers would almost certainly be empty. Wagoner wasted no time getting in touch with his counterparts at Ford and Chrysler to ensure they would be at the front of the line when Congress reconvened for a lame-duck session.

The Democrats' victory parties had scarcely ended when, on November 6, the CEOs of the Big Three, along with Ron Gettelfinger, the UAW chief, paid a visit to House Speaker Nancy Pelosi, Senate Majority Leader Harry Reid, and other Democratic leaders. For ninety minutes, the visitors pleaded for loosened restrictions on the $25 billion of advanced-vehicle incentives so they could borrow the money to stay afloat. Not surprisingly, given Obama's support from midwestern union voters, the Democrats listened attentively, but Pelosi's subsequent effusive statement of support was carefully hedged.

The next day, the automakers unveiled dire third-quarter earnings reports (GM having quietly dropped its plan to post results the day before the election). GM's in particular caused an uproar on Wall Street. It revealed that the company was now burning through a stunning

$3 billion a month—roughly $4 million an hour—more than double the losses of the previous quarter. And for the first time, GM acknowledged publicly that its cash balance would approach "the minimum amount necessary to operate our business" by the end of 2008.

Wagoner made a customary pilgrimage to CNBC, where auto correspondent Phil LeBeau didn't hold back. "The numbers are not pretty," he began. "How close is General Motors right now towards bankruptcy?"

Wagoner ducked, but LeBeau kept asking, finally eliciting a direct response: "We have no plans whatsoever to consider anything other than continue to run the business," Wagoner said. "We don't think anything positive would come out of any sort of consideration of reorganizations. I've seen pundits write this stuff, but you can't sell cars to people under that circumstance."

This wasn't spin. The GM chief executive was convinced that, while consumers might fly on bankrupt airlines, they would never buy cars from a bankrupt automaker because of the need for warranty coverage and concerns about resale value. Our task force would later learn that, on Wagoner's instructions, GM was making no contingency plans, no preparations whatsoever for a possible bankruptcy filing. Its investment bankers from Morgan Stanley and Evercore Partners had taken the unusual step of beginning to explore bankruptcy options on their own. But in October, when they'd advised GM's board to prepare, Wagoner had cut off the discussion, curtly thanking them for their time. He had similarly dismissed every other effort to convince him to prepare for a possible bankruptcy. This attitude would add materially to the cost of the eventual rescue.

The auto industry was high on the agenda when Congress returned to work on November 18. At 3:02 P.M. on that overcast Tuesday, Senator Christopher Dodd gaveled to order a hearing of the Banking Committee on the automakers' bailout request. Perhaps underrating the import of the moment, Dodd's aides had passed on storied Senate venues like the ornate Caucus Room in the Russell Senate Office Building, where the Watergate hearings occurred. Instead the session took place in a remote hearing room in the Dirksen building, a drab 1958 relic. It was packed with photographers crowded in front of the dais, attendees in rows of chrome-and-plastic chairs, and banks of TV cameras. Dodd quipped, "If I had known the interest, I would have held this at RFK" — the former football home of Washington's beloved Redskins.

The guests — CEOs Wagoner of GM, Mulally of Ford, and Robert Nardelli of Chrysler, as well as the UAW's Gettelfinger — testified in alphabetical order. Mulally and Nardelli bemoaned poor vehicle sales, and Wagoner summed up GM's problems as not of its making, as he had at Treasury: "Mr. Chairman, I do not agree with those who say we are not doing enough to position GM for success. What exposes us to failure now is not our product lineup, is not our business plan, is not our employees and their willingness to work hard. It is not our long-term strategy. What exposes us to failure now is the global financial crisis, which has severely restricted credit availability and reduced industry sales to the lowest per-capita level since World War II." As business skidded further in the weeks following the election, the automakers had dropped the pretext of requesting speeded-up advanced-technology incentives. Instead they asked Congress point-blank to open up TARP and direct the Treasury to provide $25 billion of emergency bridge loans.

That week is remembered less for anything the CEOs said than for the furor that erupted after Brian Ross of ABC News reported that the three had flown to Washington in separate private jets. Wagoner had been advised by his Washington PR person, Greg Martin, to fly by commercial jet, but he had rejected the idea. "I have meetings," he told Ross after the hearing. "I have a tight schedule."

Yet the hearings proved pivotal in other ways, providing a public display of the automakers' state of denial and revealing Washington's confusion about whether and how to help the industry. Most senators and representatives glossed over tough issues and tossed around terms like "prepack bankruptcy" without any real idea of what they meant.

And the hearings created one of the unsung heroes of the auto bailout, Senator Bob Corker, a Republican from Tennessee. I came to Washington with a bias against Corker because he had beaten my favorite Senate candidate of the 2006 election, Congressman Harold Ford Jr., after a particularly ugly campaign. Small and wiry, with an intensity belied by his soft southern drawl, Corker had been a mayor and businessman before being elected to the Senate. In that arena of show-horses and workhorses, he was proving to be a workhorse.

For Corker, the hearing was an eye-opener. Just returned from a trip to Russia and Ukraine, he was tired, had a headache, and hadn't spent more than a minute thinking about autos. But it wasn't lack of sleep that left him dumbfounded. The automakers were asking for $25 billion but hadn't even told the senators how they were going to divide it up. Nor had any of them submitted or prepared plans to show how, if the request was met, their companies could be made viable without further outlays.

Corker, getting down to business with terse, biting questions, pressed the CEOs on how the money would be split. Wagoner replied that GM wanted "our proportionate share," in a tone that irritated Corker. He asked Gettelfinger to rank the three companies' "shape," best to worst: "Ford, Chrysler, and General Motors," the union chief acidly replied. Corker hammered the CEOs over the lack of analysis in their request, and Gettelfinger over an extreme provision of the UAW contract under which laid-off workers received 95 percent of their normal pay.

For Corker, this was his chance to "own" a major issue, at least among Republicans. Returning to his office in the nether reaches of the Dirksen building, he gathered his staff and began to lay plans for a fact-finding mission to Wall Street. He would seek out the finest auto industry analysts and financiers and maybe, just maybe, come up with a rescue plan.

With Thanksgiving fast approaching, Congress ended its session without taking action on autos. Instead, in a public letter, Pelosi and Reid offered the CEOs a do-over: the House and Senate would return for a rare second lame-duck session in December, devoted exclusively to autos. But that session would take place, the letter warned, only if each company presented "a credible restructuring plan." Interestingly, the letter did not directly address the most important issue: whether $25 billion, as staggering as that sum would have seemed just months before, would even be enough.

The coda to the week happened not on Capitol Hill but on *Saturday Night Live*. The show opened with a parody of what the second set of hearings might be like. In the skit, the CEOs do not fly to Washington, they drive — and apologize to Congress for showing up late because their cars all broke down. "I was going to drive my 2009 Cadillac XLR-V, a model we at GM are very proud of," says the ersatz Rick Wagoner, "but every time I tried to start it, I just got a powerful electric shock, and the upholstery would catch on fire." The CEOs ask Congress not for $25 billion but for hundreds of billions, to be paid over in quarterly installments over five years. "As you can see, Mr. Chairman," says Wagoner, "this proposal is specific, it is detailed, and it is both short- and long-ranged." When the congressmen protest, he adds testily, "With all due respect, we are not talking about a gift or a subsidy. We are talking about *a loan.*" The skit careens on until the CEOs end up boasting that they have entire factories devoted to building lemons, and acknowledge amiably that they probably will never pay the money back. As over-the-top as it was, the parody spoke to the unpopularity of using tax dollars to rescue the automakers: by early December, most polls showed public sentiment running against the idea.

Hank Paulson kept tabs on the auto crisis, but in truth Detroit's headaches were pretty far down his list of major problems. The struggle to stabilize the financial system was gobbling auto-rescue-sized chunks of federal funding every week, and at the rate at which Treasury was bailing out banks, Paulson feared that TARP would run out of money. Congress had appropriated half of the $700 billion authorized in the law that established the program; of that $350 billion, the Treasury had already committed more than $200 billion and the rest was going fast. If one or two more financial giants failed — Bank of America, say, or the huge financial operation at General Electric — the Treasury might not have the resources necessary to stave off a systemic collapse. Paulson's worries intensified just before Thanksgiving, when Citigroup needed a second bailout — $20 billion on top of the $25 billion the Treasury had already kicked in.

All of Washington realized that the lame-duck Congress was unlikely to appropriate the second half of TARP. Bailing out Wall Street — unpopular back in October when TARP had first been passed — had become more politically toxic in the intervening six weeks. And of course President Bush, on his way out, had exhausted his political capital. Winning approval for the second half of TARP would certainly be easier in 2009, with a new President and a new, more heavily Democratic Congress.

But Paulson didn't think the matter could wait. He set out to make the case to Obama for securing the second half of TARP. He called Rahm Emanuel, Obama's chief of staff, two days before Thanksgiving.

"We need to take down the last part of the TARP and we can only do that with you and we need your help," Paulson said.

"That's not good news," Emanuel replied in his blunt fashion. He directed Paulson to call Larry Summers, the incoming President's top economic adviser. Summers questioned Paulson about TARP, and then, to Paulson's surprise, pointedly brought up autos. "You are not going to let the autos fail, are you?" Summers asked. The Democrats were moving Detroit to center stage.

Bush's White House staff, more focused than Paulson on the auto crisis, had expected this. In his first postelection press conference, Obama had emphasized his commitment to autos, which he called "the backbone of American manufacturing." He'd made the point again in his first private meeting with President Bush, pressing for help for the auto industry.

Bush's team saw that to obtain the additional TARP funding that Paulson argued was essential, they would have to rely on Democratic votes. That support, they believed, would be contingent on two things: the active endorsement of the President-elect and relief for the auto companies. But they didn't want to help Detroit unless they could attach strings — they wanted the automakers to secure concessions from major stakeholders to ensure their long-term viability. Otherwise, Bush's advisers argued, the incoming Democrats would cave in to special interests — particularly the UAW — with $25 billion becoming $50 billion or more. Meanwhile, the auto companies would do no genuine restructuring and instead end up wards of the state. To address these worries, Joel Kaplan, a deputy chief of staff, floated an interesting idea. Kaplan was a young, articulate Harvard Law graduate who had worked in the Bush White House since 2001. Paulson much preferred dealing with Kaplan and his boss, Josh Bolten, than with others among the White House's hefty contingent of rigidly ideological conservatives.

Kaplan proposed creating a "financial viability adviser" and granting him or her the power to hold the automakers accountable — they would get no long-term money from the government without show-ing they could survive as going concerns. Importantly, from the Bush team's perspective, the incoming administration would publicly em-brace that same commitment at the time of the viability adviser's ap-pointment.

Paulson responded warmly to the idea. Bailing out an industry so fundamental to the American identity and way of life was a politically charged subject. Only someone outside the usual chains of command, someone of authority and integrity — Paul Volcker, the former Federal Reserve chairman, was mentioned — could force the tough decisions the industry would need. What was more, if the White House could persuade the Democrats to agree on the choice of an adviser now, there would be someone securely in place to hold off the unions and keep the bailout in check after Bush left office. "Financial viability adviser" quickly got shortened to "car czar," an epithet that would come to cause me much grief.

Paulson and Summers went round repeatedly that week about TARP. Summers felt that Paulson hadn't truly sold the Bush White House on the importance of taking down the second half of TARP and was try-ing to enlist the Obama team in his cause instead. In the course of ev-ery conversation with Paulson, Summers brought up autos. Although skeptical about the car-czar idea, he had started thinking about possi-ble recruits, hence the call to me the afternoon before Thanksgiving.

Over the holiday, the White House stepped up its effort to engage Obama in a joint approach on both TARP and autos. Bolten phoned Emanuel to ask for a face-to-face meeting, but Rahm was reluctant. In the last presidential transition occurring during a historic economic cri-sis — Franklin Roosevelt's succeeding Herbert Hoover in 1933 — FDR had deliberately remained aloof until he was in office. The Obama team doubted that there was a workable way to co-govern. And it had stud-ied that precedent and concluded that it had little to gain politically by collaborating on any issue, let alone TARP and autos. This carefully cal-culated decision was packaged under the appealing sound bite "there can be only one President at a time."

This was a source of frustration to Bush officials, who were pleased when Emanuel, unwilling to reject Bolten out of hand, agreed to a meeting — although he did not want it to take place in the Bush White

House and specified that Summers, not he, would lead the Obama delegation. On Sunday afternoon, November 30, the two sides, mostly dressed in khakis and sports coats, gathered at the Treasury Department in Paulson's corner office, Paulson in his customary wing chair and Summers on the couch next to him. The Bush delegation, led by Bolten, Paulson, Gutierrez, Kaplan, chief congressional liaison Dan Meyer, and Keith Hennessey (whom Summers would be replacing), far outranked the team from Obama, which was still forming a staff. Paulson laid out the White House proposal: if the incoming administration would "link arms" to win approval for the second $350 billion of TARP, then the outgoing administration would support an auto rescue plan. Following this, Kaplan outlined his proposal for including an auto rescue in the uses of the second tranche of TARP. President Bush would issue an executive order appointing a financial viability adviser to administer the bailout, and the new Treasury secretary would agree to make TARP funding available only if the automakers could show that they were viable. As Summers already knew, this adviser would have broad authority to require financial plans from the automakers and to impose his own measures — including Chapter 11 bankruptcies — if the companies fell short. While the adviser would be officially selected by Bush, the Republicans made it clear that only someone acceptable to the Obama team would be named.

Summers zoomed in on TARP, probing for evidence that the added money was actually needed before Obama arrived. Next he asked a lot of questions about autos, not hiding his skepticism about the idea of a car czar. Why would Obama want to outsource a problem that was his responsibility? Bolten replied that the White House was open to other ideas, but the meeting ended inconclusively after ninety-five minutes. Paulson, ever relentless, called Summers twice the next day, and Hennessey also gave Summers a ring. The clear impression among the Bush team was that the Obama team did not want to say yes or no and was slow-walking them.

This triggered two recalculations. First, the administration decided to back off on TARP: as much as Paulson wanted the extra safety margin of $350 billion, an ugly fight over gaining access to the money could roil the markets as badly as another bank failure. Second, worried about the sufficiency of TARP, it returned to a legislative strategy that involved pushing Congress to make the advanced-technology funding available as a bridge loan to the auto companies.

"Every industry in America is hurting today. Show me one that couldn't be assisted and made more viable and more profitable with an additional $34 billion," demanded Texas Congressman Jeb Hensarling. "So why the folks before us and not other folks?" By Friday, December 5, Detroit's CEOs were back on Capitol Hill for round two.

In two scant weeks, the amount of their bailout request had ballooned from $25 billion to $34 billion. GM, at this point, wanted a $12 billion loan and a $6 billion line of credit, including $4 billion immediately to ensure survival past January 1. Chrysler wanted $7 billion. Ford, breaking ranks, said it needed no immediate cash, just a $9 billion line of credit.

In the midst of what was becoming a predictable circus, some truths emerged. Most compelling was the testimony of Mark Zandi, the chief economist of Moody's Economy.com, who had delved into the automakers' restructuring and restoration costs. According to his analysis, their recovery plans rested on too optimistic assumptions. Just to avoid bankruptcy in the next two years, Zandi testified, the automakers would need not $34 billion but rather $75 billion to $125 billion — numbers that would prove amazingly prescient.

Yet Zandi conceded that, in its battered state, the economy could not stand Detroit's implosion. Like other witnesses, he recommended that Congress provide emergency aid, though not as much as the automakers had asked. More could be offered later if the turnarounds began to work.

The hearings ended with the grudging consensus that the automakers did indeed need help, but no one in Congress knew where the cash would come from, and only a week remained in the legislative year.

A weekend of horse-trading ensued, during which President-elect Obama appeared on *Meet the Press* to reiterate his support for a bailout. "Millions of people, directly or indirectly, are reliant on that industry, and so I don't think it's an option to simply allow it to collapse," he said. By Monday, the congressional Democrats and the Bush White House had outlined an agreement, although it would take another few days to resolve the details of what a commentator called "the smallest Band-Aid that the automakers said they could live with [and] the most onerous conditions House Democrats could bring themselves to impose."

The proposed bill provided $14 billion in loans, to be drawn not from TARP but from the Advanced Technology Vehicles Manufacturing Loan Program, as the White House and other Republicans had been proposing. Also called for was the selection of a presidentially appointed car czar and the imposition of a March 31, 2009, deadline for the Big Three to submit turnaround plans. If these failed to satisfy the car czar, he could demand repayment, which would mean bankruptcy.

Speaker Pelosi had adopted the White House's approach in hopes of winning Republican votes. But by midweek, the gambit was in trouble. Although it appeared that the House would approve the bailout, the Senate posed a much tougher hurdle. Many Republican senators were itching to take a hard line on the automakers and the unions.

These murmurs of dissent prompted Bush to dispatch both Chief of Staff Bolten and Vice President Dick Cheney to the Republican senators' weekly policy lunch, where the discussion grew heated. Abandoning his customary hard-line, free-market, let-'em-fail rhetoric, Cheney warned that unless the senators took action, they risked being remembered as "the party of Herbert Hoover forever."

As disgruntled lawmakers shifted in their seats, Bob Corker, not easily intimidated, stood up. "There is no way in heck that I would support this!" he said, declaring that the White House proposal demanded too little of the automakers. Describing what he'd learned from his fact-finding mission to Wall Street, Corker said that GM and Chrysler were effectively broke. More loans without the restructuring of liabilities and expenses would be folly, he argued. He laid out a set of tough strictures that would require the automakers to cut debt by making lenders accept stock; fund employee health care plans with stock, not cash; and make wages competitive. When he concluded, the caucus erupted in applause.

"If [Bolten and Cheney] came with ten votes, they left with two," Corker said triumphantly after the lunch. He emerged with an unusual charter: Minority Leader Mitch McConnell delegated him to use the last two days of the congressional session to negotiate a more stringent bailout bill. In the rigid Senate pecking order, such tasks were almost always reserved for senior politicians.

Word of the senators' rebellion spread fast. The White House had not expected to get many Republican votes in the House, and that proved to be the case. When Pelosi's bailout bill passed the House that evening, only 32 Republicans, mostly from auto manufacturing districts, joined 205 Democrats in voting yes. The auto bailout had been sucked into a Bermuda Triangle of transition politics. A lame-duck conservative Republican President, anxious that the auto industry not implode on his watch, was allied with congressional Democrats in the face of resistance from his own party.

Treasury Secretary Paulson wasn't holding his breath for Congress to get the job done. Dusting off the contingency plan commissioned weeks before, he called to set up a lunch to discuss autos with President Bush. Paulson wasn't enthusiastic about Corker's proposal; from an investment-banking standpoint, it wasn't bad work for an amateur, but the government's understanding of automakers' problems was still too limited to justify such specific measures. What's more, Paulson suspected that the Republican leadership's support for Corker was only lukewarm; he doubted that any bailout plan could actually muster the necessary votes.

His worry now was that Bush might not follow through on using TARP. Though the President had repeatedly told his senior team that he wanted a smooth transition and did not wish to saddle Obama with a major crisis as he walked in the door, the hard-core ideologues in the White House would certainly continue to argue against a bailout. To be sure, Paulson still believed that rescuing the automakers might strain TARP and hamper the Treasury in coping with a future crisis. But in recent days, the prospect of a disorderly bankruptcy of the automakers had moved up in his hit parade of imminent threats. Paulson was becoming convinced that an unplanned auto bankruptcy could have a disastrous impact on the declining economy and the frozen financial system.

So, as Paulson lunched with the President and Kaplan in the small dining room adjacent to the Oval Office, he argued for a bailout. "GM has done no preparations to file for bankruptcy," he explained to Bush, who was eating carrots, a chopped apple, and a hot dog on a bun. "There is no private debtor-in-possession financing available. So a GM bankruptcy would be messy and would disrupt the network of suppliers," rippling through the industrial economy. Bush didn't explicitly agree, but Paulson left feeling reassured that if Congress failed to act, Bush would be open to emergency bridge financing using TARP.

Thursday, December 11, was shaping up as the biggest day of Bob Corker's young Senate career. He had started at 7:30 A.M. with a call to Fritz Henderson at GM. His quick win of the company's endorsement was not especially surprising, given that the bailout conditions Corker sought to impose involved mainly sacrifices by the UAW and GM's creditors. Ron Gettelfinger, Corker's next call, at least didn't hang up on him — he said the UAW was open to further discussions. Corker's final step of preparation was to make the short trip to the Capitol to persuade his fellow senators.

"It's showtime," Corker began in his appealing drawl as he stood on the Senate floor at 10:14. For the next seventeen minutes he reprised the argument he'd made to the caucus the day before, explaining his new conditions, which he now called covenants. "So let's go ahead and fund the request that has taken place," he pleaded. "And let's have three covenants, only three covenants. We can do this with a very short bill which we drafted. Three covenants."

Agreement on Corker's first two covenants came easily. The Democrats had no objection to the notion of converting two-thirds of the automakers' massive debt into equity — debt conversion is a standard practice when restructuring. The UAW, meanwhile, agreed in principle to accept GM and Chrysler stock in lieu of cash to help fund health benefits — it had made a similar accommodation with Ford.

Wages were another story. In exchange for federal money to keep the automakers afloat and save jobs, Corker wanted the UAW to bring Detroit's labor costs into "parity" with those of the Japanese transplants by the end of 2009. He was in effect angling for a concession that in decades of bargaining the Big Three had never been able to extract.

The senator was in constant motion, ducking in and out of the negotiation as the tension ratcheted up. The union would not commit to
a firm date before the expiration of its contract in 2011 for cutting labor
costs, and Corker would not back down. "This is the only thing standing between us and a deal and Christmas," Senator Richard Durbin of
Illinois, the majority whip, said with exasperation at the Republicans'
intransigence.

By 10 P.M. the negotiation had failed. Majority Leader Harry Reid
announced, "It's over with," going on to predict that Wall Street would
not be a pleasant sight the next day. More ominously, he predicted,
"This will be a very bad Christmas for a lot of people as a result of what
takes place here tonight."

Bitterly disappointed, Corker blamed the union, speculating that
Gettelfinger and his team never really meant to come to terms: the
UAW president, a master negotiator, knew that Bush would use TARP
as a last resort, probably without the strings that Corker was trying to
attach. And, of course, Gettelfinger was counting the days until the
union-friendly Obama administration arrived.

Gettelfinger angrily countered by saying that in recent years the
union had made several rounds of concessions to help the automakers
while creditors and other stakeholders had sacrificed nothing. "The
GOP caucus was insisting that the restructuring had to be done on the
backs of workers and retirees," he declared.

Corker may have been a little in front of his skis, but his effort was
admirable. He'd outshone his congressional colleagues in cutting
through the confusion and emotion during the early hearings. And together with the Bush team, he had homed in early on the key issue:
pumping money into either GM or Chrysler without a substantial restructuring of liabilities and expenses was foolhardy. The levers he
tried to pull — reducing outstanding debt, restructuring health care obligations, and making wages competitive — were some of the same that
we would manipulate later when the Obama task force took its turn.

The speed of the President's response the next day took the Treasury
by surprise. At 7:10 A.M. Joel Kaplan phoned Paulson from the White
House. "The President is on Air Force One," he began, explaining that
Bush was en route to Texas but meant to issue a statement before land-

ing. "He does not want the markets to come unglued on the fact that the Senate failed to act," Kaplan said.

Paulson was annoyed to have only a few minutes to review the President's statement, but he was aware that politically, Detroit was not Wall Street. While Bush had allowed Paulson and Bernanke to call many of the shots during the financial panic, autos were a heartland issue on which the White House wanted to take the lead. The Bush administration was not alone in responding to the Senate's failure to act. Canadian Prime Minister Stephen Harper pledged that his nation would "do our share" to save the automobiles. Accordingly, that morning, the Canadian government declared that it stood ready to kick in an added $2.8 billion to the proposed U.S. bailout. "We want to be part of the solution, and it will be commensurate with the production that takes place here in Canada," the industry minister told reporters.

Paulson summoned the exhausted staffers monitoring the automakers' crisis amid other duties. "You guys are now going to be working on a potential loan to the autos," he said. "The President is going to need options."

Minutes later, the White House statement came out. "Given the current weakened state of the U.S. economy," announced Press Secretary Dana Perino, "we will consider other options if necessary, including use of the TARP program, to prevent a collapse of troubled automakers." After that, Paulson's phone rang—calls from Kaplan and Gutierrez and the heads of the Big Three. Each CEO stayed true to script: Nardelli still wanted Treasury to make GM buy Chrysler. Wagoner asked to get started on a bridge loan for GM. Mulally, who stayed on the phone the longest, reiterated his concern that Washington would do something for the other automakers that would put Ford at a disadvantage. That refrain would continue ad nauseam.

The White House gave the Treasury four days—counting the weekend, that is—in which to map out options. Paulson and his team raced to answer two questions: What was the right policy, and what constituted a fair survey of options to present? A memo sent to the President on Monday night included four options. Except for the fact that TARP was now the source of the funding, the first option was very similar to the House bill—a bridge loan administered by a presidentially appointed car czar and subject to a financial viability test.

In the wake of the bill's failure in the Senate, the indefatigable Corker had been calling Paulson and the White House to urge the incorporation of his provisions in any bailout. The second option, preferred by Paulson, Kaplan, and their teams, centered on a bridge loan with conditions similar to Corker's. Finally, the memo outlined alternatives reflecting the views of the hard right: a proposal to provide TARP financing for an immediate bankruptcy and restructuring, and a proposal to do nothing at all and let the automakers fail.

The fate of the automakers was now in President Bush's hands. Tuesday afternoon, Paulson and Dan Jester, the head of his auto team, made their way to the Oval Office. During my time in Washington, I attended several such "decision meetings" and knew the inside story of others. Depending on the subject and the extent of disagreement among the President's advisers, the meetings could be either brief and almost perfunctory or hard-fought over many hours. This one fell somewhere in between.

The Bush White House was much more divided on what to do about autos than I would later experience under Obama. As a result, Jester spent much of the eighty-minute session trying to satisfy the concerns of Cheney, economic adviser Keith Hennessey, political adviser Ed Gillespie, and others favoring the harsh discipline of the marketplace. As the discussion wound down, the President went around the room soliciting recommendations from all of the dozen attendees. A handful of the more rigid, led by Cheney, had not been persuaded by Paulson and Jester. Bush was noncommittal, but in his body language, Paulson saw pragmatism trumping ideology. "Please let us know quickly," he asked the President.

That was not Bush's style. Despite his reputation for rashness, the President actually liked to chew over big decisions. Bailing out Detroit was certainly distasteful for him, especially as the last major act of his troubled presidency. He spurned bailouts on principle and privately disdained the U.S. automakers for being unable to build cars people wanted. Yet he'd already decided that letting the companies fail was off the table, and he had said so in public on December 12. As the week wore on, Paulson pestered Kaplan for an answer. "Look, Hank, this is a hard decision," Kaplan told his much older colleague.

"It's not a hard decision, it's an unpleasant decision," responded Paulson.

Ultimately the President ordered his staff to find a course of action somewhere between the more general House bridge-loan bill and the specific, mandatory conditions proposed by Corker. Keith Hennessey's compromise was to use strictures similar to Corker's but make them nonbinding, subject to the car czar's judgment. Bush went for that.

On Thursday morning, December 18, the President put GOP hardliners on notice that a bailout was imminent. Speaking at the American Enterprise Institute, a conservative think tank, he gave a surprisingly forthcoming response to a question about autos. "This is a difficult time for a free-market person," he began. "Under ordinary circumstances, failed entities, failing entities, should be allowed to fail. I have concluded these are not ordinary circumstances." In September he'd chosen to bail out Wall Street, he said, because "I didn't want to be the President during . . . the beginning of a depression greater than the Great Depression." Then he came back to Detroit: "I am worried about a disorderly bankruptcy and what it would do to the psychology and the markets. They're beginning to thaw, but there's still a lot of uncertainty. I'm also worried about putting good money after bad. That means whether or not these autos will become viable in the future."

Finally, in his customary, somewhat fractured English, he rebuffed ideologues: "Frankly, there's one other consideration, and that is, I feel an obligation to my successor . . . I believe that good policy is not to dump him a major catastrophe in his first day of office."

Because Bush had taken two days to make up his mind, there was only one day left before most of Washington shut down for the holidays — and the President wanted to announce the auto rescue on national TV before the markets opened the next morning. But lending tens of billions of dollars isn't simple. The Treasury needed agreed-upon, signed "term sheets," not just from General Motors and Chrysler but from their financing subsidiaries, GMAC and Chrysler Financial.

Those negotiations stretched deep into the night. Around 2 A.M. one of Paulson's colleagues took a call from Steve Feinberg, the chief of Cerberus, the private equity firm that owned most of Chrysler. Cerberus was proposing to turn over the automaker to the U.S. government for one dollar. Having witnessed the stalemate in Congress, the investor explained, he wanted to help resolve the crisis. The Treasury team mistook Feinberg's patriotism for a joke and just another sign of the automaker's desperate state.

Most of the staff members worked straight through. When the White House called at 7:30 to ask "Are you ready?" Jester was able to say, "We're looking good." The team delivered signed term sheets from both automakers. Characteristically, GM's paperwork didn't show up until just minutes before the President's scheduled airtime.

At 9:01 on that overcast, drizzly Washington morning, George Bush made it official, announcing the biggest industrial bailout in American history, with $17.4 billion of TARP money headed to Chrysler and GM.

The announcement happened to fall on the same day as the annual White House senior staff dinner. For this, the eighth and final such event of Bush's tenure, many former staffers had been invited as well as the current crew, so about one hundred diners gathered that evening in the East Room.

At the end of the meal, Josh Bolten rose to address the President and his colleagues. "As everyone here knows, each year the senior staff chips in to buy the President a Christmas gift," he began. "One year we bought him a high-quality chain saw. Another year we bought him an underwater camera. Last year, we all pooled our funds and bought him a top-of-the-line weed whacker for the ranch. Mr. President, this year for Christmas your senior staff chipped in and bought you . . . Chrysler!" The group burst into laughter and applause.

In retrospect, the Bush team's approach to the problem proved more thoughtful than I originally understood. For one thing, the loans bought time, not just until January 20, inauguration day, but until at least March 31, giving us a little breathing room. For another, Bush appropriately designated the Treasury secretary as the ultimate authority under the loan agreements, effectively declaring that there would be no independent car czar. Finally, adopting Corker's conditions — as imperfect as they were — provided a baseline of expected sacrifices that paved the way for our demands for give-ups from the stakeholders.

3

MR. RATTNER GOES TO WASHINGTON

My car from Washington's Reagan National Airport pulled up in front of a nondescript building on 6th Street NW where only the guards and temporary concrete barriers announced the presence of something unusual — the transition headquarters of the President-elect. Inside, Barack Obama, yet to be inaugurated, was preparing to take on America's biggest economic crisis since the Depression.

Although stepping across this threshold marked my physical entrance into political life, the hard knocks had started well before I got off the plane. Behind the scenes I was already under fire from Senator Deborah Stabenow and others from Michigan's congressional delegation — members of my own party! — who had heard of my appointment and didn't feel I had sufficient knowledge of the auto industry to help Detroit stay open for business. Perhaps my new bosses or I should have anticipated it, but we'd been preoccupied with trying to get under way amid the seeming free fall all around us. For me, the friendly fire only added to my terror about going in to lead a team that didn't yet exist on what gave every appearance of being a political and economic suicide mission.

For better or worse, history in this administration was going to be made at an accelerated pace. I could not help but imagine a disturbing scene set six months or so in the future in which President Obama, a man I admired, would have to face cameras and reporters and a lot of angry people and explain what had gone wrong: on his watch, two major automakers — iconic companies long among the largest and most important in the United States — had closed their showrooms, fired their workers, and shuttered their plants. The manufacturing sector was in turmoil. The state of Michigan was insolvent. A million or so people had been added to the unemployment rolls. The economy had received a terrible shock and was spiraling rapidly toward depression. And though I was in the background, I knew that the eyes of the President and his key advisers would be on me, because the job of my team had been to find a way to prevent this, and we had failed.

No realist could have avoided such forebodings. Chrysler and GM, both on the brink of failure, had been propped up by emergency government loans. The week after his election, in Chicago, at Obama's first substantive sit-down with his economic advisers, it was conceded that no situation on the economic front appeared thornier than the one I had been recruited to manage.

Obama had asked, "Is there any way these guys are going to avoid bankruptcy?"

"Unlikely," he was told.

"Why can't they make a Corolla?"

"We wish we knew," replied his advisers.

We would have very little time. The $17 billion in TARP funds provided by the Bush administration was draining away fast. Doubts were widespread that the automakers, required to submit "viability plans" on February 17, would make a sound case for more help.

Quite possibly ahead of us was, despite the best efforts of many, the implosion of an industry once synonymous with American ingenuity — at a moment of great vulnerability for the nation and for a new president who was inheriting a war being waged, not in Iraq or Afghanistan, but in the U.S. economy, where all the casualties were here at home.

As I hurried through the mid-January chill to transition headquarters, Secret Service agents stood guard near x-ray machines and scanners behind bulletproof glass. Upstairs, in a corner of the eighth floor, the President-elect's economic team was crammed into a half-dozen rooms. Tim Geithner and Larry Summers had offices the size of those of vice presidents at my old firm, with their names printed out on 8½-by-11 paper and taped to their doors. Obama himself occupied a space a short hallway — and a few more Secret Service agents — away.

Messy piles of paper and a mountain of leftover coffee cups testified to the transition team's long hours, but the mood was not despairing. Although the situation Obama had inherited was frightening, his victory represented a mandate for change, and change the incoming administration was determined to effect. Fixing the problems that threatened to add the Detroit automakers to the junk heap of old American dreams was very much on its to-do list. In this crisis atmosphere, the normal pomp of government was, at least at this informal moment, a quaint notion: incoming cabinet secretaries labored side by side with interns. Meetings gathered spontaneously in cramped corners. Rahm Emanuel strode the halls like a military commander.

I still faced vetting, but we needed to plan for the days ahead. With many still questioning the young President's readiness for his new assignment, the public had to perceive Obama as being on top of the challenges. Unemployment was soaring. Another new disaster on Wall Street could easily occur. For GM and Chrysler, there was the difficult, controversial question of bankruptcy, the course that most of us considered obvious, but scary to think about. No one had ever taken industrial companies of this size and complexity through bankruptcy before.

With nearly $100 billion in assets, GM alone was larger than all the U.S. airlines that had gone bankrupt in the past fifteen years, combined. And while automakers and airlines both depend on consumers, the automakers need their long-term goodwill more than any airline does. A passenger's contract ends at her destination gate. But when you buy a new car, you want to be able to count on years of warranty coverage, and to feel confident that you can eventually sell or trade in the car for a reasonable price. We could find no precedent for a company selling a product like autos keeping its customers in bankruptcy. If car buyers were to abandon Chrysler and GM, all the money in TARP would not be enough to rescue them.

What was more, with autos, the new administration was starting from scratch. On the case were two extremely diligent generalists who had been scrambling since the election to get up to speed on Detroit. They were Josh Steiner, my partner at Quadrangle, and a public-policy maven named Brian Deese. I'd worked with Josh for years but scarcely knew Brian. In the coming months, I'd end up spending more time with him than with my wife.

Young and enthusiastic, Brian was a Boston-area native and a Middlebury College graduate, with a major in politics, a minor in economics, and a radio show called *Bedknobs and Broomsticks*. He'd done stints at several think tanks and completed most of three years at Yale Law before dropping out for the Obama campaign. (At Larry's affectionate insistence, he would finish his law degree in August 2009.) After Obama won, he'd loaded his dog into his car and headed for Chicago, where he landed a spot on the transition team. (Brian's closest encounter with automaking had been sleeping in the car in the parking lot of an Ohio Pontiac plant.) A rising star, he would later be dubbed by the *New York Times* "The 31-Year-Old in Charge of Dismantling GM."

The economic meeting with Obama in Chicago at which the auto situation was reviewed had been scary for Brian. "This is basically just darkness," he sat there thinking.

Steiner and Deese had kept Obama and his top lieutenants informed as the Bush bailout took shape. The "one President at a time" policy limited their ability to make inquiries, but they'd picked the brains of members of the transition team who had restructuring experience, including Paul Volcker, who, twenty-nine years earlier, as chairman of the Fed, had been involved in the first Chrysler bailout. They'd quickly come to the same conclusion as the Bush administration, that a disorderly failure and liquidation of GM and Chrysler would be a terrible economic blow.

Steiner's and Deese's work also involved getting themselves and the President-elect's team briefed on the problems dogging the Big Three: the suffocating liabilities, excessive labor costs, overly large dealer networks, underused assembly plants, and on and on. In December, Deese had worked behind the scenes to try to help the Senate's last-ditch effort to craft an auto rescue, spreading the word that neither the Senate Democrats nor the UAW should expect the Obama administration to be a soft touch on labor matters. And they did succeed in influencing a key aspect of the Bush administration bailout — the replacement of Kaplan's idea of an independent car czar with that of a "President's designee" who would report within the normal executive-branch chain of command. Since the bailout was now part of TARP, the Treasury Department would be the official home of the Auto Task Force.

For help with financial modeling during those hectic weeks, Steiner and Deese had enlisted a thirty-one-year-old investment analyst, Brian Osias, who, despite a job on Wall Street, had volunteered his "spare time." The work pattern that emerged foreshadowed the crazy hours of our task force. At the end of a typical day, Josh and the two Brians would consult around 8 P.M., then the Brians continued with discussions late into the night. Next, Osias would hit the computer as Deese slept until 5 A.M., checking in with Osias upon rising. Then it was Osias's turn to nap — until he had to go to his office. The trio would talk on the phone again at 10 A.M.

Unfortunately for me, the notion of a car czar had taken hold in the popular imagination and in the media. After GM and Chrysler had received their initial loans at the turn of the year, attention shifted to the question of who would run the auto team. Josh Steiner, tired of juggling two jobs, was nudging Tim and Larry to replace him so he could turn his full attention back to Quadrangle. Deese was often the only one available to take calls from stakeholders in the auto world. "It was a little scary," he later admitted to the *New York Times*.

Amid the media and stakeholder frenzy, I shouldn't have been surprised that word of my acceptance on January 7 leaked almost immediately, though I'd hoped to keep the news confidential until I could inform my partners and our investors. But within a few hours, Senator Chuck Schumer called to congratulate me. How had he heard so quickly? "From Larry!"

Less than twenty-four hours later, Jake Tapper of ABC News posted a report on his website. For me, this was a potential disaster. My eighty-five Quadrangle colleagues had just been blindsided, not to mention more than one hundred investors in our private-equity funds, whom I had hoped to inform of my departure. Dismayed, I called Larry, who — to my amusement — wondered aloud whether the problem had arisen "from your end or our end."

Soon all hell broke loose. The first to take a swing at me was Bill Ford, the Ford Motor scion and ex-CEO whose company was not even on the federal dole. "It would be really helpful to have somebody in there who would take the time to have a deep understanding of our industry," he told reporters at the annual Detroit auto show. Ron Gettelfinger was quoted in the *Wall Street Journal* saying that the government should appoint someone who "knows something about the auto industry" rather than a Wall Street guy.

Politicians piled on. Michigan's two senators questioned my lack of knowledge of manufacturing and, in particular, autos. Why should they believe that a Wall Street guy who hadn't been to Detroit in three decades could handle an emergency that might wreck their state? As scared as I was, I agreed with Tim's and Larry's instincts in picking me for this assignment. This was not a managerial job; it was a restructuring and private equity assignment. And while I was not a classic restructuring guy, I had been through a number of bankruptcies. I certainly considered myself a qualified private equity investor. Equally important, I had been around the political arena for many decades, the kind of experience that Larry and Tim correctly deemed important. Others were kinder about my appointment, including Hillary Clinton, who sent me a BlackBerry message during her confirmation hearings for secretary of state: "Anything I can do to help?"

I quickly had my first taste of the popular parlor game of impugning the integrity of government officials, often without regard to facts. On January 9, the *New York Post* claimed that my appointment was being held up because of a suspicious link between Quadrangle and Cerberus, the owner of Chrysler. There was nothing suspicious: Cerberus had loaned money to a struggling portfolio company of ours that owned *Maxim* magazine. Later, in lieu of payment, Quadrangle had decided simply to give the company to Cerberus, which resolved the matter.

Yet, to my distress, the mainstream media picked up the tabloid report without independent verification. Ultimately, when my government vetters questioned me on the matter, they dismissed it as a nonissue.

What was I getting into?

Without question, I had a great deal to master. Deese shared with me the work that he, Brian Osias, and Josh had produced, and I began to read everything, from auto industry research reports to books about the history of the Detroit Three. But the only material we had from the Bush period were term sheets for the Chrysler and GM loans. Except for one of Hank Paulson's advisers who had stayed on to help Tim, we would, unfortunately, never meet with or speak to any of the Bush team.

. . .

Brian Deese greeted me on that first visit to transition headquarters. He looked as young as I'd expected from having spoken with him on the phone, and wore a workaday suit and tie and had a scruffy beard. Remarkably poised and exceptionally intelligent, he reminded me of the White House staffers I'd known as a reporter covering the Carter administration—talented politics-and-policy types who had always dreamed of passing through the White House gates each morning to work for the President.

Brian and I settled into a small empty office, a few doors away from Tim and Larry, and began discussing the daunting questions. *How should we define success? Was bankruptcy a realistic option for GM? Could Chrysler be a viable company? What did "competitive" labor costs mean? What was the most efficient and productive way to assemble an effective team, including outside consultants?*

So much was on the table that not all of it immediately penetrated my consciousness. It would be days before I realized that the problems of the auto finance companies, GMAC and Chrysler Financial, were as great as those of the automakers. No solutions to the automakers' problems could occur without a sustainable restructuring of the finance companies as well.

Around noontime, I sat with Tim Geithner as he munched what looked like a tuna fish wrap. I later learned that in the course of the morning he had received word that the Senate Finance Committee was in an uproar about his neglecting to pay Social Security and Medicare taxes earlier in his career. Yet I detected no sign of distress.

This stoicism helped me see why the President-elect had chosen Geithner in the first place. Obama's options for Treasury secretary had been quite limited. Essentially, only Larry and Tim had the necessary government experience, along with the credibility vital in the financial world. Obama could have recruited a leading business figure, but the record of CEOs at Treasury was mixed at best, as evinced by the forgettable performances of Hank Paulson's predecessors, Paul O'Neill and John Snow. Meanwhile, choosing another Treasury secretary from Wall Street, like Hank Paulson, was politically out of the question after the financial meltdown. As head of the Federal Reserve Bank of New York, Tim had facilitated the bailouts of AIG and the banks and helped to prevent a systemic collapse. That had earned him Wall

Street support, even though he was neither an economist nor a financier.

I had long heard great things about Tim and knew he had spent most of his career in public service and that he was almost indifferent to the creature comforts prized by Wall Streeters like myself. His only outside interests seemed to be tennis, basketball, workouts at the gym, and cooking at home on weekends. Like Obama, he had the adaptability of one who had grown up around the world: his dad had worked in international development, and Tim had spent much of his childhood in Zimbabwe, India, and Thailand. In the 1980s, the senior Geithner oversaw the microfinance project of Obama's mother, Ann Dunham, for the Ford Foundation in Indonesia.

Tim had followed Larry up the ladder at the Treasury Department, where he'd gained a reputation for his ready grasp of difficult issues and sound judgment. The big question about Tim during the selection process had been whether he was personally imposing enough. As Ken Duberstein, ex–chief of staff to President Reagan, told the *Washington Post,* "Tim at 47 looks 32, and you need to have . . . grey hair and gravitas. It's not that he's not qualified; it's how he looks." It was said that Obama chose Tim over Larry both to signal a step past Clinton and because of personal chemistry.

From Tim's office, I went next door to visit Summers, who was sipping one of the numerous Diet Cokes that he typically consumed in the course of a day. Far more expressive and voluble than Tim, he exclaimed several times, "This is going to be great." I'd known and liked Larry since the Clinton administration and was in awe of his intellect, vast knowledge, and ardent curiosity about unfamiliar subjects — such as the auto industry. His appetite for work was prodigious, but he was also the archetypal absent-minded professor (habitually late, chronically disorganized). Happily, his determination and drive more than compensated. As fast as his mind worked, his mouth was often in a lower gear. He could start a sentence several times before settling on exactly what to say. Early in our relationship, I had learned to resist trying to help him complete his thought. And I'd seen flashes of the intellectual arrogance that contributed to his fall at Harvard, where he was president from 2001 to 2006. But I had been delighted when Obama asked him to take on the pivotal job as director of the National Economic Council (NEC). I could not imagine the new administration tackling problems of the magnitude it was facing without Larry's help.

In due course, our conversation turned to the controversy swirling around me. "We underissued that one," Larry said, introducing me to a new bit of Washington jargon. I took him to mean that the Obama team should have anticipated the flap and acted to head it off. I offered to step aside on the spot. "You shouldn't feel any obligation to me," I said. But Larry responded that both he and Tim were convinced that my Wall Street experience and part-time political work were the right skills for the job.

I wasn't so sure. I had accepted the job welcoming the fact that I would be reporting to Tim and Larry, and now the press had turned me into a czar (which would have amused my Rattner ancestors who were fur merchants in Moscow). I felt that I had a huge bull's-eye painted on my back.

I made only one other visit to transition headquarters, coincidentally on the day the Senate agreed to the second $350 billion of TARP funding, January 15. Pushing through the second tranche of the unpopular program was a heady success for an administration that hadn't yet taken office. The news occasioned high-fives in the economics corner of the eighth floor and a victory-lap appearance by Rahm. I met Haley Stevens that day, even younger than Deese and a native of Michigan, who had wanted more than anything to assist with autos and had gotten a mutual acquaintance to send me her résumé. Haley had spent most of the three and a half years since graduating from college in one political job or another while also earning a master's degree. After the election, she'd worked on confirmations for cabinet-level appointees. Since she was already on the transition team's payroll, Deese and I quickly decided to make her our chief of staff. We would come to find her tireless, cheerful, and blessed with a social conscience and a talent for improvisation.

A little later, I met a far more senior new colleague, Diana Farrell, who was slated to join Larry's NEC as a deputy director. Like me, Diana came from business. Unlike me, she was versed in management consulting, having been the director of the McKinsey Global Institute.

While neither she nor I knew what her exact role on the team would be, Larry had inserted her to provide some senior support for Deese during the muddled early days, and I was delighted. From the start, Diana realized that GM and Chrysler were going to need much more of an overhaul than the President's political advisers and even Larry expected, a point she helpfully tried to drive home to them.

When inauguration day arrived, I deliberately remained in New York and watched Barack Obama be sworn in on TV. I had decided to keep my trips to Washington at a minimum until my appointment went through. I saw culture shock ahead: my career had involved moving to smaller and smaller firms with less and less red tape — from Morgan Stanley to Lazard to Quadrangle. Suddenly I was entering the world's largest bureaucracy, a realm of meetings and memos. The new administration was drowning in questions, often with higher priority than those of our team, and almost no one knew how to make things happen. I would have to be polite, work the system, and keep nudging. But the inefficiency sobered me. It was what Wall Street would call a risk factor.

Like nature, government abhors a vacuum. I was flooded with e-mails and calls even though my appointment was by no means official. Seemingly small matters foretold of major issues to come. For example, in mid-January GM blew its first deadline under the Bush loan agreements, failing to satisfy certain reporting requirements for its second installment of $5.4 billion. The company's accounting systems, it emerged, were simply incapable of producing data on GM's cash position in the form that the Treasury wanted. The GM bureaucracy was equally unsuccessful at revising its corporate expense policy on time. Five days later, it complied and got the money.

Automotive suppliers started to fail, which was how I discovered that the scope of my assignment was much broader than I'd anticipated. GM and Chrysler had dominated the conversations with Tim and Larry. None of us appreciated that, with auto sales down 40 percent, the collateral damage among related businesses would be vast. These companies, which provide factories and repair shops with raw materials and parts, were in deep trouble, and because of their interconnectedness, the trouble could become wildly contagious. Bailing out the giant automakers wouldn't be enough if they could no longer get the parts they needed to build cars. A collapse of just a few key suppliers could cause the Big Three (and possibly some transplants as well) to shut down abruptly, triggering widespread economic disarray. Yet no government money had been allocated to help the auto parts manufacturers. Like the seven-second delay in live television, the suppliers' problems took a little while to surface. This was because the Big Three usually didn't pay for parts until forty-five days after delivery. A slowing of the assembly lines actually made the suppliers temporarily more flush — they could collect on prior deliveries without having to spend money to fill new orders. But when the shock wave from collapsing demand caught up with them, its effect was brutal. And with capital markets frozen, they had nowhere to turn.

Most of the failures were companies that I had never heard of — like Contech, a privately owned, one-thousand-employee metal-casting company outside Kalamazoo, which declared bankruptcy after revenues fell by nearly one-third in 2008. Multibillion-dollar businesses whose names I vaguely knew — like American Axle, Lear, TRW, and Dana — saw their stocks collapse. As I later learned, the rule of thumb is that for every automaking job there are two supplier jobs, suggesting that 650,000 jobs were at risk among suppliers.

Since early January, Brian Deese had been thinking about a definition of success for our team. It was clearly not just a matter of dollars and cents. How should we balance the bailout's huge cost and risk against the need to preserve communities and jobs and limit the economic ripple effects? We quickly settled on two principles to propose to Larry and Tim. First, further government funding should come only in exchange for fundamental restructuring that made automakers truly viable and got them off the federal dole. Second, all stakeholders in GM and Chrysler — investors, creditors, employees, and retirees — ought to share the pain of such an overhaul.

This definition was notable in part for what it did not say. It pointedly did not include protecting all jobs. Or rule out bankruptcy. And it did not include industrial-policy goals, such as the development of electric vehicles. Instead it mirrored the hard-nosed approach that a private owner might have taken — except the new owner was to be the American taxpayer.

We expected objections from other parts of the administration, in the form of an "interagency process" in which Energy, Commerce, Labor, and other departments would weigh in. I braced for compromise. But perhaps because of the magnitude of the crisis, or because everyone in the new administration was equally overwhelmed, no other part of the executive branch got involved. Indeed, as we worked, Obama's "climate czar," Carol Browner, mediated between the administration and Congress on tougher fuel-efficiency rules without ever asking us to twist arms at Chrysler or GM.

The flow of auto industry issues became a torrent as I tried to calm colleagues and hand off leadership at Quadrangle. As I began to address the task force's logistical issues, from staffing and space to computers and phones, I struggled to comply with onerous vetting requirements and spent countless hours helping to search for ways to defuse questions on my qualifications.

Being vetted can be a full-time job. At Josh's suggestion, I had begun talking to my attorneys in mid-December, in part to ascertain whether public office was feasible for me. Every senior appointee has to complete two massive documents: the SF-86, an impossibly tedious security-clearance statement that requires listing—just for example—every foreign trip an applicant has taken in the previous seven years, and the SF-278, which involves the disclosure of every financial interest and obligation. Like most recent administrations, this one had added its own questions, derived from past debacles, such as Zoë Baird's failure to become Bill Clinton's attorney general after neglecting to pay the so-called nanny tax. I can't count the hours I spent complying, but I do know that the honor of working for the federal government cost me more than $400,000 in legal fees.

The vetting rules were more than a personal nuisance; they hampered our effort to assemble a first-class team. As part of his pledge to rid government of special interests, Obama layered new conflict-of-interest strictures on top of the statutory rules that applied mostly to financial holdings. He targeted lobbyists with rules that barred any candidate who had worked for an organization that would be a party to the matter that the individual would be handling in government. This seemingly logical concept had the unintended consequence of severely restricting our ability to hire anyone who knew anything about the automobile industry, a limitation that fueled the very criticism we were trying to counter.

I didn't see Larry Summers again until two weeks after the inauguration, in his new West Wing office, a 16-by-17-foot space that appeared to have been last renovated in the Eisenhower era. The view was of a white parapet perhaps two feet away. Larry didn't care; offices in the West Wing are all about proximity to "the Oval." Neither did Deese. In what must originally have been a reception area were jammed a half-dozen desks for support staff. Deese had commandeered one, and for the first few weeks was sure he'd get evicted. But eventually he was told that he could either stay or decamp to a real office, in the Eisenhower building across the driveway. Always wise, Deese also understood the value of proximity and elected to remain in a location that gave a huge boost to our efficiency by guaranteeing ready access to Larry during a period when his every moment was precious.

My visit was motivated by my growing despair. Every day had brought additional evidence of the seemingly intractable problems of GM and Chrysler — loss of market share, overwhelming structural costs, bleeding cash. Having had experience in the mosh pit of restructurings, overhauling entities the size and complexity of the automakers on tight deadlines felt impossibly daunting. Simultaneously, the Greek chorus of criticism intensified. On February 2, I saw Senator Carl Levin of Michigan, whom I knew slightly, at the swearing-in of Hillary Clinton. When I reintroduced myself, he politely but firmly announced, "If you're going to do this job, you'd better have some people around you who understand manufacturing."

My growing impulse — notwithstanding my desire to serve in a time of crisis — was to snuggle back into the comfort of Quadrangle. "I don't mind a challenge but I like to know it's possible," I e-mailed Larry. Larry can be an indefatigable and relentless salesman and batted back my concerns one by one. Among other things, after weeks of patient inquiries, I still had little idea of how many people I would be allowed or how to get them on the payroll. When I mentioned this to Larry, he asked how large a team I needed. "If we were in the private sector, I'd say fifty people," I told him, "but in a governmental context, maybe fifteen."

"But the whole NEC is only nineteen professionals!" Larry exclaimed.

In spite of all this, somehow I left the meeting willing, for the moment at least, to soldier on.

Larry and Tim and I had agreed that, to dispel the furor surrounding my appointment, the task force needed to be bolstered with someone who could balance my Wall Street credentials with credibility in Detroit. We considered veteran industrial executives, like my friends Henry Schacht, former head of Cummins Engine, and George David, chairman of United Technologies. I was eager to hire Steve Girsky, formerly a top auto equity analyst at Morgan Stanley who had also worked for both General Motors and the UAW. Steve had forgotten more about the industry than I would ever know. But a stint as an *unpaid* adviser to the UAW during bailout negotiations the previous fall disqualified him under Obama's rules.

As a potential deputy, many suggested Ron Bloom, whom I knew slightly as we'd overlapped at Lazard before he'd gone on to a totally different career. The son of leftist parents who sent him to a Zionist labor youth camp, Ron had been inspired to help workers. Yet unlike most aspiring labor activists, he went to Harvard Business School and then Wall Street. At Lazard, he and his partner Gene Keilin engineered large, creative restructurings aimed at giving workers both equity ownership and seats on the employers' boards.

In 1996, Ron became, in effect, the United Steelworkers' chief restructuring officer. Cheap steel from emerging nations was causing American steelmakers to fail, often resulting in ugly bankruptcies that left workers and pensioners in the cold. Rather than try to prop up doomed companies, Ron showed his genius in helping them consolidate, identifying and saving the jobs that would last and arranging the softest landing possible for steelworkers who were displaced. We convened at the Ritz-Carlton, where he ordered a martini—not exactly a steelworker's drink. But with his long, solemn face and warm eyes, he looked every bit the workingman's advocate. Like many negotiators, he had a ribald sense of humor. He liked to compare his style to that of the patient in a dentist's chair who grabs the dentist by the genitals and says, "Now, let's not hurt each other." His sense of humor extended to himself. "I get it," he said one day early in his tenure, as the team was filling with Wall Street veterans, "I'm affirmative action."

Like me, Ron was used to running his own show. Yet I liked him and we had a lot in common. We'd both been through many restructurings. Like me, he was soft-spoken and fact-based. We shared a firm capitalist perspective: companies had to be viable, and saving loss-makers was pointless. And we agreed on another key issue that Ron raised. "Just so you know where I'm coming from," he said, "my agenda here is to save as many jobs as possible."

"So is mine," I replied.

Finding Ron was a step forward, but my doubts deepened days later, when the White House officially refused to grant Girsky a waiver from the vetting rules.

At almost exactly the same moment, five senators — including the Michigan Democrats — sent an open letter to Obama that seemed aimed at me. They asked him to "create a group of advisors to oversee the loans and provide the insight needed to steer our domestic automakers through this unprecedented crisis." The senators said the panel should "understand manufacturing."

I'd had enough. I drafted a long e-mail to Larry listing the reasons for me to withdraw. But I didn't send it. I actually sent a shorter, milder note, offering again to step aside. "I am sorry that we are putting u in this position," Larry responded, not letting me off the hook.

Meanwhile, with February 17 looming, we tried to get organized. As Deese had done with his desk in the West Wing, Haley Stevens simply commandeered a spacious, airy room at Treasury. She had desks placed around the perimeter facing the yellow walls and put a conference table in the center. Telephone and Internet access was delayed, so we used our cell phones and wireless cards, wondering how past incoming administrations had functioned. The windows of the room looked out on the White House, a constant reminder of the pressure on us.

Officially I had no office. Not having completed the appointment process, I was not supposed to be in the Treasury building except for meetings, although many rules were bent in this crisis atmosphere. I was given the use of a cavernous office, decorated with an antique typewriter and a framed collection of 1938 currency, a dozen or so doors down from Tim's suite. History seeped from the walls. In this room, President Andrew Johnson had signed the Amnesty Proclamation on May 29, 1865, restoring the rights of those who had joined the Confederacy. A printed copy hung on the wall with his signature, although it turned out to be a facsimile.

I felt like a kid in a new school, but all the teachers were also new. It was so hard to get through the Secret Service checkpoint that on my second day, I e-mailed Haley, "Is there a cafeteria in this building? I'm afraid to go out — I may never get back in!" Everything was complicated, including communicating with Tim, who I assumed would have e-mail and a BlackBerry. But within ten days of his taking office, e-mails to his address were routed to the "Executive Secretariat," a group whose job was to manage the message flow to Tim, with rules and forms for everything. Every communication needed to adhere to a specific format and clearance process.

Meanwhile, January auto sales were abysmal — GM was down 49 percent, Ford 40 percent, and Chrysler 55 percent. The companies were burning through their money at an alarming rate. GM's cash position was skirting close to the $11 billion minimum the company said it needed to operate; Chrysler forecast that it would drop below its minimum operating requirement of $2.5 billion before March ended.

Given these figures and the Bush loan agreements, which set very specific benchmarks for the automakers to achieve by February 17, we could not delay opening a dialogue with both companies. The first call — between Ray Young, of GM, and Brian Deese, Diana Farrell, and Mike Tae, a new arrival at Treasury — revealed that GM was still dreaming. Each company was required to include a pessimistic or "downside" assumption about future auto sales, but GM's idea of a downside was 20 percent market growth. Diana tried to push Ray to think of more appropriate downside cases but couldn't make him understand. "Okay, let me try this one more time," she finally said. "Ray, I'm not sure you're hearing what I'm saying. What I'm saying is that your *worst* case is our view of the absolute *best* case, and you need to start thinking about radically different outcomes."

So concerned were Brian and Diana (I was still operating behind the curtain) that they recommended to Larry that he alert the GM board.

He agreed and called Erskine Bowles, his friend who had been one of the directors who had visited Paulson back in October 2008. We also worried that GM had too little contingency planning under way. Thanks to Wagoner's refusal to consider bankruptcy, the company had not even hired restructuring lawyers until mid-December. With Chrysler, the task force did a similar reality check, emphasizing the need for conservative assumptions about demand. Chrysler was already pessimistic in its downside assumptions, though with its sales down 55 percent, the company's planners could hardly have been otherwise.

Bankruptcy, of course, had always been the elephant in the room. It was scary even to think about. Yet if managed successfully, it could enable GM and Chrysler, under the protection of a court, to stay in business while restructuring debts, renegotiating contracts with unions and suppliers, selling or scrapping obsolete and underused plants, and otherwise positioning themselves for a fresh start.

From the first moments in December when Josh Steiner had started sharing tidbits about what he and Deese were learning, I had thought bankruptcy was inevitable. Especially at GM, there were too many actors on the stage and too many liabilities that needed to be expunged or dramatically reduced for me to believe that a purely voluntary restructuring could work. Conceivably, the company could renegotiate its labor contracts without court protection. But what about the thousands of individuals and institutions who held GM bonds? How could GM ever corral all these creditors and persuade a large majority to accept pennies on the dollar, something a voluntary restructuring would require? And what about GM's vast, overgrown dealer network — more than six thousand independent businesses across the country, each protected by contracts and state franchise laws?

Senator Corker had tried to prepare the way for a restructuring without bankruptcy by designing the three conditions that then became embedded in the Bush loans. But they proved nowhere near tough enough to ensure financial viability and impossible to implement outside bankruptcy. GM and Chrysler wasted many hours trying to comply with them, while in the end their principal benefit was to provide a baseline that all the stakeholders would understand and thereby ease the pressure on us to produce conditions of our own.

At the same time, the risks of bankruptcy were immense. I was far from being an expert, but I'd seen enough in my investment banking career to know that bankruptcy disrupts a business from top to bottom. As the automakers were always quick to remind us, customers dislike dealing with bankrupt companies; suppliers demand cash on delivery. And imagine trying to hire talented people if they know your business is bankrupt. Instead of being able to concentrate on competing in the marketplace, executives must spend much of their time huddling with lawyers and advisers and placating bondholders and banks. The longer the exercise goes on, the more distracting and expensive it becomes. I remembered the head of our restructuring practice at Lazard, a crusty veteran of scores of deals, telling me again and again that "bankruptcy should never be thought of as the solution of first choice for a troubled company." Todd Snyder, a Rothschild bankruptcy specialist who had advised on the Bush bailout plan, became our indispensable guide. He knew all the tools and techniques for effecting corporate overhauls. I was particularly gratified when he agreed with my amateur's assessment that our salvation might lie in a form of asset sale known as a Section 363, after the part of the bankruptcy code that governs it.

Section 363 allows a bankrupt company to act quickly to transfer intact, valuable business units to a new owner. (The conventional bankruptcy process restructures the corporation as a whole.) Once exotic and obscure, 363 had provided the only bright spot in the cataclysmic implosion of Lehman Brothers. It was used to salvage Lehman's money-management and Asian businesses. Though 363 had never been applied to industrial companies on the scale of Chrysler and GM, I had suggested to Josh back in December that the new team explore the option. It might offer a way to save GM's and Chrysler's best factories and brands while the courts sifted through the other wreckage.

I hated presenting problems without solutions, but we had none ready for prime time when we went to see Tim and Larry on February 11, six days before the Chrysler and GM submissions would confirm the debacle in the offing. Since we had no staff, we had to rely on Todd Snyder's people at Rothschild to prepare the presentation. Even then, the best we would be able to do was to lay out a series of options that gave a clear indication of our thinking.

I wanted to be well prepared. At 10 P.M. the night before, after the

Rothschild team arrived, we convened on a conference call to go over the possible restructuring options. Nearly all involved putting GM and Chrysler into bankruptcy. The only nonbankruptcy solution required reaching out-of-court agreements promptly with the labor unions, creditors, and suppliers, distributors, and dealers. We gave that approach the lowest probability of success. Every one of the options entailed using huge amounts of taxpayer money to sustain the companies through the restructuring period.

Most of the conference call was spent discussing the Section 363 approach, our final and best option. But the time Rothschild said would be needed was long, from six to fifteen months. I thought that would be a disaster.

We ended up having to brief Tim and Larry separately. During our time with Larry, our tough talk about bankruptcy was interrupted by an emotional interjection from Gene Sperling, a counselor to Tim. A devoted public servant and gifted policy wonk, Gene had served during all eight years of the Clinton administration, the last four in Larry's job, heading the NEC. He spoke up here as a Michigan native.

"I don't know what to tell you guys to do," he said, "but if you are not from the Midwest, you cannot appreciate the devastating psychological effect that bankruptcies would have there." Gene would repeat this admonition many times during our deliberations, a helpful reminder of the human consequences of our actions.

That seemed to strike a chord with Larry, whom I could see getting nervous. Although in December he had been one of the voices telling the President-elect that bankruptcy was probably unavoidable, the prospect clearly disturbed him more as it came closer to reality. He was particularly leery about the risk of permanent government involvement. "I hear you, Larry," I said at one point. "But make no mistake about it, you own these companies," by which I meant that the massive amount of federal aid would put the government in the auto business, regardless of who ultimately owned the stock. He ended by asking us to develop the best approach in the event bankruptcy was not available.

We briefed Tim at the Treasury; unlike Larry, he did not push back. He took it as given that we'd identified the right options and that bankruptcy was probably inevitable. To him, the question was how to cushion the shock so that consumers would keep buying cars. "We need to put foam on the runway," he said, an allusion that, as a pilot, I readily understood: airport crews use foam on the runway to mitigate crash landings. It can be effective, but doesn't always prevent fatalities.

Shortly before the viability reports were due, GM previewed for us its updated analysis. The company now forecasted needing an additional $2 billion just to survive until March 31. The Chrysler news was equally bad. The company's draft submission showed dwindling cash balances, a blunt refusal by creditors to reduce secured debt, and a dark analysis of the consequences of failure. In Chrysler's estimate, liquidating the business in an orderly way would yield around $1 billion, assuming that it had run through all the cash on its balance sheet.

Neither company was making much progress on the other requirements of the Bush loans, either. Descendants of Corker's original conditions, these provisions had been designed as key steps toward restructuring — reducing liabilities like debt and legacy health care obligations and lowering operating costs, including labor. By February 17 GM and Chrysler were required to submit signed term sheets from their stakeholders proving that these cuts had been achieved.

Admirable, but surreal. While the companies had begun negotiating earnestly with unions, debt holders, suppliers, and dealers, there was absolutely no chance of success. The unions made it clear that they would not give ground again without shared sacrifice, particularly from lenders. The Chrysler banks, meanwhile, were steadfast in their unwillingness to reduce the $6.9 billion of outstanding debt. GM was going through the motions of trying to win the support of a sufficient number of its public bondholders to reduce its debt on that front. But there was a greater chance of finding oil under the White House.

Bad chemistry with GM added to everybody's stress. Less than a week before the deadline, Ray Young called Deese to ask for a postponement on meeting the restructuring benchmarks — GM wanted two more weeks. Making that call did not show great judgment, but Young's attitude was even worse. He suggested to Deese that if GM missed its benchmarks, the *government* would look bad. To Larry these were fighting words. Had GM somehow forgotten that taxpayers were footing its bills? He called two of GM's Washington advisers the next day and received assurances that Young would not attempt any direct communication with the White House again.

Still, we recognized GM's difficulties; Chrysler had them too. On the eve of the deadline, we said uncle and waived all of the cost-reduction strictures. Had we not, both automakers would have been in default on their federal loans, and therefore bankrupt.

We faced mountains of red tape. Seemingly obvious matters, such as whether to make the reports public, needed to be considered. A procedure had to be created for receiving the plans. Our most important behind-the-scenes preparation was a memo to President Obama on what to expect. POTUS memos, as they are called (POTUS is government-speak for President of the United States), have their own special protocol. They come from cabinet-level officials (Tim and Larry, in our case) but are, of course, drafted much further down the food chain (in our case, by Deese). A good POTUS memo is short, with lots of bullet items and bold type to emphasize decision points.

Having watched GM and Chrysler unveil a succession of overly optimistic forecasts, we were determined from the start to be hardheaded in our assessments. By this time, we believed that the bailout would require at least $50 billion of additional capital, and we had serious doubts as to whether the government would receive a substantial portion of the money back. We also wanted to be sure that the White House understood that without bankruptcy as a tool, we were quite pessimistic about the possibility of effecting fundamental restructurings.

Finally, judging from the worrisome conversations with Rothschild, it seemed possible that bankruptcy, with all the attendant risks, could last at least six months. Throughout our work, we consistently strove to be as realistic as possible when communicating with our superiors and to use probabilities rather than absolutes. We tried to follow two simple rules: no surprises, and no problems without proposed solutions.

February 17 neared, but the automotive team still had not been announced — a growing public-relations headache. As early as February 2, Tim's spokeswoman, Stephanie Cutter, had sent around an e-mail warning that came to me at Quadrangle: "We're about to lose control of this story." The notion of an official task force had been floating in the

ether; Deese grabbed hold of it and convinced Larry that a group of senior staffers like Diana Farrell and Gene Sperling would be both productive and politically salable. But when Larry looked at a draft of the
plan, he said, "We can't announce a task force with a bunch of people
like staff. We can't announce staff meetings as task force meetings."

Much of the administration's disarray was understandable. Larry
and many of the domestic-policy staff had been consumed with getting
the President's stimulus package through Congress — a $787 billion af-
fair. The solution the White House eventually settled on for autos was
something called the Presidential Task Force on the Auto Industry, a
cabinet-level committee to be chaired jointly by Larry and Tim and
comprised of officials from across the administration. While it sounded
impressive, its purpose was to bury once and for all the idea of a car czar,
reassure the Midwest that autos were a top priority, establish Larry and
Tim as coequals on the matter, and free the actual task force — namely,
staffers like Brian and me — to work in peace.

This presidential task force was announced as haphazardly as it had
been planned. On February 16 aboard Air Force One, Press Secretary
Robert Gibbs told reporters that its formal unveiling "could be" later
that day and mentioned that someone named "Richard Bloom" would
be joining the staff. As it turned out, the actual unveiling wasn't until
four days later. But at least the announcement saved face — and cleared
the slate for the automakers' submissions.

When the documents finally arrived on the seventeenth (true to
form, GM missed the customary 5 P.M. cutoff by forty-five minutes), the
White House was ready with a concise statement supporting the bailout. It emphasized the need for shared sacrifice: "Going forward, more
will be required from everyone involved — creditors, suppliers, dealers,
labor and auto executives themselves — to ensure the viability of these
companies."

As we worked through the night to prepare a memo for Tim and
Larry, the substance of what we had received was clear: GM and
Chrysler showed little progress toward meeting the conditions of the
loan agreements, and their requests for additional funding — $14 bil-
lion — were based on unrealistic assumptions. Neither plan offered any
hint that bankruptcy would be necessary or desirable to achieve long-
term viability. The gaps we found reflected the two companies' weak-

nesses and personalities. Lacking a robust selection of new designs and unable to meet tightening fuel economy standards without appealing small cars, Chrysler pinned its hopes on a prospective alliance with the Italian automaker Fiat. GM still relied heavily on an imaginary rebound in demand.

Wall Street also found the GM plan lacking. (Chrysler's received no comment, as the company was privately owned.) Rod Lache of Deutsche Bank, one of the most respected auto industry stock analysts, decried the massive debt that GM proposed to continue to owe. He reiterated his sell recommendation, giving the stock a price target of zero. Within three days, the stock sank 19 percent, to $1.77 a share, cutting GM's market value to a meager $1 billion.

All that remained was for me to officially say yes to the job I had already started. I was still terrified. While Detroit melted, I dithered. This finally prompted Larry to shift into bad-cop mode, calling me to suggest that I was on the verge of "doing a Judd Gregg," a reference to the Republican senator whom Obama had chosen as secretary of commerce. Gregg had made a 180-degree turn, withdrawing his acceptance after it dawned on him that he disagreed with much of the Obama agenda.

If I withdrew at this late date, I realized, I would almost certainly never get another chance to serve in an Obama administration. I e-mailed Larry to apologize for my hesitancy. The e-mail he sent back bucked me up: "Life will work out for you either way though America will be better off if you do this." I was also grateful for an e-mail from Deese: "My opinion is of little consequence to the situation, but for what it is worth I think you are incredibly needed right now, that you will succeed notwithstanding the terrible task in front of us, and I am willing to do whatever I can internally to help make this situation one that you're comfortable taking on."

Finally, on Thursday, February 19, sitting on the couch in Tim's office watching his precious minutes tick by, I understood that the time for indecision was past. Impulsively, I closed my eyes and jumped.

The following Monday, I once again found myself standing in the cold outside a fortresslike office building, this time the Treasury Department. Shivering outside the guard shack on Pennsylvania Avenue as I waited to get in, my clearance adrift in a bureaucratic haze, I could not help but think about all the bailout's delays — and the costs for me, for the industry, and for the country.

Obama's "one President at a time" stance may have been good politics, but if his team had linked arms with the outgoing administration, as President Bush's advisers had proposed, billions of dollars could well have been saved. The incoming administration should have made its personnel decisions much faster, as many commentators had urged. The deliberate pace at which key posts were filled did not comport with the urgency of the circumstances. Tim's and Larry's appointments weren't announced until almost three weeks after the election. Much quicker action, perhaps as soon as the day after the election, would have seemed more appropriate.

Of course, if there had been no presidential election or change of administration, there would have been no costly holdups. So maybe the delays and the billions of dollars in added expense just have to be accepted as costs of democracy.

4

"F**K THE UAW"

"WHY EVEN SAVE GM?" he demanded provocatively, interrupting the conversation. Other people had asked the question in the past, but it was astonishing coming from Rahm Emanuel. It certainly wasn't the challenge we'd anticipated. We had gone into the meeting expecting the White House to oppose letting even Chrysler go, but Emanuel had put GM in play, at least rhetorically.

The viability reports had not shown any reason for hope. In fact, the situation had gotten worse. GM and Chrysler now said that they needed more money—another $14 billion right away, to be precise. This meeting with Emanuel had come together as Team Auto—the name we had chosen for ourselves to minimize talk of "czars"—continued to face the scary conundrum of bankruptcy. We would almost certainly need that process to achieve fundamental restructurings, but we feared that the medicine was so strong that it might kill the patients we were trying to cure. There was also the question of whether Obama, so publicly supportive of the automakers and sincerely committed to saving the industry, would actually allow a bankruptcy.

The White House chief of staff occupies an unusually elegant office by West Wing standards. (Rahm was known to brag that his first-floor office was eight square feet larger than the Vice President's, and closer to the Oval.) We approached its splendor assuming that Rahm would attack, in his trademark slash-and-burn style, the conclusion on which we were approaching consensus: from a business perspective, it seemed more and more doubtful that Chrysler should be allowed to continue as an independent entity.

It was when we tentatively aired the notion about Chrysler that Rahm turned and uttered his shocker: "Why even save GM?" Seated to his right, David Axelrod, the President's principal political adviser, pulled out polling results and reeled off statistics showing how much the public hated bailouts.

Ron Bloom was the first to shake off his surprise and make a counterargument. He reminded them of the tens of thousands of autoworkers' jobs at stake. But that didn't deter Rahm. "Fuck the UAW," he growled.

From the opposite end of the table, Tim Geithner pushed back, drawing on his experience with the fickle nature of public opinion. I had seen this myself, most starkly with Lehman Brothers. Right up until Lehman declared bankruptcy, public opinion, including opinion on Wall Street, had overwhelmingly favored letting the firm go down. But in the ensuing chaos, the consensus had shifted almost overnight, and the government was believed these days to have made a terrible mistake by acquiescing in Lehman's collapse.

I was sitting with my back to Rahm's door. Suddenly I saw others around the table stiffen. I turned to look behind me. The President had just walked in. Having read somewhere that everyone is supposed to stand when the President enters the room, I leaped to my feet — only to notice that no one else had. "Welcome, Steve," Obama said, shaking my hand. "Sit down." He asked Rahm to step into the hall with him for moment, and with that, my first encounter with Barack Obama as President ended as abruptly as it began. (I later learned that the President likes to roam the first-floor halls when he has a question or request for a senior aide.)

In my limited contacts with Rahm and by osmosis from others, I knew that the chief of staff ruled by a mixture of respect and fear. Policy types didn't rush to him for analytical insights on their latest idea, but no one doubted his political instincts, his toughness, or his work ethic. He ran a tight ship, with no tolerance for the infighting that often characterizes a White House staff. Nor did he accept anything less than perfection from his subordinates. As a result, there was not a lot of love from Rahm. The old Washington saying "If you want a friend, buy a dog" seemed meant for those under his supervision. And Rahm never hesitated to seize command, as he did after Tim's rocky start as Treasury secretary — Rahm had stepped in and effectively started supervising Tim on a daily basis. Such aggressiveness is fine when all is going well, but it breeds resentment that can turn into sniping when the tide recedes, as it did briefly for Rahm in early 2010 when health care reform bogged down.

He subsided as the conversation resumed, and it struck me that, despite the fireworks, our doubts were being laid to rest. We'd arrived wondering whether the White House would be willing to take a firm stance with the automakers and do the right thing with the taxpayers' investment, however risky or politically painful it might turn out to be. We left feeling newly confident that, at least if Rahm Emanuel had anything to say about it, the President would stand behind our tough approach.

The meeting had one other memorable moment. We had come armed with maps showing Chrysler's major facilities and listing the members of Congress in whose districts they sat. Rahm zoomed in on Kokomo, Indiana, one of Chrysler's most important locations. "Dan Burton is not the congressman from Kokomo, Joe Donnelly is," he declared. The chief of staff's encyclopedic knowledge of congressional districts dazzled all of us except Harry. Sitting on the couch on the far side of the office, just two days into the job, his heart sank at the thought of our having made a mistake. He sent a BlackBerry message to our advisers at Rothschild, who had prepared the chart, to find out how this could have happened. He was relieved by the response: Kokomo turned out to be split between two representatives, and the plants were, in fact, in Dan Burton's district. As the meeting adjourned, Harry sidled up to the chief of staff and corrected him. "That may be," Rahm replied, "but the workers live in Joe Donnelly's district."

That still left the question of how far the auto industry bailout should go. "We're already in Vietnam," Larry said in a separate meeting, referring to the all but certain decision to provide more aid to the automakers. "I can imagine doing something in Cambodia." By that he meant indirectly helping a few key suppliers, the equivalent of fighting from Vietnam and not sending ground troops across the border. But there he drew the line: "There's no way we're going into Laos." He wasn't about to commit the government to a full-scale invasion that involved bailing out the entire supply chain.

By now I'd learned more about auto suppliers than I'd ever imagined I would, including the central fact that they are mutually dependent on and firmly enmeshed with many other parts of the economy. Tier-one suppliers provide products that can go right into a vehicle, like a wiring harness or a set of disk brakes. Tier-two suppliers generally provide components that comprise such assemblies — say, wires or brake pads. Tier-three suppliers provide raw materials for making the components, like copper or rubber. Except it's more complicated: many suppliers play multiple roles and sell to other industries. A tier-two supplier of wires might also sell to makers of dishwashers, for instance. A company like U.S. Steel might sell steel to both tier-two suppliers for making parts and the automakers themselves, which buy lots of steel directly — for example, to fashion into "top hats," as the outer shell of a car is known.

This vast industrial ecosystem presented a far different challenge from GM and Chrysler. While many suppliers were struggling because of the plunge in auto demand, it was hard to figure out which, if any, to help. We could not deal with each company individually, so we worked instead with their trade group, the Motor and Equipment Manufacturers Association, and an ad hoc coterie of industry experts and participants. We also met with the purchasing executives of the Big Three, who certainly knew more about suppliers than any of us. Midwestern politicians frequently weighed in too, including Michigan Governor Granholm, who e-mailed me in late February to warn about the risk of runaway supplier failures and propose ways that Washington could help. Meanwhile, Todd Snyder and his Rothschild colleagues, who had many clients in the supplier community, regularly fed us horror stories about that part of industrial America.

We had gathered around Larry's government-issue imitation-Chippendale conference table. It was Monday, February 23. Even though for all practical purposes I had been working for six weeks, this was my first official day on the job. I had awakened that morning to a story in the *Detroit News,* reporting that virtually no member of the task force, including Tim and Larry, drove an American car. Happily, the *News* had given me credit for owning a Lincoln Town Car, which I had replaced with a Lexus a year or so earlier. By 8:45 A.M., I'd said a teary farewell to my Quadrangle colleagues.

Then I'd spent most of the day in Washington completing the "onboarding" process, including being sworn in. The human resources department had sent word that this needed to occur in a room with an American flag (which nearly every office at Treasury had). I was excited, thinking that Tim himself was going to do the honors. At the appointed time, I presented myself in room 2428 to find two nice ladies from HR, who asked me to face the flag in the corner, raise my right hand, and repeat after them. Nothing is ever quite what you expect. But now, at 5:30 P.M., here I was in Larry's office, an official public servant.

Our meetings with Tim and Larry had already fallen into a routine. Larry sat at one end, next to a safe that was apparently meant for classified documents but showed no sign of use. I would take the seat to his right. Brian Deese would sit across from me, with Ron Bloom to his left. The rest of the other attendees would find seats around the room. Tim would sometimes sit opposite Larry at the other head of the table. But if he was late or didn't want to get dragged too deeply into the discussion, he would choose a different chair, or sometimes Larry's couch, which generally served as the bleachers for those who didn't have speaking roles.

I was intrigued by the dynamic between the two men. Tim had been Larry's protégé throughout the Clinton administration and they got along well. They shared a technocratic approach to issues and problem solving, short on ideology and long on analysis. While Larry's IQ was on its own pedestal, Tim was certainly very smart. Both were devoted public servants with extreme work ethics. They had become close friends and tennis partners.

Yet their personal styles were utterly different. Tim was a man of few words, Larry a man of many. Tim was organized and low-key, although given to occasional bursts of profanity and odd fits of giggling. Larry was more chaotic. He seemed oblivious to time or dress. He would happily immerse himself in a meeting until someone — usually his harried assistant, Bryan Jung — pulled him out. Going to see him made me imagine what it must have been like to have him as a professor. I always felt the need to be fully prepared and careful about everything I said, because no half-baked remark got past Larry. But unlike many of the professors I remembered from college, I looked forward to sessions with Larry because his questions were always incisive and his thoughts stimulating. And I appreciated his directness.

In the Obama administration, the status of the two had been partially reversed, with Tim now in the more lofty perch as Treasury secretary. But he had gotten off to an unfortunate start: his first major address, a long-awaited speech in early February, had been a PR disaster. Intended to unveil the administration's program for restoring credit in America's banks — an ambitious, forward-looking $2 trillion plan — the speech was attacked for being too general and short on convincing detail. Far from reassuring the public, it sent the stock market down nearly 5 percent. Critics denounced Tim. At Treasury, everyone felt terrible for him. Yet the scuttlebutt in the wake of the speech was titillating. His chief spokesperson, Stephanie Cutter, mysteriously disappeared. It was at this point that Rahm Emanuel was said to have taken control of Treasury, dictating everything from Tim's public appearances to his staff picks. When Tim's calendar and phone logs from early 2009 were released, it was surprising how many times a day Tim spoke to Rahm or saw him. Many wondered whether Tim would survive.

Particularly in these difficult early days, Larry tended to take the wheel on auto matters. Tim was preoccupied with bank problems, so Larry's leading on autos seemed like a tacit division of labor. Though Larry didn't bring much knowledge of the subject, he recognized that unlike banks, the federal government was devoid of institutional expertise in autos. Most importantly, he brought his vast intellectual curiosity. Perhaps also because of his stronger personality and the fact that the meetings were mostly in his office, Larry would usually run the sessions. He was not the type to sit quietly through a presentation; we quickly learned to put our most important points first, because sometimes we would not get past the opening pages before Larry jumped in. At this particular meeting, the minute we brought up helping the supplier base, he became agitated. When he heard some of the particulars of our ideas, he was even more unhappy.

The root of Larry's response was his distaste for government intervention in the private sector. Though a good Democrat, he firmly believed in capitalism and free markets. He accepted the necessity of bank rescues and of helping GM and Chrysler, but suspected that the liberal wing of our party wanted more intervention and more bailouts. Luminaries like George Soros and Joseph Stiglitz, for example, advocated nationalizing banks. Larry was determined to draw the line between the "too big to fail" interventions and the pressure to do more. He didn't want us crossing into Laos.

Tim didn't voice an opinion, but we went away understanding that we would have to refine our thinking. A few days later, we got an unexpected intervention. As I would later witness firsthand, Barack Obama was remarkably well informed for a new President with so much on his plate. He mentioned to Larry that he had read about the liquidity problems of the suppliers in the *Wall Street Journal.* "It would be a shame if at the end of this, we saved the auto companies but weakened out the supply base and shifted the manufacturers' reliance onto foreign suppliers," Obama told Summers.

As I studied the industry in those early weeks, I learned that the car business had gone through a mini-version of the housing bubble. Auto financing had been abundant in the years leading up to the financial crash of 2008 — for a brief period in 2006, buyers could borrow more than 100 percent of the cost of a new car! And because as many as 90 percent of consumers finance their new-car purchases, easy loans kept U.S. sales hovering around seventeen million vehicles a year until gas prices spiked. At the same time, substantial gains in quality and reliability were leading consumers to keep cars longer; all told, the number of cars in America rose by nearly 25 percent in the decade ending in 2007 while the driving-age population grew by less than 15 percent. The ratio of cars to licensed drivers, long greater than one-to-one, continued to increase. In 2008, of course, the wheels had come off. The collapse of the financial markets choked credit; rising unemployment and sinking house prices sapped household budgets; and summer brought $4-a-gallon gasoline, a particular disaster for the Detroit Three, with their anemic offerings in small cars.

And I came to appreciate why automakers obsess about the total number of new vehicles sold each year (they call this the SAAR, the seasonally adjusted annual rate of sales). In effect, the SAAR is every automaker's speedometer. For any company with a competitive line of products in a business where fixed costs are high and market share tends to shift only gradually, total volume is the most important determinant of profitability. We'd started this project in the midst of the steepest falloff in sales that the auto industry had experienced since at least 1950.

By January 2009, the SAAR had collapsed to 9.6 million. Extrapolating from this trend, many pundits issued dire forecasts for at best a slow and meager recovery.

But looking at the big picture, I'd begun to feel more optimistic about the prospects for overall sales than I had at the start. Unlike newspapers, an industry I knew all too well as a former journalist and as an investment banker, no one has invented a substitute for the automobile. The driving-age population was continuing to increase by more than 1 percent a year. "Scrappage," or the rate at which cars were junked, had dropped decade by decade, from the 1970s rate of more than 7 percent a year to about 5.5 percent, which meant that the average age of cars on the road was increasing. Car buyers could put off replacement purchases, but not forever. I recognized, of course, that strapped budgets and other factors would keep many Americans away from the dealerships for a good while — GM had nearly totaled itself with overly rosy predictions of recovery. Still, the automakers' prospects weren't all bad. A key part of our task, I realized, would be to arrive at a realistic SAAR forecast to incorporate into our investment analysis.

Our inquiries had led to another pleasant surprise: U.S. automakers were no longer as pathetically inefficient as people thought. We learned this from the Center for Automotive Research, an Ann Arbor, Michigan, think tank whose experts showed up to brief us during those early weeks. Listening to them one morning in our big yellow staff room, I was idly flipping through the package of charts they'd brought when I suddenly sat up and took notice. In 2007, the Harbour Report, an authoritative statistical source on automaking, had found that the Detroit Three needed just over 32 hours of labor to build a car, versus 30 hours for Toyota. That represented a huge advance over 1995, when GM had been at 46 hours, Chrysler at 43, Ford at 38 — and Toyota at 29. And given that the Big Three tended to make larger, more expensive cars, the narrowing of the gap was all the more significant. Harbour had concluded, "General Motors essentially caught Toyota in vehicle assembly productivity."

Another somewhat outdated criticism involved labor costs. We'd discovered how difficult it is to compare such costs on an apples-to-apples basis because of complex calculations involving the value of employee benefits, the composition of the labor force, and more. Each stakeholder — the automakers, the union, the creditors, investors — provided different, often substantially different, estimates of labor costs. While it seemed clear that American automakers' costs remained higher than those of the transplants, progress had been made. Just in the run-up to its February 17 submission, for example, GM had succeeded in reducing active employee labor costs per hour from $60.64 to $52.89 (versus $51.62 for Toyota). GM achieved this not by reducing wages for existing workers but by trimming benefits and having new workers start at much lower wages.

There were unpleasant surprises as well. Most glaring was the continuing low opinion consumers held of Detroit's products. A page of analysis from Deutsche Bank captured that succinctly. In almost every category, GM products fetched thousands of dollars less than their Toyota counterparts. A GM "premium compact" sold for $3,814 less than a Toyota, a stunning gap for cars priced at less than $20,000. Consumer perceptions are often slow to change, and I concluded that closing this gap with Toyota could take years. As I digested these data, I also realized that as much as the Detroit Three had been pilloried for missing the small-car market, their failure wasn't due to complete stupidity. If it costs $1,000 or more in extra labor expense to build a car that could be sold for only about $16,000 — nearly $4,000 less than its competitor — it would be impossible to make a profit. So why build it?

To my shock, Detroit fell short of foreign automakers on most SUVs and light trucks, fetching as much as $3,500 per vehicle less in some categories. The disparity could be traced in part to memories of the decades when Detroit cars were blatantly inferior in quality. But that also was an outdated impression. For model-year 2000 vehicles, the National Highway Traffic Safety Administration received more than 12,000 complaints about GM cars, as opposed to only around 2,000 about Toyotas. By the 2009 model year, Toyota was down to slightly more than 1,000 complaints — and GM had fallen to an even smaller number. (All of this, of course, predated Toyota's massive recall in early 2010.) And while Chrysler still had none of its cars on *Consumer Reports*'s recommended list, 21 percent of GM's cars appeared, a respectable increase from prior years, although a far cry from Toyota's 77 percent. Despite all this, however, consumers still had good reason for their unwillingness to pay as much for a GM car as for a Toyota: GM cars had lower resale or "residual" value. Detroit, in effect, had created a self-perpetuating disadvantage.

Of course we saw page after page of depressing statistics showing the relentless decline in market share of the three domestic automakers. The drop from nearly 100 percent of the U.S. market until the mid-1950s was gradual until the mid-1990s, when it accelerated. From 1995 through 2008, GM had lost a third of its U.S. market share. There was absolutely no justification for the increase in market share that GM had assumed as part of its viability report. Yet it was equally apparent that there could be no permanent return to profitability without reversing the continuing loss of market share. This would emerge as the company's greatest challenge.

The last big surprise was the rising tide of imported cars. Notwithstanding the presence of the transplants, the share of "pure imports" in the U.S. market had leaped from 19.7 percent in 2005 to 26.1 percent in 2008. Why hadn't this been in the headlines? When I'd covered the Carter administration in the late 1970s, imports had been a huge source of public outcry. And these figures did not reflect vehicles assembled in Mexico or Canada; under NAFTA, the North American Free Trade Agreement, those no longer counted as imports. I'd been a supporter of NAFTA and open trade, but wearing my auto cap now made me more conscious of the loss of U.S. jobs. Still, I had enough problems on my plate without volunteering to take on new ones.

All told, my accelerated immersion into the auto industry left me convinced that there was no fundamental or structural reason why Detroit couldn't compete, at least for the huge American market. To be sure, GM and Chrysler needed massive restructuring of both operating costs and liabilities, such as legacy health care. But if this could be accomplished — and if the companies, particularly GM, could be put under new management — I believed that they could be viable and even highly successful.

The morning after my swearing-in, I made the first of many trips to Capitol Hill to visit with the anxious Michigan delegation, beginning with a stop at the Rayburn House Office Building. The meetings were ceremonial, a chance for the legislators to repeat their concerns and for us to nod solemnly, as if we needed to be reminded of the gravity of the problem. Our host, John Dingell, who had served in the House since 1955, was courteous and statesmanlike, offering many rhetorical flourishes. Sander Levin, who had been in Congress a mere twenty-five years, was low-key and almost avuncular, while his younger brother Carl, also present, had the demeanor of a senior senator. Then we crossed over the Hill to the Senate offices to meet with Debbie Stabenow, who had caused me the most grief during my appointment. She nattered on pleasantly, her thoughts jumbling as she fiddled with her BlackBerry. Leaving Capitol Hill, I couldn't help but think that all that Stabenow and Carl Levin had accomplished by their carping was to delay my appointment by several weeks, making it that much harder to deliver the help that they said they wanted for their state.

My first formal encounters with the auto chiefs had come as GM and Chrysler each appeared at the Treasury for reviews of their financial viability reports. We'd decided to subject the submissions to close examination — the same kind of "due diligence" that top private equity firms apply to potential investments. With the automakers asking for more money, in effect we faced a new investment decision, and we owed it to the taxpayers to give it the best professional scrutiny. Any political considerations, we assumed, could be factored in separately.

Chrysler came first, on Wednesday, February 25. We had of course studied the company's report and found it severely wanting. It asserted that Chrysler could survive as an independent entity by hunkering down, cutting costs and reducing debt, which struck us as far-fetched. The alternative survival path — an alliance with the big Italian automaker Fiat, which Chrysler had floated with fanfare a few weeks earlier — seemed plausible. But the report gave only the sketchiest of details, not nearly enough information for us to evaluate it. Worse, Chrysler's plan did not provide for any reduction in its $6.9 billion worth of senior secured debt, an impossibly heavy burden for a company in such bad shape.

Hollowed out by nine years of mismanagement by its German parent, Daimler, Chrysler had been acquired by Cerberus in 2007 at the peak of private equity mania. So now it was competing against much larger and better-positioned global rivals as a purely North American player, with that market in a historic slump. It had no significant new vehicles in its pipeline, and its current cars and trucks did not stack up well against the competition.

To turn the business around, Cerberus had installed as chairman and CEO Robert Nardelli, a gung-ho veteran of General Electric. I knew Nardelli slightly — he had spoken at our annual conference a year or two earlier. He was known on the business scene for his "take the hill" attitude. The son of a General Electric plant manager, he had risen through the ranks at GE to become one of three finalists to succeed the legendary Jack Welch. When Welch picked Jeffrey Immelt instead, Nardelli left to run Home Depot. Eventually it became apparent that retailing and Nardelli didn't mix. Home Depot grew during the six years he ran it, but it lost market share to rival Lowe's and its stock remained flat. Nardelli also attracted attention for his outsize compensation and his highhanded treatment of shareholders. When the board reportedly pushed him out in early 2007, his severance package was estimated at $210 million.

At Chrysler, though, he seemed quite different from what I had read about him. He was dogged and scrappy and ran the business in a hands-on, close-to-the-ground style that harked back to GE. Nardelli subscribed to Jack Welch's core business philosophy: Be number one or two in your market or get out. Chrysler was, of course, a distant number three in North America, not even counting the transplants. That spurred Nardelli's attempt, starting in mid-2008, to merge Chrysler with General Motors. (Another motivation was pressure from Cerberus and JPMorgan, Chrysler's lead bank, which were increasingly anxious to extricate their capital as the auto market collapsed.)

Much later I learned that GM was hardly the only alliance he'd attempted. He'd also been in negotiations with the two most successful auto executives in the world, Carlos Ghosn of Nissan and Renault and Sergio Marchionne of Fiat.

Ghosn, in the minds of many, is the best automotive CEO to emerge since Alfred P. Sloan Jr., the father of General Motors, who reigned from 1937 to 1956. The Brazilian-born son of Lebanese parents, Ghosn got his start as an executive at tire giant Michelin. Nissan, the unprofitable $56-billion-a-year Japanese automaker, recruited him as COO in

1999 to take over its restructuring plan. Promising to quit if he couldn't return the company to prosperity within two years, Ghosn ignored Japanese traditions by closing plants, eliminating poor suppliers, and laying off workers far more aggressively than was typical for an Asian automaker. By March 31, 2001, the end of the 2000 fiscal year, Ghosn had delivered on his commitment — Nissan booked a $2.7 billion profit, a $9.2 billion swing from the loss it had suffered just twelve months earlier. The turnaround won Ghosn, who became CEO in 2001, acclaim around the world, including Japan, where his exploits were chronicled in a comic book. In North America, Nissan increased its market share against longtime rivals Toyota and Honda and raised eyebrows by fending off UAW organizing efforts in its plants.

Then in 2005, Ghosn became a dual CEO, taking charge of Nissan's minority owner, the $55-billion-a-year Renault, while retaining his Nissan post. Officially a French citizen, he now lived much of his life on a corporate jet, shuttling among Europe, North America, and Japan.

He had approached Rick Wagoner as early as June 2006 about taking a 20 percent stake in GM, but Wagoner persuaded his board to rebuff the deal, in part to save his own job as CEO. Later, Nardelli and Ghosn started to talk, reaching a preliminary agreement in early 2008. The deal, which was never made public, drew on the same playbook that Ghosn had used to unite Nissan and Renault. Chrysler and Renault-Nissan would form a global alliance by sharing design, engineering, and purchasing, saving large sums of money. Each would own stock in the other, to provide added glue. Ghosn would succeed Nardelli as Chrysler's chairman (to his credit, Nardelli, in his efforts to save Chrysler, was selfless about his own titles and role).

Then, as gas prices soared and the U.S. auto market hit the skids, Nardelli tried to broaden the deal into an alliance that would enable Chrysler Financial to tap Renault-Nissan's financial resources. Ghosn agreed to this at first. But in the spring, when business conditions continued to worsen, he got cold feet and withdrew. What could have been a lifesaver for Chrysler was not necessarily good for Renault-Nissan.

Chrysler by now was hemorrhaging cash, and Nardelli pressed on in his quest for potential partners. The merger talks with GM stretched from July to October, when GM effectively broke them off and asked the Treasury for help. Nardelli also sounded out Alan Mulally at Ford, a longtime friend, who told him, "I love you to death, Bob, but I've got my own plan."

Finally Nardelli turned to Fiat. He had already done some business with Sergio Marchionne in early 2008. Chrysler had lacked a small car in its product line, which it needed to meet increasingly stringent U.S. fuel economy standards and to broaden its appeal to customers. Among Marchionne's great successes at Fiat had been the Fiat 500 (or Cinquecento, as it is known in Italian), a stylish, zippy little car similar to the BMW Mini but a lot cheaper. Nardelli, who had injured his back and flew to Turin wearing a brace, spent two days with the Fiat chief. They came to a handshake to produce the Cinquecento at a Chrysler plant in Mexico.

The flamboyant Marchionne was viewed by the inbred auto industry as an arriviste. Raised in Canada, he had started as an accountant and made a career in European industrial companies before finding his way to Fiat. The big automaker was virtually moribund when he arrived. Within a few short years, Marchionne blew up its bureaucracy, empowered a new generation of engineers, and turned Fiat into a growing and profitable automaker. Unlike the buttoned-down Ghosn, he was voluble, idiosyncratic — his trademark was a black sweater, worn sometimes over a dress shirt and sometimes not — and hungry for media attention. But he matched Ghosn's drive. He would cross continents more casually than most businessmen would approach a trip from New York to D.C. He showed every indication of viewing himself as heir apparent to Ghosn as the world's greatest auto executive.

When Nardelli called in early January, Sergio jumped at the opportunity, dispatching squads of executives to Chrysler's mammoth headquarters in Auburn Hills, Michigan. They worked around the clock to negotiate an alliance, using the template that Nardelli and Ghosn had developed. By January 12, the companies had agreed on a sufficiently detailed term sheet that Chrysler's CFO, Ron Kolka, called the Treasury to disclose that an important alliance was in the offing. The tentative deal, announced eight days later, was greeted with as much enthusiasm as could be summoned given Chrysler's precarious state. One industry expert called it "interesting" and said, "It helps the long-term viability."

But the glimmer of hope soon faded. Just before Chrysler's February 17 government deadline, Marchionne told Nardelli that Chrysler could not include their joint plan in its viability report, permitting only a vague description of the alliance. JPMorgan knocked another big hole in Chrysler's report by refusing at the last minute to let Nardelli factor in any reduction in the company's massive bank debt. That ought to have been a routine assumption for a business so close to the abyss.

Our task force, Team Auto, was aware of none of this, of course, but we'd soon get to know Sergio and JPMorgan well. They'd be among our biggest headaches in the race to save the company.

5

RICK, BOB, AND SERGIO

BOB NARDELLI MUST HAVE been in quiet despair as my colleagues and I gathered around the wooden conference table in our yellow-walled combination conference room and office to hear him and his executives present their plan. We were unaware of Fiat's eleventh-hour U-turn or the intransigence of Chrysler's banks, so we had no idea why the viability report was so weak — to us it seemed as if Chrysler had simply run out of cards.

This was an introductory due-diligence meeting — a financial industry procedure similar to a deposition in a lawsuit, in which the parties to a prospective deal undertake a detailed and painstaking review of the facts, numbers, and assumptions. It's a chore, not a drama, and about as exciting as an average day of C-SPAN. This session would be somewhat ceremonial, and would serve as a broad introduction for senior members of the task force, like Ron Bloom and me. In the ensuing days, Brian Osias and others would dig far more deeply, in essence tearing the numbers apart and putting them together again.

There was tension in the air as we milled around making small talk before getting down to business. The body language of Nardelli and his colleagues told me that they knew they were fighting for their company's existence and were determined to infuse every bit of salesmanship they possessed into their presentation.

At sixty, Nardelli was of medium height, with thinning brown hair and his college ring on his finger. He seemed like an ordinary corporate executive in demeanor and dress — down-to-earth and likable, ready to roll up his sleeves. His earnestness occasionally led him into odd territory, such as his habit of prefacing many of his sentences with our first names, beginning each one "Steve and Ron . . ." or "Ron and Steve . . . ," as if anxious that our attention not stray. For four hours, he and his executives gave it their best, but beneath the surface we could sense the thinness and even hear the lack of conviction in their voices. After two years of fighting to save their company, they were tired. And they must have known that they were not giving us a business plan that we could back with more government dollars.

The next day's due-diligence session, with General Motors, was disturbing in a different way. Beforehand, Haley had spent half a day finding an available space that could show PowerPoint slides. (The U.S. Treasury is ill equipped to entertain visitors from the outside world, I learned. The few conference rooms are scattered throughout the two-block-long Treasury fortress and are under the control of many different departments.) Finally she'd lined up a room in something called the Treasury Annex, a shabby building across Pennsylvania Avenue. I had walked by this building many times but had no idea it was part of Treasury. The windowless sixth-floor room in which we met was no more inviting than the exterior—cramped, drab, and gray. Inexplicably, it bore the title "Center for Excellence."

The GM folks pretended not to notice any of this. Nor, in the months that followed, did they ever give a sign of how hard it must have been to have a bunch of Wall Street recruits and government bureaucrats sit in judgment of their iconic company. Though they'd started their bailout request at the cabinet level, now that billions of dollars of TARP money had been provided and a task force assigned, they didn't throw their weight around or demand to see Tim Geithner. They seemed to regard us as a necessary hardship, to be endured as a way of securing more cash.

Before leaving our office, I asked Haley what we were going to give them for lunch. "Nothing," she replied, explaining that Treasury had no budget for refreshments at meetings, "not even for bottles of water." It seemed rather harsh to expect our visitors (not to mention ourselves) to go six hours without food or drink, so I gave Haley $100 from my wallet and told her to go to a sandwich shop. That became our regular routine when we had lunchtime visitors.

• • •

This would be my first meeting with Rick Wagoner, about whom I had so many questions and had heard and read so much. By most accounts, he had been a golden boy at GM. After graduating from Duke University and Harvard Business School, he'd begun as an analyst in 1977 in the GM treasury, where many of the company's leaders got their start. He'd risen through the ranks, including stops as treasurer and then president of GM's important Brazilian operation. In 1992, as GM went through its first near-death experience, losing almost $30 billion in three years, a boardroom coup replaced CEO Robert Stempel with Jack Smith. It was Smith who summoned Rick from Brazil and named him CFO at just thirty-nine years of age. In 2000, at forty-seven, Rick succeeded Smith and became the youngest CEO in GM's history.

Wagoner at first seemed the change agent General Motors needed. He won kudos by bringing in a former Ford executive as CFO and also recruiting automotive marketing and design legend Bob Lutz, a larger-than-life car guy who masterminded hits such as the resurrected Pontiac GTO and the Cadillac CTS, and pushed for the development of the Chevrolet Volt. Wagoner tackled tough housecleaning challenges, like pulling the plug on the moribund Oldsmobile brand. After 9/11 he championed the Keep America Rolling campaign, in which GM lured consumers with zero-percent loans—a smart blend of commerce and patriotism that brought the company much praise.

Yet, after a few years, the job seemed to wear Wagoner down. Killing Oldsmobile proved a harrowing ordeal that cost GM well more than a billion dollars, alienated many of its dealers, and discouraged further efforts at brand elimination. A 2003 effort to hold the line on GM's dwindling North American market share at 29 percent (GM executives sported "29" lapel pins) fizzled quickly. A Wagoner-backed deal to acquire 20 percent of Fiat, mostly for engine technology, became such a burden that in 2005 GM paid Fiat $2 billion to cancel it. (At our first meeting, Sergio would brag that he had taken GM to the cleaners.) That same year Wagoner tried jawboning the UAW into accepting cuts in health benefits, only to back down when the workers threatened to strike.

Born and bred as an insider, Wagoner never displayed any fortitude for remaking GM's hidebound corporate culture. He operated as an incrementalist, and a slow-moving one at that. His guiding star appeared to be an unshakable faith that GM was not like any other company; it was *General Motors*. Whatever happened to other companies couldn't possibly happen to GM.

Consequently, he fought efforts by GM investor Kirk Kerkorian to pare down or sell brands like Pontiac and Hummer — moves that, like an alliance with Nissan, could have left the company much better off. When GM stock topped $40 a share during the financial bubble in 2007, he also turned down proposals by investment banks to raise billions in new capital.

Not knowing Wagoner, I imagined that his talents included the kind of determination and work ethic that could withstand the grinding punishment of being the CEO of a company like GM. I had seen this in other CEOs and understood the value of those skills. At the same time, I couldn't help but suspect that his real genius had been in keeping the board of directors on his side as losses mounted again to the tens of billions of dollars, market share continued its grim slide, and the price of GM shares fell to single digits. Regardless, now the company was in crisis, and leadership had to be judged on results.

Wagoner greeted us with a firm handshake and a steady gaze. He looked and carried himself like a CEO — he was tall and solidly built, wore a nicely tailored suit and had a full head of brown hair. He left simultaneous impressions of amiability and remoteness. Unlike Nardelli the previous day, who had led the Chrysler presentation and shown a clear willingness to engage, Wagoner gave listeners very little to grab on to. He made a few opening comments and then turned over the floor to his lieutenants, occasionally interjecting a remark here and there but mostly presiding. While I respected the collegiality this implied, it left nearly everyone with the impression that he held himself aloof. If Rick had taken a more central role it would probably not have affected our assessment of the company, but might have affected our judgment of him. (Tellingly, not once on that day did Rick utter the word "bankruptcy," almost as if he were incapable of saying it.)

Unlike our meeting with Chrysler, this six-hour session was devoid of tension. The GM team seemed placidly to take for granted that somehow, some way, the government would agree to its requests.

As a business, we were happy to discover, the company seemed to have much more going for it than Chrysler. It had been free of the ownership changes that Chrysler had experienced. It remained the largest car manufacturer in the United States. While its vehicles were far from ideal, they were on average considerably more appealing and popular than Chrysler's. The company had global operations — some troubled, like Opel in Europe, but some highly promising and successful, particularly its fast-growing joint venture in China. (To GM's delight, Chinese consumers perceived Buick as the classiest car a person can drive to advertise success.)

Yet GM's survival plan reminded me of the old joke about the economist marooned on a desert island with a can of food but no way to open it. How does the economist solve the problem? He *assumes* a can opener. From Wagoner on down, GM seemed to be living in a fantasy that, despite the evidence of decades of decline, it was still the greatest carmaker on earth, in a class by itself. Chrysler at least had recognized the gravity of its situation, it seemed to us, and had tried to find answers. GM, after cruising to the brink of collapse and begging for government help, now seemed mostly to be marking time in expectation of an economic recovery and a rebound in sales. Its February 17 submission consisted of the same proposals the company had offered the Bush administration back in December, modestly speeded up. The same cutbacks in brands, factories, subsidiaries, blue-collar workers, and salaried employees were now compressed into a period of one to four years.

There was still no real urgency. GM did not think this necessary, as its troubles, as Wagoner had told Congress, were mostly due to market conditions. The only mention of bankruptcy was to present it in all its ugliness, an option that no sane person would pursue. The overall concept seemed to be to trim only what was easily achieved and absolutely necessary, and use taxpayer dollars to ride out the recession. Incredibly, GM now assumed an even higher rebound in car sales in 2012 than it had back in December. The company seemed oblivious to the fact that its original request, in November 2008, for $10 billion to $12 billion in aid had grown steadily and was now at $22.5 billion to $30 billion. All told, the presentation, delivered with one of the largest PowerPoint decks I had ever seen, made it apparent to me that Wagoner and company had not come to grips with that stubborn tin can.

Every industry has its own drivers and idiosyncrasies; if our sessions with Chrysler and GM did little else, they helped me learn more about automaking. I was astonished, for example, to learn how the Detroit Three accounted for labor costs. Broadly speaking, the operating costs of any business can be divided into two buckets: variable and fixed. Variable costs are those that change with the level of production: if you make more vehicles, you need more parts and steel.

Fixed costs are those that tend to remain constant regardless of how many units you produce: items like interest and rent payments and the salaries of permanent staff. Most businesses account for wage workers as a variable cost because the companies hire and lay off workers based on production. But at GM, Ford, and Chrysler, it wasn't that way. They accounted for labor as a fixed cost—under the UAW contract, autoworkers got paid nearly the same whether they built cars or not. (The companies actually maintained "rubber rooms" where idled workers could job-hunt, watch TV, and work crossword puzzles while they collected pay.)

The evident absurdity of this state of affairs sapped morale and had a perverse effect on how the U.S. automakers did business. With fixed costs so high, they had an incentive to build as many cars as possible so as to reduce the average cost per car. Similarly, with variable costs relatively low, additional cars could be made without much additional expense. These factors played a major role in Detroit's addiction to discounts and incentives. The end result was what no businessperson would want—a low-profit-margin business that is vulnerable to any slackening in consumer demand.

I also learned how the automakers' size and power had helped mask their weakening position. At one end of the pipeline, these giants commanded favorable terms from their suppliers—they could wait to pay their bills. On the other end, they used their clout to force dealers to pay for cars before they even reached the dealers' lots. All this provided a massive cash flow benefit, as well as a powerful incentive for the automakers to stuff dealerships with as many vehicles as possible.

The list of only-in-automaking business practices went on and on. In addition, I had to race to master a whole new vocabulary—words like "homologation" (conforming a car to U.S. safety and environmental standards) and "subvention" (reimbursing the finance companies to offer low or zero-percent financing on cars). Yet I felt that being a new-comer to the industry wasn't such a terrible thing. I could look at Detroit's practices with fresh eyes and compare them with those of more profitable industries, such as information, entertainment, and communications, where I had spent much of my business life.

Now that the task force was officially open for business, there also began a parade of visits from auto industry stakeholders. Surprisingly, everyone from auto executives to union chiefs to suppliers came to us believing that the government should solve their problems. Some of our visitors were testy; all left disappointed that the government wasn't going to be everybody's piggy bank. The GM bondholders were typical of this. As part of the TARP loan agreement, GM was expected to slash its $27 billion of unsecured public debt by two-thirds. This meant getting investors to exchange at least $18 billion in bonds for much riskier GM stock. There was no way for GM to force them to do so: under the usual bond indentures, a lender's entitlement to interest and principal cannot be abridged without its consent. That meant GM needed volunteers.

But this raised a classic "free rider" problem, as economists call it. Why would any bondholder agree to have its investment dramatically reduced when, if other investors accepted the offer, it could keep its full entitlement? No company had ever achieved such a sizable debt reduction involving so many bond issues and thousands of bondholders outside of bankruptcy. GM had been talking to representatives of its biggest bondholders for weeks, without any progress, seriously jeopardizing its chances of being found viable on March 31.

Now these advisers appeared at our door, armed with a proposal. I almost fell off my chair when I saw that their solution to this dilemma was for the Treasury to guarantee some of the new debt. I held myself to a few polite questions, but I was seething. Yet another stakeholder asking for a handout.

Such sessions underscored the need to expand our team — quickly. I took a giant step in that direction by hiring somebody I found via e-mail: Harry Wilson, a fiercely driven young expert in corporate restructurings. His was one of the many unsolicited résumés I'd received when word of my possible appointment began to leak. Harry had grown up in a Greek immigrant family in a river town in upstate New York, where he'd seen his mother get laid off three times from textile mills as they'd closed one after the other. Harry had been the first in his family to earn a college degree, from Harvard, and he'd gone on to earn an MBA at Harvard Business School. He had done private equity deals and industrial restructurings at four distinguished Wall Street firms. And he was a registered Republican! His e-mail touched me, especially these lines: "Steve, I will end on a personal note. There is only one reason I am sending you this email: I have a very deep interest in public service, particularly given the good fortune I have enjoyed in my own life, and . . . I think my skills and personal characteristics are an ideal match for those needs. In short, I can't think of a better way for me to serve my country in the near term than this role, and I think our country needs all the talented people it can get (regardless of political affiliation)."

Harry's employer references were glowing. But just because he had put his hand up for a job didn't make him easy to convince. The burly thirty-seven-year old, who looked like a fairer, younger version of Al Gore, had a whole list of questions and concerns that reflected the diligence and care that we would later see in his work. Was the task force free to attack the auto industry problem without regard to politics? he wanted to know. Was its goal with GM and Chrysler the fundamental restructuring that both companies sorely needed? I told Harry candidly that while I believed that the President, Tim Geithner, and Larry Summers were committed to doing the right thing, only time would tell if the administration would withstand the political pressure to pull punches, particularly from strong supporters like the UAW. There were risks, I admitted, but the opportunity to work on such an important matter far outweighed them.

After thinking it over, Harry agreed to join the team. Now all we had to do was get him hired. As he began the same vetting ordeal that Ron and I had gone through, one of the TARP chiefs made a transformative observation. If the task force was going to continue to oversee the deployment of TARP money, he said, then the staff should be on the payroll of TARP, which had its own streamlined hiring process. Even better, TARP had more money for hiring than did the Treasury, whose budget had been strained to the breaking point by the financial crisis. So we were able to bring Harry on board in ten days — overnight, by D.C. standards. Importantly, his addition cemented the principle that our hiring would be done without regard to political views and ensured that Team Auto would be something of a team of rivals.

The flow of ideas and suggestions from outside the task force continued to climb. Some served as useful affirmations of, or correctives for, our thinking. Others were bizarre. A friend passed along an e-mail from an architect suggesting that GM and Chrysler get out of autos and manufacture housing instead. An otherwise sensible acquaintance forwarded an e-mail from an investment group purporting to want to put "$50 billion to $150 billion" into the auto industry. "This seems important enough to pass on," he wrote.

We labored to find an acceptable solution to the supplier crisis in time for our next meeting with Larry, set for Monday, March 2. "Given Larry's concern about Laos, I'm particularly worried about going to him with a structure that he will have an easy time poking holes in," I said to Deese from home on Saturday night. The issue ate up most of the next thirty-six hours. By the time we appeared in Larry's office late Monday afternoon, we had boiled down our supplier ideas to two. The more modest idea — if you can call a $5 billion to $10 billion proposal modest — was a kind of insurance fund that would guarantee payment to GM's and Chrysler's suppliers. Suppliers would have to pay a hefty fee to participate, but we believed such a program would relieve them of a major worry.

Our second idea, far more ambitious, would be a kind of mini-TARP — a fund to provide so-called debtor-in-possession, or DIP, financing for suppliers that declared bankruptcy. (DIP financing enables a bankrupt company to keep the lights on and pay other essential bills while it reorganizes.) We had qualms about the scope and workability of this idea. Which suppliers would qualify? Where would we draw the line? How would we screen dozens or hundreds of applicants? "I ran a fund and it is a big undertaking," I said to Todd Snyder, who was pushing the idea.

The discussion moved fast once we got into Larry's office. We quickly agreed that the administration's goal should be not to save suppliers per se but to save only those that were of critical importance to the automakers. This decision evolved into a mantra for dealing with the myriad parties besieging us with requests: "We cannot solve the problems of every company in every industry."

As often happened with Larry, the meeting ranged beyond the immediate agenda into a discussion of the many other issues facing us. Diana sat thinking how the auto problem just kept "radiating out" to include not only suppliers, but dealers, finance companies, and on and on. Focused on our suggestion that GM and Chrysler be treated differently from one another, Larry told us he wanted us to come back to him with a preview of how the movie was going to end for all the companies that needed help, from GM on down.

Over the next few days, we scrambled to fast-forward our thoughts to what the announcements that we knew were coming by March 31 might look like. Even at that early date, we found ourselves in agreement about most of the important issues. For starters, it was abundantly clear that neither GM nor Chrysler had demonstrated viability. Neither had extracted sufficient sacrifices from its stakeholders. We were skeptical about Chrysler's prospects as an independent company and inclined to believe that a partnership with Fiat was its only real hope. We saw GM as more likely to survive, but were convinced that new leadership would be required. My thought was to replace Rick Wagoner and divide his responsibilities between a new chairman and an interim CEO. I also felt that much of the board should be replaced.

Though I'd met Wagoner only once, to my mind there was no question but that he had to go. It wasn't personal; it was business. We did not know of another industrial company in history that had burned through so much cash as fast as GM had on his watch. It had vaporized $20 billion in twelve months and was in the process of burning another $11 billion in the first quarter of 2009, all of which was now coming out of the pockets of taxpayers. Even more compelling was the fact that GM said it would need still more bailout money to tide it over. After nearly a decade of experience as a private equity manager, I believed in a bedrock principle of that business: put money behind only a bankable management team. To my mind, no private equity firm on the planet would have backed Rick Wagoner or GM's current board.

I knew Rick must have many admirable qualities, the foremost of which was an unshakable belief in his company and himself. Yet he also set a tone of friendly arrogance that seemed to pervade the organization. His performance at the Senate hearing the previous November had been typical; he and his team seemed certain that virtually all of their problems could be laid at the feet of some combination of the financial crisis, oil prices, the yen-dollar exchange rate, and the UAW.

We gave considerable attention to timing. On the one hand, as we all knew, any reorganization would take time, and two of such magnitude could be lengthy indeed. On the other hand, every day that went by meant more taxpayer money was going down the rat hole. We played around with timetables in thirty-day increments, starting with thirty days for each company to get its act together: Chrysler, to secure the Fiat partnership; GM, to scrap its rosy scenarios and retool its plan. Because of its scale and complexity, GM would then need more time, at least an additional sixty days, to win the necessary concessions from its creditors, suppliers, and unions. Chrysler's fate was clearer: if it failed to bring about the Fiat partnership, it would be liquidated. If GM failed to achieve the necessary concessions from its stakeholders, the result would be bankruptcy. We didn't yet know exactly what a GM bankruptcy would mean, but we could see no alternative to it. And we began to muse about how to be sure GM moved forward with more energy than was its custom. One idea was to send a team to Detroit to "monitor" the company's progress. We chose that word to avoid giving the impression that the government would be stepping in to run GM. But as events unfolded, I am sure that Harry Wilson never thought of himself as a monitor. By the time he was finished, neither did anyone at GM.

Of course, developing a straw man would be easy. For us to pin down facts and be certain we had a detailed plan that would succeed would be a lot more difficult.

I had my first face-to-face encounter with Sergio Marchionne a few days later—a trim, likeable guy with a high forehead, wire-rimmed glasses, and the ever-present black sweater. He gave an elaborate description of the turnaround at Fiat. Then his team laid out a plan for saving Chrysler, with frequent interjections from Sergio, acting as a kind of color commentator. Assume that consumer demand doesn't recover but stays flat at ten million vehicles for eight years, they began.

They showed how, just by adding Fiat's small-car designs to its lineup, Chrysler would gain market share and make enough money to survive. They had Chrysler's market share growing by close to 40 percent. If you accepted that, and then assumed that overall demand would recover in less than eight years, Chrysler would obviously make a lot of money.

Sergio knew how to turn on the charm and was selling hard, but we weren't buying it. "Those are nice assumptions, but where are you going to get that market share? Who are you going to take it from?" Harry asked. "They're going to respond over time with new models of their own." Sergio didn't really have an answer to that. Nor had our guests given much thought to how a combination of the two companies might be structured. For its part, the Fiat team was also disappointed in the meeting; they thought our lack of experience in the auto industry showed.

"Why don't we just give him the company?" I said in exasperation after I got back to my office with Ron, Harry, and our younger colleagues. "I don't think there's a deal here." I asked the others what they thought, and the consensus was that I should go back to Sergio and ask if Fiat would put up capital. I made that phone call, and Sergio essentially said "No way." Plainly, if we wanted to do business with Fiat, the American taxpayer would have to bear all the risk. The rescue of Chrysler might have ended right there had not Sergio seized on an invitation to come back for a do-over. He returned the following week with a much more careful and detailed presentation that gave us confidence about his understanding of the company and his ability to turn it around.

The next day brought my first meeting with the cabinet-level Auto Task Force, in the West Wing's Roosevelt Room. Nearly all the attendees understood this session was purely ceremonial, but a couple — such as Energy Secretary Steven Chu — weren't yet versed in the ways of Washington and thought they were there to provide substantive input. After the meeting adjourned, as we walked through the reception room of the West Wing on the way back to Treasury, Larry paused to review a few items, including the work that was under way on SAAR, the seasonally adjusted annual rate of sales.

While the red tape of the federal government can be maddening, it can often be offset by the extraordinary resources available to analyze a problem. In leading our SAAR work, Harry Wilson had drawn on economists at Treasury and the Council of Economic Advisers, as well as a team of experts from Boston Consulting Group. I was relieved that the conclusions largely mirrored my own general thoughts. While we were probably facing a depressed SAAR of 10.5 million to 13.5 million for 2010, we could anticipate an eventual recovery to 15 or 16 million.

The discussion became more animated as we stood explaining our work on SAAR to Larry. Diana, recognizing that we were standing in a place where our private business might be overheard by waiting visitors, kept shushing our group, to little avail. Finally, Darienne, the receptionist, came over and told Larry that he could not use her waiting room as a meeting area. In Deese's experience, that was not an unusual occurrence, as Larry had a tendency to hold court there. Looking around at the waiting room, I thought the West Wing deserved better. The room had a tattered feeling, with its heavy-duty beige wall-to-wall carpet and worn furniture. It looked as if it had been lifted from the pages of *Reader's Digest.*

We knew we could function most efficiently by staying put in D.C., yet we realized from the outset that we'd have to make at least one trip to Detroit to avoid more criticism from the heartland. By early March, we could delay no more. All the same, we were determined not to waste more than a day, and so arranged a packed itinerary that would touch all the right bases. To satisfy the futurists, we would visit GM's Technical Center and drive its next-generation vehicles. For traditionalists, we would tour an old-line Chrysler assembly plant. And to acknowledge the importance of labor, we would visit with UAW leaders at their headquarters, Solidarity House. I was half asleep as I debarked from my Northwest Airlines flight at 8 A.M. at Detroit's Metro Airport. I was stunned to find myself in one of the most modern and luxurious terminals I had ever seen. Somehow, I'd imagined that a burned-out city would have a burned-out airport. As I passed a newsstand in the concourse, the blaring headline of one of the local newspapers caught my eye: "Hear Us Out, We're in Crisis."

We knew that every aspect of our trip would be scrutinized, so we'd pondered at length how to get around the Motor City. We didn't like the idea of having GM or Chrysler pick us up, and didn't want to show favoritism in our choice of a car to drive. We'd settled on what seemed like a neutral option: we rented a Ford Escape from Budget. (Haley had made sure it had a GPS, since none of us knew our way around Detroit.) Ron drove, with Brian, Diana, and me as passengers.

Our first stop was Solidarity House. As I had told Ron when we first met, I believed in saving jobs. I had also written op-eds about America's growing income inequality and about the declining real wages of workers. I believed that organized labor could be a constructive part of the solution as long as it focused on those issues, rather than on featherbedding, trying to protect workers who were not pulling their weight, and blindly fighting technological change. During my eight and a half years at the *New York Times* I'd been a card-carrying member of the Newspaper Guild and had watched the company's eleven unions make all those mistakes. They'd ended up hurting both the workers and the *Times*.

With that experience, and having also absorbed the conventional wisdom that the UAW was a big part of the auto industry's problems, I arrived at Solidarity House expecting to be harangued. The building was eerie. It had been built of steel, glass, aluminum, brick, and stone in 1951 — the year before I was born — when the UAW had 1.2 million members; Walter Reuther, its legendary president, had proudly called it "the labor university of the future." But now the UAW was down to just above 400,000 members and Solidarity House looked like a man whose clothes were too big.

Soon after we reached the main conference room, however, where Danish, orange juice, and coffee awaited, my mood changed. Ron Gettelfinger and his team greeted us, dressed in casual clothes, with the UAW logo emblazoned on the left breast pocket of their button-down shirts. It was a visible contrast with our business suits. And far from browbeating us, they gave a thorough presentation that included as many details and figures as investment bankers would have used. (I later learned that my old firm Lazard had helped prepare it.) The presentation argued that the wages of workers at GM and Chrysler were competitive with those of the transplants, as the Bush loan agreements required.

Gettelfinger himself intrigued me. He'd been UAW president since 2002, and with his trim frame, white brush mustache, and crisp manner of speech, he hardly fit the mold of a union boss. Raised on a southern Indiana farm, he'd started as a chassis-line repairman at Ford's Louisville, Kentucky, assembly plant in 1964. He earned an accounting degree, attending night classes at Indiana University, and by 1979 had worked his way up to UAW plant chairman. He became known for forcing union concessions and forging better relations with management, moves that helped persuade Ford to keep the plant open.

Unlike many UAW leaders who gained a following through an outsize personality, Gettelfinger rose through relentless attention to detail and unflinching honesty. His entourage was minimal and he was close to few people. He didn't drink, didn't gamble, had quit smoking, and usually brought his wife, Judy, along on business trips. As president, he banned the Friday golf outings that UAW officials traditionally took with their management counterparts. He felt they were unseemly and sent the wrong message to union members.

In 2003 — when GM posted its best full-year profit under Rick Wagoner — Gettelfinger had negotiated a national contract that protected many members' wages and benefits. Nearly every year after that had been spent in retreat. Gettelfinger agreed to concessions that had been anathema, from two-tier wages that committed new hires to a lower pay scale, to making billions of dollars in health care cuts that involved reopening a contract with GM that was already in place. He told the rank and file in a 2006 speech: "The challenges we face aren't the kind that can be ridden out. They're structural challenges, and they require new and farsighted solutions." Hiring Lazard reflected his perceptiveness. Although the move angered some members who mistrusted Wall Street, Gettelfinger knew the union had to be ready in the event GM's problems spiraled out of control. I left thinking of what Margaret Thatcher once said of Mikhail Gorbachev: "We can do business together."

From Solidarity House we drove to GM's fabled Tech Center in suburban Warren. A car with a news photographer flanked us, his camera clicking away. More interested in architecture than in cars, I knew that the Tech Center had been designed by the great architect Eero Saarinen in the late 1940s and was known around the world as an icon of modernism. On that score, it didn't disappoint. Wagoner and his team took us on a tour to see models of new vehicle designs. He paused to show off the electric-powered Volt, which looked fine on the outside but had an interior that seemed like an Apple iPod knockoff.

Next it was time to drive. I knew that car manufacturers share a marketing principle with airplane makers: put a reviewer behind the wheel or at the controls, and you generally get a positive result. I was no exception. With Rick riding shotgun — clearly a veteran of many such test drives — I navigated the campus of the Tech Center. The Volt drove surprisingly well and accelerated far better than I'd expected. It was noiseless and smooth and did not noticeably shift gears. Other prototypes we tried — fuel cell cars and hydrogen-powered cars — elicited similarly positive reactions.

After the fun, we settled into a conference room with Rick and his team. In deference to government ethics rules, we each handed over $11 in cash to a GM aide and in return got a box lunch and a receipt to turn in to Treasury for reimbursement. We discussed the prospects of the Volt, and it quickly became clear that the car had commercial clay feet. At least in the early years, each Volt would cost around $40,000 to manufacture (development costs not included). But in size, features, and performance, it would have to compete with the Chevy Malibu and similar cars, which sold for around $20,000. Because of legislation passed in 2008, buyers of plug-in electric cars would receive up to a $7,500 tax credit — a big incentive, but not enough to bridge the cost gap. The bottom line was that there was no way for the Volt or any next-generation car to have a positive impact on GM's finances any time soon. Certainly not within the five-year framework that private equity firms typically use to evaluate investment opportunities.

We touched on many other subjects, including the difficulties of GM Europe. But on the whole, the session was staid, genteel, and devoid of drama, reflecting the company's personality and that of its CEO. A casual eavesdropper would never have guessed that this company had gone off the edge of a precipice and was now in free fall.

As we finished lunch and got up to leave, GM's security people reported that a flock of reporters and camera people had staked out the Tech Center's main gate. GM sent us out the back way, which Diana thought was an odd decision, since the whole point of our trip was to be seen. When we pulled up at the Chrysler factory a few miles away, the media were waiting there too. Reporters shouted questions and cameras zoomed in on us through the fence as we walked from our Escape; we spied a news helicopter circling overhead.

We began with Nardelli and his colleagues in the plant manager's office — a decrepit conference room with binders and trophies lined along the shelves, which reminded us of the office of a high school basketball coach. The contrast with the setting at GM could not have been more stark. Chrysler had wanted us to go to its design center, in its modern, monumental headquarters complex. But Auburn Hills was a long drive to pack into a crowded day, and for symbolic reasons, our Detroit visit required a factory tour, so here we were at the Warren Truck Assembly Plant, where Dodge Ram pickups were put together.

The tone of the meeting was also a far cry from our session with the GM execs, in part because we had come with a stark message that seemed very much in keeping with this aging facility: while our public posture would remain that we were continuing to study the Chrysler submission, our real assessment was that the standalone Chrysler plan simply didn't work.

The Chrysler executives pushed back hard. Diana — the former management consultant — was struck by the differences between the two cultures. In contrast to the mildness we'd encountered at GM, the Chrysler executives came across as rough and edgy, almost defiant.

As we went down a set of narrow metal steps to begin our tour, Nardelli looked over his shoulder at me on the stair above him. "Your assessment just wasn't fair," he said. He felt that we'd given him and his company short shrift in more ways than one. Chrysler was the last stop on our itinerary, and because we'd arrived late, our visit was rushed. His team had gone to great trouble to bring its latest models from Auburn Hills to Warren; for security reasons, prototypes were not usually allowed outside the design center.

Nardelli led us to a large white room in which a half-dozen gleaming vehicles were arrayed in a semicircle on the concrete floor. The purpose of this showing was to convince us that the cupboard was not as bare as everyone thought. We walked among the vehicles — sedans and trucks and even a Fiat 500 — as the Chrysler people talked about advanced hybrid power trains and new, environmentally friendly diesels.

But by this point our goal was not to miss our flight back to the mountain of work that awaited us in Washington. So we only had time for what amounted to auto speed dating, a quick hop from car to car.

The factory itself was an old-line Depression-era assembly plant, built in 1938. We raced through this as well. I wanted to stay longer — watching truck bodies drop onto chassis in the modern equivalent of Henry Ford's assembly line is a thrill for more than just young boys. I also found myself looking at the workers, a mix of old and young, male and female, black and white. I was well aware of Detroit's 22 percent unemployment rate (it would soon reach 29 percent) and its lack of virtually any new jobs, never mind high-paying ones for manufacturing workers. These workers, I realized, were dependent on us, their futures in our hands. If we failed, and the automakers collapsed, they would be jobless, perhaps for the rest of their working lives.

After running the press gauntlet again, we dashed for an evening flight back to D.C. As we drove to the airport, we passed through downtown Detroit at rush hour. It felt like a ghost town. "Where is everyone?" one of my colleagues asked. The stark images of a seemingly evacuated city and the weary faces of assembly-line workers stayed with me, and I would think of them often in the ensuing weeks.

6

THE B WORD

"BANKRUPTCY IS NOT our goal." The words seemed to just pop out of my mouth.

At the behest of the White House, I'd found myself on the phone with some reporters from Detroit while on my way in from the airport on a Monday morning in March. All went fine until one asked about bankruptcy for Chrysler and GM. I should have been prepared for this obvious question, but wasn't.

I hesitated, trying to reconcile my preference for directness with the indisputable need to avoid further destabilizing two already fragile companies. And the last thing I wanted was to be dragged into some kind of horrible media free-for-all.

Dealing with reporters, I had to get used to how the rhythm of journalism in Washington had changed. During my years as a *Times* reporter, the Washington crew typically faced a 6 P.M. deadline for all but the most important stories. So unless late news broke, we had evenings free for the carousing that journalists back then enjoyed. But reporting these days goes on 24/7, with questions often posed and answered by e-mail. Throughout the day, our press people replied to questions themselves or asked for our help. There was no more stopping at the cocktail hour. By mid-evening, the next day's newspaper stories would appear on the Internet, triggering rounds of pushing and pulling between our communications team and the reporters to try to move errors, misunderstandings, or excessive harshness to a happier place. We would awaken in the morning and open the print editions to see whether our labors had borne fruit.

The tone of the relationship between the media and the government had changed too — it had grown more mistrustful and cynical even than after Watergate. No matter what we did, our competence, our motives, and, at times, our integrity were questioned.

The game was rough, but the White House press office had decided it was time for us to play it. We needed to make the case to the public that the task force was getting things done. That was why I had found myself in that airport car on the phone with the *Detroit News* and the *Detroit Free Press,* being questioned about one or more of the automakers having to declare bankruptcy.

I went ahead and said what had come to mind: "Bankruptcy is not our goal. I've been in and around bankruptcy for twenty-six years as part of my private-sector work. It is never a good outcome for any company, and it's never a first choice." I knew that I was on the edge of being disingenuous, but no formal decision had been made about bankruptcy and the decision would be the President's, not mine. So great was our concern about scaring off car buyers that we did not want to take any chances by throwing around the B word.

Sharpened to a sound bite — "Bankruptcy is not our focus; bankruptcy is not our goal" — my ad lib became our mantra.

Yet all the while we were preparing for it.

The day after our return from Detroit I'd met Matt Feldman, a bankruptcy lawyer whom we'd recruited because TARP's nine-attorney legal department had no one available with cutting-edge experience in restructuring. I didn't know Matt but Harry and Ron did, and he had also been recommended by a mutual friend on Wall Street. Nonetheless, hiring a lawyer at Treasury presented its own complications; TARP or no TARP, I was told, only the general counsel was permitted to hire attorneys. We eventually ground through the bureaucracy, trying to take advantage of Matt's expertise as best we could along the way.

So skittish was the White House about any talk of bankruptcy that when Matt's firm put out a press release proudly announcing his joining the task force, I was ordered to reprimand him for breaching protocol. I knew that Matt had nothing to do with the release — it was an innocent effort by his firm to brag a little — so I chose to ignore that particular instruction, the only time in my government career when I did so.

Matt Feldman was our last senior hire. Balding and cherubic, he had the maturity, steady nerves, and persistence that we'd require in dealing with the strong and stubborn personalities of a dominant industry. Matt also had terrific judgment on business issues well beyond questions of law. And he would prove to be as fine a restructuring lawyer as I have ever met.

We now had plenty of chiefs but no Indians. Harry proposed that we launch an investment-banking-style recruiting drive. It didn't faze him that we had only a couple of weeks to hire people, instead of the usual six months. On March 13, he blasted out an e-mail to his entire network of Wall Street contacts. "The work is incredibly intense," Harry wrote. "The amount of work is massive, the timelines are tight and the level of focus is also very high." And he added "compensation = government wages." When Matt read it, he thought it was so tough that no one would respond; Harry's view was that we wanted only highly talented people with an extraordinary sense of commitment. His e-mail was a way to select for them. We were soon deluged with hundreds of applicants, the vast majority from people we hadn't solicited directly as Harry's e-mail ricocheted around cyberspace.

We spent part of a morning reviewing piles of résumés and settled on a small group of candidates to invite to Washington for interviews. They had to pay their own way; unlike an investment bank, Treasury had no budget for reimbursing candidates' travel expenses. Nor was there anything like relocation or temporary-housing allowances for those we hired. Five of our new colleagues (including Ron and Harry) settled at the Woodward, a former office building a block from the Treasury that had been renovated to accommodate just the sort of short-term residents we expected to be.

In hiring, as in many other matters, we would have preferred a more conventional schedule, to make sure we picked the very best. But I'm a believer in the principle of Malcolm Gladwell's book *Blink:* you can often make equally good decisions in a fraction of the customary time. (Warren Buffett has shown that superb investing need not entail the months of due diligence and deliberation that private equity firms typically apply to a deal. Buffett has been known to make successful multibillion-dollar bets on the basis of a few meetings or phone calls.)

As we filled out the team, I thought of it as a firm rather than as a governmental hierarchy with gradations of seniority and titles bordering on the ridiculous — we wanted no "principal deputy undersecretaries" or the like. There were five partners (Ron, Harry, Brian, Matt, and I) who each had clear responsibilities but who functioned as a team. Matt ran our mini–law firm, with the assistance of Paul Nathanson, a superstar who had worked for me at both Lazard and Quadrangle before going on to Harvard Law School and a Supreme Court clerkship for Chief Justice John Roberts. We had diligence/restructuring teams for GM (headed by Harry) and Chrysler (headed by Ron with help from Brian Osias). Wall Street and the auto finance companies became my bailiwick, and to guide us with the latter, we recruited yet another Brian, Brian Stern, a youthful but experienced pro in financial institutions.

The White House belonged to Brian Deese, whose physical proximity to Summers and precocious understanding of policymaking were invaluable assets for navigating the byzantine decisionmaking process. Among many other things, I would learn an entirely new language from him, the lingo of the West Wing. "Litigate" meant to debate a decision or the wording of some document or speech. "Lean into" referred to encouraging the media about a particular line of speculation. "Wave off" was the opposite. To get "caught trying" meant receiving credit for having attempted something (like saving Chrysler) but failing.

Our recruiting effort succeeded in part because it coincided with a slow time on Wall Street. But far more significant, I found, was the desire of people to serve. With one exception, none of our new arrivals had any government experience or had ever thought much about coming to Washington. All shared the urgency that had finally prompted me to close my eyes and jump: the nation was going through a financial crisis, and for those of us with relevant qualifications, this was our chance to help. As Harry wrote in his e-mail, "I believe the opportunity is both unique and tremendous."

Washington veterans marveled at our hiring. I made a point of bringing as many of our new colleagues as I could to meetings in the West Wing. Even Larry was impressed. "Where did these people come from?" he asked on more than one occasion. "Every time you come here I see different faces, but they all seem to know what they are talking about." Our growing team attracted a different kind of attention in the halls of the Treasury. Never mind that we were part of TARP and our hiring didn't impinge on Treasury's tight budget; eventually Mark Patterson, Geithner's no-nonsense chief of staff, suggested that a task force of fourteen was, as Larry had cautioned weeks before, large by government standards.

By early March, I had settled into a routine that would continue until the end of my government service. I had sublet a cozy furnished condo on 23rd Street that had the advantage of access to room service from the Ritz-Carlton Hotel (to which it was attached) and to a Reebok Sports Club. I would get up at 5:30, take a quick look at the e-mails that had arrived overnight (inevitably, a pile from Harry), and be on a treadmill at the gym in time to catch the opening of *Morning Joe* on MSNBC at 6 A.M. The reports were filled with gloom, with the stock market below 7,000 and people debating whether we were in a recession or a depression. By seven, I would be back to shower, dress, scan the newspapers, and wolf down a bowl of Cheerios or an English muffin, all in order to get to the office in time to prepare for our daily 8 A.M. Team Auto call. Lunch was a tuna fish sandwich or a chicken caesar salad at my desk, a big change from the Four Seasons restaurant in New York, on the ground floor of the Seagram building, where Quadrangle had its offices. I'd get back to my condo between 8 and 9 P.M., eat some takeout food or order room service, and respond to the e-mails and other tasks that had piled up during the day. Answering government e-mails from home took some doing. The Treasury's e-mail system had layers of security that made it difficult to navigate remotely. (I'd been given a top-secret clearance — complete with a security briefing — but I never needed it for my job.)

I had anticipated this ascetic life and soon came to enjoy it, though it was a long way from the glamour of Washington that many envision. An unexpected benefit was that my caloric intake was so reduced that I lost five pounds during my time in government. Another happy surprise was that Team Auto was sufficiently autonomous for many of us to be able to commute home on weekends. I didn't mind spending most of Saturday and Sunday on conference calls or answering e-mails or commenting on drafts as long as I could be with my family for meals.

My teenage children didn't have much interest in cars or car companies — these were city kids. But having grown up in a politically active household, they were curious about government life. They particularly wanted to find out how it compared with the TV show *The West Wing*, reruns of which they watched endlessly. (I've never seen a single episode.) One weekend when I was stuck in Washington, my twin boys, who were seniors in high school, came to visit. They'd been to the White House (and the Oval Office) during the Clinton years and now wanted to see the Treasury building where I worked. Built in the mid-nineteenth century, the Treasury has all the feel of the important monument that it is. The department has an in-house curator, and the building's long and eventful history is displayed on its walls. As my boys and I walked the cavernous halls on Saturday morning, I enjoyed as much as they did looking at the vintage photographs, some of significant events, some of the building and its neighbors over the years. We also toured the portraits of former Treasury secretaries on the third floor, each with a surprisingly frank caption explaining the individual's successes and shortcomings. And we visited the ornate marble Cash Room, a banking hall where in the past money could be redeemed for gold and silver, and which was also the scene of President Grant's inaugural ball. (Since arriving at Treasury, I had been to the Cash Room for two ceremonial events: Tim Geithner's swearing-in and his disastrous first bank speech.)

The toll on my colleagues, who had more limited financial means and many of whom had young children, was far greater than it was on me. Every evening around six, Ron, Matt, and Harry would don headsets and call home to talk to their school-age kids. Ron would make the five-hour drive each week from his home near Pittsburgh in his 2003 Mustang (making him one of only a couple of task force members who drove an American car). When Matt Feldman told his wife he was joining the task force, she replied, "Let me understand this. You're moving away, you're leaving me with four kids, you're resigning your partnership, you're giving up 98 percent of your income, and you're asking me to be excited about that? I'll support you, but don't expect me to be excited about it." My young colleague Sadiq Malik spent his first month on a friend's couch in the Virginia suburb of Rosslyn. I tried to ameliorate the sacrifices as best I could, such as by paying for a stocked refrigerator and cabinet of cookies, granola bars, and the like to sustain the team during the late nights.

Even Harry Wilson, tough as nails, experienced low points. He had given up a treasured early retirement to go back to a life of hundred-hour weeks, and he and his family were feeling the strain. Two weeks after joining Team Auto, having been told he couldn't go on the Detroit trip because of lack of space, he mistakenly took a worried comment that I made during a Sunday conference call as personal criticism. That night, as he said goodbye for the week to his wife and four daughters, most of them broke down in tears. Bombarded on all sides, he lay down on his bed and cried. The next morning, after a mostly sleepless night, he took the first flight to Washington, miserable as he contemplated another week of back-to-back meetings.

For my part, after spending January and February feeling like a piñata at a fiesta, March came as something of a relief—but only partially so. My fears now focused on the substance of what we were trying to do and the enormous responsibility on our shoulders. I would sometimes sit bolt upright in the night, realizing that the fate of an entire industry—one that constituted a full 4 percent of our economy and was responsible for millions of jobs—rested heavily in my hands. The thought did not make for restful sleep.

Ironically, although I'd just been described in a *Washington Post* article as "fearless" and "self-confident," my indecision over taking the auto job demonstrated that I was as filled with doubts and questions as anyone. Later, I would learn that Tim had described me as having a low pulse rate, which was literally true, although it often didn't feel that way. Tim meant that I didn't fluster easily. In that respect, I realized that he was right. Once I took the auto job, I didn't shirk from decisions. It was our responsibility to make them.

While I was saying publicly that bankruptcy was not our focus, behind the scenes we were working intensively to figure out the best way to effect the critical restructurings. From the start, we had been the (mostly) happy recipients of much unsolicited advice. The question of how to deal with the two insolvent automakers whose businesses would never survive the long, slow grind of a conventional bankruptcy was fascinating to a crowd of experts.

Many of the suggestions were impractical, even when they came from sophisticated practitioners. Others revolved around the idea that we should push for passage of special bankruptcy legislation to speed us along. We asked our lawyers to draft a wish list of what such a law would include. Given the complexity of the subject, it was evident that if nothing else, passing legislation would involve an unacceptable delay. Many of the procedural steps in the bankruptcy code that we would be seeking to strip away had themselves been added to correct perceived past abuses, so whether Congress would have been amenable to changes was far from clear. Moreover, merely asking Congress to amend the bankruptcy code could well have triggered the consumer strike that we were working so hard to avoid. Finally, we were advised that efforts to shortcut bankruptcy procedures could well run afoul of the "takings clause" of the U.S. Constitution, or at least lead to prolonged litigation over the law's constitutionality, resulting in delays that would almost certainly exceed those involved in a Chapter 11 filing.

At the core of our problem was timing. Rothschild initially estimated that even a Section 363 sale of assets, the fastest possible bankruptcy, would take between six and fifteen months, time that I did not believe we either needed or had. I tried editing the timeline with Todd Snyder and his colleagues, challenging their assumptions at each step. When that didn't work, I asked Matt Feldman for help. Matt looked at the Rothschild analysis and had the same reaction I did. "This timeline is crazy," he thought. "It's way too long." The weekend before our trip to Detroit, the three of us had a series of phone calls. Matt found himself sitting in his study in Westport, Connecticut, watching his forsythia shrubs begin to bloom, being asked by Todd to support a timeline that he didn't believe in to a senior colleague he hadn't yet met.

Bit by bit, we whittled down Rothschild's opening bid to a period that we thought the automakers could survive. A week later, Matt was ensconced in a Treasury Department conference room with a whiteboard, working through structure and timing with John Rapisardi and his team of bankruptcy lawyers from Cadwalader, Wickersham & Taft, who was advising us. Feldman pushed them to a critical breakthrough: unlike most 363 sales, which include a marketing period to ascertain whether a better offer might be lurking in the bushes, we would propose no marketing period, thereby dramatically shortening the process.

Matt's argument was that everyone in the solar system knew these automakers were effectively for sale. If another buyer existed, it would have come forward by now.

We discussed none of this with General Motors or Chrysler. Instead we zeroed in on their principal challenges. For GM, management was the issue; for Chrysler, sheer survival.

Chrysler's creditors had been pressing us for weeks for a chance to make their case. Their anxiety was easy to understand. In May 2007, at the height of the private equity bubble, JPMorgan, Citibank, Bear Stearns, Goldman Sachs, and Morgan Stanley had agreed to lend $10 billion to Cerberus to help fund its purchase of Chrysler and Chrysler Financial. It was one of those Rube Goldberg financings that private equity guys and aggressive lenders dream up when times are flush. For a little under a year, all seemed to go well — Chrysler even paid down about $3 billion of the debt. But as the creditors prepared to sell the remaining debt to other banks and investors, as would have been routine, the credit markets began to fail and the value of the debt fell.

JPMorgan was in the deepest. In acquiring Bear Stearns when the investment bank collapsed in March 2008, it inherited another hefty chunk of Chrysler debt, bringing its total exposure to $2.7 billion. That was many times more than any bank, even one as gigantic as JPMorgan, would ever want to hold in a single loan, never mind one to a troubled automaker. Worse, JPM was rumored to have much more auto-related exposure on its books. So as industry sales headed south, the Chrysler loans, not surprisingly, commanded the attention of JPM's top operative.

That was James Bainbridge Lee Jr., known on Wall Street as Jimmy Lee, or just plain Jimmy. Almost exactly my age, Jimmy had had one employer since graduating from Williams College in 1975. He had started as a trainee at Chemical Bank and had survived a series of mergers to end up in the highest echelon of one of the world's megabanks. He looked and acted the part. He was partial to elegantly tailored suits and white-collared shirts. He hated being "caricatured" — as he put it — by the way he dressed, and while profiles of him often mentioned suspenders, he insisted that he hadn't worn them in more than a decade. Jimmy was one of the most effective "clients' men" of our generation, an articulate peddler of advice, money, and service. His office at JPMorgan headquarters, at 270 Park Avenue, was a combination command center and personal shrine, with banks of monitors, tickers, and screens, plus shelves of mementos of his many megadeals. He had long aspired to run a bank, but in recent years had settled into a happy life, proud of his position in the executive suite two doors down from CEO Jamie Dimon and of his ability to deploy billions at a moment's notice. At a celebration of Jimmy's thirtieth anniversary with the bank, Jamie toasted the man "who has lent more money than anyone on Wall Street and" — dramatic pause — "gotten most of it back."

I had known Jimmy since the mid-1990s and enjoyed watching him work his magic. Not surprisingly, he'd started calling me almost from the first day that my name had surfaced for the auto job. Each time we talked, Jimmy would bring up the proposition he'd been pushing for nearly a year, since JPMorgan had first realized that its huge loan was in trouble: a merger of GM and Chrysler. Many thought the idea made sense because a merger would eliminate redundant product lines, factories, and jobs; Jimmy liked it because he believed it would shore up the fast-eroding value of his loan. Long after Rick Wagoner had vetoed the idea the previous fall, Jimmy was still tirelessly arguing for a merger, like a dog that would not let go of a bone.

In our phone calls he also relentlessly reminded me that creditors deserve to be paid. "When you lend somebody $6.9 billion," he would say, "you expect to get $6.9 billion back. And not a penny less." I listened knowing that Jimmy's position was patently ridiculous. Chrysler debt was trading at around 15 cents on the dollar (admittedly, infrequently), and according to Chrysler's own analysis, the liquidation value of the company was perhaps as low as $1 billion. Clearly, Jimmy didn't believe that the Obama administration would be willing to push back and let the banks take over Chrysler rather than cave in to their demands.

Jimmy was eager to get together and talk. When, after several phone calls, he realized that I was too busy to come to New York, he made arrangements to visit the Treasury. Normally he'd have made the trip by corporate jet, but in the era of TARP — JPMorgan had received $25 billion of government aid — Jimmy felt obliged to go commercial. He chose the Acela express train for himself and his associates, and arrived at the Treasury around noon on March 13, muttering about the breakfast burrito that he had consumed en route. I loved the idea of Jimmy slumming on the Acela, forced to make do with a breakfast burrito.

We received our guests in the Diplomatic Reception Room, an odd, ornate space meant for Treasury secretaries hosting high foreign officials, and the only vaguely suitable room that Haley could find for us that day. Couches and comfortable chairs surrounded a fireplace at one end of the room and a nineteenth-century glass-topped mahogany meeting table occupied the other. All this was the furthest thing imaginable from a sleek, state-of-the-art financial conference room. When the JPMorgan delegation arrived, a Treasury technician was doggedly trying to hook up a Polycom speaker phone so Matt could listen in. (We had by now discovered that the Treasury mess would provide food and refreshments for meetings as long I paid for them myself.)

Jimmy and his team had brought a flip-chart book extolling the virtues of a GM-Chrysler combination. I realized that as a staunch Republican who, like many businessmen, distrusted Washington, Jimmy was worried that the Obama administration would side with the UAW and reject any merger that involved eliminating jobs. He seemed particularly suspicious of Ron Bloom, with his union cred, and he and his associates addressed most of the presentation to me and Harry, as potentially more sympathetic ears.

We listened politely, knowing that given the management problems at GM, a merger simply wasn't in the cards. As Matt struggled to follow the conversation via the balky Polycom, he was wondering, "Are these guys like on planet Pluto? How could they possibly think that someone could effectively put these companies together? GM and Chrysler can't even run their own businesses." I shared that view, but just three weeks into my job and sitting across the narrow table from Jimmy, I wanted to seem open-minded. So I said as mildly as I could, "This may be an option, but we've talked to GM, and GM does not want to buy Chrysler. As the government, we can't just say 'You have to.'" Harry and I also pointed out how difficult executing such a complex combination might be on a short deadline, especially over management's objections. Well, Jimmy said, if we liked the idea, JPMorgan had a lot of people who were very familiar with the auto sector and would gladly help.

Jimmy and his colleagues left feeling better than they'd expected.

"Steve and his team kind of understand this stuff and maybe we've got a shot at doing this merger," he thought, riding back to New York on the Acela. For my part, I'd heard nothing to change my view that whatever the theoretical merits of merging Chrysler into GM, GM's current management wanted no part of it—and any new leaders we put in would have their hands full even without a merger. (If we had supported a deal, I don't know whether the UAW would have been able to use its political muscle to block it. I do know—as underscored by Rahm's expletive about the UAW—that no one in the Obama administration ever asked us to favor labor for political reasons.)

The following Monday, I shifted my focus from the emotive characters surrounding Chrysler to their stoical counterparts at GM. The issues there were utterly different. We never contemplated letting GM fail, and because of the company's enormous size, no merger or alliance could save it. We had to address GM's dysfunction head-on, and a key to that was upgrading the leadership.

For starters, I knew we would need a new chairman. I had long been of the view that the roles of chairman and chief executive officer should be separate, as European companies have historically done. Without such a separation, I believed that there would be insufficient checks on the CEO and the management team. A lack of good governance was certainly part of GM's problem.

My search for a chairman was not going well, however. I'd been quietly gathering names—mostly from private equity firms and investors who had achieved success by backing results-oriented management teams. At Larry's urging, I also sought help from perhaps the most admired former CEO in America: Jack Welch. I didn't know Jack all that well and was gratified when he agreed to take my calls. I was intent on landing a world-class former CEO who could serve for five years—which meant no older than sixty-seven, since GM's mandatory retirement age for directors was seventy-two. Jack knew almost every big-time retired CEO and played golf with many of them. I discovered I could turn to him the way I might have turned to an extremely wise headhunter. I'd call with a candidate's name, and Jack would quickly say "Great guy," or "Lightweight," or "Dope"—in most cases reinforcing my own, much more tentative impression.

A big problem was that public resentment toward top executives was just then at full boil. For example, on March 19 a congressional panel interrogated Ed Liddy — the stalwart ex-CEO of Allstate who was a dollar-a-year volunteer running the wrecked insurer AIG — as if he were a common criminal. One of my top prospects for the GM chairmanship was scheduled to visit me in Washington a few days later; after he saw what happened to Liddy, he canceled. I called him and, grudgingly, he agreed to let me come see him at his home in the Midwest. I flew there the following Monday — but he wouldn't change his mind. (Later I learned that his golf buddies had kidded him, "What on earth would you go to GM for? Do you want to end up like Ed Liddy?") It was clear that lining up a chairman before our March 31 deadline would be exceptionally challenging.

There was even less room to maneuver in replacing Rick Wagoner as CEO. In a perfect world, we'd have liked to look outside the company or outside the industry, as Ford had done in recruiting Alan Mulally from Boeing. Yet following through on such a search would take months and be very risky. GM didn't have that kind of time. Meanwhile, the obvious internal candidate was Fritz Henderson, whom I'd met when GM had made the presentation to us in the dingy Treasury Annex. He'd impressed me as smart, energetic, down-to-earth, and more open to change than Rick. His knowledge of the business seemed encyclopedic. Yet something he'd said to Harry on March 11, during Harry's first trip to Detroit, stuck in my mind. Harry had asked at one point, "How would you characterize the culture of General Motors?" Fritz had meandered for a bit, talking about the company's good people, then paused. "You know, it's the only firm I've ever worked for," he said. "It's the only culture I know."

I knew Rick and Fritz were planning to return to D.C. in mid-March. I called Rick and asked to see them together and then to meet with them separately. I had no specific agenda for the three-way meeting; it was mainly a pretext to get time alone with each, and it came and went without incident. But when Rick came back at 4:30 that afternoon, he still had Fritz in tow. Somehow our signals had gotten crossed. We had an awkward moment until Fritz excused himself and retreated to the local Starbucks, where he sat thinking that management changes surely must be in the works.

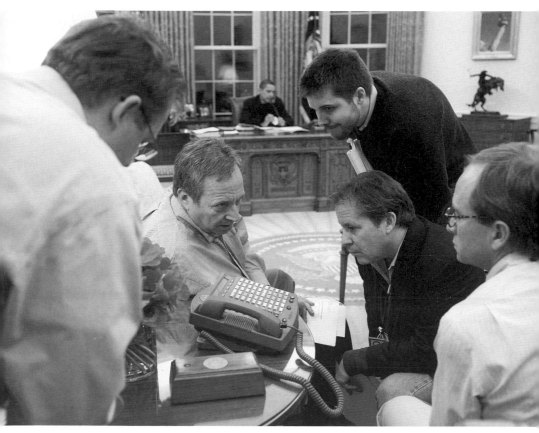

We hunched around a balky speakerphone in the Oval Office, listening in as Barack Obama briefed legislators on his first major action on autos. He'd been President barely two months. That's Larry Summers, chief economic adviser, with the wrinkled brow; I'm at far right. At left is Press Secretary Robert Gibbs; between Summers and me are Brian Deese, standing, and Gene Sperling. Official White House Photo by Pete Souza

They begged for a bailout but arrived by private jet: from right, GM CEO Rick Wagoner, Chrysler CEO Bob Nardelli, and Ford CEO Alan Mulally, with United Auto Workers chief Ron Gettelfinger, testifying before a Senate committee in November 2008.

President George W. Bush and Treasury Secretary Hank Paulson smiled outside the Treasury on the October 2008 day Congress passed TARP, the $700 billion financial rescue fund. Tens of billions of those dollars would soon flow to automakers.

With GM and Chrysler teetering, the Senate could not muster the votes for a bailout, but Bob Corker, the Republican junior senator from Tennessee, emerged as the unlikely architect of tough guidelines adapted by Bush and later Obama.

I was intrigued by the dynamic between Summers (left) and Treasury Secretary Tim Geithner, who jointly oversaw our task force. Tim had been Larry's protégé in the Clinton administration, yet their styles were different. Tim was a man of few words, Larry a man of many. Tim was organized and low-key; Larry was more chaotic but his intense interest in autos thrilled us. Stephen Crowley/The New York Times/Redux

A big flap erupted when I was named what the media kept calling the "car czar." Critics asked, what did a financier know about making cars? So I needed a deputy who could balance my Wall Street credentials with credibility in Detroit: Ron Bloom, who had served as chief restructuring officer for the United Steelworkers. (Above, me in a March 2009 TV interview; below, Ron at a Senate hearing in June.) Jay Mallin/Bloomberg News/Getty Images; AP Images/Susan Walsh

America's biggest, fastest industrial restructuring depended on Harry Wilson, who quarterbacked the overhaul of GM; Matt Feldman, our resident genius of bankruptcy law (the image is from *American Lawyer* magazine — the 363 on the tire refers to the section of the bankruptcy code whose application by Matt was groundbreaking); and Brian Deese, who secured for Team Auto a foothold in the White House (that's the entrance to the West Wing behind him) and contributed his policy expertise.

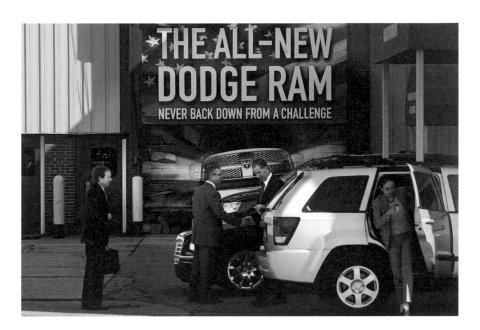

Team Auto's whirlwind tour of Detroit on March 9, 2009, included a visit to a Dodge Ram assembly plant. That's Diana Farrell of the task force at right, Ron Bloom (center, right) shaking hands with a Chrysler official, and me (left) fretting that we were running late. Seeing the assembly workers whose jobs were in jeopardy was a sobering reminder of the gravity of our task; I thought of them often in the ensuing months. Marcin Szczepanski/Detroit Free Press/MCT/Landov; AP Images/Carlos Osorio

General Motors world headquarters in Detroit's Renaissance Center, seen from a mostly abandoned warehouse district. As both city and company crumbled, GM's leaders reigned in splendid isolation from a thirty-ninth-floor executive suite. Bill Pugliano/Getty Images

General Motors Chairman and CEO Rick Wagoner in his Detroit office on March 19, 2009, three days after our first one-on-one meeting.

Fabrizio Costantini/Bloomberg News/Getty Images

Bob Nardelli, chairman and CEO of Chrysler, on his way to a Senate hearing in December 2008.

AP Images/Kevin Wolf

Ford Motor Company CEO Alan Mulally at an international automotive congress on January 12, 2010, in Detroit. Under his leadership, Ford avoided bankruptcy and didn't need a bailout; he is the only one of the three who still has his job.

Bill Pugliano/Getty Images

The strain of multibillion-dollar negotiations showed on the faces of five men, all very different, who were key players in the crisis: Ray Young, GM's hapless chief financial officer; Fritz Henderson, who after working at GM for his entire career served as CEO for 247 days; Ron Gettelfinger, chief of the United Auto Workers; Sergio Marchionne, Fiat's hot-tempered CEO, designated by Barack Obama as Chrysler's last hope; and Jimmy Lee of JPMorgan, who was obliged on his trips to Washington to forgo the corporate jet and ride the Acela.

By permission of Michael Ramirez and Creators Syndicate, Inc.

David Horsey/SeattlePI.com

On June 1, 2009, President Obama announced the ultimate overhaul: the Treasury was forcing General Motors into bankruptcy, and when it emerged, the company would be 61 percent taxpayer-owned with a chairman and four new board members selected by the U.S. government. To keep car buyers from fleeing, the President established government-backed warranties, and his Cash for Clunkers program was aimed at spurring demand. Meanwhile, editorial cartoonists needed no further encouragement.

Chrysler lowered the boom on inefficient dealers in June, canceling franchises and ordering dealers to take down their Dodge and Chrysler signs. Some 800 of the company's 3,200 "stores" were closed.

Reuters/Joshua Lott/Landov

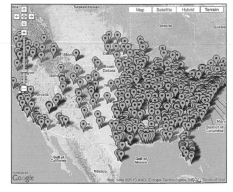

Ed Whitacre (top), the flinty Texan I coaxed out of retirement to become chairman of the new General Motors, evoked memories of Lee Iacocca by going on TV as the company pitchman. Soon after this commercial ran, the board pushed out Fritz Henderson and Ed took over as CEO. I was disappointed in summer 2010 when he left after nine months in the job. But his successor, Dan Akerson, another Team Auto recruit, also embodies the no-nonsense, disciplined approach GM needs to survive and even thrive.

Courtesy of General Motors

When our work was completed, I took Team Auto and friends to a Mexican restaurant for margaritas and farewells. From left: Matt Feldman, Brian Stern, Meg Reilly (Treasury spokesperson), Paul Nathanson, me, Ron Bloom, Mara McNeill (Treasury attorney), Brian Deese, Dustin Mondell (Rothschild banker), Clay Calhoon, Lindsay Simmons (Treasury attorney), Harry Wilson, Sadiq Malik, Sally Wrennall-Montes (Treasury assistant), Rob Fraser, Haley Stevens, David Markowitz, and Brian Osias. Courtesy of Paul Nathanson

Rick and I faced each other uneasily at my conference table. He was impassive; I was nervous. While I had interacted with many CEOs in my Wall Street career, I'd never, in effect, conducted a job interview with the head of one of America's largest corporations. I asked him to describe his management team, the individuals' strengths and weaknesses, and how he saw it evolving over time. He said that Fritz was being groomed to succeed him, although after only twelve months as president, he would benefit from more experience. I was looking for an opportunity to gently shift the conversation around to Rick, but couldn't find one. So I just asked, "And what about your plans going forward?" Rick seemed to be expecting the question. "I'm not planning to stay until I'm sixty-five," he said (he'd just turned fifty-six), "but I think I've got at least a few years left in me." He paused and added, "I told the last administration that if my leaving would help save General Motors, I'm prepared to do it." My sense was that he left the meeting thinking he'd persuaded me of his importance to GM's turnaround, in part because of the lack of a qualified replacement.

Fritz came by the following morning. Balding, mustachioed, slightly stocky, he seemed an unprepossessing fifty-year-old corporate guy. But when he spoke, there was knowledge and intelligence in his voice. We ate lunch at my conference table — chicken caesar salads from the Treasury mess (paid for by me, of course). I kept the conversation general, just trying to get to know him and gain a sense of whether he was up to the job of replacing Rick. Fritz put his cards on the table. "Last summer I turned down a very attractive CEO job because I felt I had a responsibility to see GM through its problems," he said. He was equally direct about compensation; his salary had been cut by 30 percent and he hadn't received a bonus since 2005. "I understand the situation," he said, "but at some point, I need to focus on my family's financial security."

Fritz represented a conundrum. He was not only a GM lifer but also the son of a GM lifer. Born and raised in the Detroit area, he had attended the University of Michigan and, while he had moved around the world during his career at GM, he was a Detroit auto guy through and through — not exactly fresh blood for a company that needed sweeping change. Yet there was much about him to like. (I enjoyed razzing Harry about the fact that unlike him, Fritz had been a Baker Scholar at Harvard Business School, an honor based solely on grades and restricted to the top 5 percent of each class.) And I was intimated by the prospect of trying to recruit an A+ player from outside, not to mention the time and disruption that an intensive search would entail. We needed to be ready by March 31 to tell the world who would be the new CEO of General Motors.

7

"IS THIS UNANIMOUS?"

TIM AND LARRY TRIED valiantly to help us parse what seemed like an endless thicket of decisions. But with the economy in deep trouble and financial markets hitting new lows, we were inevitably left to our own devices more than they, or we, would have liked. Larry jokingly called Team Auto a "social experiment"—we were like a petri dish left out on a laboratory counter to see what would grow.

Tim's time was in particularly short supply. He was locked in endless meetings—including a seven-hour session on a Sunday with all the economic team, as well as, for a substantial part of it, the President—trying to figure out whether to start nationalizing banks, and if not, what more should be done to prop them up. In the month of March alone, he testified before Congress six times, announced two massive new liquidity programs, unveiled a regulatory reform plan, and made a day trip to Medellín, Colombia, for the annual meeting of the board of governors of the Inter-American Development Bank. I couldn't begin to imagine how he coped with the stress.

Later, after our auto effort proved successful, many commentators would ask why the administration couldn't have taken a similar approach to the banks. This question flared most emotionally around AIG, the rogue insurance giant to which the Treasury and the Fed ended up committing $182 billion to stave off chaos and make creditors and counterparties whole. Even sophisticated critics almost always missed the crucial point: for banks, unlike automakers, bankruptcy was not a useful tool for reorganization, as the Lehman Brothers disaster had so vividly demonstrated. And as we quickly learned in autos, without bankruptcy as a tool for reorganization, it was nearly impossible to achieve shared sacrifice among the stakeholders.

That was the nub of what was angering the public and weighing on Tim: the absence of shared sacrifice. The hundreds of billions of dollars that the government was committing through TARP was protecting the financial system, but collaterally also rewarding the creditors and counterparties. In a perfect world, instead of having their risk essentially eliminated, these creditors and counterparties should have suffered along with everyone else touched by the crisis.

The Obama administration also opted not to change the management teams at the banks and financial companies. As I went about my business, I overheard fragments of the internal debate on this subject in the hallways of Treasury and the White House, but I stayed out of it. Based on sound advice from former Treasury Secretary Robert Rubin, I had gone to Washington resolved to stay focused on my assignment and not poke my nose into other business. Had I been asked, though, I'd have reiterated my belief that, with rare exceptions, a CEO who leads a company into a state in which its only recourse is a government bailout shouldn't be in his job.

So while Tim tried valiantly to make time for us, we ended up working much more closely with Larry. I was pleasantly surprised by his fascination with autos. But a lot about Larry intrigued me.

Of all the people who I encountered during my stay in Washington, he was among the most colorful and the most interesting. Though we were longtime friends and I had always felt that I had his respect, I was well aware of his reputation for bumptiousness and approached my role as one of his charges with a bit of trepidation. But working for him turned out to be stimulating, enjoyable, and harmonious. Like me — with more justification in his case — Larry didn't suffer fools. He was attentive to the opinions of people he respected, particularly those who offered well-reasoned analyses in matters outside his expertise. Titles and résumés meant little to him; he listened to what was said and decided whether the speaker seemed worthy of attention. Thus he regarded Deese's views on certain matters to be far more valuable than those of higher-ranking colleagues. Harry, too, quickly came to burn brightly on Larry's radar screen. Smart young colleagues adored him, and I could see why Larry had been popular among Harvard students while warring with some members of the faculty.

In our discussions, I tried to keep to my home turf of finance and business. It was hard to challenge him on economics, certainly for me but also for bona fide economists like Christy Romer, the chair of the Council of Economic Advisers. Alan Krueger, the affable chief economist at Treasury, was perhaps the Washington economist whom Larry respected most. He'd been a student of Larry's at Harvard and had received an A+.

I tried to decide whether Larry had always been great to work for or whether the searing experience of being pushed out as president of Harvard had changed him. In part based on what I heard from a few of his former colleagues from the Clinton-era Treasury Department, I concluded that some of his rough edges must have been sanded down. Also, he had arrived in Washington this time with a chief of staff, Marne Levine, who had both Larry's respect and very sound judgment. When he returned from a meeting in the West Wing, fuming about stupid ideas that had been put forward, Marne could calm him and keep him from flying off the handle. Larry visibly worked hard to control himself. At one meeting I attended, a junior colleague in the bleachers (the couch on the other side of his office) offered an unsolicited comment. "That's one of the silliest . . . ," Larry began, but then caught himself and said, half under his breath, "That's the old Larry. The new Larry says, 'Have you thought about it this way?'"

Having been a star debater at MIT, he loved to argue. In many instances, of course, he used argument to express his views and try to win others over. But in other cases, he seemed to take a contrary position just to be sure all the pros and cons were hashed out. At still other times, he appeared to argue because he wasn't sure himself what he thought. For instance, I heard him take both sides — sometimes in the same conversation — on the efficient-markets hypothesis. This principle holds that because markets are always processing all available information, it's futile for an investor to try to "beat the market." In the aftermath of the 1987 stock market crash, Larry had drafted a paper against the theory; the analysis began: "There are idiots. Look around." Yet when Harry produced a set of projections for GM showing high potential returns for a prospective stockholder, Larry invoked efficient-markets theory to push back, arguing that if Harry's projections were accurate, we would already have a line of investors waiting outside our door.

His metaphors were vivid and so was his manner of speech. Once Diana Farrell began to offer an opinion, but before she passed the midpoint of expressing her thought, Larry interrupted to say (not harshly), "I've already considered that idea and rejected it." This so amused our younger colleagues that for weeks afterward they would say to one another, as they debated one proposal or another, "I've already considered that idea and *rejected* it."

Larry was an economist, however, not a businessman. Occasionally I thought he didn't have the best perspective on financial markets or business. I wasn't sure that he wanted to be told bluntly that he was wrong, especially by a subordinate. So I would gingerly try to correct his minor mistakes (Chrysler had *lenders,* not bondholders) and to nudge him ever so gently toward my views on business and finance. Our discussions were the high point of my Washington experience; I would leave convinced that there could be no happier future circumstance than the chance to work for him again.

Every few days, often in late afternoon when Larry's schedule was lighter, a delegation from Team Auto would troop over to the White House to squeeze ourselves around the cramped conference table in his office.

That was where we first presented our bill — a mid-March back-of-the-envelope estimate of how much the auto bailout was going to cost. I wanted to have a "budget" at the earliest practicable opportunity, with the notion that we would update it as our thoughts were refined by additional work. Coincidentally, the overseers of TARP had asked to see our numbers. They were getting ready to receive the results of the bank stress tests and were evidently feeling the same dread that Hank Paulson had experienced five months earlier, that TARP might not have enough money to cover all needs. Rahm began intimating that the auto bailout might have to seek new funding from Congress, probably a nonstarter under any circumstance (as the Bush administration had found) but surely impractical on our timetable. After a few anxious days, the issue receded as early signals from the stress tests came in.

Our first, rough estimate for the "auto caper," as Ron Bloom liked to call it, was $100 billion — $75 billion on top of the $25 billion the government had already put in. Within that total, we'd earmarked $50 billion for GM and Chrysler, $40 billion for their affiliated finance companies and for "consumer support programs" to cover warranties and encourage buyers not to abandon Detroit, and $10 billion for suppliers.

What I found offensive about these numbers was that less than three months earlier, the CEOs of GM and Chrysler had sat before Congress insisting that less than $20 billion would solve all their problems. Economist Mark Zandi's dramatic calculation of $75 billion to $125 billion, so startling at the December 2008 hearing, had proved far more prescient than those of men who should have known their business far better than any economist or government bureaucrat.

Larry barely batted an eye — we had just begun our work, so neither he nor we were in a position to put much certainty behind any estimate. And there was no immediate need to whittle down the numbers. The existence of TARP allowed us to contemplate committing tens of billions of dollars freely, a surreal contrast to the normal process of prying money loose.

The toughest issue on the table was what to do about Chrysler. Could it be saved? Should it be saved? The questions were debated at nearly every meeting. Finally, on March 13, the matter came to a head. Shortly after 4:30 on that chilly afternoon (though the cherry blossoms were ready to bloom), we gathered around Larry's table and took our regular seats, I at his right and Deese at his left. Filling out the table were Ron, Harry, Diana, Gene Sperling, Alan Krueger, and Austan Goolsbee. Austan, a forty-year-old economics professor from the University of Chicago, had been an adviser to Obama from the beginning of the long march to the White House. In appreciation for his steadfast support, the President had named him to one of three slots on the Council of Economic Advisers. Perhaps in part because of his special relationship with Obama, Austan never shrank from speaking his mind clearly, directly, and forcefully. He liked to go by the numbers, using the rigorous analytical approach for which the Chicago economics department was known.

Regarding Chrysler, there was no doubt as to what Austan (and CEA chief Christy Romer) believed. He began by recapitulating the dismal state of the auto industry that we had been living with for the previous ten weeks. He went on to address the impacts on employment of a potential Chrysler liquidation. Of course the loss of Chrysler would not mean that fewer cars would be sold in America; Chrysler's lost production would be taken up by other automakers. The question was, which ones would benefit?

Austan and his team had concluded that Chrysler's product line overlapped much more with those of GM and Ford than with those of foreign-owned companies. In their view, most would-be Chrysler buyers would likely turn to other domestically produced brands. Thus Chrysler's demise would actually *boost* GM's and Ford's odds of surviving the current Great Recession.

We all knew that Chrysler's liquidation would immediately vaporize nearly 300,000 jobs — 40,000 at Chrysler and the balance among its suppliers and dealers. But Austan argued passionately that once other automakers raced into the gap, the net loss would be a fraction of that, perhaps a small fraction. The Chrysler skeptics had other strong arguments for letting the company die. It was the weak number three among the U.S. automakers. Continuing to bail it out would send the wrong signal about the Obama administration's inclination to make hard decisions when confronted by corporate sob stories.

Harry took the economic analysis and translated it into financial implications for GM. Goolsbee believed that GM would capture more than a quarter of Chrysler's customers, or about 300,000 additional cars sold per year. That would strengthen its business and reduce the amount of taxpayer capital it would need. Harry's quick calculations showed that if Chrysler went away, GM's pretax profit could be increased by about $2.4 billion a year. That could add more than $10 billion to GM's market value, a meaningful increment for whoever ended up owning shares.

No one challenged the accuracy of Harry's figures or those of the Council of Economic Advisers. The case for saving Chrysler was based more on political and social reality. For example, while the net job loss might ultimately be as low as the CEA suggested, on day one of Chrysler's liquidation, those 300,000 jobs would disappear. Moreover, the job loss would be directly associated with an Obama decision, while the jobs regained would be invisible.

In addition, the government would still face huge costs in letting Chrysler fail — for instance, Michigan's state unemployment insurance fund might go broke and need bailing out. Deese offered an argument that resonated with Larry: Given the uncertainty in our economy, it was better to invest $6 billion for a meaningful chance that Chrysler would survive than to invest several billion dollars in its funeral. (The hole in this argument was that we could invest $6 billion and still have to pay for the exact same funeral.) He and other defenders also extolled the potential benefits of the Fiat alliance and of preserving "optionality" for later moves, such as an eventual merger with GM.

Back and forth the arguments flew. For Austan Goolsbee and Alan Krueger, the CEA's analysis was compelling. Harry, meanwhile, was particularly emphatic about the positive effect Chrysler's demise would have on GM. Goolsbee and Wilson were also concerned about Chrysler's weak product line and its ability to turn the corner, even under Sergio's strong leadership, before its cash ran out. Diana, taking the perspective of a management consultant, wondered rhetorically why the government would be in the business of saving losing companies.

On the pro-Chrysler side, Gene reminded us that liquidation would shatter entire communities. Ron emphasized the need to preserve as many jobs as possible. Brian asked why, from a policy and political perspective, we would let Chrysler go if we had reasonable confidence that it could be saved. I saw the sense in all these diverse views and felt torn.

Larry pressed us to attach probabilities to our recommendations and countered with odds of his own. Like Bob Rubin, with whom the concept is most closely associated, Larry is an enthusiast for "probabilistic decisionmaking," a method for weighing uncertainties. He asked how likely we thought it was that federal money would keep Chrysler alive for eighteen months (essentially past the midterm elections) and for five years (potentially through another business cycle).

At one point, he confessed that as we gave our answers, he was discounting our probabilities based on what he thought we would say. For example, knowing that Ron was in favor of saving Chrysler, Larry lowered the probability Ron assigned to the success of the alliance with Fiat. The opposite for Harry. Plainly, Larry was loving this debate.

I was truly undecided. The economic and financial analysis for letting Chrysler go seemed compelling to me, as did Diana's logic. But I knew I was expected to form an opinion based on all of the factors, not just the numbers. Finally, Larry turned to me and said, "I know where everyone else is on this. What I'm trying to figure out is where you are." I continued to wiggle. Deese, whose judgment I respected enormously, was looking at me across the table as if to say, "Are you out of your mind? If we have a way to support Chrysler as a viable business, we can't let it go down in this economic mess."

Larry called for a show of hands. His question was precise: "If you assume that the probability is 50 percent or greater that Chrysler would survive for five years, would you save it?"

Diana was unhappy with the phrasing, because she thought Larry was stacking the deck — forcing those who believed Chrysler's chances were actually slim to assume a higher probability. She had suspected that he wanted to save Chrysler and now was sure of it. While she recognized that under Larry's formulation she should be voting to save Chrysler, she voted against it anyway, as a kind of protest. Austan felt sandbagged too — he thought that if Christy had been present to vote, and if Deese, a junior staffer, had been barred from voting, a further bailout for Chrysler would have stood no chance.

As it was, the vote was 4 to 3 against a further Chrysler bailout (with Bloom, Deese, and Sperling in favor) when Larry turned to me again. I was still unwilling to commit. Frustrated, he asked, "If you were President, what would you do?" This was an effective reminder that the man I'd signed on to serve did not have the luxury of sitting on the fence. I could not duck the question put this way, so finally, reluctantly, I cast a "51–49" vote in favor of the bailout. With that, the tally was tied, so Larry's became the deciding vote. He approached the question from a seemingly simple standpoint: Which would be the bigger mistake, saving Chrysler, which would keep a very fragile competitor to GM alive? Or letting it go, which might decimate the U.S. economy?

Larry listened closely to the "two good companies instead of three" argument that the opponents made and also worried about giving Fiat a "free option." But in the end, for him, this calculus was simpler than his courses at Harvard had been: once he was convinced that Chrysler could get through at least a couple of years, he believed the risks of letting it go represented more of a gamble than the economy should be subjected to at this critical time. As he later described it, "You could think of it as a cheap form of stimulus at a time when the economy clearly needed stimulus." We had all come a long way from the dark days of early March when, having concluded that Chrysler was not viable as a standalone company, we would have guessed that liquidation was the most likely outcome.

When the meeting ended, as we filed out of the office, Larry pulled Krueger aside. Quietly he told him, "I hope you understand that it's different being the decisionmaker than being an economic adviser. There are other factors I have to consider." He knew how strong the case was that Alan and Austan had made, and didn't want his star student to think he'd gone all wobbly.

Larry recognized that Chrysler was a close enough call that the President needed to be briefed, and asked us to craft a short memo. The CEA, worried that its views wouldn't be fully represented, wanted to send its own memo of dissent. But Larry vetoed that, declaring that there would be only one memo to the President, and it would fairly portray both sides of the debate. Our memo to Obama was "litigated" extensively with Larry before being dispatched the following week.

The memo was still being worked on and Chrysler was still on Austan's mind as he prepared for a President's Daily Brief in the Oval Office on March 18. Neither he nor Alan Krueger had heard anything further about Chrysler since the vote in Larry's office five days earlier and assumed the decision had been made to save the company. They feared that they would not be told until the last minute to avoid more disputation.

The topic for Obama that morning was an update on Wall Street, and Austan was present on behalf of the President's Economic Recovery Advisory Board (PERAB) — nongovernmental advisers, led by Paul Volcker, whose job was to give Obama a "ground-level sense" of the economy outside what he called the echo chamber of the Washington bureaucracy. Access to the President's Daily Briefs was, of course, restricted and generally didn't include Austan. In this case, Christy had told Austan, "You can go, but only to observe on matters affecting PERAB, and you're not allowed to say anything."

The briefing was uneventful until the end, when Austan was startled to hear Summers describe to Obama our decision to move up the announcement of a $5 billion receivables guarantee program for auto suppliers to the very next day. We'd wanted to hold off until the end of March, so that the President could announce the program with his other auto industry decisions. But the supplier crisis was real and urgent, and the pressure to respond was enormous, so we'd sped up the launch even though the mechanics of implementing the program were still far from complete. "Okay," said the President, taking it in. "That sounds sensible."

Whoa, thought Austan. "Mr. President," he interrupted, "just be aware that the second we announce we're going to save the suppliers, everybody is going to assume we're saving the auto companies too. Have we really decided that? If not, we've got to figure out how we're going to message this thing."

"Of course," Summers said curtly, and the meeting moved on. As soon as the session adjourned, he cornered Goolsbee outside in the corridor and exploded, "You *do not* relitigate in front of the President!"

"I was not litigating in front of the President," Austan shot back. "He hasn't seen that program and it has nothing to do with the financial rescue." Larry felt that the freewheeling Austan was off base. The CEA had been aware of the plans to help the suppliers, and there wasn't anything about the program that mandated a rescue of any or all auto companies. The President would still have a free hand when that larger issue reached his desk.

To make matters worse, Austan inadvertently was never informed that the carefully balanced Chrysler memo was about to be delivered to the President at almost that very moment, as Larry had promised. Austan continued to boil based on his impression that the views of the dissenters were not being reflected, a concern that would only grow in the coming days.

Now that it was clear that Larry wanted the Chrysler rescue to proceed, I worked hard to make sure he understood how much was still left to do on the matter and how much uncertainty remained. We had issues to resolve with Fiat, had not begun to negotiate with the UAW, and of course Jimmy Lee and the creditors were still demanding 100 cents on the dollar. We had carried out so little due diligence on Chrysler as a business that to invest now would be, by private equity standards, negligent. As smart as Larry was about so many things, I wasn't sure private-sector dealmaking was his strong suit.

The Fiat negotiations were not going well. Although Chrysler had unveiled the alliance with great fanfare on January 20, we viewed that announcement as a beginning rather than an end. In particular, we remained concerned that Fiat was putting no money into the deal. This was bad business and bad politics. The agreement called for the Italian automaker to get an initial 35 percent ownership stake in return for providing Chrysler with technology and management expertise. I worried about the potential backlash from billions of dollars of U.S. taxpayer money going to an automaker that would be managed and partly owned by a foreign company. Worse, for Fiat the deal was risk-free—if the alliance didn't work, it could walk away with no penalty.

We struggled to persuade Sergio to put up some cash. But as much as the ambitious CEO wanted Chrysler, that was where he drew the line, at least in part because Fiat was facing its own financial challenges. Eventually, after hard bargaining, Ron succeeded in carving back Fiat's initial ownership stake to 20 percent, requiring the company to meet meaningful milestones before receiving additional shares and limiting its ownership to no more than 49 percent until the entire Treasury investment had been repaid. All in all, I felt it was a fair deal, and nothing that has transpired since then has changed my mind.

The launch of the $5 billion receivables guarantee program for suppliers on March 19 would be the first pronouncement from the Auto Task Force, so I wanted to be sure that we put our best foot forward. Our team worked hard to be sure we had all the mechanics right; Mara McNeill, a Treasury lawyer, became our unsung hero on these critical issues. We wrote a public fact sheet, rehearsed questions and answers for calls with reporters, and helped Tim's staff craft an announcement that made it seem as if we had our act together. His statement hit all the right notes. "The Supplier Support Program will help stabilize a critical component of the American auto industry during the difficult period of restructuring that lies ahead," it read. "The program will provide supply companies with much-needed access to liquidity to assist them in meeting payrolls and covering their expenses, while giving the domestic auto companies reliable access to the parts they need."

This unveiling was received better than I would have predicted, even in the heartland. Senator Carl Levin, crusty as he was, called the program "good news." Governor Granholm announced, "Today's action will minimize unnecessary job losses."

Meanwhile, I was pleasantly surprised to see a quote from David E. Cole, chairman of the Center for Automotive Research, in the next day's *New York Times*. "I am convinced they have decided that a major bankruptcy in this industry is not going to happen if they can help it," Cole said. Only ten days from the President's March 30 speech, and the industry's closest observers did not know what had, for all practical purposes, already been decided.

Unfortunately, however, Senator Corker was furious. He called Summers to remind him of a promise that he and Deese and I had all forgotten. Back in January, as part of the horse-trading to get legislative approval for the second half of TARP, Larry had sent a lengthy, painstakingly negotiated letter to congressional leaders that promised, among many other things, that additional TARP funds would flow to the auto industry only "in the context of a comprehensive restructuring." Of course the Supplier Support Program failed that test. Corker didn't stop at a phone call. He issued a statement saying that the program was "a violation of trust and another sleight of hand by this administration." (Ironically, Corker had voted against the second half of TARP because he thought Larry's letter had not been strong enough; he'd wanted a promise that no more TARP money would go to the auto industry — period.)

It was the first time I'd ever seen Larry shaken. Deese felt terrible too, knowing that responsibility for avoiding such slip-ups generally fell to the person in his role. (Belatedly I realized I also bore some blame. I'd been present at transition headquarters the day the letter went out and knew of the auto industry paragraph. But I'd been so ignorant of the ways of Washington in those early days that I hadn't registered what was going by me.)

The only positive aspect of the episode was that Larry asked me to follow up with Corker and do my best to mollify him, which led to a strong friendship between us. In the course of a sangria-fueled Mexican dinner one warm spring night, Corker asked me, "You seem like such a sensible fellow, why are you a Democrat?" "Three main reasons," I said, ticking off my views that Republicans had favored the rich at a time of growing income inequality, abandoned fiscal responsibility, and held unfortunate positions on social issues such as a woman's right to choose abortion.

As events unfolded, I became convinced that we had gotten our supplier policy right. In particular, we were correct in resisting the many pleas to bail out failing companies — to invade Laos, as Larry would have put it. Suppliers continued to go bankrupt that spring, but the financial markets reopened just enough to provide debtor-in-possession loans, enabling the normal Chapter 11 restructuring process to work. We also encouraged the automakers to provide DIP loans to their most critical suppliers when the banks refused, and quietly supplied GM and Chrysler with extra funds to enable them to do so. The outcome was far better than we would have achieved with bailouts. Once we drew the line on federal intervention, the supply base was forced to merge, shrink, and otherwise restructure itself to a size that realistically reflected the industry's prospects. And we were faithful to our goal of saving only those jobs for which there was sound economic justification.

Our payment guarantee program, meanwhile, was scarcely used. To instill market discipline, we had made the money so expensive that suppliers thought twice before signing up, and ended up tapping only $413 million of the $5 billion we had allocated. But it had the desired effect of reassuring both companies and communities; as a bonus, the Treasury made a little money for taxpayers on the fees.

We were acutely aware of the taxpayer money being sucked every day into Detroit. For Chrysler, each additional month of life support was going to cost $500 million to $1 billion, money that the Treasury would never see again if the company ended up liquidating. GM would cost even more — as much as $2 billion a month. So we wanted the President to impose the tightest possible deadlines for the automakers to come to terms with their stakeholders or seek the protection of the bankruptcy court: thirty days for Chrysler and sixty days for GM. We gave GM an extra month in part because we were quite certain that it would not end up in liquidation (minimizing the risk of a "good money after bad" problem) and in part because the company was so complicated. In a perfect world, Harry would have allotted himself and his team six months to perform due diligence and restructure the business (and in our earlier straw man, we had proposed a total of ninety days for GM). But on March 19, our lawyers at Cadwalader uncovered a sobering fact:

the company had a $1 billion bond payment coming due on June 1. If we allowed GM to make that payment, we'd be awarding 100 cents on the dollar to bondholders who were entitled to only pennies. Yet if the company failed to pay, under the law as few as three of its thousands of creditors could force it into a chaotic and potentially fatal uncontrolled bankruptcy. This was an unwelcome extra incentive to work fast.

I knew that by the end of March we had to formalize our recommendations in a "presidential decision memo" and presumably sit down with Obama as he made up his mind. But I had no idea how all of this would work. As usual, I deferred to Deese, who'd never been party to a presidential decision either, but at least had a desk in the West Wing and *seemed* to know what he was doing.

As Deese was getting under way, a surprising notion drifted over from the White House: the powers that be wanted the announcement to be made by Ron and me on March 27—an idea that struck both Deese and me as insane. This was arguably one of the most important actions that the administration was likely to take in its first hundred days, and it seemed unimaginable that it should come from anyone other than the President. Eventually wiser heads prevailed. The President would speak to the nation on March 30, a day before heading off on his first overseas trip. A gaggle of cabinet members would then fan out across the Midwest to drive home the fact that Washington was coming to the rescue. We never learned the origin of the original rollout plan but assumed it was advisers leery of political fallout from such a controversial set of announcements.

What little I knew about presidential decisionmaking included an appreciation that a decision memo was intended to give the President all the background, arguments, and data he needed. By now, our views were well honed: we wanted fundamental restructurings on a short timetable, almost surely involving bankruptcy. By now as well, the economic and political risks were seared into our brains. We had also refined our budget for the "caper" to a range of $76 billion to $88.5 billion, startlingly close to the final figure of $82 billion.

Importantly, after last-minute lobbying by Austan and Christy—who were still unaware that the first memo had gone to the President—the memo included the views of those opposed to saving Chrysler, the sole area of disagreement among the President's advisers. Wherever the

President came out on these recommendations, we knew it was going to be a high-stakes game of brinksmanship.

On Thursday morning, Larry summoned Ron and me to his office in the West Wing. We were talking about various loose ends when Larry abruptly put on his suit jacket and said, "Let's go downstairs." The next thing I knew, I was in the Oval Office for the second time in my life (the first had been during the Clinton years, as a "friend of Bill," to show it to my kids). The room was yellower and brighter than I remembered, almost like a movie set. But this was no movie. President Obama and a clutch of key advisers were there waiting, and the sole topic of the morning's Daily Brief was to be autos. In the hectic pace of life in the West Wing, no one had told me!

The room was packed and the seating protocol intrigued me. Of course the President sat in his wing chair in front of the fireplace. Vice President Biden was not in attendance; his matching chair remained empty. Those who had significant roles in the meeting filled two facing sofas. Another five or six aides — some very senior, including Rahm Emanuel — occupied a row of straight-backed chairs facing the President. Still another clutch of aides, including Deese, stood around the periphery.

Larry began formally, "Mr. President, we're here today to review the decisions that you need to make regarding the auto industry," and then started to tick off the main issues. After just a few moments, the President said, "Larry, I've read the memo." (Indeed he had, as I recognized when he started citing figures from the final page.) The conversation quickly turned to the only major area of disagreement, Chrysler, about which the President had also been informed in our shorter, separate memo a week earlier.

The group was still in the early stages of reprising the arguments that we'd been having for days in Larry's office when the President asked about our conclusion. "Is this unanimous?" he said.

"Well, no, the CEA doesn't agree," he was told. Christy explained that Austan had pushed to have the opposing view presented.

"Where's Goolsbee?" the President asked, realizing that the most vocal spokesman for the opposition wasn't in the room. Christy had asked Larry for permission to bring Austan along, but Larry had refused, citing a decision by Rahm at the outset of the administration that

Christy would represent the Council of Economic Advisers. Austan was in his office in the Eisenhower building, across West Executive Drive. A summons went out from the President's assistant Katie Johnson, and after a few minutes Austan strode in. The Oval Office was so full that Austan tried to become the fourth person on a three-person sofa. After a few minutes, the President waved him into Joe Biden's empty chair. That put him awkwardly between the President and Larry. "I understand you don't agree with this recommendation," Obama said.

"Yes, that's true," Austan replied.

"What's your best argument?"

Austan seized on a hometown metaphor: "If you try to land at O'Hare, you've got runways going both ways. We're trying to land planes at the same time. If you try to keep Chrysler in production, that's going to seriously damage our efforts. It's going to make doing GM substantially more costly. You might even threaten Ford."

The President asked Christy to review the net job loss from a Chrysler shutdown, but just then Katie came in with a note. The Daily Briefs are intended to last only about twenty minutes, and she was signaling Obama to move on to his next meeting. "This is too important to decide in a rush," the President told us. "We need to get together again later."

We reconvened early that evening, in the windowless Roosevelt Room, the only real conference room in the West Wing available for general use. Obama took a seat in the middle of the long table, with Larry directly across, me to Larry's left, Diana to my left, and Ron to Larry's right. Tim chose the end of the table in front of the fireplace, with its painting of Teddy Roosevelt on horseback above the mantel. Flags lined the wall behind Obama, giving him a particularly presidential air. Other senior aides filled the remaining seats: Rahm, Axelrod, Robert Gibbs, Romer, Peter Orszag, Valerie Jarrett, and others.

By protocol, unless they had speaking roles, less senior aides took the couch and upholstered chairs behind where I sat; tonight Brian and Harry and others were there. (For meetings where all the seats were taken, people would stand near the couch — no one wanted to be out of the President's line of sight.) There was a no-BlackBerry rule — attendees were supposed to deposit the devices in a small basket outside the door, with a yellow Post-it to identify the owner. A few regulars, like Peter Orszag, chose to ignore the rule. (Like many of us, Orszag carried both a government BlackBerry and a personal one. His were strapped to his belt like a pair of six-shooters.)

Having spent most of my professional career trying to avoid unnecessary meetings, I was unprepared for the Washington game of jockeying to attend as many as possible, especially with the President. I would watch regular White House meetings grow larger and larger, until Rahm would issue an edict like "principals plus one"—meaning that each cabinet-level attendee could bring one aide but no more. The rule would last for a meeting or two and then attendance would slowly creep up, beginning the cycle anew.

Larry had alerted me that he was going to start this session by asking me to describe what would happen if the administration stopped funding Chrysler. While Larry favored a rescue, he wanted to establish a baseline, a clear understanding of the consequences of inaction. The previous December, Vice President Cheney and his lieutenants had been confused on this critical point, in thinking that without government funding there could be an orderly wind-down or a traditional Chapter 11 bankruptcy reorganization. "Chrysler would run out of cash in a matter of days," I explained matter-of-factly. "It would have to close its doors, cease paying suppliers and employees, and immediately liquidate. Thirty thousand workers will be out of work on day one, and it will cascade from there."

The President and his aides took the information calmly, and the conversation began, retracing in considerably more detail the broad points that had been made that morning in the Oval. Besides Tim and Larry, we hadn't had much contact with Obama's senior lieutenants, and I was curious to see what thoughts and opinions they would offer. With them now at the table, the discussion took on a more far-reaching and political cast. David Axelrod reviewed the latest polling data, repeating points he'd made earlier in the month about public opposition to bailouts, though less emphatically, and balancing that with data about the likely political fallout of a meltdown in Detroit. Press Secretary Gibbs had apparently been somewhat unsettled by what he'd heard in the Oval Office that morning. He had e-mailed Deese in the course of the day to ask for data on the unemployment rate in a handful of key metropolitan areas. Now, in this meeting, he referred us to a map that was part of our handouts. "We talk about a great depression being 25 percent unemployment," he began. He pointed to places on the map. "There's 18 percent unemployment here. There's 24 percent unemployment here. For these guys, it already is a depression." Rahm was quiet, intervening only to repeat his memory trick of identifying the legislators in whose districts large Chrysler facilities were located. Tim remained totally silent, as was his custom when he was comfortable with where a meeting was going. I knew Harry was itching to chime in from his perch, but Diana had warned him that he wasn't allowed to speak.

The President was mostly listening, although at one point he observed that being tough with Chrysler would be a lot easier if the government hadn't just bailed out the banks, particularly Citigroup.

After perhaps forty-five minutes, the key points had been made. Larry turned and asked me to give the President my assessment of whether the Chrysler-Fiat alliance could be completed successfully. This was another question he had flagged for me beforehand; my caveats about the uncertainties of dealmaking had registered and he wanted Obama to hear them. "I would put the probability at 50 percent, Mr. President," I said, "but in my experience, deals generally get worse, not better."

That seemed to put a damper on the group and there was a pause. The President looked around the room and said, "Does anyone else have anything to say?" No one did. The President rested his chin on his hands for a few seconds. Then he looked up and said, "I've made my decision. I'm prepared to give Chrysler thirty days to see if we can get the Fiat alliance done on terms that make sense to us." He turned to me and Ron and added, "I want you to be tough and I want you to be commercial." We took that to mean that we should insist that all of our conditions be met in a way that was prudent from the taxpayer's standpoint.

Not wanting the Chrysler discussion to end on such a down note, Deese — who is anything but shy — piped up from the couch. "I think it is worth recognizing that there are positive attributes associated with the Chrysler deal if it gets done," he said. "It's not all negative, including the fact that while Fiat hasn't committed money, they have committed themselves with their technology, including a commitment to build a forty-mile-per-hour car in the United States." People began to laugh, and it took a couple of beats for Deese to realize what he'd said and start laughing along. Building a forty-mile-per-gallon car would indeed be significant—but a forty-mile-per-hour car probably wouldn't improve Chrysler's prospects very much.

I found President Obama's decisionmaking style to be consistent with his "no drama Obama" reputation and on a par with the best CEOs I had spent time with on Wall Street. In addition to having done his homework, he remained engaged on a subject far from his comfort zone and probably equally far from his zone of interest. He was decisive when his advisers were divided, supportive when they were not. Perhaps most important, he showed courage in making a tough, politically risky decision.

And notwithstanding the disagreement over Chrysler, those more expert in presidential decisionmaking than I—including Chrysler opponents such as Diana—felt that the process worked well. Both sides got their say and the President decided. For my part, I was also somewhat shocked to realize that I was, at fifty-six, the oldest person in the room.

The President accepted our other recommendations without comment, and after a brief discussion about preparing the public announcement for the following Monday, March 30, the meeting adjourned. In hindsight, it is remarkable that our proposed management changes—including the ouster of Rick Wagoner as chairman and CEO of GM—never came up. Within a few days it was to figure large in our lives.

Larry had raised the management question with us early on and in his Socratic way, probing our assumption that Wagoner had to go. But Larry had never seriously questioned the need for new management; for him, it was a matter of who, when, and how. Initially Larry was of the view that, for the sake of continuity, Wagoner should stay until he'd seen GM through the traumatic bankruptcy. To us that seemed a terrible idea. We argued that planning and executing the restructuring was effectively the first chapter in GM's future, and therefore it was critical to have a new CEO who would "own" the result. In due course, Larry came around to our view.

We never talked about who should do the firing. Throughout its rescue operations, the Obama administration had wanted to minimize at least the appearance of intervention in the private sector. Had I thought to flag this question for Larry, he might well have suggested a quiet word with trusted GM board members. Alternatively, he might have asked that Tim do the firing, as Hank Paulson had dismissed the heads of Fannie Mae and Freddie Mac. (None of the previous dismissals had created any fuss.) But when the question never came up, I simply concluded that this unpleasant task was up to me.

So I'd made preparations on the assumption that the President would approve our plan and that I'd have to inform GM right away. We'd asked Rick and his colleagues to come to Washington the next day on the pretext of being briefed on the President's upcoming announcement. As part of their itinerary, I'd scheduled a private meeting for myself with Rick as soon as they arrived at Treasury. I knew that the GM board held a conference call every Friday at noon during the crisis, and I wanted to tell him before then.

While inscrutable, Rick turned out not to be oblivious. He had divined from our previous conversations that his future was in doubt. That morning, he spoke to George Fisher, GM's lead director, with whom I had served on the board of Brown University. "I had good experiences with Steve at Brown, and Steve would know that it was in the government's best interest to keep you around," Fisher reassured Wagoner, emphasizing his view that GM was finally producing more realistic projections and plans.

Promptly at 9:15, Rick arrived and took a seat on the red fake-leather couch in my office. I took a chair from my conference table and placed it opposite him. I went straight to the point. "In our last meeting," I said, "you very graciously offered to step aside if it would be helpful, and unfortunately, our conclusion is that it would be best if you did that." He took the news impassively and at first did not say a word. I later learned that coming on the heels of the Fisher conversation, he was devastated.

I told him of our intention to make Fritz the interim CEO while we looked for a permanent replacement. Rick reacted to that, cautioning me against hiring an industry outsider to run General Motors. "Alan Mulally called me with questions every day for two weeks after he got to Ford," he said.

Next we talked about the GM chairmanship. I hadn't succeeded in finding an outsider for the job and the day before had suspended my search. Instead I'd pored over the list of board members in hopes of identifying a director who could make a credible interim chairman. Kent Kresa stood out. I did not know him, but he had the right pedigree. He'd been successful as chairman and CEO of the defense contractor Northrop Grumman and had served on the GM board since 2003, long enough to know the company and not conspicuously overlong. Larry, it turned out, knew him slightly from a foundation board on which both had served and had a good impression. I'd made a couple of calls to friends who also gave positive feedback. So now I asked Rick if he would be willing to see if Kresa would step in as interim chairman for a couple of weeks. Rick concurred and graciously agreed to ask him.

As this awkward conversation drew to an end, Rick suddenly asked, "Are you going to fire Ron Gettelfinger too?" I replied that I was not in charge of firing the head of the UAW. There wasn't much more to say. I offered to let Rick meet alone with his colleagues, who were waiting upstairs in a conference room to start the briefing session, but he said no, we should stick to the schedule. (I don't know when he planned to tell them.)

A long walk together through the halls of the Treasury would have been uncomfortable for us both, so I asked my assistant to help him find the meeting room while I gathered my colleagues, and made sure to give them a head start. But my assistant was new to Treasury, and it took them almost that long to find the conference room. When Rick walked in, Ray Young half jokingly asked his boss, "Do we still have jobs?"

"You do," said Wagoner. Though he hadn't planned to, he told them what had just occurred — which is how Fritz Henderson learned he was to become interim CEO. Rick had barely delivered the news when Harry, Ron, and I arrived.

We had no way to know what we had walked in on, and my colleagues and I plunged into our briefing about the President's forthcoming speech. Henderson, who had suspected the management change was coming, was now dwelling silently on the word "interim." "This is not going to let me be effective," Fritz thought. Then he put the worry aside and forced himself to pay attention to what we were saying about the deadlines and conditions that the President was about to impose — deadlines and conditions it would be his responsibility to meet. "The probability of bankruptcy just went up a lot," he realized as we described the plan.

But Ray — whose lack of common sense seemed limitless — did not get the message. As we finished, he fretted aloud that GM would have to reconsider the timing of its bond-exchange offer. Harry gently suggested that a lot of things at GM would now have to change, but Ray still wasn't getting it. I couldn't help myself and snapped, "It should be obvious that the bond exchange is the least important thing we have to worry about." Fritz rested a hand on Ray's forearm and quietly said to him, "We'll come back to this."

Rick said not a word ("He looks shell-shocked," Harry thought), and the uncomfortable meeting soon came to a merciful end. After I got back to my office, still unaware that Rick had delivered the news, I waited what I thought was a reasonable interval for him to do so and then called Fritz's cell phone.

"What do you think?" I asked.

"Thank you for your confidence in me," Fritz replied. "Let's talk about one thing which I don't think is right — making my title interim CEO. You can fire me any time you want, but at least give me a chance to succeed."

"Let me think about that," I said.

Fritz hung up, thinking, "Steve gets this, but he's got to go through a bunch of hoops to change this, because the decision has already been made that I would be an interim and that would have to get undone." When he didn't hear back from me right away, he was even more sure of his initial instinct. In reality, my bosses didn't much care whether Fritz was called interim or not, so I didn't need to clear it with them. While I understood Fritz's concern, my hesitation about agreeing to his request on the spot reflected my inexperience with such matters and my desire to consult my new guru Jack Welch before responding. When I caught up with him, his reaction was instantaneous. "Fritz is right," Jack said. "If he's called interim, he won't have a chance."

That afternoon, I received a call from a furious George Fisher, calling in his capacity as GM's lead director. (Like most Fortune 500 companies, GM had a lead outside director in an effort to provide a counterweight to the combined chairman and CEO.) George was a gracious man who had been CEO of both Motorola and Eastman Kodak. Unfortunately, as his conversation with Rick that morning indicated, as lead director he had been pretty much blindly supportive of Rick. "We are absolutely convinced we have the right team under Rick Wagoner's leadership to get us through these difficult times and on to a bright future," Fisher had said in August 2008, immediately after GM announced a $15.5 billion quarterly loss. Now he lashed out at me for firing Rick. "I think you are doing a lot of right things, but I think this is wrong," said Fisher, who privately found our actions "abhorrent."

He also felt — with some justification — that the selection of Kresa as interim chairman was a slap in his face. I had expected this and had deliberately not asked Kresa or anyone else to take Fisher's place as lead director, which I pointed out. "I noticed that and appreciated it," Fisher said, calming down as he spoke. Of course, with Kresa as a non-executive chairman, the lead director's role had been rendered moot.

Shortly afterward, I got a call from Bob Joffe, the tall, bespectacled sixty-five-year-old former presiding partner at the law firm of Cravath, Swaine & Moore, who had been advising the GM board for many years. Bob was a good friend; we had labored together in the political vineyard as ardent Democrats. He was also a terrific lawyer and counselor who conveyed gravitas and judgment. "The board is pretty upset," Bob reported. "They feel that you've taken away their most important responsibility," by which he meant the hiring and firing of the CEO. There was talk of a mass resignation, Bob said. "I think it would mean a lot if you would be willing to get on the phone with them tonight," he suggested.

By the time I joined the conference call that evening, the GM board members weren't as enraged as I'd feared. Still, I was glad not to be with them in person. There were a number of hostile questions, particularly from some of the longest-serving directors who had been most complicit in GM's decay. I explained that in bringing our decision about Rick to him first, I was trying — perhaps erroneously — to give him the dignity of presenting his departure to the board himself, in whatever context he chose. After about a half hour, the questions petered out and the board excused me to continue its deliberations.

Later, Bob Joffe called to say that my willingness to let the directors vent had been effective in quelling any nascent mutiny. I was relieved. I had been trusted to implement decisions that would normally be executed at much higher levels of the government. A mass resignation on the eve of the President's speech would have been more than an embarrassment; it could have crippled the auto rescue effort and been a particular disaster for me. Fortunately, all of the directors agreed to stay on through the restructuring, and several later told me privately that we had made the right decision.

I called Fritz the following day to let him know that "interim" would be dropped from his new title. It wasn't until much later, though, that he told me the story of his flight home to Detroit on Friday — a somewhat surreal journey during which he and Rick sat next to each other, one row away from a well-known automotive journalist. They didn't exchange a single word about the day's events. When new CEO and former CEO debarked at the sparkling terminal where Team Auto had arrived just eighteen days earlier, Rick went off silently with his security guard. He and Fritz would never have a conversation about what had transpired; from then on in public, Wagoner maintained an aura of silence and impassivity.

But behind the scenes, as the initial shock wore off, Wagoner was on an emotional rollercoaster. On Saturday morning, in a fury, he called a lieutenant. "I don't think this is even legal," he fumed. "I am going to go to the board and see what we can do. I'm thinking I should fight this." The next morning he called again, but he was calm. "I need to make it easy on Fritz. I'm not going to fight this," he said. Then, amazingly, he spoke of all the work he still had to get done and how he planned to go to the office at the Renaissance Center on Monday to watch Obama's speech. Colleagues called, pleading with him not to go. Wagoner liked to triangulate advice — it was part of his style as a manager. Once enough people told him not to go to work, he relented. An aide urged instead, "Get in your car with Kathy and drive as far away from Detroit as you can." Wagoner and his wife left almost immediately for their South Carolina vacation home.

For us the weekend was a blur of paperwork — drafts of the President's address, talking points for outreach calls, fact sheets, and formal responses to the viability plans that GM and Chrysler had submitted on February 17. To forestall errors and misunderstandings, we shared drafts of the responses with the automakers, expecting — and getting — considerable protests about some of our language, especially from Chrysler, because of the flat statement that it was not viable as a standalone company. Many of us, including me, remained uneasy about giving Chrysler a lifeline, and we included in the fact sheet six difficult conditions the company would have to meet to qualify for the additional $6 billion of assistance that we were contemplating.

Harry, meanwhile, had had a surreal conversation with GM's Ray Young in which Ray tried to negotiate several points in our formal response to GM's viability plan. He was effectively trying to remove or blunt our many criticisms of GM — criticisms that industry observers had been voicing for years. Harry listened patiently for a while, but finally exasperation took over. "Ray," he said, "this isn't a negotiation. These are our firmly held views. Of course you're free to disagree, but we haven't spoken to any industry observer who feels any better about the plan than we do."

On Sunday night, when we assembled in the Oval Office to hear President Obama make his courtesy calls in advance of Monday's speech, I was more than a little awed by what we had unleashed. My friend Arthur Sulzberger sent the first news flashes to my BlackBerry. I texted back, "I'm sitting in the Oval Office!" feeling the unreality of the moment.

For the President, of course, it was another evening of work, more momentous than some but less momentous than others he would surely face. And yet it marked a turning point in American industrial history — a turn, I hoped, for the better. After his calls were completed, we fanned out in preassigned groups to other rooms in the West Wing for follow-up work. Deese and I conducted a background briefing call for reporters. More than a hundred members of the media dialed in to listen to a "senior administration official" preview the next day's announcements by the President.

On the verge of the largest industrial restructuring in history, accompanied by massive government financial support, the first question was "Why did you believe it was necessary to ask Chairman and CEO Wagoner to step aside?" From there, the questions mushroomed across the full range of our actions, but with a disproportionate number still focused on the fate of Rick Wagoner.

Simultaneously, Larry and Ron spoke with the "auto caucus"—interested members of the Senate and House. When we reconvened afterward in Larry's office to compare notes, he was concerned about what he had heard. "I think we need something more on the demand side," he said. For all of Larry's reputation as an academic, his political instincts were sharp. And his instincts were now telling him that we'd been thinking too much like wonks—obsessively dwelling on financial restructuring and doing too little to promote a broad auto industry recovery.

We brainstormed how to fix the problem. It was Deese who surfaced the idea of trade-ins for gas guzzlers. The notion of boosting overall sales by offering rebates on trade-ins of old, fuel-inefficient cars had come up during the late-2008 discussions about a stimulus package and again in our early work on autos. A similar program had been a hit in Europe, where the German government had offered the equivalent of a $3,200 rebate for consumers willing to scrap cars at least nine years old and buy newer ones. But we'd dismissed the idea because such a program would require legislation, which we doubted could be enacted quickly enough and which might also distract Congress from more important parts of the President's agenda. Under tonight's circumstances, however, rebates suddenly seemed like a pretty good idea. "Let's try it," Larry decided. Brian labored through the night to work out a plan and insert new language into the President's speech, thus giving birth to Cash for Clunkers.

The speech was set for 11 A.M. We assembled in Larry's office shortly beforehand and, following custom, trooped downstairs to the Oval to see if the President had any last-minute questions or requests. Of course, this was unlikely—his speech by now was loaded into the teleprompter and he didn't have to worry about questions from the press because there would be no Q&A. Going to see him was just another manifestation of the White House obsession with racking up face time with the President.

After a few minutes, we trailed Obama to a staging area in the State Dining Room. Gathered there were members of the Presidential Task

Force on the Auto Industry — the secretaries of energy, transportation, labor, and the like, as well as Tim and Larry. They were reporting for duty as what the communications department called potted plants. Often White House image makers don't want the President to make an important, controversial announcement by himself. So they arrange potted plants behind him to convey an added note of gravity and consensus. A protocol officer carefully lined up the officials and, just a few minutes behind schedule, they marched out to the foyer of the White House, where the announcement would take place. Brian, Ron, and I were left standing by ourselves in the State Dining Room; we had not been deemed worthy to serve as potted plants! I didn't care — this was another aspect of Washington that I found unappealing. We made our own way to the foyer and stood behind the camera crews, craning for a glimpse of the President as he delivered his remarks.

The speech was clear and direct. "Let there be no doubt," he said, "it will take an unprecedented effort on all our parts — from the halls of Congress to the boardroom, from the union hall to the factory floor — to see the auto industry through these difficult times." But our groundbreaking rescue plan ended up having to compete with the news of Rick Wagoner's ouster, word of which had leaked to the media on Sunday and was getting more attention than it should have. I was stunned by commentaries suggesting that the government was somehow overreaching by replacing a CEO who had lost $11 billion of taxpayer money in three months — and had been asking for more. No private-sector investor would have put up with that; it was commonplace to make large infusions of new capital contingent upon a management change. Larry professed to be less surprised, while acknowledging that the reaction was stronger than he would have predicted.

Rightly or wrongly, the notion of Washington exerting its grip on an industrial icon was unnerving to many people. Governor Granholm called Rick a "sacrificial lamb." The *New York Times* published a truly moronic op-ed piece by William Holstein arguing that GM would now be "deprived" of Wagoner's expertise. Happily, several respected commentators praised our decision, notably Paul Ingrassia, a Pulitzer Prize–winning auto expert. His op-ed in the *Wall Street Journal* was headlined "Wagoner Had to Go: We Heard More Realism from the President Yesterday Than We've Heard from Detroit in Years."

From my standpoint, the controversy over Obama's decision to offer more assistance, contingent on the automakers' meeting strict deadlines, was more expected. Senator Corker, still smoldering over supplier assistance, called it a "major power grab." The *Journal*'s editorial page started referring to GM snarkily as "Obama Motors" and "Government Motors." David Brooks on the *Times* op-ed page dismissed the deadlines as empty threats and concluded: "It would have been better to keep a distance from GM and prepare the region for a structured bankruptcy process. Instead, Obama leapt in. His intentions were good, but getting out with honor will require a ruthless tenacity that is beyond any living politician." I suspected Brooks had no clue what a "structured bankruptcy" meant. All the same, I was gratified at least that both the *Times* and the *Washington Post* praised the President in their editorials.

The single most interesting reaction I heard came not in the media but by telephone. I had barely returned to my office after the President's speech when Jimmy Lee of JPMorgan called. "We need to talk!" he barked.

"I thought there was nothing for us to talk about," I said innocently. "You said '$6.9 billion and not a penny less,' and that's not going to work for us."

"That was then and this is now," he said.

I chuckled silently and continued to play dumb. "What changed?" I asked.

"I didn't realize how important this was to the President," Jimmy said, somewhat fatuously.

I was surprised by how quickly Jimmy had picked up the phone, but not by his shift in attitude. This was precisely what we had hoped to accomplish when we'd urged the President to set a firm deadline for Chrysler, with liquidation to follow unless all the stakeholders agreed that the sacrifice would be shared.

8

JIMMY TURNS BRIGHT RED

WHILE OBAMA'S SPEECH cut off Jimmy Lee at the knees, it embold-ened Sergio Marchionne. His company, after all, had just been desig-nated by the President of the United States as Chrysler's last and only hope for survival — which gave Sergio the kind of negotiating advantage that most dealmakers can only dream of. The very next afternoon, the Italian-Canadian CEO stood before the assembled leaders of Chrysler, the UAW, and Team Auto in a Treasury conference room and told us, "This is a totally new ballgame."

His investment banker, Andrew Horrocks of UBS, proceeded to read a list of demands — "opportunities," he called them — for saving money, mainly from Chrysler's contract with the UAW. You could feel the tension in the room ratchet up. To comply with the TARP loan re-quirements, Chrysler and the UAW had already spent a lot of time ne-gotiating a so-called all-in compensation rate to bring UAW-Chrysler workers in line with workers at the Asian transplants. What was more, Fiat had already agreed to many of the terms.

But now Sergio and his team, after taking a closer look at the deal, decided "there is some air in it." They thought Chrysler's and the UAW's assumptions about future sales were overoptimistic. Fiat also suspected that Chrysler's labor negotiators had grown too cozy with their UAW counterparts — Chrysler's president, Tom LaSorda, and its other chief negotiator, Al Iacobelli, both had union members in their families. Eventually, Sergio would demand that one of his Fiat exec-utives sit in on all labor talks, "to be his eyes and ears." So now Fiat wanted more concessions, such as a variable wage rate that would tie compensation to productivity gains — an idea that the UAW had always detested.

I watched Ron Gettelfinger's face flush and the muscles in his jaw tighten as he realized Sergio wanted to recut the entire deal. Finally he spoke up.

"You people," he said, his voice rising, "are the people with two houses. And we're common people, we're average people. We're just trying to make a living, and too much is being asked of us." He was angry at the task force, angry at Chrysler, and especially angry at Fiat. Pointing at Sergio, Gettelfinger said coldly, "We had an agreement."

The mood of the meeting lifted just once. As the group reviewed the Chrysler-Fiat alliance, we came to the provision that Chrysler would build and market Fiat's popular minicar, the 500, in America. A participant turned to General Holiefield, a massively built man who was chief of the UAW's Chrysler unit, and asked, "Can you fit inside that, General?" The room erupted in laughter.

I watched to see how Ron Bloom, with his long experience in labor negotiations, was reacting to all this; he was attentive and seemed surprisingly unperturbed. Afterward he told me to think of most of what happened that day as posturing—now that it was behind us, the real horse-trading could start.

Fiat and the UAW were now mainly Ron's responsibility. He and Harry and I had divvied up the mountain of work that Team Auto would have to complete in order to meet the President's conditions and deadlines. Harry got General Motors. He was to spend most of April in Detroit, working with executives and squads of consultants to hammer out a turnaround plan—a realistic one, this time, that wouldn't waste taxpayer money. Meanwhile, Ron and I would concentrate on Chrysler, which had to be brought to terms or liquidated by May 1. While Ron took the lead on Fiat and the UAW, my job, besides monitoring everyone's progress, would be dealing with Chrysler's banks and the finance companies of Chrysler and GM. I also needed to recruit two new chairmen and a slew of new directors for both companies.

I entered the byzantine world of the fincos the very next day, April Fool's Day, as it happened. We faced off in a Treasury Department conference room against an imposing lineup of businesspeople: the top management from Chrysler Financial, GMAC, and Chrysler, plus Steve Feinberg and the guys from Cerberus. They all knew more about automotive finance than we did. We were trying to fly solo without having taken flying lessons, I thought, and I hoped we wouldn't crash and burn.

Pretty quickly I discovered that the fincos posed a bigger problem than I'd imagined. Auto finance companies are a lot like banks, but there is one crucial distinction: Banks rely on deposits from consumers and businesses for most of the money they use for loans. Finance companies have no such depositors unless they happen to own a bank; instead they must depend on large borrowings from banks and investors for the cash that they lend to car buyers (known as the retail trade) and auto dealers (known as wholesale or floor-plan borrowers).

I began to understand how the collapse of the financial markets had created havoc for automakers. As a result of the credit crunch, both GMAC and Chrysler Financial had seen their ability to borrow from banks severely curtailed. To raise added funds in recent years, the fincos had also made heavy use of securitizations, in which their loans to consumers and dealers were bundled, sliced up like a layer cake, and sold off in tranches, typically to investment funds. This market, too, had imploded in 2008, cutting off another key source of funds. As a result of all this, the fincos had drastically reduced lending to consumers and dealers, a major factor in the steep falloff of car sales.

GMAC was much larger than Chrysler Financial—$155 billion in assets versus $22 billion—and its problems were greater. In its glory days, armed with a strong credit rating, it had fallen into the same bad habits as other elite financial outfits, such as GE Capital and AIG. Like an occasional smoker who gradually acquires a three-pack-a-day habit, GMAC began to abuse its cheap capital, branching out aggressively into other kinds of lending—in particular, residential real estate at the height of the housing bubble.

For a while this led to McMansion-size profits for GMAC's residential capital unit, ResCap, but by the end of 2007 it was gushing red ink. GMAC had already lost its investment-grade rating and now had to pour in billions to keep ResCap afloat, weakening its ability to make car loans.

Things only got worse. By autumn 2008 GMAC's own survival was in doubt, and it came running to Washington for help. Initial relief took the form of GMAC's being granted 'bank holding company' status by the Federal Reserve. This unorthodox move made the big lender eligible for the same sort of emergency support that Goldman Sachs and Morgan Stanley received when they became bank holding companies. It also paved the way for an injection of $5 billion of TARP money. Further, GMAC hoped for access to other support programs, particularly those administered by the Federal Deposit Insurance Corporation.

But the FDIC had wanted no part of the huge auto lender. An independent agency that, like the Federal Reserve, is not under the direct control of any branch of government, the FDIC was established during the Depression chiefly to insure consumers' savings accounts and put an end to 1930s-style bank runs, which it had done. Then came the current crisis, which saw the Bush administration turning to the FDIC for help. In response, the FDIC offered something called the Temporary Liquidity Guarantee Program. I had read about the TLGP but had no idea what it did. I learned that, in return for a fee, it enabled cash-strapped banks to sell bonds and commercial paper backed by an FDIC guarantee, allowing the banks to raise fresh capital at exceptionally low rates.

It wasn't hard to see why the FDIC and GMAC were at loggerheads. The FDIC had thousands and thousands of conservatively financed community banks as its members and looked with distaste on the gargantuan, messy octopus of GMAC. If it extended loan guarantees to GMAC and then the finance company collapsed, the FDIC could well be on the hook for billions of dollars of debt. In addition, even before becoming a bank holding company, GMAC had made itself a pariah in the industry as the owner of a small, fast-growing online bank, now known as Ally Bank, which had been using the Internet to aggressively market certificates of deposit with high interest rates. The FDIC's members hated this competition. The FDIC sympathetically took the view that the high interest rates offered by online banks (there were others besides Ally) jeopardized the bricks-and-mortar banking system by squeezing profit margins. It had stepped in to limit the total deposits that Ally Bank could accept — a stricture from which GMAC now sought relief.

As I sat listening to our visitors, I was seized by the enormity of the finco problem. Chrysler Financial was the immediate headache. Its $22 billion balance sheet wasn't large by bank standards, but unlike GMAC, it had no bank and no depositors. In early January 2009, Chrysler Financial had also been given a slug of TARP money — $1.5 billion — to enable it to keep making consumer loans. But that money was running out.

Then we learned, to my horror, that putting Chrysler into any form of bankruptcy would have severe consequences for Chrysler Financial. A very large proportion of its remaining bank credit lines would immediately be withdrawn. In order to keep Chrysler Financial in business, we might have to replace all of its $22 billion of borrowing facilities with taxpayer money. But there was more: we would face very much the same problem with GMAC, which was six times larger than Chrysler Financial.

The Cerberus delegation arrived on a damp, cloudy spring day hoping for a merger with GMAC and Chrysler Financial, lubricated by TARP money. Cerberus owned 40 percent of GMAC and 80 percent of Chrysler Financial, and saw this as a gambit to salvage whatever equity value remained, particularly in Chrysler Financial. I could imagine the tactic helping Cerberus. What I did not see was how merging two cash-strapped institutions into one even larger cash-strapped institution could help the taxpayer or revive automobile financing. I found myself adopting the same rationale that Rick Wagoner had invoked in opposing a GM-Chrysler tie-up.

I was profoundly worried that the story would end right here. A company that I hadn't even known our team was responsible for might well cause Chrysler's demise. I was dwelling on this when I heard Al de Molina, the CEO of GMAC, throw out an idea: Why not let GMAC take on the job of financing new purchases of Chrysler vehicles, at both the consumer and the dealer level? Under this scenario, Chrysler Financial would go into "runoff mode," continuing to hold the loans that it had made but not making new ones. It wouldn't need new capital. Best of all, the fine print of its credit agreements would permit such a step — even if Chrysler itself went into Chapter 11.

De Molina of course had his own agenda. The big, assertive Cuban-born banker envisioned that such a combination would cement GMAC as too big to fail and force the FDIC to help. A former Bank of America executive, de Molina made no secret of his ambition to make GMAC a banking giant. Almost from the start, he had clashed with the man who was effectively his boss — Cerberus's soft-spoken and seemingly tentative Steve Feinberg, who now sat fidgeting as de Molina made his case. Feinberg didn't care whether GMAC was large or small; he just wanted to make Cerberus's investment multiply. The only way he saw to preserve that investment, given the reality of the financial and economic crisis, was to cut, not expand. The consequence was palpable tension between Feinberg and de Molina, whom people within Cerberus had taken to referring to mockingly as Ricky Ricardo.

I think of myself as pragmatic and solution-oriented. The wisdom of de Molina's idea — never mind what I thought of the two men — was immediately apparent to me. Walking out of the meeting with Ron Bloom, I pulled aside de Molina and said, "This looks like a possible path." My despair had faded a bit, at least for the moment. Having GMAC take over lending for both firms might solve the finco problem. If the numbers worked, the FDIC and the Federal Reserve would still have to agree, of course, but I naively assumed that that would be the easy part.

The second day of April brought another crew of financial heavyweights, Chrysler's banks, led by the inimitable Jimmy Lee, fresh off the Acela and another breakfast burrito. Today was our day to talk — Ron Bloom, Matt Feldman (our veteran bankruptcy lawyer), and I were to lay out the terms we wanted from Chrysler's creditors if the company was to get further federal aid. Jimmy, representing the bankers, and I faced each other across the table, our colleagues flanking us like mobsters protecting their bosses. The airy, brick-walled conference room where we gathered had once been part of the Treasury's attic. Jimmy had brought high-level representatives of Citibank, Goldman Sachs, Morgan Stanley, and Elliott Associates to hear firsthand what we had to say. Before coming to the Treasury building, they had gathered in JPMorgan's Washington office and agreed to spend the afternoon in "listen mode."

Fiat and Chrysler were on hand too — the bankers needed to understand the projections and business prospects of Chrysler in its new alliance with Fiat in order to analyze any proposal we might make. So we first gave the floor to Sergio, who sat at the far end of the table in his black sweater. He launched into a disquisition, filled with hyperbole and flourishes, about his unique ability to turn around Chrysler. No specifics about how he intended to do that were offered. Instead he painted, in considerable detail, all that he perceived had gone wrong under Bob Nardelli, who sat at the other end of the table looking dyspeptic. Although Bob was still the CEO of Chrysler, it was understood that he and his lieutenants would leave as part of a Fiat alliance. He had come to view Sergio as a bullying egomaniac, but he put great store in self-discipline. He had been pleased at the kind words that the President included about him and his team in his March 30 remarks and had resolved to soldier on through this ugly process as quietly and with as much dignity as possible.

Jimmy Lee felt vindicated for not having tried harder to negotiate an earlier resolution with Chrysler. "There is no management," he thought. "It's Sergio and the government. We saved ourselves a lot of blood, sweat, and tears, and now we're finally dealing with the owners of the company."

I said nothing until we turned to the central question, the $6.9 billion of debt for which Jimmy had been demanding full repayment.

"We had in mind for you a much lower number, $1 billion," I told him, explaining that this was equal to the amount the banks would likely receive if Chrysler were to liquidate. The money would be in the form of loans owed to the banks by the restructured Chrysler.

Jimmy seemed genuinely stunned. He turned bright red. For many seconds there was silence in the crowded room. Even the Fiat delegation was shocked. We had not shared our proposal with them, and they had been assuming the loan would be negotiated down to $2 billion to $2.5 billion.

"What about equity?" he finally asked. In the usual restructuring, senior lenders who are not going to get all of their money back receive a big helping of equity as part of their consideration.

"We have other plans for that," I replied.

This information made our already stingy offer seem worse. Jimmy became apoplectic. He demanded to know why, if the government thought banks important enough to give them tens of billions in TARP money, it wanted to squeeze them on this deal. He also demanded to know why the UAW should get any consideration, since it was well below the banks on the priority list of who would get paid in a bankruptcy.

Ron responded to that, bluntly telling him, "I need workers to make cars, but I don't need lenders." Matt then chimed in, emphasizing that from the Treasury's perspective, the bankers had little negotiating power. "If you don't like our proposal," he said, "you can credit-bid," meaning they could foreclose on their loans, seize Chrysler, and operate or liquidate it themselves — costly, messy, politically charged options that we believed these lenders would never seriously consider.

Finally Jimmy resorted to a threat. "I've got one of the toughest bosses on the Street," he said, meaning Jamie Dimon, the JPMorgan CEO. "He may want to call the President!"

"Feel free to have him call," I said, unperturbed.

Behind the dramatics, Jimmy must have been recalculating fast. He had assumed that by my asking Sergio to extol the Fiat-Chrysler combination, we were talking up the value of Chrysler equity — yet now we were offering none. In fact, I had not ruled out the possibility of ultimately offering the banks some equity to get the deal done. But that could be negotiated. Most important, beyond the particulars of equity or the terms of the loan was building their enthusiasm for the prospects of Chrysler under Sergio's leadership. That's why I'd wanted Sergio to make the presentation.

What I didn't know at the time was that Jimmy and his boss Jamie had met with Sergio back in January. They hadn't been impressed by the Sergio show and doubted whether he could rise to the massive challenges of Chrysler.

Jimmy seemed to understand what I was trying to do and played along, asking to see the projections and business plans that Fiat was developing. "If you want an answer other than no, something like a counteroffer, then we need those new numbers," he said. We agreed. As the meeting drew to a close, Jimmy asked if we could have a word alone. We stepped into the corridor by an elegant open stairwell, looking down five stories to the Treasury basement. "Putting aside the very, very generous offer," he said sarcastically, "I think I can get all the banks to do a deal." Achieving unanimity among the lenders would mean that at least one reason for a bankruptcy filing would be avoided.

"I don't really think you can," I replied.

While hardly a bankruptcy expert, I was unaware of any situation in which unanimity had been achieved in a creditor group this big — Chrysler had forty-six lenders, including several aggressive hedge funds that might prefer to fight to the death. We parried for a few more minutes and then Jimmy was on his way back to the Acela.

Just as Ron viewed the opening clash of Fiat and the UAW as obligatory theater, I discounted what Jimmy had said. And I felt no urgency to reengage him in the coming days. Of all the hurdles we faced, the banks were the smallest. When the time came, either they would agree to something reasonable or they could take over Chrysler. We had agreed to make every effort to save the company, but my ambivalence about its prospects was such that I wasn't all that bothered by the possibility of getting "caught trying."

Ron, it turned out, had been a bit too sanguine about the Fiat CEO. We really were dealing with a new Sergio, not the urbane charmer who had assured us in March that he saw no impediment to an agreement with the UAW. As the days ticked by toward the April 30 deadline, Dottore Jekyll became Signore Hyde. Yes, there was a charmer in Sergio. But there was also someone else.

His next negotiating session with Gettelfinger, held at the Chrysler-UAW training center in Detroit, was a disaster. Sergio started lecturing Gettelfinger about the need for the autoworkers to accept a "culture of poverty" instead of a "culture of entitlement," attacking, among other things, retiree health care benefits.

"Why don't you come and sit with me and tell a seventy-five-year-old widow that she can't have surgery and that you killed her husband?" Gettelfinger snapped. The discussion became more emotional and nastier as Sergio revealed in greater detail the changes he wanted in the UAW contract. "Tweaks," he kept calling them. But a quick, back-of-the-envelope calculation by Bloom showed that Fiat was really demanding what amounted to as much as $5 an hour off the contract. The meeting ended in a shouting match. Sergio went off to shop in an Apple store — he is obsessed with Apple — to cool off.

Sergio's attitude toward his Chrysler counterparts changed too. "From puppy dog to pit bull" was the way one executive described the transformation. Congenial conversations in March about Fiat-Chrysler technology sharing gave way to tense April talks in which Sergio would demean and swear at the Chrysler officials. "Do you think I am fucking stupid?" he'd ask rhetorically.

Gettelfinger, the veteran labor negotiator, took all this in stride. He sensed a performance in progress and knew that, despite Sergio's bluster, Fiat really wanted the deal. And Sergio knew that Gettelfinger was a realist. The UAW chief may well have put off Corker and the Republicans, thinking President Obama would offer a better arrangement, but now that Obama had threatened on national TV to liquidate Chrysler unless all parties came to terms, Gettelfinger was cornered. He understood that we needed to be able to tell taxpayers that any new Chrysler contract satisfied the conditions of the TARP loan, including parity with the Japanese transplants. (To that degree, the Bush administration was getting its wish to "rule from the grave.")

An even bigger motivator was fear. The continuing deterioration in the auto business was terrifying for all of us. More than once, I would think of Rahm Emanuel saying, "Never let a crisis go to waste," as we used the growing economic catastrophe to achieve changes and sacrifices that would have been impossible in another environment. And we had the advantage that for the Obama administration, this was something of a "Nixon goes to China" moment, as Rahm had signaled with his short, crisp dismissal of the UAW in his office a month earlier.

By the time the labor negotiation moved back to Washington, I had begun to think of the Treasury building as Uncle Sam's Fix-It Garage. Although we were still facing potentially insurmountable problems, the task force seemed increasingly like an actual entity and our jobs like actual positions. Down in the basement, we settled into the "skunk works," as Ron called it. My partner Josh Steiner had told me that status in Washington had much to do with offices and staff. While I had worked hard to build our team, I couldn't have cared less about my office. I was very comfortable in my basement lair. In the anteroom of my office, cubicles had been built for the "partners" (Ron, Harry, and Matt) and for Haley. A few doors away, two other sizable rooms had also been carved into cubicles for our more junior colleagues. And we had nice government-issue signs outside our doors: "Auto Task Force" they announced. From my desk I could gaze through barred windows onto the Washington Monument and the Mall and, in the other direction, to the small parking lot where Tim Geithner's gold Suburban pulled up by his private entrance. For security reasons, he took his SUV even to go across the street to the White House. I would often see him come and go several times a day, cell phone invariably clamped to his ear.

I was on the phone plenty myself, fielding calls from a dizzying array of interested parties, led, of course, by the Michigan politicians. Like many other stakeholders, they had been unnerved by the President's tough March 30 speech and particularly his use of the B word. As clear as Obama had been, the delegation chose to concentrate on the possibility of avoiding bankruptcy rather than the prospect of entering it. Our running joke was that the Michigan politicians were progressing through Elisabeth Kübler-Ross's five stages of grief—denial, anger, bargaining, depression, and acceptance. Except that just when we thought we had nudged them to the next step of understanding the need for bankruptcy, they would fall back a stage.

Ron Bloom decided to tackle the most visible labor issue first: so-called legacy costs. The UAW was notorious for its "Cadillac" retiree benefit plans, which in essence guaranteed free medical and dental care and prescriptions for life. (Such plans had made General Motors the largest purchaser of Viagra in the world.) In casual conversations after I took the auto job, my friends would often ask, "What are you going to do about the medical benefits?"

Happily, we had a road map. In 2007, Chrysler had taken a major step when the UAW agreed to create a trust—a Voluntary Employee Beneficiary Association, or VEBA—to assume responsibility for retiree health care benefits. This relieved the company of the uncertainty of this huge, ever-growing, and unknowable expense. Under the plan Chrysler was committed to make an additional one-time contribution of $8.8 billion to the VEBA, and in return would have no further obligation. All future benefits would be paid by the VEBA. If the $8.8 billion proved insufficient, that would be the problem of the VEBA, the UAW, and the workers.

The Corker amendments would have taken the arrangement one step further and required that the UAW agree to convert $4.25 billion of this debt into Chrysler equity. In the December negotiations, the UAW had signaled its willingness to say yes (it had reached a similar accommodation with Ford in February 2009), but the collapse of the legislation ended the discussion. Until now.

Starting with VEBA enabled Ron Bloom to sidestep Sergio to a large degree. Fiat had already agreed to accept a 20 percent ownership of Chrysler with the opportunity to earn another 15 percentage points. Of the 65 percent of equity not yet allocated, we—the U.S. government —wanted no more than a nominal percentage. Some might well go to the creditors, but we knew that the banks' appetite for Chrysler equity was small, because the shares of a restructured Chrysler would have little immediate value. So most of the equity was actually unspoken for, and Tim and Larry readily acquiesced in giving 55 percent ownership to the VEBA. (As Bloom designed the deal, "giving" was a relative term; in the unlikely event of excess profits on the VEBA's equity, this overage would revert to the Treasury.)

We expected headlines blaring "UAW in Chrysler Driver's Seat." In fact, we'd made sure to do everything we could *not* to have the UAW control Chrysler. For starters, the VEBA equity was held by the health care trust, not the UAW. And the stock had no voting rights. All we gave the VEBA was the right to designate a single Chrysler board member with the approval of the UAW. Negotiating these terms was easy. Neither the UAW nor the VEBA had any interest in controlling or owning the struggling automaker; rather, they wanted to sell their equity as quickly as possible.

Structuring a note to satisfy the other half of the VEBA's approximately $8.8 billion total claim was more complicated. Given the restructured Chrysler's heavy liabilities (even after bankruptcy), Ron felt that payments had to be back-loaded. And they were. Chrysler's annual payments to VEBA would rise from $300 million in 2010 to a staggering $823 million in 2019. Ron reasoned that by that date Chrysler would either be healthy enough to make the payments or be liquidated. If the latter transpired, the UAW's retirees would have lost their health care anyway.

With all components of the VEBA package valued fairly, we calculated that the UAW was taking a significant cut on its health care claim, at least 40 percent. Indeed, for the retirees, the shared sacrifice called for by President Obama had arrived without delay. Large reductions in benefits would start in July 2009, including the elimination of vision and dental plans.

Yes, the UAW accepted pain and risk. More surprising, however,

Fiat also granted concessions that amazed the Chrysler representatives, including CFO Ron Kolka and restructuring adviser Bob Manzo. Perhaps to its detriment, Fiat had relied on Bloom, whom it credited with understanding VEBA's intricacies, for guidance on how to handle the issues. And if Fiat was expecting the Chrysler team to protect its interests, it should have known better. The attitude of top Chrysler officials toward Fiat executives, especially Sergio, hovered between disdain and outright hatred. Manzo and Kolka felt it was not their job to take sides, just to answer questions Fiat or the UAW raised. For example, they watched the Fiat negotiators accept provision after provision — such as interim cash payments until the new agreement took effect in 2010 — that Chrysler would have resisted. Fiat also didn't try to further reduce the health care benefits for retirees and agreed to make bigger up-front payments. Sergio himself was rarely in the room — he was much more interested in the wage negotiations with Gettelfinger, which were starting again down the hall.

On Good Friday, as Fiat's representatives, UBS investment banker Andrew Horrocks and deal lawyer Scott Miller, closed in on an agreement with the UAW, their BlackBerrys started to buzz. They ignored them, until they saw that the caller was Sergio's lieutenant, Alfredo Altavilla, who ultimately sent a curt text message with an unmistakable order: "Leave."

Outside on a beautiful spring day, Horrocks and Miller found Sergio and Alfredo standing by the Willard Hotel. Sergio was smoking a cigarette; his talks with Gettelfinger had blown up yet again. He and Alfredo had not only stormed out but also called a halt to the VEBA talks.

"I needed some air," said Sergio as he smoked. "Let's cool down over the weekend."

But not everyone was ready to close it all down. When Horrocks's cell phone buzzed again, it was an angry Ron Bloom. "Where the hell are you two?" he bellowed. Horrocks explained what had happened. "Don't leave, come back," Ron pleaded.

Soon Sergio relented, and after another couple of hours the terms were completed: a historic VEBA agreement that would permanently remove retiree health care liabilities from Chrysler's balance sheet and give the VEBA a 55 percent stake in Chrysler.

In accordance with UAW tradition, Ron Gettelfinger came into the room to finalize the deal. He was accompanied by General Holiefield and Steve Girsky, the Morgan Stanley auto-analyst-turned-GM-insider-turned-private-equity-investor, who was advising the UAW.

Horrocks stood and reached out to shake Gettelfinger's hand. "I know if Sergio was here he'd want to shake your hand," he said.

When Gettelfinger didn't extend his hand toward Horrocks, the room went uncomfortably still.

"This deal hurts people, and that's something Sergio needs to understand," said Gettelfinger. "This is *not* a time to feel good."

After a few more awkward seconds, Holiefield reached across and shook Horrocks's hand.

Horrocks mentioned the incident to Bloom the next day, saying it had upset him. But Bloom replied, "Don't take it personally. To Ron, you just undid one hundred years of collective bargaining."

Despite the progress on legacy costs, everything else was at a standstill. The wage negotiations were stalled, and Fiat still hadn't produced the projections it had promised Jimmy and the banks. Less than three weeks remained.

Bad blood between Fiat and Chrysler was the source of the delay as Sergio and Nardelli squared off over their divergent views of the business plan. Sergio wanted to lowball the numbers and downplay Chrysler's prospects to make his job easier. He wanted to ensure that he inherited Chrysler with as much taxpayer cash and as little debt on it as possible. To that end, he pressed for the inclusion of absurd assumptions that implicitly repudiated not only Nardelli's previous leadership but also the facts contained in the February 17 submission, which Sergio had signed off on—before backing out at the last minute.

Back and forth the two sides went, making little progress as precious days elapsed. Sergio argued with Nardelli. Sergio's deputy Alfredo Altavilla argued with Tom LaSorda. Even Fiat's investment banker Horrocks and Chrysler's restructuring consultant Manzo fought.

While it was understood that Nardelli and his team would be leaving, they retained substantial leverage. All of us felt it important to have the old management team's "buy-in" for the new business plan, particularly since Sergio wanted more money from the Treasury than Nardelli had said was necessary. Sergio was aware too that, as a foreign company, Fiat would benefit from the "air cover" of support from the Americans who'd been running Chrysler.

When neither side had budged by late Friday night, April 10, Ron Bloom decided he'd had enough. He ordered the two junior members of our Chrysler team, Brian Osias and Clay Calhoon, to fly to Detroit first thing Saturday and not to come back without a set of projections to give to the banks. Horrocks, speaking for Fiat, told Clay that the meeting wouldn't be at Chrysler's headquarters in Auburn Hills but would be held instead at a nearby hotel. Perplexed, Clay called Manzo to ask about the reason for the odd change. Manzo was dumbfounded; Fiat had not informed Chrysler of the meeting. He was furious. After days of trying to work out a unified set of projections, Manzo now felt blindsided.

After a flurry of angry phone calls, the Saturday meeting was moved to Chrysler and the Chrysler team was invited to join. By 11 A.M., Osias and Calhoon convened more than two dozen Fiat and Chrysler executives and advisers around the large table in Chrysler's fifteenth-floor boardroom. The executives were almost all middle-aged industry veterans. Osias was thirty-two years old and Calhoon was twenty-six, and both looked younger than their years.

"We're going to sit at this table until we're done," Calhoon announced.

No one left until two o'clock Sunday morning. By then, only one matter remained: an estimate of the incentives that Chrysler would have to offer consumers ("cash on the hood," in industry parlance) in order to meet the sales projections. Cash on the hood had become a emotional issue. In recent years Chrysler had led the industry with incentives as high as $4,000 cash back on some SUVs. Sergio, unfortunately, had ridiculed the practice. Leaders from the old regime agreed that the incentives were too high, but felt that Sergio had no sense of the need for them in a marketplace that was not his own and that had grown to expect them. Rather than try to sort out the disagreement, Osias and Calhoon let the exhausted executives go home — and made them come back later on Easter morning. They deadlocked all the same, and it took a call that day from Ron to Sergio to put the cash-on-the-hood issue to rest.

The head butting led Ron reluctantly to conclude that Fiat and the UAW would never reach agreement on their own. He summoned both parties to Washington and installed them in separate rooms on different floors of Treasury. A third room was reserved for Nardelli and company, who would spend the following days overseeing Chrysler via their cell phones and BlackBerrys and cooling their heels. For most of a week, Ron was Henry Kissinger shuttling between the North and South Vietnamese. Fiat and the UAW both understood that Chrysler's wages would have to be competitive with those of the transplants. Now that Sergio had committed to a projection of future sales, there was finally a quantitative basis on which to negotiate.

We knew from the outset that reducing hourly pay for active autoworkers would be confrontational beyond imagination, so we were relieved when it turned out that base wages were not that different between the Detroit Three and the Japanese transplants. Ron found other aspects of the contract where it would be easier to ask for cuts. Apart from cash income, UAW members enjoyed a gamut of benefits that added substantially to the automakers' costs. Another big burden for the automakers was the UAW work rules. These required both GM and Chrysler to maintain scores of job classifications. A worker at Chrysler could not so much as tighten a screw if it was not in his job description.

Ron focused on expanding a provision that new employees — so-called tier-two workers — could be hired at a lower wage. This category had been created in 2007 as a way to lower Detroit's labor costs without penalizing existing workers. It allowed for a limited number of new workers to come in at $14 per hour, versus about $28 per hour that existing UAW members earned. But because the automakers had been mainly laying off rather than hiring, few tier-two workers were actually on the domestic payrolls. To bring Sergio's projected costs down, Ron persuaded Gettelfinger to raise the limit on the number of tier-two workers that Chrysler would be allowed to hire. Of course, for Sergio's costs actually to decrease, Chrysler's business would have to grow enough to need new workers.

As the third week of April ended, an agreement between Fiat and the UAW at last seemed within reach. Ron knew he had to close the deal — hardly a given with Sergio, who as a "volunteer" was liable to back away again at any time. But Ron realized that he had a trump card to play.

He went to Sergio and said, "How about if I can promise you labor peace? Not just through this contract but through another contract after that? If I can tell you that there won't be a strike, that's especially valuable, because you want to change the culture." Ron offered other goodies as well. These included a commitment to keep wages frozen for the life of the contract, through 2011, and a commitment to have any open issues at the end of the next negotiation be subject to binding arbitration based on maintaining competitive wages with the transplants. Yet even with these enticements, Sergio was hard to pin down. First he said yes, then no, and then he decided to go back to Italy for the weekend to think about it. There he had been hailed by the Italian media as a conquering hero for Obama's decision to designate Fiat as the savior of once mighty Chrysler. Finally, near the end of the weekend, Sergio called Ron and authorized him to make the proposal to Gettelfinger.

Ron sat down with the UAW chief the following morning. He knew that his "ask" would not seem quite as big to Gettelfinger as his "give" had seemed to Marchionne because the union chief was operating under the mistaken assumption that the conditions of the TARP loan agreement, including the no-strike clause, would automatically stay in effect. Nonetheless, Ron also knew that he was asking the UAW to make the biggest concessions in its history. "This is the best I can do," Bloom told Gettelfinger, outlining the terms he'd given Sergio and using every ounce of his credibility as a labor negotiator. "I know you don't want to do this deal, but then we need to go home and Chrysler is going to liquidate." Gettelfinger thought about Bloom's proposal for an hour and agreed.

9

CHRYSLER'S LAST MILE

As THE CHRYSLER-FIAT deadline neared, Harry Wilson started push-ing a very smart, very different alternative. It was interesting enough to do more than distract us. It made us question: Was Fiat really the partner we wanted for Chrysler? We were certainly frustrated with Ser-gio, who kept trying to recut the deal and whose refrain had become "I don't have to be here, you know." But it wasn't just that which made the plan proposed by our determined colleague compelling. Harry offered a way to save hard-hit American taxpayers a lot of money, give GM a better shot in the long term, and still avoid a full-scale Chrysler liqui-dation.

Of course we'd already dismissed the idea of a GM-Chrysler merger, but what if, Harry suggested, GM were to take over Chrysler's top brands? He had always believed that the taxpayer and the U.S. auto in-dustry would be better off if Chrysler LLC disappeared. That was still his logic as he sketched out what we soon called Plan B, although in my mind I occasionally bumped it up to Plan A.

In Harry's scenario, GM would absorb the best parts of Chrysler and the rest would be eliminated in an orderly way — goodbye out-dated product lines, obsolete plants, unneeded dealerships. At the top of the list of assets worth saving was Jeep, a brand known all over the world and whose customers stayed loyal despite the fact that the prod-ucts were less than innovative and often lagged behind both interna-tional and domestic rivals in handling and fuel economy. Some in GM saw Jeep becoming a poor man's Range Rover overseas.

Chrysler also remained the top American maker of minivans, the cat-egory it had pioneered and once dominated. By this time, its minivans were built in Windsor, Canada, so the jobs were more Canadian than American. And the vehicles weren't so great — comparably equipped Honda Odysseys and Toyota Sierras could command thousands of dollars more at retail. But from GM's standpoint (the company having long since abandoned its own woeful minivans) car-shopping soccer moms would at least consider Chryslers.

Finally, there were Dodge Ram pickups, like those we'd watched being built during our plant tour in March. Ram was the reddest of red-state brands, prized for its testosterone image.

By mid-April, Sergio's outbursts were becoming extreme. He made a major issue of the fact that, along with a small network of Chrysler dealers and distribution centers in Europe (complete with hundreds of millions of dollars of valuable inventory), Fiat would be taking on responsibility for 1,200 employees. Though he'd been reminded several times that the people were part of the deal, when the subject came up once more, he erupted as though he were being bilked. "Do you think I am fucking stupid?" Sergio screamed at his own right-hand man, Alfredo Altavilla. "That is not why I fucking brought you here!" The tirade got so bad that Ron and others quietly got up and left.

In another city, Harry was presenting his idea to GM manufacturing chief Gary Cowger, who called Fritz Henderson. Fritz — a chief proponent of a GM-Chrysler merger in the past — was now CEO and in a position to act. On April 16, he phoned me to signal GM's interest. We sent Brian Osias and Clay Calhoon back to Detroit to develop the concept. For the young bankers, this meant round-the-clock number-crunching for the second straight weekend.

The resulting analysis was a sobering reminder of how much we were about to gamble on Fiat's rescuing Chrysler. Plan B required substantially less government funding up front. In place of the $8 billion of TARP money that was slated for Plan A, GM would need less than $4 billion to acquire the brands — $2 billion to buy them from Chrysler and the balance for additional working capital. This represented an immediate saving of $4.5 billion.

What was more, just as Harry had argued in mid-March, eliminating Chrysler as a competitor would add substantially to GM's value. By 2014, its profits would be billions of dollars higher, meaning substantially greater value for the Treasury's investment in GM, potentially $8 billion to $12 billion more.

"This is just wrong," Ron Bloom burst out. "This is not what I came here to do!" Team Auto had convened in Larry Summers's office on the morning of April 21. Ron had arrived in a buoyant mood from having at last succeeded in uniting Sergio and the UAW. But his equanimity dissolved when Larry revealed himself as willing to hear Harry out on Plan B.

"The President gave us a direction," Ron countered emphatically. "He told us to save Chrysler. If we want to have a backup, that's fine. But we shouldn't make Plan B into Plan A." Next, Ron reminded us that the job losses under Plan B, though not as great as in a full liquidation of Chrysler, would still be severe. And he noted that many of the jobs saved would be minivan assembly jobs in Canada.

Always torn about saving Chrysler, I experienced new waves of ambivalence after Harry offered up Plan B. If Larry had been seriously interested in changing course, I would have happily seconded him. But despite his curiosity about the backup scenario, he gave no indication that Plan A was no longer Plan A.

After Ron cooled off, he concluded that "you can't beat something with nothing" and resolved to stay focused on getting the Fiat deal across the finish line.

Beyond the UAW agreement, there were other enormously complex issues to resolve. Under Matt Feldman's watchful eye, Chrysler and its team of lawyers were racing to complete the documents for an unprecedented use of the bankruptcy code. The company's filings — to be made on the morning of a speech by Obama that was currently being planned — were going to include more than twenty different bankruptcy petitions as well as the corporate documents to create a new Chrysler that would be the proposed buyer of the assets worth saving.

The majority owner of this new entity would be the VEBA. Fiat, the Canadian government, and of course the U.S. Treasury would also have equity stakes. (The unwanted assets would be left behind and liquidated by the old Chrysler, which would change its name to Old Carco

LLC.) Matt knew that this aggressive use of Section 363 would provoke legal challenges, and wanted to be prepared.

Meanwhile, Brian and Clay, with twenty specialists from Cadwalader, were working out the particulars and prepping documents for Chrysler's deal with Fiat. Chrysler's finances were tangled, as you might expect of a huge business that had changed hands repeatedly. (In eleven years it had gone from public company to Daimler subsidiary to being majority-owned by a private equity firm.) Still to be negotiated were billion-dollar questions including Daimler's lingering commitments to the Chrysler pension fund, the disposition of loans made by the Canadian government to help keep Chrysler solvent, and so on. On all fronts, the effort was in high gear.

Chrysler's time was running out, and when the White House reserved a TV slot at noon on April 30 for a presidential speech, we felt the added heat. Already, presidential speechwriter Adam Frankel had begun trading talking points and drafts with Brian Deese. The idea would be for Obama to emphasize themes he had introduced before: the importance of America's automakers, the gravity of their problems, and the need for shared sacrifice by all stakeholders to make them viable businesses and avoid wasting taxpayer money.

All this would set a context for the Fiat-Chrysler solution. The President would play down the fact of Chrysler's going into bankruptcy; that was just a necessary step toward revival. Still worrisome was the possibility that bankruptcy would vaporize consumer demand for Chrysler cars and trucks and make the deal with Sergio a hugely expensive fiasco.

Knowing the Fiat deal could still implode, Harry fine-tuned Plan B. His enthusiasm infected Osias and Calhoon, who shared his skepticism about Chrysler with or without the Italians. The thought of lending billions to a company whose long-term survival was uncertain worried them all. Brian and Clay wanted to revisit the costs and the net job losses of dismembering the business.

It was as if a team of doctors trying to save a patient were suddenly considering euthanasia.

Austan Goolsbee jumped in again too. He and the Council of Economic Advisers produced an analysis of the employment impacts of Plan B. Their original estimate for a Chrysler liquidation had been a net job loss in a wide range, anywhere from about 15,000 to 125,000. Now Goolsbee said that the job loss from Plan A would be around 25,000 and the loss from Plan B would be about 60,000, a difference of around 35,000 jobs — and a far cry from the 300,000 that had practically knocked Larry off his chair when the subject of a Chrysler liquidation first came up. Of course as with a liquidation, Plan B would entail substantial disruption along the way to its relatively small net job loss. And supporters of Plan A, like Deese, wondered whether the CEA had skewed its analysis to support its position. Some private economists, such as Mark Zandi, had projected far greater job loss from any dismemberment of Chrysler.

I watched all this with bemusement. On April 25, after Osias and Calhoon delivered their detailed financial projections to Harry, I tried out some simple math on my colleagues. By their reckoning, we were talking about putting in $15 billion less now and ending up with something like $12 billion more in 2014, for a delta of $23 billion without discounting.

When no one argued with my math, my stomach started to tie itself in knots. Plan A was very costly. At risk was perhaps $17 billion of taxpayer value — for what? The preservation of 35,000 jobs (that is, $500,000 per job), and the real but nebulous benefit of sparing our country more economic dislocation and the shock of another piece of bad news.

On April 26, a sultry spring Sunday with pollen so thick you could see it accumulate on windowsills, we filled the seats in Tim's small conference room for a final powwow before the President's fast-approaching national address. For all practical purposes, Sunday was a workday for Tim — he had been shuttling crisis teams in and out all day, particularly those working on the banking problems.

Larry, in khakis, had walked over from the West Wing. Most of Team Auto was present too, having decided to work all weekend as crucial problems remained unresolved. Two belonged primarily to me: I had yet to get regulatory approval for the Chrysler Financial–GMAC deal, and I had yet to finish the creditor negotiation. I took the opportunity to run by Larry and Tim our strategy with Jimmy and the banks. But the main issue on the table was a go/no go decision on Plan A.

Harry had detoured to Washington on his way to Detroit to make an impassioned plea for Plan B, bringing along an assortment of Power-Point slides, which made me fear he had been spending too much time at GM. More importantly, he brought the backing of Osias and Calhoon, who encouraged him to push for the more cost-effective solution offered by Plan B.

Besides the testimonials and the numbers, Harry had marshaled other interesting evidence, such as an analysis suggesting that Chrysler's disappearance need not completely destroy its dealers. Most of the jobs and profits in a dealership come not from sales of new cars but from service and used cars. Both would be needed if Chrysler liquidated.

Ron was not left to fight on his own. Deese, savvy at playing the angles of public policy, reiterated his arguments about the billions of dollars of potential social costs (in unemployment insurance claims and the like) that a shutdown would trigger. Matt Feldman emphasized that switching to Plan B at this late date would severely complicate the bankruptcy process, resulting in added cost and delay. He believed that these complications could easily eat up all of the savings that the proponents of Plan B had set forth.

For the most part, the arguments were familiar and neither faction would budge. So inevitably came the big question: Should the matter be brought to President Obama again?

Tim and Larry were at a seeming impasse. A rarity. "This is all very interesting, but we're not going to risk the Fiat deal," Larry declared.

"Shouldn't the President hear this one more time? Shouldn't he have a shot?" asked Tim.

Larry demurred, but Tim tried again, insisting, "Maybe he should."

With that, they thanked us and adjourned. I assumed that Tim and Larry had silently agreed to take their disagreement offline. And when we heard nothing more afterward, I realized that whatever the merits of Plan B, the clock had pretty much run out. Plan A had to be made to work.

The day was hot by the time I went back upstairs to see Stephanie Cutter, Tim's media chief, and the air conditioning in her office was broken.

The *New York Times* had asked to interview me for a story on Obama's first one hundred days. Stephanie would oversee the conversation to keep me out of trouble. I had nothing to contribute regarding the dramatic overall sweep of events. However, the *Times* had homed in on the auto rescue — of interest to all Americans and, unlike other Obama crises, a tale with a clear beginning and middle. For the White House, the subject posed a challenge. Obama, torn among many battles, had probably spent the least amount of time on the auto front. Unlike many issues involving multiple departments with different mandates and agendas, autos were firmly in the hands of Tim and Larry, who never had a disagreement requiring Obama's attention. The only significant question for him to adjudicate had been whether to save Chrysler, and he had been able to satisfy himself on that and decide quickly. Yet the White House publicists were eager to show the President at the center of the action, and they'd been working hard to spin the *Times*'s story that way.

Stephanie put reporter Jim Rotenberg on the speakerphone and he started firing with questions about our interactions with the President — what decisions we had brought to him, who said what, where the points of disagreement were. Periodically, Stephanie, working her BlackBerry, would hear a question deemed too close to private White House business. Motioning to me not to answer, she would snap at Rotenberg.

The resulting article, "Early Resolve: Obama Stand in Auto Crisis," framed the President's intervention as "a case study in the education, management, and decision-making of a fledgling president." Without getting a single fact out of place, the piece showed him just as the White House had hoped: studying the issues in depth, delegating effectively, being decisive when necessary and frank about his beliefs. "With supreme faith in his ability to explain anything to the country, Mr. Obama shrugged off concerns and said he would openly signal that bankruptcy was a possibility," it read. On Rick Wagoner's ouster, the story reported that Obama "had advisers deal directly with the car companies and never spoke with the GM chief executive he effectively fired." It went on to add that the President "had no problem with anyone knowing he had toppled a giant."

I knew that line in particular would please the White House. At the time, some commentators were questioning the President's toughness, and Rahm Emanuel used every opportunity to counter that perception. He had poked his head into Larry's office before one of our press briefings to say, "Be sure you tell them that the President was muscular."

My personal dealings with the media were far less pleasant. A situation involving my firm, Quadrangle, back in New York, was increasingly drawing attention, and the sort of goodwill that Obama then generated as a matter of course seemed for me to be, at that moment, in very short supply.

Years before I'd become a public servant, we had hired a "placement agent" named Hank Morris to help raise money from New York State and other public pension funds. I had known Morris, a political consultant, for years. Both of us had worked on Chuck Schumer's first campaign for Senate in 1998. Before Quadrangle offered Hank the assignment, I'd checked him out with Chuck, who had confirmed my impression that, in a realm filled with shady characters, Hank was a straight shooter.

That wasn't how it turned out. On March 19, Hank and David Loglisci, the chief investment officer for the New York pension fund, were indicted on 123 counts of fraud. The Securities and Exchange Commission filed a parallel complaint. All of us at Quadrangle had been cooperating for months with the probes, and my involvement had been fully disclosed to the White House during the vetting process at the time of my appointment, a fact later confirmed by Press Secretary Robert Gibbs. The indictment named Quadrangle as a Morris client and described its role as a money manager for the pension fund. But the story remained mainly local.

All that changed on April 15, when the SEC amended its complaint, adding details about Quadrangle's involvement. This time, the roof fell in. The press went crazy, bombarding us with questions and casting my conduct in the worst possible light. White House reporters asked Gibbs about me the next day. "He's not accused of doing any wrongdoing," Gibbs replied. "And is not likely to face any criminal or civil charges as it relates to this. And a pending investigation was something that he brought up to us." Even that didn't help. I continued to be deluged with questions.

Now that I was in the national spotlight, New York Attorney General Andrew Cuomo and other state officials pressed the inquiry further. My daily chores suddenly included late-night conference calls with lawyers and former Quadrangle colleagues as we attempted to make our case to the authorities and the press. During my many years in business, I had certainly been criticized, but I had never before had my integrity questioned. Nothing in my entire professional life had been as painful as that episode.

None of this improved my appetite for dealing with a player who had emerged as a threat to Team Auto's whole endeavor. Not Jimmy, who lacked the leverage to block us on Chrysler and had nothing to do with GM. Not Sergio or Ron Gettelfinger. The new headache was Sheila Bair, the powerful chairwoman of the FDIC, which we needed to complete the GMAC and Chrysler Financial deal. Everything else in our charter depended on that. Without GMAC's help, Chrysler would have no way to finance ongoing sales and the restructuring would fall through. General Motors's survival would also be jeopardized.

I'd become aware of Bair's central role gradually, while arranging for GMAC to take over Chrysler Financial's lending activities. I had expected that obtaining the regulatory approvals would be easy. After all, didn't we work for the same government? Didn't we all want to save the economy from further shocks? That naiveté fell away quickly.

GMAC had three regulators: the Fed, the FDIC, and the state of Utah, where its Internet bank, Ally, was chartered. Since the Federal Reserve and the FDIC were independent agencies, for the first time in our "caper," we could not use executive authority to direct the bureaucracy. No one—not the secretary of the Treasury, not even the President—could tell Ben Bernanke or Sheila Bair what to do. So the potential impediment at this point was not the recalcitrance of outside stakeholders but that of government colleagues.

We didn't need much from the Fed, primarily just relief from something called Rule 23A, a Depression-era regulation prohibiting banks from lending money to "affiliated companies." GM still had a significant stake in GMAC, but from our first meeting with Fed general counsel Scott Alvarez, we sensed a desire to help. Scott and his colleagues were diligent and careful—they made clear that they wouldn't support a full merger of Chrysler Financial and GMAC. Yet they also signaled that they shared our desire to solve the auto crisis.

The FDIC, more directly and intimately involved with the bank subsidiary, had the authority to lift limits on deposits that GMAC had agreed to at the end of 2008 and controlled access to the TLGP. Its cooperation on both fronts was essential to GMAC's plan for providing financing to GM and Chrysler customers. Our initial encounters were worrisome. Two Team Auto members, Brian Stern and Rob Fraser, had a Sunday session with the Fed also in attendance, where the FDIC was unyielding. A few days later, Deese and I accompanied Brian and Rob to FDIC headquarters to try to make some progress. But Bair's lieutenant Chris Spoth and her deputy general counsel Roberta McInerney listened, gave away little, and promised no cooperation beyond checking with their boss.

The only specific objection raised by Spoth was GMAC's financing of dealer inventories, which he viewed as excessively risky. The irony was that of all the possible reasons to worry about GMAC, "floor plan" was the least of them. In theory, GMAC can lose money on floor plan if a dealer won't or can't pay, but the deck is stacked in favor of GMAC. If a dealer defaults, GMAC has the right to seize the unsold cars and return them to GM for full value. What's more, most dealers are *personally* liable for floor-plan loans, a tremendous incentive to make good on the debts. The historical loss rates on floor plan had been close to zero. The new risk, of course, was that GM itself might no longer be around to honor its repurchase agreement. But the President of the United States had just stood up to tell the world that a GM liquidation was unthinkable. What was the FDIC so worried about? We couldn't figure it out.

It took me a while to understand that we were caught in the web of Sheila Bair's own agenda. She was a lawyer from Kansas who, like Ben Bernanke, was a Bush administration appointee. Like Bernanke, she had also been an academic, though of lesser distinction. Unlike Bernanke, she was a politician too — in 1990 she'd lost a Republican congressional primary in her home state.

Bair made her mark at the FDIC as an articulate early advocate of forceful action in the subprime mortgage crisis. At a time when the Bush administration was still wedded to its free-market, noninterventionist stance, she stood her ground. In 2008 *Forbes* named her the second most powerful woman in the world after German Chancellor Angela Merkel. A few pundits even touted her as a possible Treasury secretary for President Obama. But inside the bureaucracy she had a reputation for being a sharp-elbowed, sometimes disingenuous self-promoter. My colleagues who dealt with Bair during the banking crisis found the experience frustrating.

Bair's concern was the safety and soundness of GMAC. We had told the regulators that we intended to recapitalize the company based on the results of stress tests then under way. The goal of stress testing, orchestrated by Tim for the nation's nineteen largest bank holding companies, including GMAC, was the restoration of confidence in the banking system. If a company's capitalization was found wanting, it would be required to raise enough additional money to weather a full range of economic storms. Ideally, investors would put up the funds, but implicit was the assurance that Washington would provide capital if the private market wouldn't. GMAC was in such weak shape that its only possible source of capital would be TARP.

Based on the stress test results — not yet public but available to us — we had budgeted $13.1 billion of new capital for GMAC. Of that, $4 billion was to support the lending it would take over from Chrysler Financial. Bair didn't believe those sums were enough. She suspected GMAC to be weaker than the stress test revealed, and didn't trust de Molina's ability to deliver what he promised. She also shared the FDIC members' antipathy toward GMAC for its aggressiveness in Internet banking.

So the FDIC withheld its approvals, muttering about more capital. Making things worse, Spoth hinted at but would not spell out his boss's demands. We made so little progress with him that I finally asked Tim to intercede. A summit meeting was booked for April 28, just two days before the President was to speak on television. It was in Tim's small conference room, in the early evening of another unseasonably warm day, that I first came face-to-face with Sheila Bair — a small, trim woman about my age with brown hair, brown eyes, and an unsmiling, sour demeanor. According to Washington protocol, this was a "principals plus one" meeting. Sheila brought Spoth. Tim and I represented Treasury, leaving me without my finco experts Brian and Rob. Bernanke and Alvarez participated by phone.

One could hear bemusement in Bernanke's soft voice coming through the speaker. His tone suggested that he was wondering, "Why are we even here?" The Fed was already prepared to meet a key demand by Bair, that GMAC be able to use dealer loans as collateral to borrow at the Fed's "discount window." But this meeting was about Bair's needs. An effort was under way in Congress to increase from $30 billion to $100 billion the credit line at Treasury used by the FDIC to backstop its deposit-insurance fund. Bair made it clear that in exchange for helping GMAC, she expected Treasury's support for the legislation. Such horse-trading is routine, and I didn't question it. I just wished that she or Spoth had been more straightforward and had brought it up weeks earlier. But Tim readily acquiesced.

Next came a recital of grievances about GMAC. Weirdly, Bair attacked dealer financing anew, making it sound as if floor-plan lending were the reincarnation of subprime. It was as though we had not, just days before, explained to Spoth why floor-plan financing is about the least risky activity an auto finance company undertakes. He remained silent, and though I was incensed, so did I. As a "plus one," I didn't think it was my place to take on Bair in the presence of Bernanke and Geithner. The moment the meeting ended, I rushed down to see Brian Stern and Rob Fraser, wondering if I had somehow misunderstood everything I had heard about floor plan. They assured me that I hadn't.

Clearly, the issue of the auto finance companies — which two months earlier we had viewed as the tail of the dog — was now a Great Dane of a problem. Soon to come was the news that Bair did not merely want Tim's support for expanding her credit line; she wanted the legislation passed by Congress before she would agree to help GMAC. That wasn't going to happen in the next forty-eight hours.

We agonized. It seemed insane to let Chrysler go down over her agenda. But Chrysler could not stay in business unless its dealers and customers got financing, and without FDIC approval, there was no way to provide it. We had fallen short on a key condition for not pulling the plug.

In close consultation with Larry and Tim, we decided the rescue was worth an additional gamble. We committed $7.5 billion of TARP funding to GMAC without waiting for the FDIC's cooperation. In exchange, de Molina agreed to take on Chrysler Financial's lending for two weeks so that the automaker could continue to sell cars. Two weeks would be long enough, we hoped, for the FDIC's legislation to pass or for Bair to come around.

I reckoned that the odds were on our side. For one thing, we'd held back $5.6 billion of the $13.1 billion earmarked for GMAC — additional capital that both de Molina and Bair wanted to see invested in the auto lender. Even if the GMAC arrangements fell through and we had to liquidate Chrysler in another two weeks, the consequences of having waited would not be severe. Keeping Chrysler on the dole for the extra days would cost taxpayers perhaps $500 million — a mere rounding error in the context of TARP's $700 billion. And people who bought Chryslers in the interim would be protected — we had a warranty guarantee program already in place.

Above all, I was banking on Bair's self-interest. Being obstructionist had worked for her up to now. But as soon as she realized she was in danger of becoming the visible face of GMAC's paralysis and Chrysler's demise — as well as of the potential collapse of GM because it, too, depended on GMAC — I hoped that the hostages would be released.

Jimmy Lee phoned so often that I got to know the voice of his assistant, Sylvia, who always placed his calls. And, with the President's speech and Chrysler's Chapter 11 filing just days away, I heard from Sylvia a lot. We'd kept tightening the screws on JPMorgan and the other creditors. At Matt's good suggestion, we'd ordered Chrysler to fund its day-to-day operating deficit, as much as possible, using its cash on hand rather than TARP money. Normally, as a company nears bankruptcy, its board reserves "cash collateral" to cover wind-down expenses. But we wanted Chrysler running on empty so that the lenders would realize they would have to put up money if they forced the automaker to liquidate.

A week after we delivered the joint Fiat-Chrysler business projections, Jimmy and his lawyer called with the creditors' counterproposal to my offer of $1 billion. It was ridiculously high: a mix of new debt and other securities that represented only a small haircut from the $6.9 billion face value of their claim. I rejected it out of hand, causing Jimmy to squirm. The Chrysler debt was a matter of huge consequence for JPMorgan. Every morning for months, Jimmy had a standing meeting with his team to strategize and plan their next move.

With me, he became even more relentless, issuing frequent reminders that JPMorgan had not caused the financial crisis; on the contrary, it had bought Bear Stearns at the government's urging to try to help. Tim had instructed me not to be taken in but to maintain strict neutrality. I was not to demand anything of JPMorgan just because it had received an infusion of TARP money; nor was I to show it favor because of Bear Stearns or anything else. I just kept reciting my arguments about liquidation value, the lenders' freedom to seize Chrysler if they wanted, and so on. Matt kept a back-channel dialogue going with Jimmy's lawyer, Peter Pantaleo, inching toward the settlement that I always believed was inevitable.

By all accounts, the politics within the lender syndicate were fierce. Dozens of smaller creditors were suspicious of the four lead banks (which they dubbed the "TARP banks"), fearing that their obligations to the government would prompt them to make unusual concessions. Little did they realize that the big banks, which together held 70 percent of Chrysler's debt, were squabbling among themselves. JPMorgan had the most to lose — $2.7 billion in loans. Citi, by contrast, had been selling off its Chrysler position since mid-2008, dumping more than $1 billion worth to hedge funds and others at around 65 cents on the dollar. Goldman Sachs had been selling too. Back in August 2008, when GM and Chrysler discussed a merger, three of the four had expressed a willingness to accept 60 to 80 cents on the dollar for their Chrysler debt. The sole holdout was JPMorgan. This led the others to suspect — incorrectly — that JPMorgan had put off marking down the loans and recording its losses.

Bankers from Goldman and Citi had advised Jimmy Lee to make the best of a bad situation. Privately they felt his brinksmanship was embarrassing and potentially costly. Citi especially wanted to avoid a liquidation. Its analysis showed it would recover no more than 20 cents on the dollar in that instance. Citi also feared losing business in its branches in states like Michigan and Ohio, where consumers might blame it for Chrysler's demise. (In late 2008, Citibank CEO Vikram Pandit had met with Sergio to tell him, in essence, that Citi was willing to cut a generous deal to help keep Chrysler afloat.)

With a week to go before the President's speech, I decided it was time to try to close the deal with Jimmy. On April 23, I bumped our offer to $1.5 billion; almost instantly Jimmy came back at $2.5 billion. I responded with the final offer that Tim and Larry had signed off on: "Two billion, take it or leave it."

"If it's cash, I'll take it," Jimmy said.

This was out of the ordinary. In the usual restructuring, Chrysler's lenders would receive their $2 billion as new loans. But Matt had learned through his back channel that cash would be high on Jimmy's wish list, and we had cleared that with Tim and Larry too. Even so, I decided to play hard to get.

"Cash isn't normal," I told him. "You should be getting new paper." This triggered a diatribe from Jimmy about the dangers of government involvement in the private sector. He got so pumped up that he announced that "in the future, we are going to think twice about doing business with a company under the government's wing. We are going to review all our dealings with companies that could come under government control or have big unions." (That "review" would last until July, when he realized that GM would likely be an abundant source of banking business in the future and called to ask my advice about soliciting it.)

Finally I relented and agreed to Jimmy's cash request.

I could foresee how the game would play out. Jimmy would go back and try to sell our terms — roughly 29 cents cash on the dollar — to the other forty-five lenders in the two days that remained. While some would not agree, most would, and we would have a strong sign of support from the lender group to help sway the bankruptcy court judge.

The next morning, the last day before the President's speech, I got my first look at the text. I tried to offer as few comments as possible, as I remembered Peggy Noonan, in her memoir of her time as President Reagan's speechwriter, ridiculing the bureaucratic "mice" who nibbled away at her prose. I didn't want to be a mouse.

I was barraged with questions as we assembled the final elements of the announcement package. Most of the burden fell on Deese and, of course, Matt Feldman, but I had my hands full putting in place our $7.5 billion stopgap to support GMAC in the absence of cooperation from the FDIC.

And then, just after lunchtime, Jimmy called with a startling request.

If we were willing to modestly increase the consideration to Chrysler's lenders, he believed he could get all forty-six to agree. He asked us to put up $2.5 billion in cash in return for 100 percent participation by the creditors. Jimmy, it seemed, had gotten himself sideways with many members of his lending group. He had cleared our $2 billion offer only with the other three "TARP banks" and for some reason had delayed informing the other lenders until several days had passed. When the rest of the lenders found out, they were livid, particularly a group of hedge funds that Jimmy — as old school a banker as remains on Wall Street — regarded as junkyard dogs.

Whatever his motives, his proposal, if we accepted it, could have a very strong impact. For many weeks we had seen no alternative to bankruptcy for Chrysler — the only question was what kind. Best case, our 363 transaction would be completed quickly and a "new Chrysler" would emerge as a leaner, more viable business in a promising alliance with Fiat. Worst case, Chrysler would liquidate through a Chapter 7 proceeding.

But even the best case was far from risk-free. Experts had been predicting that any form of bankruptcy could take months and months. No matter how fast we could push the 363 sale through, we knew that Chapter 11 would be costly and distracting. Having been humiliated by Sergio, Bob Nardelli and his team were miserable at the prospect of trying to manage the business for any longer than absolutely necessary. And we all still worried that bankruptcy would decimate Chrysler vehicle sales.

Yet avoiding bankruptcy seemed so unlikely that we hadn't so much as studied the numbers of a case where all the secured lenders were on board. I summoned Team Auto in a state of high anxiety. "Let's get in on a single page, where we can look at it," I instructed Matt and the Chrysler team. "We need two columns, with everything we can quantify about the costs and benefits of the two paths." My hope was that the benefits of avoiding bankruptcy would sufficiently outweigh the costs to justify our raising our offer enough to close the deal. If Jimmy was asking for $500 million, I thought that $250 million would satisfy him.

Very quickly, the page filled with numbers. To my amazement, the totals at the bottom of the two columns were much closer than I would have guessed. For example, closing unwanted dealerships would be difficult and costly without Chapter 11 protection — they'd have to be bought out one by one. But when bankruptcy expenses like lost sales and administrative costs were added, the two approaches were about a wash. Hovering over all this was the unquantifiable risk of disrupting consumer demand. All in all, Chapter 11 was not the place we wanted to be if it could be avoided for $250 million.

It was very late to come to this revelation. As I called Tim and Larry to strategize, my mind raced ahead. Team Auto would have to stay up all night helping rewrite the president's speech, plus the fact sheets and supporting materials, all of which were ready to go. Instead of present- ing Chrysler's bankruptcy, Obama would now say, in effect, "I am de- lighted to announce that after arduous negotiation, in an unprecedented shared sacrifice, all of Chrysler's stakeholders have reached agreement. This will enable the company to go forward with manageable operating costs and liabilities, and without the taint of bankruptcy. As President, I have agreed to commit $8 billion to support Chrysler's plan to achieve sustainable profitability, to the benefit of its workers, its customers, its communities, and our nation."

Tim and Larry agreed that I should respond to Jimmy with an of- fer of $2.25 billion — an additional $250 million. But the offer was good only until 6 P.M., I told Jimmy, because of the President's speech. He had just a few hours to win over all the creditors and deliver the hold- outs.

There was nothing more to do now except carry on with the final preparations for bankruptcy and wait to see if Jimmy could deliver. Jimmy gave the controls to his bespectacled head of syndicate, Andy O'Brien, who began working the phones. They soon assembled more than thirty consents. As 6 P.M. approached, Jimmy reported he was still short more than a dozen answers. He asked for more time, which I doled out in increments, extending the deadline to 6:30, then 7:00, and finally 7:30.

As 7:30 neared, we were hearing through the grapevine that Jimmy was not going to get all of the consents in. I decided that time was up and called to thank Jimmy for having tried. "I've got just five left," Jimmy pleaded. "Give me more time, Steve. I can get them." Reluctantly, I replied, "I can't, Jimmy. I'm sorry." We would go forward with the bankruptcy. His final request was that the President publicly recognize JPMorgan's efforts to be constructive.

Later in the evening, Matt was able to piece together what had happened behind the scenes, and it became clear that I had made the only decision possible. Not only had the holdouts—a handful of hedge funds—demanded $500 million to sweeten the deal, they had also wanted all the extra money for themselves, to the exclusion of the other lenders. That crazy proposal—which cost the creditors the $250 million that I had offered—was pushed by a lawyer named Tom Lauria, whom the hedge funds had hired. I had never heard of Tom Lauria, but Matt knew him well professionally; he regarded Lauria as one of the most undisciplined members of the bankruptcy bar, a self-promoter who would say or do almost anything.

My decision did not sit well with Chrysler, whose board of directors was in almost constant session as bankruptcy neared. Bob Manzo, the company's representative, continued to push for a deal. E-mailing Bloom and Feldman that night at 8:44, he urged them to reconsider the holdouts' proposal.

"That's too close to not exhaust every avenue to get this done," Manzo wrote. Feldman was furious that Manzo had gotten in the middle of the negotiations. "I'm now not talking to you," he fired back. "You went where you shouldn't."

Manzo tried to make amends, but Feldman ignored his e-mails and calls as he worked into the night putting the final touches on the bankruptcy petition. He finally responded to Manzo at 3:54 A.M. "It's over," Matt's e-mail said. "The President doesn't negotiate second rounds. We've given and lent billions of dollars so your team could manage this properly. I've protected your management and Board and now your [sic] telling me you're going to try to put me in a position to have to bend to Lauria. That's BS."

At daybreak in Detroit, two hours later, Chrysler President Tom La-Sorda e-mailed Manzo to ask if their last-ditch intervention had been successful. Manzo was direct: "Tom. Not good. Tried most of the night with no luck. These Washington guys want to show the market . . . that they can be tuff."

That, of course, was not at all how we saw it. Nothing would have pleased us more than to avoid the bankruptcy of a major U.S. auto-maker.

The White House protocol resembled the one we'd followed a month earlier: a preliminary briefing for the media, outreach calls by President Obama from the Oval Office, then the televised presidential address. I had a chance to review his speech one last time. Despite his theatrics, Jimmy ultimately had been a positive force, and I had taken the mouse-like step of inserting a thank-you to JPMorgan. I was also pleased to see that the White House had added language to echo some of the last-minute battles behind the scenes. Notably, the speech now included a searing criticism of "investment firms and hedge funds [that] decided to hold out for the prospect of an unjustified taxpayer-funded bailout." I was quite angry that a handful of investors had pushed Chrysler into bankruptcy (while costing themselves their share of the extra $250 million), so I welcomed that language.

We took some time in the Oval Office beforehand to underscore for the President the remaining uncertainty with GMAC and the risks that it held. Not wanting to publicize our difficulty with Sheila Bair, we had fudged the situation in the President's speech and in the fact sheet. The latter read: "The U.S. Government is supporting the automotive re-structuring initiative by promoting the availability of credit financing for dealers and customers, including liquidity and capitalization that would be available to GMAC, and by providing the capitalization that GMAC requires to support the Chrysler business." In his calm way, the President took this in stride, and happily the media never probed the weasel wording to find out what was really going on with GMAC.

After President Obama completed his outreach calls, we made our way from the Oval Office to the first floor of the White House to as-semble behind him as he announced to the nation that we were putting Chrysler into bankruptcy. This time, Ron and I merited inclusion as potted plants.

• • •

Sequestered in the West Wing for much of the morning, I was unaware of the drama that had unfolded for Matt Feldman and the bankruptcy team. Matt was working with Brian Deese on more White House talking points when his BlackBerry began buzzing. He saw a slew of urgent e-mails from Manzo. Matt stepped outside to call. "What happened?" he asked.

"You're never going to believe this," said Manzo breathlessly. The pressure of events had apparently gotten to Chrysler's bankruptcy lawyer, Corinne Ball. "She stood up at the board meeting and told the board that there was a real risk that Lauria was going to file an involuntary and that it would be a breach of the board's fiduciary duty not to file immediately to preserve venue."

Translated, this meant that she thought the holdouts would try to block us from filing the Chrysler case in New York federal court, which had the most experienced and professional bankruptcy judges. Instead they would file in a friendlier court. The White House was aware of this risk but didn't think it worth adjusting the plan.

"You've got to be kidding," Matt said. "Where is she?"

"She took her briefcase and the pleadings and headed downtown," Manzo replied. Feldman, mystified, called Corinne on her cell phone.

"Have you filed yet?" he asked.

"I just handed the clerk the petition," she said. Feldman, who knew everybody in the bankruptcy court, asked her to put the clerk, Vito, on the phone.

"Hey, Matt," Vito said.

"Have you put the petition on the system yet?"

"No, I was just about to."

Once the petition was keyed in, it would hit the Internet within twenty minutes. The President was not due to speak for ninety minutes. Matt asked Vito to give the phone back to Corinne.

"Corinne, Vito is going to hand you back the petition. You do not want to preempt the President. If you preempt the President, I'm telling you, I don't know that the financing is still available. You cannot do this."

"You don't understand," Corinne insisted. "There are reporters all over the place. They saw me go in. We've got to file." Matt asked her to put the clerk back on the line.

"Is there a place you can have Corinne sit so the press won't see her for the next hour?" Feldman asked.

"I have a desk in the corner," Vito said.

Just then a line from *Dirty Dancing* popped into Feldman's head: *Nobody puts Baby in a corner.*

"Put Corinne in the corner," he told Vito.

And there she sat until President Obama uttered his first words.

The news of Chrysler's bankruptcy was explosive, of course. "Chrysler Pushed into Fiat's Arms," declared the *Wall Street Journal.* "Obama Vows Swift Overhaul as Chrysler Enters Bankruptcy," said the *Washington Post.* As we regrouped in Larry's office after the President's speech, Larry was unhappy with Obama's words about the hedge funds, thinking them unnecessarily harsh. He'd reviewed the speech in advance and blamed himself for not having spoken up. "I should have said something," he fretted.

For my part, I hadn't adequately anticipated the extent to which the President's statement, together with our disparate treatment of the various stakeholders, would constitute another frightening message to a Wall Street already shaken by repeated attacks from Washington.

What particularly upset the financial community was the fact that the senior lenders, who were "secured" and who ranked first in line among Chrysler's creditors, would not get all their money back, while certain unsecured creditors — most controversially, the UAW's VEBA — would be paid in part for *their* claims. Under the strict rule of priority in bankruptcy, senior creditors are intended to be paid in full before any other stakeholder gets a penny.

But bankruptcy law also provides that a new investor — which the government was, in effect — can allocate its capital however it chooses. We believed that it was in the taxpayers' interest to give Chrysler equity to Fiat in return for its technology and management. And we believed that giving the VEBA a mix of debt and equity was also good business — as Ron had told Jimmy, you need workers to make cars. And while the $2 billion that Chrysler's banks were getting was far less than the face value of their loans, it represented more than 100 percent of Chrysler's assets, as the company's liquidation value indicated. By that measure, they were getting more than they deserved. In fact, every

single creditor of Chrysler received more than it would have in a liquidation.

What our critics also failed to recognize was that many creditors
with the same rank as the VEBA got treated *better* than the VEBA. For
instance, Dodge and Chrysler car owners with warranties were unsecured creditors too. Yet we gave them 100 cents on the dollar, because
what consumer would buy another Chrysler if the company didn't
honor its warranties? Similarly, most Chrysler suppliers received full
payment, because without its suppliers, Chrysler would no longer be
able to make cars. The 50 to 60 cents on the dollar we awarded the
VEBA hardly seemed overly generous by comparison.

We would spend many hours during the ensuing months trying to
explain that the shape of Chrysler's restructuring had nothing to do
with the heavy hand of government and everything to do with the fact
that Treasury was the investor of last resort, the only source of capital
prepared to finance Chrysler. Even Jimmy understood this: "Treasury
was holding four aces and I was holding the two of clubs," he would
tell Wall Street colleagues. For our part, we reminded the skeptical of
the golden rule of Wall Street: He who has the gold makes the rules. Or
as my father used to say to his unruly children: "He who eats my bread
sings my song."

10

HARRY WILSON'S WAR

DETROIT'S RENAISSANCE CENTER — built in 1977 by Henry Ford II as a headquarters for his grandfather's car company — was supposed to be a symbol of a revitalized Detroit. That didn't pan out. Detroit's decay continued and Ford decamped to suburban Dearborn. The center's seven glass towers still dominate the skyline, but views from the upper floors reveal a lunar landscape of abandoned buildings and deserted streets that, for most, have symbolized this once thriving city for decades.

Now General Motors headquarters occupies Tower 300 of the RenCen. At 9 A.M. on April 8, Harry Wilson and two Team Auto associates stepped off an elevator there, having fortified themselves with breakfast sandwiches at the McDonald's in the food court below. In the conference room on the thirty-seventh floor, the first cohort of GM executives was waiting, their backs to an expansive view of the Detroit River and the colorful electronic billboards of the modestly more prosperous city of Windsor, Ontario, beyond. Joining our Treasury trio was a clutch of consultants from Boston Consulting Group (BCG), led by Xavier Mosquet, as well as two bankers from Rothschild.

For the next eleven hours, the task force members watched a parade of GM executives flash tables, charts, and bullet points on the projection screen. Whether any of it meant anything would take time for Harry and his two assistants to figure out. Both were young Wall Streeters who had joined Team Auto just two days before. David Markowitz was a thirty-six-year-old University of Michigan graduate whom Harry had known from Goldman Sachs. As driven as Harry, he was also just as analytical and unaccepting of second-rate work. Yet the two were stylistic opposites: David's quiet personality and almost rabbinical manner complemented Harry's gregariousness. Sadiq Malik, at thirty, was a skinny, intense Pakistani American who had graduated near the top of his class at Dartmouth, taken a Harvard MBA, and worked at the Blackstone Group and other Wall Street firms.

The trio had arrived armed with a five-page, day-by-day outline of everything they intended to accomplish with GM over the next four weeks. Harry's objective was to tear General Motors apart and reassemble it as a profitable business. Everyone involved agreed that a total overhaul was necessary. The "viability plan" delivered by GM in February had proven management incapable of dispassionately and analytically creating an achievable business plan. While Ron and I contended with Sergio, the creditors, and the swarm of Chrysler-related problems, Harry's mandate was to design what we had taken to calling "Shiny New GM."

It was obviously a monster challenge. GM's was an antique, closed corporate culture. Old-fashioned notions of hierarchy definitely applied here. Above the floor where Harry's team set up shop were two floors of executive suites that could easily have been in a different tower — or a different city. The company's twenty or so top brass drove each morning into a private parking garage, where their cars would be fueled and cleaned. The half-dozen most senior executives used a special card to ascend in an elevator that would not stop at any other floor (no mixing with hoi polloi) before reaching thirty-nine, where they reigned in splendid isolation. Below, on thirty-eight, were no offices, only the boardroom, the executive dining room, conference rooms, and a guard, who sat behind an imposing round console receiving visitors.

The Obama administration had never seriously considered just letting GM liquidate. America's second-largest industrial company (after General Electric) was deeply woven into the very fabric of America, with its generations of workers, its networks of suppliers and dealers, its historical resonance and symbolism. GM embodied the intimate connection between the free capital markets and the social and political contract on which they depend. It could not be allowed simply to disappear. Beyond that, our early work had led us to believe that the company's problems were, to a considerable degree, of its own making — and fixable. It was the job of Harry and his team to verify this hypothesis while ensuring that we had a sensible plan to end GM's decades-long pattern of careening from crisis to crisis.

Something approaching hope was not out of the question. Despite its disarray, GM was still the source of more than 12 percent of all the new cars and trucks on earth. Its 243,000 employees were spread across 140 countries; GM and its partners actually built cars in 34 of them. In the United States, the company operated from 207 locations in 35 states — not counting dealerships, which were, of course, all over. Everything about GM was supersized; in the course of our work we would learn that the company was party to more than a half million contracts.

Harry knew what he was up against. His first official act with the task force had been to ask for GM's financial model, a kind of megaspreadsheet that companies use to monitor and forecast revenues, expenses, profits, and other important business metrics. GM took days to respond. When it did, the model was useless. Unlike a normal model in which a user can change an assumption and see how the effects ripple across the business, GM's spreadsheet was "value pasted" — the numbers had been entered manually and no underlying formulas tied them together. "Why can't they send us something where the links work?" Harry complained to our Rothschild advisers. "We should ask them to stop playing games."

Harry's first visit to GM, on March 11, had given him a jarring sense of the weakness at the top. At a meeting of high-level executives, he asked CFO Ray Young how much cash the company needed to operate day-to-day. "Eleven billion," Young replied.

"That seems astronomically high," Harry said. "How did you get to that number?" Being Harry, he'd already calculated that for an automaker of GM's size, a cash requirement proportionate to those of Ford and Chrysler would be in the $6 billion to $7 billion range.

Young explained that GM was using a formula based on sales volume, and started walking Harry through the calculation. But as he cited the figures, it was plain that they didn't add up to anywhere near $11 billion.

"You realize that's six to seven billion dollars," Harry pointed out.

Young seemed genuinely puzzled. After a long and very awkward pause, he stammered, "I'll have to get back to you." Harry was dumb-founded.

It hadn't always been like this. GM's treasury department had a reputation for brilliance dating back to Alfred P. Sloan. It was Sloan who had pioneered the notion of using tight financial controls to keep track of its far-flung and disparate divisions. Based in New York, in the vaulting white marble GM building across from the Plaza Hotel, the General Motors treasury was also known as the cradle of CEOs. Rick Wagoner and Fritz Henderson started their careers there, as had others. In my early days on Wall Street, I heard much about GM's treasury staff, which was viewed as cutting edge and among the best anywhere. But GM's sagging fortunes thinned the talent in the ranks. Many good people had retired or quit, and others who might have once been recruited had opted for more lucrative, glamorous jobs on Wall Street.

From the beginning, Harry and his team encountered financial systems as decrepit as Detroit itself. As GM's financial position weakened, it had cut back on funding for its finance group. When it bought Ross Perot's Electronic Data Systems, it turned responsibility for running information technology over to EDS. In 1996, it spun out EDS but left it to manage GM's information technology, which resulted in GM not controlling its own central nervous system. Complications arising from that decision meant that the company needed weeks, not days, to figure out its cash. To assemble the corporate balance sheet, executives had to e-mail around the world and then stitch together a patchwork of reports. Not surprisingly, different countries had different systems.

GM's Latin American operations had a better handle on cash and cash forecasts than did other parts of the empire. But even in Latin America, it was unclear where the money actually was deposited. "No one had a list of all of the GM bank accounts worldwide," a GM adviser told us. By their own estimate, treasury executives spent 80 percent of their time gathering data and only 20 percent analyzing it. (Harry never did get the financial model he'd asked for, because it did not exist. Rothschild ended up jury-rigging one to serve the task force's needs.)

GM faced analogous problems with its accounting operations. The company often had to restate its earnings and was the subject of repeated inquiries from the SEC. In March 2006, for example, GM announced that it needed to revise its profit figures for the previous six years, as a result of having used questionable accounting techniques. As recently as January 22, 2009 — as I was in the midst of deciding whether to take the auto job — GM agreed to settle SEC civil charges relating to its accounting. That a global company could have so shoddy a bookkeeping system was mind-boggling. Such problems led to poor decisionmaking.

GM was continually driving without headlights and kept behaving as though cash were not an issue. The summer that gas prices soared and all-important SUV and pickup-truck sales slid, it belatedly suspended its $1 per share dividend. But it invested in Michigan real estate, laying out $626 million to buy the RenCen, and $200 million more for office buildings in Pontiac. Depressed by Rust Belt malaise and the growing credit crunch, the prices must have seemed like bargains.

It didn't take long for Harry and Fritz Henderson to collide. The day after President Obama told the nation that GM would be on a sixty-day deadline to reinvent itself, the new CEO called to assure Harry that GM was reworking its turnaround plan and would have something for him by the end of the weekend — five days hence.

"Wait a second," the thirty-seven-year-old Harry said to the CEO of the world's second largest automaker. "We're talking about a *wholesale revision*." He didn't want the GM team to burn precious days producing yet another mediocre plan. This time, nothing short of perfection was acceptable. There was no time to waste on another mediocre plan. Fritz deputized Troy Clarke, the head of GM North America, to deal with Harry and to enlist other top executives to help.

Harry gave Clarke and Gary Cowger, the company's worldwide manufacturing chief, pep talks by phone the following day. "We have a once-in-a-lifetime opportunity to re-create this company," he said. "You've got to not be constrained by historical habits and practices. You have to think about it and say, 'If we were to start this from scratch, what makes sense for this business?'" Harry came away enthusiastic that the GM chieftains understood both his mission and his desire to approach the task as a colleague rather than an adversary. But in truth, the thirty- and forty-year veterans he was talking to were wary at best.

In Harry's mind, rebuilding GM from the ground up meant starting with the "badges" and "nameplates," automobile-speak for individual brands (of which GM had eight in the U.S.) and models (forty-five). He felt GM's mission was pretty straightforward — it needed to sell quality cars at a competitive price, a simple objective that had eluded the Big Three for decades. So he wanted to know how well positioned each vehicle was — its price, profitability, capital requirements, next-generation design, and so on. He imagined each model as having its own business plan; it could be evaluated to see how strong the product was, and if you totaled up all forty-five, you would see how good GM was as a whole.

On that April morning on the thirty-seventh floor of the Renaissance Center, where the new GM began, the trio from Team Auto watched as slides began to flash onto the screen at the far end of the room. Immediately they realized that the presentations were as interesting for what they didn't show as for what they did. Charts of vehicle sales included no historical data, only projections — which consisted, almost without exception, of upward-sloping lines.

Charts of selling prices showed no comparative data, as if there were no such thing as Ford, Honda or Toyota. This was a puzzle. Why would GM present the data in such a useless manner? Whom were they trying to fool? Or did they just not think about historical numbers and comparative data in a systematic way? It seemed incredible that no board members or senior executives had ever demanded such basic rigor to inform their decisionmaking. We never knew for sure, but concluded that it was just another expression of GM's "get along, go along" culture. (To the GMers' credit, when Harry insisted that all analyses include historical and comparative data, they readily complied.)

We knew before setting foot in Detroit that GM had a badge and nameplate problem. It had too many of each without enough clear differentiation in consumers' minds. Sloan's original vision — "a car for every purse and purpose" — had mushroomed into confusion. Sloan had organized an array of five brands that did not compete with one another but rather offered customers alternatives at different price points. As a family moved up the economic ladder, the "ladder of success," it could also ascend through GM's product line, remaining loyal customers at every step.

The first rung was Chevrolet, and so it has remained. GM's mass-market volume leader accounts for more than 70 percent of GM's total sales in the U.S. Pontiac, Oldsmobile, and Buick occupied the next rungs up. The top rung was Cadillac, which Sloan made into a synonym for affluence. The ladder worked brilliantly in the company's heyday, but as GM's dominance eroded and it began to cut costs, it could no longer keep the brands sharply distinct. Instead of complementing one another, they began to jostle and overlap, competing for resources within the company and cannibalizing one another's customers. The addition of specialty brands like Saturn, Hummer, Saab, and GMC complicated the management challenge.

Meanwhile, Toyota was pursuing a different strategy. While it had twenty-nine nameplates (compared to GM's forty-five), it had only two brands. As a result, Toyota could effectively spread its marketing costs over a large number of nameplates within one brand. By offering more nameplates, Toyota was essentially offering more product choices within each brand. This drew more customers into Toyota showrooms and was a key reason why Toyota dealers were much more productive than GM's.

The problem of too few nameplates per brand was exacerbated by GM's financial woes. Each nameplate requires a certain amount of capital to develop, test, produce, and market to customers. To conserve cash, GM started to slow its product replacement cycle. While agile competitors would come out with new versions — called "refreshes" in the industry — every couple of years, GM was taking longer to renew its products. GM brands started looking "empty" and its showrooms stale. Sloan's strategy of "a car for every purse and purpose" had become GM's weakness.

To his credit, Rick Wagoner had recognized that he had too many brands to feed. After becoming CEO in 2000, he eliminated Oldsmobile. And GM had also analyzed eliminating Pontiac, Saturn, and Saab. The proposal made it all the way to Wagoner, Henderson, and marketing chief Bob Lutz, but all set it aside. According to Fritz, killing Oldsmobile had cost more than $2 billion; there would be smaller, but still sizable hits if Pontiac, Saturn, or other struggling brands were jettisoned. In essence, GM didn't have enough money to fully fund these brands or to put them out of their misery — a brutal financial Catch-22.

But when the economic tsunami hit in 2008, selling or killing brands

—Saab, Saturn, and Hummer this time, and sharply scaling back Pontiac—became part of GM's viability plan. Harry's question was whether still more should go. GM had blocked out less than an hour for each presenter, but with Harry's grilling, sessions ran as long as two hours. For each brand, he wanted to take nothing for granted but rather to build a business case from the ground up. What was its position in the market? What was its selling proposition? How did it compete? And on and on, as only Harry could do.

Lunch was sandwiches and chips provided by GM, for which the Treasury team paid in cash to comply with ethics rules. As the afternoon wore on, Troy Clarke asked when Harry wanted to see him and Mark LaNeve, GM North America's sales and marketing chief.

"Ten o'clock will be fine," Harry replied.

"Okay, ten tomorrow it is," Clarke replied.

"No, I mean ten tonight," Harry shot back.

When the sessions finally ended late that evening, David, Sadiq, and the BCG team went to dinner at the Coach Insignia, atop the RenCen Marriott. Harry stayed behind, making notes. By the time he left his desk to go to the rooftop restaurant, the elevators had been shut down and he was left to order room service by himself.

The next morning, the team turned to human resources. Harry was pleasantly surprised to learn that in its personnel review process GM held its own with the best in corporate America, such as General Electric. Reviews were 360 degrees, meaning that each individual was evaluated by subordinates and peers as well as by supervisors. But Harry saw what was wrong with this seemingly attractive picture: at GM, there were no real consequences. Poor performers were rarely demoted or fired. "It was feedback but not with accountability," Harry concluded. Welcome to Generous Motors.

This was the antithesis of what Jack Welch had practiced at GE. Welch was legendary for his view that the top 20 percent of employees should be "loved to death" and the bottom 10 percent should be moved out—humanely, but moved out.

GM's cultural problems extended well beyond personnel decisions and the splendid isolation of its top brass. Its decisionmaking was notoriously bureaucratic, slow, and lacking in analytical rigor. A grandly titled Automotive Strategy Board sat atop many layers of management. It convened for two full days every month, yet decisions were rarely reached in one session. Instead, the Strategy Board meetings became grand productions, with pre-meetings for days to prepare for the actual meeting, and charts sent in advance to be vetted, edited, and sent back for final changes. "It was like a meeting of the UN," a longtime GM executive told us.

Among the slides that the human-resources executives showed our team was one entitled "GM's Values." It listed all the right buzzwords — innovation, speed to market, teamwork, and the like. But as Harry and his colleagues looked at it, they realized that the company didn't practice most of those things. The lack of accountability meant that words, not actions, were paramount.

A top-down, hierarchical approach pervaded those upper floors, where real life dared not intrude. Wagoner, Henderson, and Lutz involved themselves in decisions that should have been left to executives several layers beneath them. It was well-known lore inside GM's communications department that in the 1980s, a brochure called "This Is GM" could not be completed until CEO Roger Smith okayed a final color change.

The GM treasury, esteemed though it once was, was famous for meddling. As one of the few GM departments that could peer into every silo, from manufacturing to marketing to purchasing, it challenged small-bore capital allocations at the plant level and dictated how purchasing should handle a small, troubled parts supplier. When a supplier went into bankruptcy, which happened with great frequency in 2007 and 2008 as auto sales slowed, the treasury would hold up minor contract modifications that the supplier was trying to finalize — a process more in line with the duties of a midlevel supply-chain manager. As a result, Rick, Fritz, and other officers faced a mountain of daily decisions. Trivial issues loomed large while big ones got lost. Presentations on major issues to board meetings and executive meetings were often reduced to one or two PowerPoint slides and then put off or passed over lightly. A general aversion to decisionmaking permeated every meeting.

GM's inability to cut bait on poor brands exacerbated the problem. Sales executives complained of spending too much time trying to figure out what to do with Saab, with its tiny thirty thousand units of sales a year. Or devising PR campaigns defending Hummer against *New York Times* columnist Thomas Friedman, who at one point wrote of the stagecoach-sized SUV, "[Hummer] gets so little mileage you have to drive from gas station to gas station."

The command-and-control culture produced managers unwilling or unable to question bad decisions. In meetings with Team Auto, when asked about areas under their direct supervision, executives would typically defer to Fritz or ask to wait until they'd checked with a senior colleague before answering.

This dysfunction hurt GM's products. A prime example, unearthed by BCG, was how the company designed a vehicle's interior — the place where the consumer spends the most time. The interior is usually among the last elements of a design to be budgeted and completed as a model nears launch. So if a design went over budget, as it often did, financial metrics dictated that the instrument panel or the cup holders be cheapened. A typical cost-cutting measure, which could save about $150 per vehicle, was to use hard plastic inside instead of soft plastic, which consumers strongly prefer. At other automakers, midlevel design chiefs or product planners would be able to block such a false economy. At GM, it took an edict from Bob Lutz to make the cheapening of interiors less than the norm.

Harry was forced to end the second day's inquiries early — at 6 P.M. — because he had invited Cal Rapson, the head of the United Auto Workers' dealings with GM, to dinner. Labor relations had been a relative bright spot at the company. After a crippling strike in 1998, management had dropped its belligerence and worked to cooperate. And while executives were still condescending in their attitudes toward the union, GM had enjoyed relatively peaceful labor relations for years. Critics thought Rick Wagoner had given away too much in the process, however, and with him gone and GM in crisis, Harry saw tough negotiations ahead. He'd sought out Rapson on Ron Bloom's advice.

Having Googled Harry, Rapson arrived at dinner wary. A florid, heavyset sixty-four-year-old with a brushy white mustache, Rapson was a machinist who'd grown up in Flint and worked with the UAW for nearly forty years. He knew that Harry had contributed generously to

Republican candidates and had gone to Harvard—two strikes against him, in Cal's mind. But as they sat in an Italian restaurant on the Ren-Cen's ground floor, overlooking the river, Harry described his working-class roots. He also talked about how he thought automaking was a great American industry, which could be fixed if people made the tough decisions to get it back on track. Right now, he maintained, there was a historic opportunity to do that, and Harry was willing to give up a portion of his life to help. Cal began to relax. Hearing Harry's motives made it easier to ask the questions he had to ask.

"I gotta tell you," he said, looking out at the river, "this management plan is crazy. There's no way we can take the cuts that they're proposing. They're closing good plants. They're laying off good people. We can't stand for that."

"Cal, I have to be honest," Harry replied. "Our big beef with the management plan is we don't think it goes far enough. It's like all the other restructuring plans that GM has had over the years. It *kind* of deals with *some* of the issues, but not enough, and ultimately leaves the company unlikely to succeed. The difference between this restructuring and previous restructurings is that this has to be the last one, because there is no appetite for another."

"We can't possibly do that," Cal protested.

Harry promised to go out of his way to ask the UAW's advice: "We're working very closely with management to develop a plan. Then we're going to come to you and walk you through exactly why we came to the conclusions we came to. If you've got better ideas, we'd love to hear them—there's no pride of authorship here. If you've got better alternatives, we'll work through them."

Rapson didn't like hearing this, of course. But the decision of whether the UAW would cooperate with Team Auto or use its political power to fight it wasn't his; that would be up to Ron Gettelfinger.

Our plan called for Harry, David, and Sadiq to spend two or three days each week in Detroit, so the following Tuesday they were back, delving into GM's manufacturing. Making a car involves three stages: stamping (sheet metal into body parts), power train (building the engine and transmission), and assembly. There was a substantial mismatch between GM's assembly plants and its power-train plants. The larger of the problems that this created was excess capacity, which amounted to wasted money. But Harry and his team also focused on the potential for inadequate capacity in some areas; this would cause bottlenecks in the event of a rebound in demand. GM's challenge would be to "right-size"—to match its manufacturing to detailed forecasts, model by model.

These were issues that the company would have to solve for itself. For Team Auto, plant closures were such a hot potato politically that we steered clear of those decisions (which tended to be dictated by things like which brands and nameplates were being eliminated). I was repeatedly questioned about this by the press, and honed another sound bite that I would repeat verbatim every time the question was asked: "No plant decisions, no dealer decisions, no color-of-the-car decisions."

Happily, when the team began touring factories, they were pleasantly surprised. For one thing, the relationship between labor and management at the plant level was truly collaborative, much better than it was higher up. For another, the manufacturing process was consistent and disciplined. GM had studied Toyota's state-of-the-art production system and replicated it, adding some improvements, at all of its plants. "Show me your oldest plant that's within driving distance," Harry had commanded his minders, leery that he was being shown only the best plants. They took him to the Flint Truck Assembly Plant, a facility opened in 1947. It was dingier and the lighting was worse than in newer facilities on their tour, but the production system was exactly the same. This corroborated the productivity data we had been studying back at Treasury. For once, GM's numbers were both rosy and real.

Harry also was struck by the pride he encountered among the UAW members, many of whose families had worked at GM for generations. The competence of the plant managers impressed him too. They seemed to be on top of their production processes, effective partners with labor leaders, and constantly looking for ways to improve operations. On the other hand, he was appalled to find that the plants had "segregated" bathrooms—one set for salaried workers, one for hourly workers—a caste system that struck Harry as wrong on the face of it and certainly a factor in GM's checkered history with labor. But the bathrooms were the exception. Overall, Harry thought, here in the guts of the operation, GM's day-to-day workings were solid. It was the head that was rotting.

When the team turned next to sales and distribution, the worries returned. GM had a dealer problem — we'd known that all along. Like Chrysler and Ford, it had way too many, a legacy of the automakers' long history dating back to a rural America. Latecomers like Toyota boasted much more modern and efficient networks. While GM sold about 30 percent more vehicles in the United States than Toyota, GM had four times as many dealers, roughly 6,000 compared to 1,450. Thus the average GM dealer sold 450 vehicles, compared to 1,500 for the average Toyota dealer. In Charlotte, North Carolina, seven GM "stores" (as dealers are known in the industry) sold roughly the same number of cars as the area's two Toyota dealerships. Chrysler's numbers were even worse. As a result, GM and Chrysler dealers were generally dramatically less profitable, had less cash to invest in their stores, and projected a substantially less attractive retail experience to customers. For the many Americans who thought the automakers owned the dealers, this affected the brand perception and ultimately hurt sales.

Driving around on weekends, I began to look out for dealerships and would often see older, smaller, shabbier Big Three stores a short distance from large, gleaming dealerships belonging to Toyota or Honda or another of the transplants.

In typical GM fashion, its effort at dealer streamlining had been too little too late. It had cut about four thousand dealers in the ten years between 1995 and 2005. But during that period, GM's share of the U.S. market had tumbled from 33 percent to 26 percent — meaning the downsized network was not much more efficient than the one with which GM had started. The treatment of dealers in GM's viability plan was more of the same. It called for the elimination of two thousand dealerships by the year 2014. Like a morbidly obese man who doesn't see why dropping twenty-five pounds in five years isn't enough, GM was too slow at shedding its flab.

In fairness, the problem wasn't merely GM's ingrown culture; it was legal too. American car dealers are protected by state franchise laws that essentially require the dealer's consent to terminate the franchise — a one-sided arrangement if ever there was one. Thus closures were not just slow, but expensive; franchisees basically had to be bought out. GM had budgeted almost $2 billion for the proposed next phase, an average of about $1 million per dealership. From our perspective, with bankruptcy came the silver lining that, under court protection, the company would have the right to tear up whatever franchise agreements it needed to.

On April 22 Harry and his lieutenants ended up at the Tech Center, where some of us had gone a month earlier to drive the Chevy Volt. That experience had been fun but irrelevant to GM's near-term survival. The briefing GM delivered to Harry was a lot more practical. It centered on the 2008 Malibu, a midsize Chevy that was competing successfully, for a change, with the likes of the Toyota Camry.

The presentation compared the 2008 Malibu to its mediocre 2006 predecessor. In redesigning the car, GM's product group had, under Vice Chairman Bob Lutz's leadership, for once defied the finance department and won approval to spend an extra $300 to $600 per car on flourishes like higher-quality interior moldings and best-in-class finishing. Those little upgrades struck such a chord with consumers that GM was able to hike the average selling price of a Malibu by $3,200. Retail sales went up by almost 50 percent. The *New York Times* described the Malibu as "a super Accord, but from GM." The Detroit auto show voted it North American Car of the Year. This simple but important redesign would generate hundreds of millions of dollars of additional profits for GM every year.

At the Tech Center Harry had his first encounter with Lutz, who had godfathered the redesign. An industry legend, Lutz was known worldwide as the quintessential American car guy. He had worked for each of the Big Three (this was his second stint at GM) as well as for BMW, and had been the impetus behind such iconic vehicles as the Dodge Viper and the Ford Explorer. A seventy-seven-year-old onetime Marine Corps fighter pilot, Lutz still drove fast cars and flew his own single-engine military training jet. In GM's bland culture, he stood out like spiked hair at a church picnic.

Harry had admired Lutz ever since hearing him speak at Harvard Business School, and it didn't take long for the two to bond over lunch in the food court. They traded notes on the Marine Corps (Harry had gone to Officer Candidate School at Quantico). As Lutz pulled a Swiss Army knife from his pocket and used the blade to open his sandwich, Harry asked, "If you had to fix GM, what would you do?"

"I'd hire three guys just like me but twenty-five years younger," Lutz growled.

"Who out there is like that?" Harry persisted. "Who could be the change agent for GM?" Lutz could come up with only two names in the entire company.

Lutz, whose years at Chrysler had been under Lee Iacocca, had preferred the Chrysler culture because if people didn't like what you did, they'd tell you to your face. GM was more civil. Middle managers would smile, nod, and keep doing what they had been doing for years. The expression "grin-fucking" was popular around GM.

Also remarked upon was the "GM nod," which referred to the dynamics of big meetings. A decision would be made. The supervisor in the room would ask, "Does everyone agree on this? Have we made a decision?" All the GM people would nod. But afterward, e-mails would pour in from the attendees or their subordinates, questioning the decision, its implications, or how it would be carried out. This would prompt a restudy of the issues. Weeks or months would pass until the once final decision eventually came undone.

The thirty-seventh-floor conference room became the office for the three auto task force members during their trips to Detroit. Unfortunately, it lacked Internet service, and when they asked about this, they were told that the necessary approval process for visitors was too cumbersome to navigate. Harry couldn't believe it. He represented GM's largest creditor and soon-to-be owner, yet the company wouldn't or couldn't connect him to the web so he could do his work. In the end, he and David bought wireless cards with their own money.

The tension between Team Auto and GM quickly mounted. Harry was pushing for fast answers — trying to determine in a few weeks how best to fix GM. But the automaker wasn't built for speed — its systems didn't produce information quickly, nor were its executives used to newcomers challenging them with theories and ideas they'd never heard broached before.

Harry's bluntness didn't mesh well with the GM way. Frank questions like "Why would you ever do that?" or "How exactly does that work?" would elicit replies like, "Well, we've always done it that way." The old-timers at GM resented Harry and his young team. They felt that the Treasury guys lacked industry knowledge and were sometimes asking the impossible. And they sensed that Treasury was starting from the assumption that the GM executives "were a pack of morons," as one onlooker put it. Yet there was little open conflict. That was not the GM way.

Some of the most stubborn opposition came from chief planner John Smith. A forty-one-year GM veteran and group vice president, Smith was a Missourian who had gone to Harvard and come up through the GM treasury. He controlled the company's sales and market-share statistics and assumptions — the ultimate levers of power at GM, because these numbers shaped multibillion-dollar decisions on everything from the manufacturing footprint to parts purchasing to cash on the hood. Smith would often reject data requests from the task force, saying, "We know what we need to do." BCG came in for its share of resentment as well, nicknamed by one GM official "consultants gone wild."

For their part, my task force colleagues thought that having Smith in such a critical job — which included responsibility for certain deals — typified all that was wrong with GM's personnel decisions. He was a man of modest ability who mostly sought to maintain the status quo. Later, members of the new board would privately dismiss him too.

While the tension between Smith and GM's new minders was most palpable, veterans like Lutz, Clarke, and Cowger, all former Wagoner lieutenants, felt that GM had made great progress before the financial crisis at turning itself around. They believed they had done yeoman's work keeping the company afloat despite its crushing liabilities and handicaps. To hear Harry and his even younger aides imply that the company was slow, inept, and out-of-date was insulting, to put it mildly. "Who does this little prick think he is?" they would sometimes mutter after a meeting with Harry.

But not everyone connected with GM responded this way. Longtime advisers from firms such as Morgan Stanley, Alix Partners, and Evercore generally nodded in agreement with Team Auto's requests and prescriptions, which often echoed their own past recommendations to their reluctant client.

Despite his early clash with Harry, Fritz Henderson (who of course owed us his promotion) was receptive to the task force. "Listen to these guys and fully vet their ideas," he would tell his executives, sometimes reminding them, "They have the money." So GM did finally respond to Harry's insatiable appetite for information — the sales and marketing staff alone produced thousands of pages of documents, on everything from the dealer network to residual values.

The debate about brands was painful nonetheless. When a consensus was quickly reached to eliminate Pontiac altogether, that left GM in North America with four brands — Chevrolet, GMC, Buick, and Cadillac. Were further reductions needed? Harry approached the question with an open mind, asking for two-brand and three-brand strategies as alternatives, and assigning BCG to collaborate with GM on the analyses. This didn't work out so well. After days of frustration, the consultants announced that they thought GM was tilting its numbers to favor the four-brand status quo.

To the GMers, the very identity of the company was at stake — how much more of its heritage must GM sacrifice to earn the right to survive? Tensions rose higher in mid-April when Harry asked GM to consider absorbing Jeep, Dodge Ram, and Chrysler minivans. In high-level meetings, GM executives would sometimes abruptly leave to talk among themselves outside the conference room, leaving Team Auto to wonder what was going on.

The two-brand option was the first to fall by the wayside after analysis showed that the GMC name was too valuable to jettison. GMC trucks are essentially the same as Chevy trucks, yet they fetch several thousand dollars more per vehicle. Whether to keep Buick was a much tougher call. To GM's thinking, Buick was needed as an intermediate step for buyers trading up from a Chevrolet and not yet ready for a Cadillac. But our team had trouble seeing this borne out by market statistics, and Buick had a very thin product line.

GM also invoked Buick's enormous popularity and prestige in China. There, unaccountably, it had become the car of choice for top-ranking technocrats and successful entrepreneurs. But that argument didn't convince Harry either. "I don't think Chinese consumers care whether Buick sells in the U.S. And if they did, it would be a bad thing for our China sales," he declared, noting how weak Buick's North American sales had been recently.

The stickiest aspect of Buick for us involved dealers. Modern car dealers typically carry multiple brands, and within the GM universe this meant there was a whole cadre of franchisees selling Buick, Pontiac, and GMC. Taking away Buick on top of Pontiac would leave these dealers with only GMC. We couldn't compensate them by adding Chevrolet to their mix because that would cannibalize their GMC truck sales. Nor could we offer them Cadillac; with its upmarket positioning, the fit wouldn't be good.

In the end, Harry reluctantly agreed to let Buick live, and GM was able to keep the four-brand strategy it wanted. A saving grace was that Buick was planning to introduce two new models in the near future that held great promise, holding out hope that the brand could be at least partially revived. But Harry attached a condition that surprised GM executives: he insisted that dealers' franchise agreements be modified so that if Buick was later shut down, the contracts could be terminated at a manageable cost. Characteristically, the GM executives hadn't thought of this eventuality. They were more interested in the rosy upside possibilities of keeping Buick than in protecting GM in the event it continued to decline. Harry's investment background had trained him to think about managing the downside just as much as the upside.

When Harry was in Washington, he would come into my office and perch on one of the government-issue wooden chairs opposite my desk. We'd catch up on the progress of his due diligence and take a few minutes to talk about the bigger challenges of restructuring GM. Pulsing with energy, Harry generally leaned forward when he was sitting, and spoke in a rapid, soft tone. We both understood that while a quick trip through bankruptcy could repair GM's balance sheet, unless we somehow fixed the culture, the company would slide back toward the abyss.

Harry hated the mediocrity he was finding. He told me how at one review session, Mary Sipes, the chief product planner for GM North America, said she was happy with plans for a particular model because her team had dubbed it "credible."

"Shouldn't the standard we're shooting for be 'compelling,' not 'credible'?" Harry asked. Above all, GM needed an attitude transplant. Its people were so used to losing, to watching market share erode and seeing their vehicles outclassed and outsold, that mediocrity became a self-fulfilling prophecy. Harry was fond of a Vince Lombardi quote: "Winning is a habit. Unfortunately, so is losing." Changing GM's psychology became a key goal for the team.

Typical of the cultural challenge was a lack of focus on shareholder value. In all our time interacting with GM executives, we never heard any of them utter that all-important term. Chatting after one lengthy session on the thirty-seventh floor, Troy Clarke told Harry that earlier that day, Ray Young had given the senior leadership a quick tutorial on equity value and "total enterprise value." Troy said he'd been fascinated to learn that if they cut annual operating expenses by $8 billion, they would add approximately $36 billion to GM's worth! He was so pleased by this discovery that he did not notice that Harry was aghast. How could the head of GM North America not understand how value is created for shareholders? The sad truth was that no one at GM thought like an owner.

Reminders of GM's lack of financial discipline were always crossing my desk. The Bush loan agreements required the company to ask for the Treasury Department's approval of any nonroutine expenditure of more than $100 million. Requests from GM's treasury usually arrived in the form of a PowerPoint deck, a handful of pages with no backup analysis or other justification. It was GM's arrogance and sense of entitlement at their worst. The company expected us to take its word for each submission and rubber-stamp the funding, which would of course have to come out of taxpayers' pockets. Close advisers to GM had noted a similar fecklessness for years. At board meetings, $1 billion often seemed the smallest significant amount. Proposals to spend, say, $500 million on this project or $300 million on that would show up on slides as $0.5 or $0.3. Presented that way, a half-billion-dollar expenditure could seem hardly worthy of discussion.

The most frequent beneficiary of GM's lax spending was Delphi, the troubled $18-billion-a-year parts maker that GM had spun off ten years before. Delphi had been languishing in bankruptcy since October 2005, but remained GM's sole supplier of such critical components as steering assemblies. By exploiting that dependency, Delphi had succeeded in extracting huge concessions from GM — a total of $12.5 billion since the spinoff.

In early March, we faced our first Delphi request. GM wanted to pay the parts maker $150 million for operating funds to tide it over for a single month! That ask was coupled with another involving a complicated proposed transaction to buy back the steering business from Delphi, also explained in a single page of PowerPoint. All told, GM would be providing more than $350 million, money it would probably never get back. Yet so certain were GM and Delphi of our acquiescence that Delphi had already issued a press release announcing the agreement.

When Harry asked the GM team how the $350 million would serve Delphi, he was told that it would cover Delphi's operating losses for a period of time, probably two months.

"Then what?" Harry asked. He was told that Delphi would likely be back at that point, its bankruptcy unresolved and asking for more money. "How long has this been going on?" he asked.

"A long time."

Harry wanted to meet with Delphi's management to try to reach a resolution that would bring the company out of bankruptcy, end the threat to GM's supply and production, and minimize the use of taxpayer cash. At a hastily called meeting with GM and Delphi representatives, he looked across the table at a senior Delphi executive who was demanding a massive cash infusion from GM and asked, "Why is this a good deal for GM? Why would we ever want to do this?"

"Because if you don't, we'll shut you down," the Delphi official replied.

Harry had been through enough negotiations to know that you can't give in to threats. "We're not going to do it," he said.

When Harry reported on the meeting, I immediately agreed. A phrase from history flashed into my mind, America's repudiation in 1799 of extortion demands by the Barbary pirates: "Millions for defense, but not one cent for tribute!" This had led to a two-year undeclared war.

As Team Auto delved into Delphi, we discovered one of the most convoluted financial messes any of us had ever seen. The prolonged bankruptcy had produced a capital structure with layer upon layer of debt. Effective control of the business rested with a group of hedge funds, some of which had bought in when Delphi looked like a bargain. They were frustrated with management for not making any fundamental changes to Delphi during its long bankruptcy and were anxious to recover their capital in any way they could. Delphi was also mired in long-running discussions with the Pension Benefit Guaranty Corporation, the independent federal agency that insures private pensions, about its grievously underfunded pension plan.

Privately we told GM that we were going to hit the pause button on Delphi until we figured it out. Though Delphi was important to GM, the sheer volume of outstanding work dictated that we had to prioritize. Ray Young and his associates were not happy; they didn't like being second-guessed and were more scared of Delphi's threats than we were. In their "spare time," Matt and Harry began to sort through the rat's nest. They soon learned that Delphi was exaggerating its need for cash. It was sitting on sufficient rainy-day capital in a sequestered account that the hedge funds refused to release. GM and the hedge funds tried to bridge their differences, but negotiations broke down.

While engaged in this maneuvering, we also undertook contingency planning in the event of an actual Delphi shutdown.

"How long could you keep the factories running if they cut you off?" Harry asked Troy Clarke, GM's North America chief.

"We couldn't," Clarke said.

Incredibly, GM had never tried to stockpile critical components in the event of a Delphi shutdown, nor had it done any meaningful work to create alternative sources of supply. Harry was stymied until later that day, when he and Clarke began a discussion of GM's upcoming production plans, which included a summer shutdown that is routine for automakers. The normal shutdown was four weeks, but this year GM wanted to make it longer to reduce the bloated supply of cars on dealers' lots.

"Wait!" said Harry. "If you shut down, doesn't that eliminate the impact of Delphi's threat? Suppose we make the shutdown even longer?"

By mid-April, we presented Larry and Tim with a plan that we believed would turn the tables and force Delphi into a reasonable negotiation. Would Delphi or any of its investors really want to be perceived as holding GM hostage at such a precarious economic moment? After our confrontation with the Chrysler banks, Larry was at first hesitant to pick another public fight, but Tim backed our strategy, and Larry came around.

On April 23, GM announced it would shut down thirteen North American plants for an extended period. While the closure was partly aimed at reducing the bloated supply of cars on dealers' lots, the accompanying news release — drafted in large part by us — was blunt. Unless Delphi came to terms with GM, it said, "Delphi or its lenders could force GM into an uncontrolled shutdown, with severe negative consequences for the U.S. automotive industry."

Shortly thereafter, the creditors released cash to provide liquidity to Delphi. We had won round one. The negotiations with Delphi continued, but with Matt and Harry forcing GM to bargain hard and strike a deal that satisfied GM's operating needs at the lowest cost to the taxpayer. They began laying the groundwork for GM to take back control of the steering-assembly business as well as of four "keep sites" — Delphi factories that made other key components.

GM's far-flung international empire was its other great cash sponge. We regularly received requests to fund subsidiaries abroad, and just as regularly rejected them. While we were legally permitted to approve these requests — and some may have represented good business decisions — I knew that part of my job was to be sensitive to the politics, particularly where taxpayer dollars were concerned. I developed what I thought of as "the *Washington Post* test": How would the public react to a headline that said the Obama administration was in effect allocating hundreds of millions of dollars of public money to shore up GM Australia, or GM Korea? We managed never to violate this principle, but GM Europe tested it most sorely.

GM Europe, with its flagship business in Opel, was a major automaker in itself. It had $34 billion in annual sales, making it about 70 percent the size of all of Chrysler. It sold about two million vehicles a year, employed 55,000 people across the continent, and was GM's biggest international headache. Not surprisingly, it and other European automakers were suffering many of the same woes as their U.S. counterparts, with the complexity of European regulation and politics layered on. Like its Detroit parent, Opel was broke and in urgent need of capital.

Opel's main creditor was something called the General Motors European Treasury Center, or ETC. This was a kind of offshore kitty where GM pooled excess cash from subsidiaries around the world, sort of a central bank for its non-U.S. operations. The ETC would lend the money, in turn, to other subsidiaries in need. Over the years, Opel had borrowed more than $1 billion from the ETC, and a failure by Opel to repay these debts would hobble other, healthier operations in places like Brazil and China.

We wanted the German government to do as ours and Canada's had done — pony up to rescue one of its biggest employers. With our encouragement, GM informed the German government in mid-March that it was willing to cede majority control of Opel to anyone willing to put up the 3.3 billion euros (approximately $4.4 billion) that the business needed to turn itself around. But while the government expressed a willingness to help, it faced domestic opposition. Instead of being on a postelection honeymoon like President Obama, Chancellor Angela Merkel was just six months from her next trip to the polls. She decided that bailing out Opel would be political suicide unless the company could arrange at least a modest infusion of fresh capital from commercial sources, ideally GM or, alternatively, a private investor.

No European nation wanted to see its Opel facility close, but neither was any eager to put up cash, certainly not without assurances that its jobs would be preserved. I was witnessing a small example of what I had written in op-eds: Europe is not a nation but a collection of countries loosely affiliated by ambition (to be like the United States) and fear (of repeating past mistakes, including two world wars). Each country worked furiously to protect its own interests — ambassadors would call on us to lobby the Germans to treat them fairly in the Opel situation! — but closing factories and shrinking capacity, though needed just as urgently in Europe as in the United States, was almost unthinkable. European mores placed too much emphasis on preserving jobs, however uneconomical they might have been.

The Germans continued to pester us for aid; we kept asserting our unwillingness to let GM divert capital to a European problem, particularly in the absence of meaningful European support. Eventually, Germany agreed to provide a 1.5 billion euro bridge loan to enable Opel to seek a private-sector partner. (I was amused to note that this bridge loan included the condition that none of the money was allowed to "leak" from Opel back to the United States.)

From GM's perspective, Opel posed a tough dilemma. If forced to give it up, GM would cease to be a global company at a time when Ford and other rivals were trumpeting their ability to produce models that could be marketed around the world. In addition, GM's midsize-car design and engineering operations were based in Europe and would have to be replicated if Opel was severed. (Korea would have been the most likely place.) But given the sensitivity to how TARP dollars were used — not to mention the bigger challenges GM faced — we felt we had to take a hard line. Opel was secondary; we needed to concentrate on building Shiny New GM.

Throughout these sometimes fraught dealings with GM and Chrysler, Ford made sure it was never completely out of mind. Alan Mulally phoned Tim regularly and often sent emissaries to me. Ford's message was always the same: We're struggling too, but we're fixing the problems ourselves. Don't penalize us because we didn't take your money. At the same time, Mulally was generally supportive of our work — he knew that the failure of GM and Chrysler would wipe out much of the supply base and make it difficult or impossible for Ford to produce its cars.

One of Mulally's delegations showed up at Treasury in late April: Lewis Booth, a crisp Englishman who was the CFO; Tony Brown, the tall, heavyset, mustachioed African-American global purchasing chief; and Ziad Ojakli, a compact, garrulous Brooklynite and former Bush White House official who was head of governmental affairs and seemed never to stop talking. "Our plan is working. We are viable," Booth told us as we sat around the conference table in the yellow-walled room 2428.

All three had been in the main conference room at Ford headquarters a month earlier, the day President Obama briefed the nation about his decisions on Chrysler and GM. The Thunderbird Room, as it was called, was adorned with eight clocks, showing the time at Ford installations around the world, and black-and-white photos of the Model T and Henry Ford. Mulally had turned it into Crisis Central as he and his team grappled with the present dramatic downturn.

Like GM and Chrysler, Ford had been fighting a losing battle for more than thirty years to maintain consumer confidence and auto sales. Despite the boom in SUVs, it had spent many recent years bleeding cash while shedding jobs and plants. Yet because of its bold decision in December 2006 to raise $23.5 billion by hocking everything it owned, the company that had long trailed GM now found itself just enough better off not to be in the throes of an impending bankruptcy.

All the same, the deepening recession was brutal. Ford, like GM, was saddled with too many dealers, uncompetitive labor rates, and a dependency on gas-guzzling trucks and SUVs. Ford had burned through nearly $21 billion in 2008. In January 2009, after reporting a $5.9 billion fourth-quarter loss, it drew down its remaining $10.1 billion line of credit. It had a quarterly cash drain of about $5.5 billion, and if business didn't pick up within a year, Chapter 11 would threaten it too. Meanwhile, its giant finance arm, Ford Motor Credit, was paying sky-high interest rates for the capital it needed.

Before the crisis, the Thunderbird Room had been the site of once-a-week meetings in which the top two dozen Ford executives around the world — from marketing to product development to Ford Credit to human resources — would deliver rapid-fire reports on their operations. Now the meetings were happening every day, sometimes twice a day, and often on Saturdays and Sundays too, as the executives confronted the effects of collapsing sales and the question of what would happen to Ford if its Detroit rivals went down in a heap.

Mulally was a relative newcomer. A former Boeing executive who'd lost the race to become CEO, he was a Kansas native who sprinkled his speech with expressions like "neat" and "gosh." That Boy Scout demeanor concealed a fierce drive to win. Bill Ford Jr. had given him the reins in September 2006 when the forty-nine-year-old scion decided he wasn't the right guy to ruthlessly pare down and fix his great-grandfather's century-old business. The massive borrowing initiative was already under way; Mulally encouraged Ford, who remained as chairman, to raise even more. At the time, the received wisdom on Wall Street and in auto circles was that Ford's fundraising was an act of desperation, necessary because Ford was so far behind GM in product development and modernization.

The new CEO's second boost to the company was working with Bill Ford to sell off Land Rover, Aston Martin, and Jaguar, high-end brands the company had acquired. They'd been meant to become the center-piece of Ford's growth strategy, but instead they had cost billions of dollars, in one fix-it attempt after another, and were a constant distrac-tion for management. Ford pursued a dual strategy in response to the bailout. In the press and congressional hearings, it applauded Wash-ington's efforts to help GM and Chrysler. Mulally had gone to Wash-ington in November and December 2008 to support his rivals and to underscore the need for a healthy U.S. auto industry.

The second part of the strategy was more private and less benevo-lent. Ford did everything it could, in its business operations and its lob-bying, to ensure that it would not be hurt by the rescues. "Disadvan-taged" became the watchword — as in "we should not be disadvantaged by what the government does to help GM and Chrysler."

This aspect of the strategy was tricky, because Ford in essence wanted the benefits and advantages that GM and Chrysler were poised to get, namely a cleaner balance sheet, lower labor costs, and access to cheap money from the Fed. But it didn't want the negatives, like the ex-ecutive-compensation restrictions, the elimination of the Ford family's super-voting stock that allowed them to control the company, or the stigma that came with taking taxpayer money. And of course it didn't want to consider, or even let anyone think it would entertain, a Chapter 11 bankruptcy filing.

Senior executives like Booth and Brown closely tracked what the government did to aid GM and Chrysler. They monitored press re-leases, statements, Chrysler and GM submissions, and news stories about the task force. They watched how developments at the two au-tomakers compared with Ford's own efforts. Special attention was paid on five fronts: labor, dealers, suppliers, debt, and credit. Ford's status vis-à-vis its Detroit rivals was a regular and frequent topic in the Thun-derbird Room.

Mulally interrupted this particular meeting — now four hours in — for Obama's speech. The President's image came up on the oversize screen, and the executives around the large circular table listened as he delivered his restructure-or-liquidate ultimatum to Chrysler and GM. Some, like Ojakli, wondered whether government-backed warranties would be enough to keep customers buying. When Obama finished, Mulally flipped off the TV and said, "This is our time to be humble and focused. We need to show that what we are doing here works."

So Ford moved aggressively to keep pace with the forced restructurings. In April it reduced its debt by $9.9 billion by offering a mix of cash and common stock, one of the largest debt exchanges in corporate history. It won relief from the UAW akin to what GM and Chrysler achieved (although the rank-and-file members voted down the new Ford contract in the fall of 2009.) It cut hundreds of dealers. To Ford's giant purchasing arm, which spent about $65 billion annually for everything from steel to seats to floor mats, Obama's speech had already brought relief it could not have secured by itself. By Ford's estimate, some 70 percent of its suppliers also did business with Chrysler, GM, or another big automaker. A free-fall, Lehmanlike collapse by a major rival could take down a supplier and shut down Ford as well; to protect itself as best it could against that eventuality, Ford had reserved hundreds of millions of dollars for supplier support. Obama, with his implicit promise that the White House would not let GM and Chrysler collapse, enabled Ford to free those reserves and apply them to other headaches.

My own sense, watching these executives operate, was that Ron Gettelfinger had been right. Months before, asked by a congressman to rank the automakers' leadership, he'd testified under oath that Ford's was the best management in Detroit.

By late April, Harry had the rudiments of an operating plan for GM. It dramatically accelerated and magnified the restructuring the company had originally proposed. Pontiac, Saturn, Saab, and Hummer would be eliminated almost immediately. By concentrating GM's focus, the number of new launches and "refreshes" of existing models could be increased from thirty-nine to forty-four over the coming five years. There would be five hundred fewer dealers four years earlier than in the previous plan. Plant closures would be accelerated by six to twenty-four months. A further 8,000 hourly workers and 1,250 white-collar executives would go. All told, the restructuring was expected to reduce North American operating costs by $8 billion a year. And while GM had been comfortable with a plan that allowed the company to break even at U.S. sales figures of 11.5 to 12 million a year, Harry was prepared to fight to cut costs until GM could break even in a 10-million-sales environment, still slightly higher than the depressed levels of early 2009.

The plan was far from ready for public consumption when, on Friday, April 24, Harry got a late-afternoon call from an anxious Walter Borst, the treasurer of GM, and a half-dozen members of his team. "We need your signoff," Borst said. They were racing to file the bond exchange offer, and they seemed to think they had to include the restructuring plan. We'd long since taken for granted that GM would need a trip through bankruptcy court, and most of GM's leaders understood that too. Knowing that the exchange offer was doomed to fail, we had ignored this bit of Kabuki theater up to now. But the GM finance people persisted in going through the motions, attending to the minutiae of regulations requiring any major change in plans to be included in the prospectus.

Harry, as it happened, was taking a rare break. He had gotten home to New York early and was playing in the back yard with his kids. He also had discovered, after many rounds of questioning, that the company had the option to delay including the details of the restructuring plan for up to two weeks. So he was in no mood for GM silliness.

"Guys, what do we think the probability of this deal happening is?" he asked, referring to the bond exchange. No one around the speakerphone at GM would give an answer.

"Give me a number," Harry persisted. "Is it less than 50 percent? Less than 10 percent?" Still no answer. He found it incredible that the company was consuming so much time and energy on a plan and no one would hazard a guess as to whether there was any chance it would ever be used! In Harry's mind, this was the exact problem with General Motors—large numbers of people running hard toward a goal of limited or nonexistent value and thus distracting from the really important priorities of the business. "I will give you a number. I think less than 5 percent. And so because we have a massive amount of work to do for a bankruptcy filing that is highly likely in the next several weeks, and I think this has an extremely low probability of happening, I cannot spend several hours going through comments on a prospectus that won't do anything to help this company."

Larry had pushed us from the start to play down Team Auto's role and keep the emphasis on GM and Chrysler managing their own affairs. That ended up being partly true of GM, in the sense that Harry and his team tried to set parameters and assumptions for its executives in the hope that they could then produce the specifics of a restructuring plan. In reality, the talent and determination of Harry, David, and Sadiq were what really drove the process. As we drafted press statements and fact sheets, I would constantly force myself to write that "GM" had done such and such. Just once I would have liked to write "we" instead.

11

EPIC BANKRUPTCY

―――――――――

"THIS TIMELINE IS impossibly aggressive. It's never been done before," Harvey Miller, the seventy-six-year-old senior statesman of bankruptcy attorneys, told Harry Wilson.

"Well, we don't have a choice," Harry countered, thinking of the President's deadline. "We can get it all done."

At 9 A.M. on the day after President Obama announced that we had put Chrysler into bankruptcy, more than three dozen well-dressed lawyers, bankers, and GM officials gathered in a conference room on the fifteenth floor of the General Motors building in New York. Dozens more had dialed in by speakerphone.

For the men and women present who had made bankruptcy their careers, General Motors was shaping up as the Big Show, the most massive industrial bankruptcy in history. The filing deadline was June 1, just a month away, and even veterans like Miller were intimidated. Privately, he had approached Matt and Harry a few days before with his concerns that GM's management was still in denial about the prospects of a bankruptcy filing and wasn't working hard enough to prepare.

Harry, chronically sleep-deprived, had a fierce adrenaline rush from the pressure. GM sought to open the meeting with a 150-page document. "What's this?" Harry asked. "The agenda," came back the reply. Harry, almost laughing, said, "You can't run a meeting with a 150-page agenda!" and moved on to the list that he and Matt had compiled.

He had before him an eight-page spreadsheet of several dozen topics that needed to be addressed in the bankruptcy — everything from GM's more than 500,000 supplier contracts to its relations with sovereign governments around the world. He had assigned responsibility for each item to individuals from the government group and GM. Next to those names, he had columns for next steps, deliverables, and due dates. In deference to GM, Harry started the meeting by framing bankruptcy as the fallback plan — GM officially still held out hope that it would find enough takers for its bond exchange offer to avoid Chapter 11. But no one else in the room saw that as a serious possibility, and by this point, privately, neither did Fritz nor most other top GMers. Then Harry dove in and began working through the list, item by item, to be sure everyone knew what would be expected.

Next to him was Matt Feldman, our stalwart bankruptcy sage. Minutes after the Chrysler petition was filed the previous day, Harry had gone to him and said, "Feldman, now you're mine." Though exhausted, Matt had dragged himself to New York for this all-day meeting.

The bankruptcy plan Matt envisioned for GM was an outsize version of the one he'd designed for Chrysler. With the help of many billions of taxpayer dollars, GM would separate its assets into two companies. "Old GM" would retain the factories, equipment, brands, and real estate that the business no longer needed. Its sole purpose would be to dispose of these assets, using the proceeds to repay the creditors that the other company, Shiny New GM, had left behind. The new company would own all the assets GM *did* want to keep. Free of crippling costs and debts, this new business would go forth as a streamlined, revitalized competitor on the world automotive scene. We meant it to be not only viable but also highly profitable.

The meeting ended at 6 P.M., having stretched nine hours. Even though it was Friday night, Harry didn't stop; he had booked a session with Carl Icahn, the legendary corporate raider and multibillionaire, who had lately expressed interest in acquiring a stake in Delphi. Icahn's offices were a couple of elevator rides away, on the forty-seventh floor. Matt dutifully accompanied Harry on the short journey, but was soon called back to Connecticut over a family matter. He was not sorry.

Harry, who liked to have an aide-de-camp by his side, summoned Sadiq Malik to Icahn's office as soon as Matt left. The meeting, while not producing any meaningful progress, lasted until after midnight, nearly killing the young analyst, who was too scared of Harry to take a bathroom break.

. . .

Neither Ron Bloom nor I attended that kickoff meeting in New York. My modus operandi has always been to delegate to younger colleagues whatever they can handle, and I felt comfortable with Harry's ability to manage the situation. Ron, however, having ushered Chrysler toward resolution, was eager to turn to GM. This marked the start of the only serious interpersonal conflict at Team Auto. Although Harry and Ron certainly had ideological differences, the friction between them was more a matter of style than substance. Both were take-charge guys. Harry saw GM as his baby; Ron, seventeen years older and officially the auto task force's deputy, viewed himself as senior to Harry.

The tension flared in Washington the next week. Ron went to Harry and said, "Let's sit down and divide up how the GM work is going to get done."

"Why do we need to divide it up?" Harry asked. "It seems to be working fine."

"Well, you've got some expertise, I've got some expertise, why don't we sit down and talk about it?" They walked down the long basement hallway to the Treasury cafeteria to chat.

"If you think I'm doing something wrong or something's not working well, let's talk about that," Harry said as they found a table. "But if all you want to do is take ownership of a process that's going really well, I don't think that makes any sense."

Ron repeated his thought about different skills.

"Tell me what your different skills are," Harry countered.

"I've done this before."

"I've done this a lot before as well. But if you think I am doing anything wrong, I'd be happy to address it."

Harry was not the only Team Auto member to feel some discomfort about Ron. After working shoulder to shoulder with him on Chrysler, Matt considered him too often dictatorial. Harry, having watched that interaction, was concerned that the same difficult dynamic could develop with GM. He also had a strong view that deal terms worked best when there was a clear leader with accountability. Nonetheless, Harry recognized that there was an enormous amount of work to do on GM and indicated that he was open to carving off pieces of the project. They agreed that Ron would spearhead our dealmaking abroad, particularly with the governments of Canada and Germany.

But when Ron said he also wanted to take over the talks with repre-sentatives of GM's major bondholders, the conversation got hot.

"Frankly, Ron, I think I've done more bondholder negotiations than you have," Harry was saying. "But also, I have to say, these guys don't like you."

"What do you mean?"

"They think you totally sold out to the unions. They don't trust you. They don't think you can be an honest broker. Whether that's true or not, that's what they think." This set Ron back. He reflected for a min-ute, concluding that he did not want to risk putting his ego ahead of the salvation of GM. "Okay. Let's set that aside and talk about the UAW."

Harry welcomed Ron's involvement on that front. He believed, as we all did, that Ron's knowledge of labor issues and his credibility with Gettelfinger were invaluable. But Harry insisted on playing an equal role. As long as Ron didn't treat him as a subordinate, he said, they could team up on the UAW talks.

The confrontation seemed to settle the differences between Harry and Ron, but after returning to our work area, Harry quietly issued or-ders that every GM-related e-mail to Ron must also be copied to him to make sure he stayed in the loop.

As Harry and his team crunched numbers for GM's financial restruc-turing over the next few days, they discovered a large flaw in our plan. In overhauling Chrysler, we had "invested" the $8 billion of new tax-payer money almost entirely as debt on the new company's balance sheet. We'd assumed we would do the same with GM. But GM, they realized, was going to require far more new money than Chrysler, even allowing for the automakers' difference in size. Harry's preliminary estimates showed that Shiny New GM would need at least $30 billion, on top of the $15.4 billion the Treasury had already put in. Yet that much new debt would leave the company groaning under a poten-tially unmanageable load of fixed liabilities — much like old GM. Harry couldn't find a way out of this.

After wrestling with the problem, Harry bounded into my office one morning waving a sheaf of papers. "We've been thinking about this the wrong way," he said. "We've got to equitize most of our debt." I immediately understood the Wall Street shorthand: he was proposing that instead of lending most of the money to GM as we had done with Chrysler, we infuse the bulk of our money into GM by buying stock. *This would mean that the government would own General Motors.*

I bought the logic of what he was saying. Leverage can be a good thing — I had made my living for nearly a decade in leveraged buyouts, and the businesses we'd worked with had almost all thrived. But debt can be particularly risky for companies in cyclical, capital-intensive industries like automobiles. A streamlined, relatively debt-free GM would have the flexibility and financial cushion to succeed. Yet I was also painfully conscious of a promise I'd made early on to Larry: "Don't worry. We're not going to end up owning GM." If Harry's analysis checked out, the question would be how to sell this turnabout to Larry.

This would bring us into one of the hottest controversies of the financial crisis. Nationalization had been in and out of the headlines since autumn, when the Bush administration had seized majority ownership of AIG. It turned the failed insurer into a joint operation of the Treasury and the Fed; nominally the company had a board of directors and CEO, but Hank Paulson and Ben Bernanke oversaw all the important decisions.

In February, as the economy and the stock market continued to slide, calls for outright nationalization of banks had increased. The calls came from a motley assortment of sages. Not surprisingly, leftish economists like Paul Krugman and Joseph Stiglitz were heard from frequently and loudly. But former Fed chairman Alan Greenspan, a lifelong champion of laissez-faire, weighed in, telling the *Financial Times,* "It may be necessary to temporarily nationalize some banks in order to facilitate a swift and orderly restructuring." Spicing the mix was a band of hedge fund and vulture investors, who argued that based on any fair valuing of assets, many major banks were insolvent and should be taken over, just as the FDIC had done in many, much smaller circumstances over the years.

Tim and his Treasury team strenuously resisted. As repugnant as it was to leave troubled banks in the hands of those who had brought them to the edge of the precipice, Tim fervently believed that his plan for stress tests of the nineteen big banks, capital infusions, and other programs to remove troubled assets from their balance sheets was the safest way to restore the banks to financial soundness without risking panic in the markets.

But the pressure on the administration to do something more — anything more — was intense. Members of the President's inner White House circle, none of them banking experts, had relationships with many Obama supporters and donors who purported to have that expertise. With the stock market in seeming free fall, they barraged the White House with calls, e-mails, and memos.

On Sunday, March 15, President Obama had gathered his closest advisers, his economic team, and his banking experts in the Roosevelt Room to try to thrash out what to do when the stress test results landed and what else, if anything, to add to the medicine being administered. The discussion on that damp, chilly afternoon was heated; after a few hours, the President went upstairs to take a dinner break with his family, imploring his advisers to try to come to a consensus.

The group veered close to having the government take control of the two most troubled banks, Bank of America and Citigroup, which was already partially owned by the government by virtue of past rescue efforts. If the stress test results were unfavorable, the more aggressive attendees argued, the government's capital should come at a high price in terms of ownership and potential control. Larry Summers was tempted by the idea. As an academic, he well understood the intellectual argument that a bank with more liabilities than assets was an insolvent bank.

Taking over a couple of banks would not, in itself, necessarily be a disaster, as the AIG experience had demonstrated. What was unnerving about the March 15 discussion was that some advocated, as part of this proposed takeover, not making all the creditors of the two banks whole. Of course, just as we had done with Chrysler and were planning to do with GM, not giving all the creditors of an insolvent institution 100 cents on the dollar is fundamental to the bankruptcy process. But among the differences between banks and car companies is that the banks' creditors included counterparties to trillions of dollars of various derivative and swap transactions. The collapse of Lehman Brothers had nearly brought down the financial system when traders became terrified of being counterparties with anyone. Seeing creditors get more than they deserved was distasteful, to be sure, but compromising the counterparties of Citi and B of A would surely have had even more cataclysmic results. Fortunately, cooler heads prevailed, and when the Sunday meeting ended, seven hours after it began, Tim's plan remained intact.

Harry and I agreed on a strategy for making our case for government ownership of GM. We were not going to argue policy or politics with Larry; we were going to argue business. By the time we sat down with him on May 11 to talk about how to invest the public's money, I'd boiled down the message to something simple: "We can either get nothing for something, or we can get something for something." By that I meant that if we didn't take equity for our money, we would be shortchanging ourselves, since GM could not support more debt.

Harry was passionate. And after many years as an investment banker, I thought I was a pretty good salesman too. We started by explaining to Larry that foreign automakers, particularly the Japanese, operated with far less debt than GM would have even if he accepted what we were about to propose. Then Harry presented two contrasting scenarios. The first provided for the new Treasury money to be invested entirely as debt. Not surprisingly, even as far out as 2014, GM would be much more highly leveraged than its rivals — basically wrapped in a financial straitjacket. Any significant hiccup in the economy had the potential to send that GM spiraling into oblivion. The second scenario assumed that most of our money would go in as equity. A small portion would go in as debt, which would be fully paid off by 2014.

"*This* GM can compete and win," Harry said. Having spent the past month overseeing the rebuilding the automaker's plans from bottom to top, he was certain of GM's promise. He spoke of the potential for huge value, possibly recouping the entire investment, or more, by the government if it held GM shares.

Next came the most difficult aspect of our pitch. The way the math worked, Harry explained, the government would end up owning not merely a piece of GM's equity, but a majority stake of about 60 percent; in other words, it would control the world's second-largest automaker. Furthermore, said Harry, we thought GM should be set up as a privately held company. It would have only two other initial shareholders, the Canadian government and the UAW's VEBA, with a slice of equity reserved for the old GM bondholders. Not having GM shares trade publicly would have a side benefit: it would insulate GM from the constant pressures and attention of the stock market until it regained its footing. This could be private-equity-style investing at its best — a focused, efficient company with no public shareholders to distract it from completing its turnaround.

I could see Larry recoil. Any kind of government ownership was bad enough, but owning a majority interest was worse. And by making GM privately held, we would be delaying the government's ability to cash in its shares, because the automaker would first have to do an initial public offering. To make matters still worse, Larry sensed, correctly, that Harry's ambitions extended beyond just restructuring GM; with his boundless self-confidence, Harry wanted to make sure that the plan for Shiny New GM was executed perfectly. If that happened, the GM team's numbers showed that the equity of General Motors could be hugely valuable.

Larry was wary of jumping to conclusions. His comfort in our ability to restructure the companies was not matched by a similar confidence in our ability to manage them. And while Larry had his own doubts that markets were always efficient, he found it hard to believe that the value of GM's equity could really grow at more than 40 percent a year for the next five years, as Harry was predicting. "If this equity was so valuable, there would be a line of people down Pennsylvania Avenue waiting to buy it," Larry argued. In fact, no one seemed interested in GM equity, at any price. While I didn't necessarily feel all of Harry's optimism, neither did I believe that markets are always efficient. If that were true, there would be no Warren Buffetts, no investors who clearly delivered superior returns over a long period of time.

Once again, I felt pulled in opposite directions. I shared Larry's concern about government involvement in the private sector and recognized the Pandora's box aspects of what Harry was proposing. And I, too, had trouble believing that an investment in GM would appreciate anywhere near as much as Harry claimed. On the other hand, all of us on Team Auto wanted to give the company the best possible chance to succeed. Having Harry let go of GM the moment it exited bankruptcy, followed by a fire sale of the government's stake, didn't seem very sensible.

Larry soon bowed to one argument: there was no reasonable alternative to government ownership of GM. (So desperate were we to avoid government ownership that we half-seriously considered a proposal by Gene Sperling to give the GM shares to America's public libraries.) But Larry was unyielding on our second assertion — and, in retrospect, rightly so. He was determined to have the government's involvement be as short and nonintrusive as possible. Coincidentally, as the date to receive the results of the stress tests on the banks approached, Larry had launched a project known as the "USG as Shareholder." Anticipating the possibility that the stress tests would reveal the need for large capital infusions into the banks that could be provided only from TARP, Larry had asked Diana Farrell to lead an effort to establish rules for how the government would manage these potential investments. She assembled some of the administration's best policymakers, ranging from Gene Sperling to Herb Allison, the former Wall Street CEO who had come on board to run TARP. Now that the possibility of owning GM suddenly seemed imminent, Diana asked me to join.

Having directed the McKinsey Global Institute think tank, Diana was in her element. She knew the issues intimately, and her collegial manner fostered a thorough, efficient policy process. We deliberated four or five times, meeting in whichever space happened to be available in the crowded West Wing. At one point, to my surprise, I saw on my calendar that our next meeting would be in the Situation Room, the legendary White House command post established by John F. Kennedy after the failed Bay of Pigs invasion. We descended to the basement, making our way through a warren of twisting halls and small offices. The command complex was said to occupy a basketball-court-sized five thousand square feet, but the Situation Room itself was cramped and bunkerlike, barely big enough for a long polished wooden table, which seated fourteen and was flanked by extra rows of chairs. The ceiling was low and the walls were lined with display panels and communications gear, all switched off while we were there. Beyond an open door to one side, I could see military technicians huddled over screens in a darkened room, monitoring who knows what.

As Diana's work proceeded, the results of the stress tests arrived, revealing, as the Treasury and the Fed had expected, a need for large infusions of capital, although less than what had been expected. Meanwhile, the markets had improved sufficiently that almost all the banks were able to raise the cash they needed from investors, allowing them to avoid the dread grasping tentacles of TARP. But we knew that for GM, Chrysler, and GMAC there was no escaping TARP, so much of the work of the "USG as Shareholder" group ended up being applied to Team Auto's companies.

Still determined to limit the government's involvement as much as possible, Larry kept a close eye on the group's work. Tim also joined the meeting in the Situation Room and seemed to share Larry's concerns. As it emerged, the policy envisioned government ownership as a three-phase process. In the first, brief phase we'd be very active, setting business goals and guidelines and picking executives and directors. Once this rebooting was done, we would step back and let the board and management run the company. Finally, we would sell our stake "as soon as practicable" to recoup the taxpayers' money. (I had bargained for the word "practicable" in lieu of the more felicitous "possible" because I thought it connoted less of a rush for the exit.)

Choosing leaders to transform GM's culture was at the top of my long list of tasks. We had already made a major bet on Fritz Henderson, who had been the only responsible choice available to us in March. I very much wanted him to succeed. Yet while I had acquiesced in his request to have "interim" removed from his title, as the weeks passed I concluded that his chances were no better than 50–50. I was determined to bolster Fritz with a strong board and, particularly, a strong chairman.

Kent Kresa, the interim chairman, had been gracious in accepting the job under the difficult circumstances of Wagoner's dismissal. He was dedicated and energetic, but at seventy-one he was only one year away from GM's mandatory retirement age for directors. Moreover, after more than five years on the board, I doubted that he was enough of a change agent for GM. This was why I had asked him to serve only for a couple of weeks as I continued to look for a longer-term chair.

Once President Obama made his March 30 announcements, there was no longer any need to keep the search secret. I stepped up my calls, drawing often for advice from Welch and from Tom Neff, the dean of executive recruiters, whom GM had retained. Nevertheless, it was not an easy task. All of the other obstacles I had encountered in March remained, particularly the scarcity of distinguished former CEOs who were still young enough to serve for at least five years. Of the long list of people that we reviewed, Ed Whitacre stood out.

I had met Ed once or twice in my work as an investment banker in media and telecommunications, but I knew him better by reputation. Our backgrounds could not have been more different. Ed had been raised in Ennis, Texas, the son of a railroad engineer and union member. He grew up playing baseball and football and hunting, pastimes that never appealed to me. He'd been the first in his family to attend college, studying engineering at Texas Tech. Along the way, he got a summer job at Southwestern Bell that involved hammering in fence posts and measuring telephone wire, and after graduation he signed on full time. His record at the company was extraordinary, leading Southwestern's transformation from a backwater regional player into today's AT&T through a balanced mix of strong management and strategic vision.

His reputation was for toughness. I remembered having once read a *Business Week* story that described him killing rattlesnakes on his Texas ranch (he would pin down the snake with a stick and crush its head with a rock). His flinty image was reinforced by his lean, six-foot-four frame, his full head of gray hair, and his laconic speech. Ed believed that we are born with two ears and one mouth and we should use them in roughly that proportion.

When I reached Ed, he had no idea why I was calling or even that I was serving in the government. As far as he knew, I was still in New York doing media and telecom deals. My proposition startled him. His first reaction was not encouraging: "I am happily retired and I don't know anything about cars." But I thought I heard a hint of uncertainty in his voice and persisted in a follow-up call a day or so later.

As an investment banker, I spent many years comfortably peddling my products and trying to recruit talent to our firm. That was business. In my new role, I felt passion and tried to convey it. "This company needs to be saved," I said. "This country needs this company. We've got a mess on our hands and you can help."

For the second time, he replied, "I don't know anything about cars and I don't think I'm qualified to do this." Yet even more than in our first conversation, I sensed a chink in his armor.

Ed was headed to Singapore for an ExxonMobil board meeting, but we agreed to talk when he returned. I was twitching with excitement about the possibility of reeling him in. In our phone conversations he had lived up to my impression of his directness and clarity of thought and so I waited anxiously for his return. Harry was just as anxious. He viewed GM as his baby and saw fixing the culture as being just as important as fixing the brands or the UAW contract or the manufacturing footprint. He lobbied me relentlessly in his soft, determined way with ideas for remaking the board.

I shared his views but didn't want us to get ahead of ourselves. First we needed a chairman. When Ed returned from Singapore, I could tell that he had mulled over my offer and concluded that he was open to it. This was typical Ed; he didn't need a lot of talk or meetings to make up his mind. On my next call, he asked point-blank what would be the government's role in the company, making clear that his interest was dependent on GM being run without interference from Washington. I assured him that the Obama administration was committed to that. After a few more conversations, he confirmed that he would be willing to serve. I was ecstatic.

Now I needed to get the interim chairman on board. The challenge, however, was that Kent Kresa was loving his role and wanted to stay until his mandatory retirement in 2010. I called Ed to see if he'd consider joining as vice chairman for a year and then succeeding Kent. But Ed held his ground. "I'm sixty-seven," he said. "I don't have that many more years in me."

I'd dealt with tricky personnel questions over the years but never with such high stakes. I consulted Larry, who was still unnerved by how swiftly I'd dismissed Wagoner and by the strong media backlash. "Let's avoid another public execution," he said, urging me to find a graceful and invisible way to ease Kresa out. Left to his own devices, Larry probably would have stuck with Kent for another year. But I agreed with Harry. With the future of General Motors on the line, I didn't want the fear of a messy transition to become the enemy of the perfect.

Larry urged me to ask Jack Welch's advice. So I called Jack, and after hearing me out about Kresa, he said, "This isn't something you can do over the phone or even in a meeting. Take him out for dinner, have a couple of bottles of wine, talk to him about his life and his family. Then see if you can make this his idea."

As it happened, Kent, who lived in Los Angeles, was scheduled to be in Danbury, Connecticut, for a board meeting a few days later. I was sure Jack would commend me for offering to go to Kent rather than asking him to come to Washington. I made a reservation at a quiet restaurant I knew (as it happened, I had a house in the area) and flew up to meet him.

We had our wine. We talked about our families. Kent commented on how pleasant the dinner was. Then he pulled a list from his jacket pocket and talked enthusiastically about people he hoped to recruit for the GM board. I felt like a fiancé about to tell his bride that the wedding was off. Kent was such a dedicated, nice guy. I gently explained the problem: I didn't want to lose Whitacre, and in any event, changing chairmen just one year after bankruptcy seemed wrong to me. But Kent brushed away my concerns. He left saying how much he had enjoyed our evening and how much he looked forward to working together.

My effort to apply Jack's formula had been utterly unsuccessful. Now what was I going to do? Still mindful of Larry's admonitions, I decided to bring Ed and Kent together to see if they could work it out on their own, and orchestrated a meeting in Washington. When the two arrived at Treasury at 5 P.M. the following Wednesday, I escorted them to the Map Room (a conference room whose clutter undercut the grand name) and left them to talk. An hour later, I returned to find that neither had given an inch.

I felt there was no longer any choice. My determination to get the right result outweighed my fear of public controversy or Larry's wrath. I asked Ed to step out of the room while I spoke to Kent alone. I explained that while we were all grateful for his willingness to serve, given that he had only a year left, we couldn't pass up the opportunity to have Ed as chairman for the next five years.

"Well, I guess that's it then," he said and stood up. I could see his feelings were hurt, and I didn't blame him. As he left, he ruminated aloud about leaving the board early. That could lead to the media flap that Larry was hoping to avoid. In the ensuing days, I would call Kent regularly to try to persuade him to stay, and asked other board members to do the same. In the end, he remained and was gracious and helpful in the transition.

Ed had gone off to get ready for dinner with me, so I had a little time to deal with another urgent matter that had bubbled up earlier that same afternoon. The media had seized on a report of my personal finances and I'd become the story of the hour.

I had known from my arrival at Treasury that my financial disclosure form, all forty-seven pages of it, would be publicly available. The substance didn't worry me — my holdings had been closely vetted and approved — but I dreaded the possible invasion of privacy. As weeks passed and no reporter thought to ask for the information, I was beginning to hope it might never happen. But today that had changed. Bloomberg News obtained the form and broke a story headlined "Obama Automobile Adviser Rattner Worth at Least $188 Million." The reporters had culled from the thick document a handful of disclosures they thought hinted of conflicts of interest, such as the old speculation about my investments with Cerberus. The story also included an unequivocal statement from Jenni Engebretsen, the senior Treasury press person: "Like all employees, Steven Rattner was required to comply with financial conflict of interest rules, including divestitures where needed, and he has done so fully."

My phone and BlackBerry were still buzzing when Ed and I regrouped at Bobby Van's, a steakhouse up the street from Treasury. I was ready to share a couple of stiff drinks. I was hoping we'd get to a quiet discussion about GM, Ed's new role, and the tasks before us. But my cell phone kept ringing as Jenni responded to press inquiries well into the evening. All the major media did stories; all echoed the details that Bloomberg News had chosen. Jenni and I were struck by the incongruity: here we were in the midst of this huge auto crisis and the reporters covering it were more interested in my finances than in nearly everything else we were doing. To me it exemplified everything that was wrong with the media: gossip trumps substance.

I'd picked Bobby Van's on the theory that Ed, being Texan, would want red meat. But he had just spent several days on a ranch and ordered fish. I kept apologizing about the calls and my resulting inability to focus on our important business at hand. At last they tapered off and we managed to talk. I liked his honesty and self-confidence. With Ed, there was no guile. As dinner progressed, it became clear that for Ed — who cared about our country but was too sensible ever to volunteer for a job like mine — stepping into GM was a form of public service. He intended to put an end to the nonstop board meetings and teleconferences of recent years — GM's board would learn to do its business in crisply run, once-a-month events. "A board should have dinner one night, meet the next morning, and be on a plane by 2 P.M.," Ed said. We ended the evening agreeing, naively, that this was a realistic approach.

Coincidentally, the way we had laid out the timetable, Chrysler's bankruptcy ended up paving the way for GM's. Chrysler's sales held up far better than we expected, and would end up higher in May than they had been in April. People were still buying Chryslers, perhaps encouraged by the warranty guarantees and other safeguards we'd put in place. Meanwhile, the public seemed to be getting used to the idea that bankruptcy doesn't necessarily mean total ruin. And I felt far more comfortable that we had our arms around things than I had two months earlier, when I'd felt I was looking over the edge of a cliff.

May was consumed with the same complex prebankruptcy stakeholder discussions as we'd had with Chrysler — to my relief, GM's were less operatic. Instead of Sergio to contend with, we had the phlegmatic Fritz. Instead of Jimmy Lee, we had thousands of faceless bondholders represented by two coolly professional firms, the investment bank Houlihan Lokey and the law firm of Paul, Weiss, Rifkind, Wharton & Garrison.

But the Chrysler precedent also made it hard to change aspects of the process we hadn't liked. I felt a little bit of buyer's remorse about the Chrysler-UAW contract. While it was a vast improvement over previous agreements, I wasn't sure we had used our once-in-a-lifetime opportunity to full advantage. I respected Ron Gettelfinger's determination to protect workers' interests. And I sympathized. My many op-ed pieces over the years had warned that income inequality in America was an enormously important moral issue and that real wages for blue-collar workers had been declining, even in years of prosperity. At the same time, if these automakers couldn't be made competitive, we would have no jobs, an outcome much worse, to my mind, than jobs that were lower paid.

So I told Harry — who scarcely needed encouragement — that when it came to GM, we should be tougher on the UAW. But this just showed our ignorance of how organized labor works. Like the unions in many industries, the UAW used "pattern bargaining" in dealing with Detroit's Big Three. Once a contract was resolved with one automaker, the other two would generally accept the main provisions. Especially on wages and work rules and other matters affecting active workers, the concessions we had achieved with Chrysler became not only the floor but also the ceiling for most of what we could accomplish with GM.

Retiree medical benefits, paid through the VEBA, were a different story. In his crusade to cut GM's debt, Harry decided we should persuade the UAW to convert its entire $20 billion claim into GM stock — by which he meant not relatively safe and interest-bearing preferred stock, but mostly common shares. His view was that this would fully align the retirees (and the workers as future retirees) with the health of the company and help create a better partnership between management and labor than had existed in the past. It would also result in a far better balance sheet for GM, increasing the probability of success — a win-win proposition. (He was so excited about his idea that at one point he started explaining the difference between preferred and common stock to me!)

This would be a much more dramatic change than what had been negotiated with the Chrysler VEBA, where half the claim was converted to stock. Fritz, who was all for union concessions, thought the idea ludicrous and told Harry so — in essence, we were asking the union to bet its retirees' ability to pay their family doctor bills on the success of Shiny New GM. But Harry got Fritz and Ron Bloom to agree to give it a try.

Harry spent many hours pitching Lazard, the UAW's adviser, on the future value of the stock. Then, on May 19, the two sides faced off across the rectangular table in the Treasury's Griswald Library — Fritz and Ron Gettelfinger seated directly opposite each other; Ron Bloom down at one end, flanked by Harry and Sadiq; the UAW advisers at the other end. Despite his skepticism, Fritz delivered the proposal with seeming enthusiasm. In lieu of its $20 billion claim, the VEBA would own 15 percent of GM, plus $5 billion in preferred stock. In other words, three-quarters of the health-fund claim would be converted to common.

Gettelfinger barely said a word. He let the Lazard people respond. They rejected the offer, asking for a $10 billion note (similar to what we had agreed to with Chrysler) plus much more common equity. The gap was huge and the meeting had to end — Fritz and Gettelfinger were due at the White House for Obama's announcement of new national fuel-economy standards. But while Fritz hustled out of the room, Gettelfinger lingered until someone tapped him on the shoulder to remind him to get to the White House.

"The President can wait," he said through clenched teeth, obviously unhappy about all the UAW was being asked to do by an ostensibly friendly administration.

The deal he was being offered was worse than what the UAW and GM had discussed just a few months earlier, during the preparation of the viability plan and before Team Auto had set to work. Especially galling to Gettelfinger was that the UAW had been instrumental in helping Obama win key states, like Ohio and Indiana, that had large concentrations of union members and retirees. It chafed to hear Ron Bloom, on occasion, preface an offer with a pompous phrase like "I am empowered by President Obama to . . ." To Gettelfinger, Bloom was a Johnny-come-lately to the Obama effort, and yet here he was telling the UAW on the President's behalf what it must accept or do.

Ron, Harry, and Sadiq went down to the basement and crowded into Sadiq's cubicle to figure out the next step. The tension between our two alpha males was palpable. Harry felt that Ron was not sufficiently frugal with taxpayer dollars; Ron felt that Harry was utterly unrealistic about what the UAW could possibly accept. Finally, they agreed to propose the same 15 percent of Shiny New GM and $5 billion of preferred, but also to throw in a note for $2.5 billion.

The negotiation resumed late that night with a smaller group at the Washington office of our law firm, Cadwalader. Periodically, one of the principals would emerge to confer with aides before diving back in. Sadiq, who was set up near the conference room, crunched new scenarios on his laptop whenever Harry asked. Bloom found Harry's approach amusing; Harry would parse Sadiq's numbers as if they were the Dead Sea scrolls. To Ron, no analysis could definitively say what was fair or unfair; it came down to where a deal could be negotiated and whether it felt satisfactory. Notwithstanding their different methodologies, Ron and Harry gradually sweetened our offer. Gettelfinger reduced his demands, but hated the idea of a predominantly common-stock deal. At the start of the talks, Gettelfinger's hope had been to get as much cash as possible for the union's health trust — he needed the certainty of payments from GM or the government to keep paying out billions in health care benefits to his more than 330,000 GM retirees and surviving spouses in the U.S. He had no wish to own stock in GM. If the UAW had to accept an equity stake to get the deal done, he wanted it to be temporary, with the government agreeing to buy back the shares soon. But that wasn't going to happen. Bloom and GM dug in their heels.

Harry tried to position himself in the role of truth teller to both GM and the UAW. He called out Fritz on a profit-sharing formula that GM had rigged, Harry felt, to limit payouts to UAW members. He also told GM to quit exaggerating the compensation gap between UAW workers and those at Toyota, Honda, and Nissan plants. Meanwhile, he chastised the union for its notorious Viagra payments and the Jobs Bank, telling Gettelfinger, "You guys make yourselves look bad with that stuff."

Gettelfinger would have none of Harry. At one point, when Harry mentioned that his mother had worked in textile mills, Gettelfinger interrupted and snapped, "Harry, I don't want to hear your stories about factories." When Harry held forth on how the auto industry was broken and needed to be fixed, Gettelfinger asked sarcastically, "Excuse me, what is your name again?"

Later, he stopped Harry to ask, "I know you are an expert on autos, but have you ever met my retirees?" Harry took the needling in stride and kept pushing a predominantly common stock settlement.

By the time the meeting broke up, around 3 A.M., Ron and Harry had upped the bid to 17.5 percent of common, $6.5 billion worth of preferred, and a $2.5 billion zero-coupon note. Gettelfinger rejected that too.

Harry was upset as they left, but Bloom was sanguine: "I've seen him do this," he told Harry. "I'll call him tomorrow and he'll agree." The next morning, Bloom called Gettelfinger and threw in some warrants, or rights to buy GM stock later at a very high fixed price. The warrants still didn't provide the cash Gettelfinger wanted, but at least they guaranteed the UAW an additional share of the upside if GM turned out to be more valuable than anyone expected.

Gettelfinger's adviser from Lazard, Andrew Yearley, told him and his aides, "This is the last offer. It is decision time." Gettelfinger announced that he needed to think. He left the hotel to walk the streets on a delightful spring morning, the temperature still in the sixties and the humidity blissfully low.

There was no easy option. Gettelfinger could reject the offer, publicly calling out Obama for forcing large, unfair benefit cuts on older, retired Americans. But that would be the UAW putting a gun to the head of the administration and GM in a time of economic crisis and might cause a political backlash. Yet if he accepted the deal, his retired members would feel the cutbacks. Gettelfinger had promised many of those same retirees in 2005 and 2007 — the years of previous GM contract talks — that they would not lose benefits or see their copays rise. Now he'd have to stand in front of them and deliver the bad news. One of his aides confided to Yearley that Gettelfinger "always takes these decisions very personally."

After about two hours of walking, Gettelfinger called Bloom and told him the UAW would accept the deal. He wasn't happy about it and ended the call by swearing at Bloom. Later he told his aides, "Everyone is sacrificing here. I think we can sleep at night knowing we did the best we could for our constituents."

Throughout all this, I had been holding my breath. No one outside Team Auto — not the UAW, not the company, not the press — seemed to realize that the balance of power was vastly different than it had been in the case of Chrysler. In taking on the UAW's Chrysler agreement, we were wielding a stick: President Obama had gone on national television and said that without a shared sacrifice by all stakeholders, the government would provide no further funding to Chrysler, leading to certain liquidation for the automakers and massive job losses for the UAW.

But with GM, Obama clearly wanted the company saved. His public statements, like "We cannot, and must not, and we will not let our auto industry simply vanish," and "I'm absolutely confident that GM can rise again," left us with no doubt that fixing GM was our mission.

Suppose Gettelfinger had simply refused any or all of our demands? We could still force GM into bankruptcy, which would void the UAW contract and, in theory, free GM to start over, either with the UAW or by hiring replacement workers. But I had meant what I'd said to the Chrysler banks when they'd whined about the amount of equity going to the retiree health trust: to make cars, we need workers. We did not believe that hiring non-union laborers to replace skilled UAW members was practical. The assembly of cars by GM involved hundreds of individual teams of five to six people executing highly specific tasks in forty-five- to fifty-second intervals. Nor did we believe that Barack Obama would be willing to discharge the autoworkers the way Ronald Reagan had fired the air traffic controllers in 1981. The idea that a Democratic administration would engage in union-busting was unimaginable.

So even in bankruptcy, we'd have been right back at the table with Gettelfinger — only then GM would be hemorrhaging cash and consumers would likely be holding off on buying GM cars until they saw the outcome of the standoff. It would have been a disaster.

I kept wondering why Gettelfinger didn't call our bluff. We had no backup plan, no notion of what we would do in that event. And we hadn't had much time to think about it. Fortunately, though he bargained hard on many issues, he stayed at the table and never threatened to blow up the whole deal. Although he kept his own counsel, his advisers speculated that he understood that the companies had to be fixed, and that as long as other stakeholders were sacrificing, he would go along. It's equally possible that he didn't realize how much leverage he had.

The deal gave GM substantially more financial flexibility than Chrysler had, and far and away the healthiest balance sheet among the Detroit Three. Instead of having to pay interest on a $10 billion note, as the VEBA had initially proposed, the company would be on the hook only for 9-percent-a-year dividends on the preferred — payments it could skip in a pinch. Though I couldn't prove it, I believed Harry's efforts had paid off. If he hadn't applied his powers of persuasion to selling the future value of GM shares, we probably would have been forced to give the VEBA a much larger percentage of the company.

Next it was Fritz who wanted to push the UAW harder. For years he'd been itching to revamp the UAW pension plan — its members were among the dwindling minority of American workers who still enjoyed traditional defined-benefit pensions, in which benefits are guaranteed no matter what they cost the employer. GM's pension expenses, much like its health care costs, had been rising for years, with cycle after cycle of union negotiations driving costs ever higher. ("Any little change," Fritz told me, "was like writing a $5 billion check to future retirees.") The market meltdown had compounded the funding challenge.

Fritz knew he couldn't ask for outright pension cuts; he wanted to freeze pensions as they were and have further benefits come in a plan similar to an IRA. Those changes alone would be worth billions to GM. But we had declined to address union pensions in the Chrysler negotiations, and when Fritz broached the subject to Gettelfinger late in the GM negotiations, the UAW chief turned him down flat: "We aren't going to sit in this room if pensions are on your list."

"OK, we'll get to that another time," said Fritz, who had been through countless difficult talks with the UAW leader.

When they heard about this, Ron and Harry discussed calling the UAW back to the bargaining table. But they concluded that attacking the union's sacred cow after virtually every other issue had been resolved could jeopardize the whole agreement. Failing to make meaningful changes in the pension plan became Harry's biggest regret. He felt it especially keenly in an airport bookstore two weeks later, when he noticed Roger Lowenstein's *While America Aged: How Pension Debts Ruined General Motors, Stopped the NYC Subways, Bankrupted San Diego, and Loom as the Next Financial Crisis.*

I felt about the GM bondholders the same way I'd felt about Jimmy Lee at Chrysler: they had made a poor loan and deserved to be treated accordingly. In a conventional bankruptcy, the GM bondholders, who were junior creditors, would get little or nothing. Nevertheless, the firms representing them were fighters. They launched a populist PR campaign, pointing out that among the bondholders were not only workers' pension funds but also people of limited means. "GM Bondholders

Are People Like You and Me" read the headline of a *Wall Street Journal* op-ed, ostensibly written by a retired blue-collar worker. There was truth to this: GM had marketed some of its bonds to individuals, selling them in face amounts as low as $25. Thus it had thousands and thousands of small bondholders. Unfortunately, there was neither logic nor a mechanism for treating them differently from the institutional investors, which held some 80 percent of the debt.

It didn't take Harry and Matt long to discover that we were in a difficult negotiating spot. Back in April, in order not to be accused of foot-dragging on GM's bond exchange plan, we had offered to give bondholders a 10 percent stake in GM in exchange for 90 percent of the bonds. But that was before we decided to invest our new money as equity, which had the effect of making a 10 percent stake hugely more valuable because the new GM would not be up to its axles in debt.

Why should the bondholders get this windfall? I wanted to adjust the percentage so the dollar value of our offer stayed the same. But Harry and Matt resisted the idea.

"They're fixed on the 10 percent," said Harry.

"Ridiculous!" I said. "Ten percent is worth at least twice as much now as it was before. We need to dial it back to less than 5 percent."

"They're not going to buy it. They'll think they're getting less value, not just a smaller percentage."

"But this isn't Joe Six-Pack you're talking to," I protested. "They're very sophisticated advisers. I think they'll understand." To my surprise, Harry and Matt disagreed.

We didn't have to reach a deal with the bondholders, I pointed out. Arguably, they didn't deserve anything, and we could fight it out in bankruptcy court. This prospect made Matt very unhappy. A knockdown dragout fight with the bondholders would mean delays and uncertainty, and possibly billions of dollars more to hold GM together if the bankruptcy process stalled. On the other hand, Matt pointed out, by making a deal with bondholders representing at least 51 percent of the debt, we would eliminate a major risk of delay in bankruptcy court.

Reluctantly, I saw the logic of their argument and told them to proceed. Naturally the bondholders still wanted to negotiate right down to the wire; in the end Harry became convinced that even 10 percent of the equity would not get us an agreement and pushed me to sweeten the pot with some warrants. Even more reluctantly, I agreed to that too. We valued the package at about 12 to 15 cents on the dollar, more than what they deserved (zero) but considerably less than the 33 cents that Corker and Bush had been prepared to let them have.

The capital structure of Shiny New GM was finally taking shape. It was radically different from what we'd imagined, as though we'd set out to build an Impala and ended up with a Volt. Rather than a small stake, the Treasury would own 60.8 percent, and the remaining 39.2 percent would be split among the VEBA (17.5), the bondholders (10), and Canada (11.7).

But while the percentages took shape, the overall capital need remained a moving target. All through May, Team Auto struggled to nail down how much we'd have to inject into GM at its bankruptcy filing. The company's list of needs was vast, and every few days new items would pop up, further evidence of its lack of a real handle on its finances.

The uncertainty was unnerving for our Canadian allies. They had been standup partners from the start. They'd matched the U.S. government's total $12 billion Chrysler investment with $3 billion of their own, a sum roughly proportional to the percentage of Chrysler production across the border. And while GM mattered less to the Canadians — it had fewer employees there — they were committed to making a comparable investment in this restructuring too, which was where the headaches began.

On May 12, the first time we met with the Canadians about GM, Ron and Sadiq told their emissary, Paul Boothe, that the GM investment would total $50 billion (counting the $15.4 billion already put in and $34.6 billion of new money to come), and warned that the figure could grow. Then Ron talked with Boothe about how much Canada would contribute. They agreed on $8 billion to $10 billion. It would be the single biggest investment the Canadian government had ever made in a business.

In exchange, the Canadians wanted GM to sign a "vitality agreement," a guarantee that the new GM wouldn't turn around and cut its Canadian production and workforce. Ironically, we had inserted just such a provision into Chrysler's agreement with Fiat, for fear that Fiat would cut too many American jobs. Boothe made it clear that a vitality agreement was a political necessity for the prime minister. Harry thought signing such an agreement was bad economics and bad for the business. If we were going to truly let GM operate as a private company, we shouldn't be tying its hands, he argued.

In addition, the UAW had made concessions in its negotiations with GM to allow a small car that was to be built in Korea to be built economically in the United States instead. This was a source of excitement for Rahm Emanuel, who saw the evident political advantage in such a development. (When finally announced, the new plan generated far less public notice than we had hoped. Critics suggested that we had pressured GM to shift production to the States.)

The decision on the small car meant that the percentage of GM's cars headed for sale in the U.S. that also got assembled in the U.S. was expected to rise to 70 percent from the current 66 percent. Nonetheless, the question became part of another emotional meeting in Larry's office. As had been the case with Chrysler, Ron and Harry took opposite sides. To Ron, what was the point of saving GM if we weren't going to safeguard American jobs? While I sympathized with Harry's view, this ultimately became a practical decision: if the Canadians weren't going to invest without a vitality commitment, then obviously we needed to give them one. And in my mind, giving them one and not taking one for ourselves failed the *Washington Post* test.

To the Canadians' dismay, though, the all-in number kept going up. Boothe, an affable, gray-haired, goateed economist whose title was senior associate deputy minister of industry, would come to Washington only to have to fly back to Ottawa to tell his bosses the new number and get clearance. A week later, the number rose to $54 billion. Then, on May 27, it reached $59 billion, with Canada now on the hook for nearly its full $10 billion.

Harry was partly responsible, unbeknownst to the Canadians. He felt that GM's inadequate financial controls posed large risks for the business and heavily discounted all of the cash projections he received from management. He was convinced that GM needed a margin of safety to offset these poor controls. If we paid in too much, he figured, as 60.8 percent owners American taxpayers would get back most of any excess and the Canadians would get their share (although the 27.5 percent "leakage" to other shareholders annoyed him no end).

Our Canadian partners grew grumpy as the funding requirement increased. Both the commonwealth government in Ottawa and the provincial government of Ontario dispatched teams to monitor the bankruptcy preparations. Team Auto didn't have enough staff to tend to them all. One evening during the hectic final week, our young colleagues David and Sadiq found themselves in a conference room at Weil, Gotshal & Manges, Treasury's legal adviser, explaining to a dozen Canadian officials why we'd just added $5 billion to the deal.

The Canadians were also concerned about GM's management. Sergio had impressed Boothe much more than had Fritz, and the emissary had told colleagues, "These GM guys don't have the same sense of fear that Chrysler does. I would feel better if GM had a Sergio." Fritz was moving too slowly, in Boothe's mind, and seemed like just another GM guy rather than the fresh blood the company needed.

As the bankruptcy filing neared, Boothe expressed these concerns to Feldman and Markowitz. "We know you are driving the bus here, but we are uncomfortable with him," he said and added, "We don't have anyone else who could do it, but we don't think it is him."

My month was spent juggling pieces of everything. Senators and representatives peppered me with calls, lobbying to keep open GM facilities in their states or districts. Often these calls sounded pro forma, as if the legislator were checking a series of boxes so he or she could attest that everything had been tried. Other calls were aggressive, occasionally hostile. I knew better than to antagonize congressmen so I always listened politely. Sometimes the monologue droned on so long that I could get a number of e-mails answered.

I was also obliged to take courtesy meetings with ambassadors from countries where GM operated, as well as meetings for the sake of bureaucratic ritual, such as the procedure for finalizing TARP investments. Still other meetings were favors to people important to the administration, like my session with a group from Utah who had no money but a great idea to manufacture an electric Hummer. If nothing else, such visits were a constant reminder of the scope of the auto crisis. One day, an old friend who had become CEO of Avis Budget came by and explained how the collapse of the auto finance market threatened his company's ability to pay for the cars it needed for its business.

GMAC hung over me as a huge piece of unfinished business that could torpedo everything else we were accomplishing. I spent days with Brian Stern and Rob Fraser figuring out how to structure and value the capital infusion that GMAC was going to need. Even more frustrating was continuing to do battle with the FDIC. As a way to keep the pressure on, we had proposed that GMAC take on the Chrysler financing business for only two weeks, seemingly plenty of time to tie up loose ends with the FDIC.

But the FDIC kept retrading and piling on new asks. Sheila Bair's designated negotiator was Chris Spoth, the rather meek career FDIC official whom we had previously encountered. He seemed to have no authority whatsoever. More than once, we would come to an understanding on a point that we would confirm by e-mail, only to receive an e-mail back the next morning denying that an understanding had been reached. At another juncture, the FDIC asked for a letter saying that Treasury would stand behind GMAC no matter what, and then kept changing the language. Tim thought the new language would make the FDIC look weak and tried, unsuccessfully, to reach Bair. "I'll write whatever you guys want, but I really think this is counter to your objective," he told Spoth. Of course Spoth needed to check with Bair. "You're right, let's go back to the other language," he responded a few minutes later. (Bair would duck even Tim when she wanted to; once her office said she was on a plane when in fact she wasn't.) Bair also wanted a letter from Tim thanking her for assisting our effort; we took to calling this the "great American letter."

Most frustrating was that after agreeing to provide the help we were seeking, the FDIC came back and increased the amount of capital that it wanted GMAC's bank (Ally) to maintain to far beyond that required of any other bank. The excessive capital requirement would have many negative repercussions. It would reduce GMAC's liquidity at the holding company and therefore its financial flexibility. Perhaps more importantly, it lowered the bank's lending capacity, the opposite of what we were trying to achieve. And it reduced GMAC's profitability and therefore the value of the $13.1 billion of new TARP money that we were preparing to invest. So the FDIC's unreasonable requirement would cost U.S. taxpayers significant money. Whose side was the FDIC on, I wondered. We whittled back the duration of the higher capital requirement a bit but ultimately had to swallow and agree. We had no alternative.

The political pressure on Team Auto steadily increased. The impacts of Chrysler's restructuring were beginning to be noticed and objected to. For instance, Chrysler had decided to leave behind workers' compensation claims in its Old Carco, which effectively left the state of Michigan holding the bag for more than $100 million in obligations, prompting angry calls from the governor. Another commotion was triggered by a botched announcement by Chrysler about closing eight U.S. plants: it mistakenly gave the impression that an engine factory was being shut in order to move production to Mexico.

The politics around GM, with its greater size and complexity, not to mention its iconic status, promised to be even more intense. Our long to-do list was full of pitfalls. One day Fritz called me to propose moving GM headquarters from the Renaissance Center to GM's Tech Center in suburban Warren, where we had driven the Volt back in March. The move would cut costs, he said, as well as symbolize the leadership's determination to become more down-to-earth and hands-on. I thought the idea was great, just the kind of action I was hoping to see from Fritz. But when I described it to Deese, he went nuts. "Are you out of your mind?" he said. "Think what it would do to Detroit!"

Though small in financial implications for the company — the headquarters was worth perhaps $165 million, compared to the $626 million that GM had paid for it just a year earlier — GM's departure would be a major blow to Detroit. In a one-year period, the once proud city that was already suffering with one of the worst unemployment rates in the country, and among the worst murder rates, would see two of its biggest employers go bankrupt, its flamboyant ex-mayor Kwame Kilpatrick convicted of perjury, and its NFL franchise, the Detroit Lions, become the first in football history to go 0–16.

Deese had some people analyze what a mostly vacant RenCen would mean to Detroit real estate. The estimate: a double-digit hit on already deflated real estate prices. Fritz proposed donating the RenCen to the city — though who would actually use it was unknown.

Leaving the RenCen made strategic sense, however, and was supported by Harry and David. The Tech Center had lots of empty space and much larger floors, so more departments and people could sit near each other, improving teamwork and communication in a culture that desperately needed more of both.

The debate, not surprisingly, soon moved beyond Team Auto. Gene Sperling was one of many to fight the move. "It's over for Detroit if you do this," he yelled in a meeting at Treasury. "Don't do this to Dave Bing"—the city's new mayor, a former NBA star and successful auto-supplier entrepreneur. "He's a good man trying to do a good thing." The city relied on GM for $20 million a year in tax revenue, Gene pointed out, and the blowback would be fierce. Deese checked with Larry, who in turn spoke to Rahm, and word came down that the move would be a bridge too far. Fortunately, this unique intervention into a specific GM matter was never leaked to the press, saving us from having to explain how it comported with our policy of letting GM and Chrysler manage their own affairs.

We'd so far been able to avoid the scalding controversy over executive compensation, but no more. The issue found us as we worked through a $7.9 billion assortment of GM obligations called "other pension and employment benefits." Lumped under this innocuous-sounding label was a dizzying hodgepodge of programs, including pension plans for thirteen "splinter" unions, most of which no longer had any active workers at GM. This last item alone was costing GM more than $300 million a year.

But also on the list were pension obligations for senior executives —including $22.1 million owed to Rick Wagoner. Like many big companies, GM provided a so-called supplemental pension for highly paid executives. While GM's basic pension plan for all employees was backed by nearly $100 billion of investments, this "SERP" was not backed by anything except the company's promise to pay. Of course no one—not the company, not the executives, not the high-level retirees—ever imagined that GM could go bankrupt, because in bankruptcy these retirees had the same lowly status as bondholders. In other words, retired GM executives could see this hefty benefit wiped out. We knew we could try to prevent that by making the same argument we'd used to justify funding the VEBA: just as you need workers to make cars, you need executives to run the company, and wiping out the pensions of retired executives would demoralize active ones. But the atmosphere around executive compensation was way too charged for us to take that position.

This was an issue above my pay grade, so I put it on the agenda for one of our late-afternoon updates with Larry. He pounced on it as if the future of the Obama administration rested on our response. Large reductions would be required, he said; that much was clear. To maintain the fiction that such decisions were being made by GM and not by us, Larry set forth four principles for GM to follow in cutting the $7.9 billion obligation. Perhaps we shouldn't have been surprised when GM came back with a proposal that was blatantly tilted in favor of the executives at the expense of the splinter unions. It took many days and several rounds of discussions to arrive at changes that fit within Larry's dictates. The executive pensions would be cut by two-thirds.

But this meant that Rick Wagoner was owed $7.1 million. Larry's first instinct was that Rick should get little or nothing, given that GM had gone broke on his watch. "Do you know what a senator gets for his pension?" he asked me, implying that no public servant would understand why Rick should get millions. I felt bad for Rick; he certainly had failings as a CEO, but he had put his heart into the job and believed in GM so strongly that he had never cashed out any of his stock. I argued that Wagoner should be treated no better or worse than the other retired executives. In the end, Larry agreed.

Larry generally kept Rahm and the President informed of potential flashpoints in Team Auto's work, but he blocked out time during the President's Daily Brief on Friday, May 29, for a last-minute review. Three days hence, on June 1, the President would announce that the federal government was putting General Motors into Chapter 11. Larry didn't want to take the chance there'd be a political surprise.

Unlike the first time Larry had dragged me to the Oval Office, I arrived at the White House knowing we were scheduled to meet with the President. I also had been told to expect cameras—NBC was on the premises shooting a special called *A Day in the Life of Obama's White House.* As I approached the West Wing entrance, I could see a video crew taping the arrivals. Making my way to Larry's office, I encountered camera crew after camera crew crowding the tight confines of the West Wing. (I later learned that thirty-two cameras were prowling the White House that day.)

We headed downstairs to the Oval, where we stood waiting by Katie Johnson's desk. Promptly at 10 A.M., the door opened, Hillary Clinton emerged, and it was our turn. With NBC in tow, we took our seats on the couches and chairs facing the President. The briefing began with pleasantries and then the President asked Larry to open the discussion without any "market sensitive" information. Larry did his best under the awkward circumstances until, mercifully, Rahm evicted the cameras and we got to work.

We reviewed for the President the progress on the restructuring: the improved cost structure, the reduction in labor costs, the additional $30.1 billion that we proposed to inject. He was familiar with all these items, and I moved through them briskly, saving the most worrisome for last.

While a majority of GM's bondholders had accepted our final proposal, we expected dissidents to fight us in court, just as the Chrysler lenders had done. In this case, there was a chance they would renew their campaign portraying GM and the administration as callous toward small investors.

Next we discussed the UAW's latest public stance. Rather than use the bankruptcy to focus on job cuts (polls showed many Americans thought UAW workers were overpaid), the union was highlighting the fact that GM, like many manufacturers, had been gradually moving production out of the United States to countries with lower labor costs. The union was complaining that the restructuring would transfer more production to Mexico and Asia.

This was technically true, we told President Obama. However, the production was coming from Canada, not the United States, and the move had been set before the restructuring agreements. We explained the vitality commitments and other arrangements now in place to protect jobs in both countries henceforth.

Larry and Diana outlined the "USG as Shareholder" policy, which would be unveiled in fact sheets accompanying the President's speech. We also had an unspoken understanding that, following an initial public offering by Shiny New GM, the government would sell at least 5 percent of its shares each year and be completely divested within eight years. This had been heavily litigated between Team Auto and Larry. Harry and I hated the idea of committing to stock sales that might not be financially optimal, but Larry had been adamant, and understandably so. The President seemed pleased.

Finally, we came to executive compensation. I briefly sketched the background, trying to avoid the mind-numbing complexity of splinter unions and SERPs to get to the item that we wanted to be sure President Obama signed off on: Rick Wagoner's pension. I explained the arrangement that would pay him $7.3 million over five years, and I could see the President's jaw muscles tighten. Suddenly I felt that I was indeed in the presence of a community organizer; the President plainly had difficulty with the notion of writing a check that was about one hundred times the annual income of a GM worker to the CEO who had brought the company down. Obama grimaced and reluctantly acquiesced. I found it striking that the President of the United States had spent more time on an issue of executive pay than on the question of whether to dismiss a major CEO in the first place.

The cloudy, humid day ended with a scramble. GM, which had been trying to sell Hummer for months, had found a buyer — a Chinese company that none of us had heard of. Deese and I were both a bit unnerved by this, as some purchases of U.S. businesses by companies with headquarters in places like the Middle East and China had become controversial. We immediately decided to take the matter to Tim and Larry, and gathered in Larry's office late that afternoon. His first instinct was to worry. Down at the other end of the table, Tim suddenly interjected, "Guys, if this were a British company, would we be having this conversation?"

"No," we replied unanimously.

"Okay, then. End of conversation."

With that, we scattered for our weekend of work. Deese, who lived in Washington, stayed at his small desk at the White House working on fact sheets and talking points and revisions for the President's speech. Ron drove home to Pittsburgh to spend Saturday and Sunday in marathon calls with German officials, patiently reiterating our position that no more U.S. taxpayer dollars would flow into Opel. Harry, Matt, David, Brian, and Sadiq camped in New York at the law offices of Weil Gotshal, GM's bankruptcy adviser. Harry jetted off on the last flight to Boston on Friday night to spend a few hours at his Harvard reunion before returning on the first flight to New York on Saturday morning. "He just wants to bask in the glory of his big assignment," grumbled a banker who had felt Harry's lash. I hunkered down at my house north of New York City for two days of nonstop e-mails, phone calls, and faxes.

As we prepared, one small concern was that Tim Geithner was scheduled to be in China on the day of the President's address. To me, this seemed like no big deal — it wasn't as if he were off playing golf — but the communications folks fretted about it. On Saturday afternoon, my cell phone rang. I heard static and then official-sounding voices. Finally, one asked me to hold for Secretary Geithner. I realized that Tim was calling from his plane on his way to Beijing.

"Is everything okay?" he asked.

"Fine," I replied. The conversation ended almost as soon as it began. I was puzzled until a day or so later, when I saw in a press report that an "administration official" had said that Tim was in regular contact with the Auto Task Force during his trip. Now I understood. (I would later learn that the ever-attentive press department also had nixed a Ping-Pong match that Tim had been scheduled to play on Monday, the day that the President would be speaking.)

For Matt, these hours were critical, as he supervised what would be a devilishly convoluted bankruptcy filing. The documents described in intricate detail the two GMs that would be created out of the 290 GM legal entities that existed.

Left behind as the old GM — shares of which would continue to be traded publicly and whose name would be changed to Motors Liquidation Company to avoid confusing investors — was a company that would be massive in its own right. For example, MLC would own 127 properties, almost all in Michigan and Indiana, with more than forty-eight million square feet of floor space, nearly the size of eight Pentagons. Many of these had been out of service for years, legacies of the era when GM commanded half of the American car industry. We would also leave behind 5,000 assembly-line robots, 200 miles of conveyor belts, even a small golf course. And we were leaving behind liabilities:

$27 billion of unsecured debt, hundreds of millions of dollars of environmental liabilities, splinter unions' retiree benefits, and unwanted supplier contracts. Even without any active operations, Motors Liquidation would stay in business until all of the assets had been disposed of and all of the claims against it resolved, a process that Matt believed could take two to four years.

Shorn of these extraneous assets, Shiny New GM would emerge to operate the 121 properties that would remain in the U.S. and would employ more than 200,000 workers around the world. The company would be dramatically reconfigured, with $65 billion of liabilities stripped from its balance sheet and its annual structural costs in North America reduced by $8 billion.

While I would later have a tinge of regret at not having achieved greater concessions from the stakeholders, we had far exceeded the requirements that Bob Corker and the Bush administration had established as part of the initial bailout. Instead of the two-thirds reduction in unsecured debt mandated by the Bush loan agreements, we eliminated all of these obligations. Instead of equitizing half of the GM VEBA, we converted 87.5 percent to stock. And so on. None of this would have been possible without President Obama's determination to do the right thing. While both Tim and Larry had assured me of this in the course of our early discussions, I had gone into my assignment nervous that political pressures would ultimately compromise the outcome. I shouldn't have been. When President Obama told us on March 26 to be tough and commercial, he meant it. Without his standing firm, we surely would have ended up with a far worse result.

A major concern for us now was making sure GM would not have to seek court protection for any of its subsidiaries around the globe. Our tight timeline for getting through a U.S. bankruptcy was challenging enough; engaging other countries' bankruptcy procedures was sure to slow down, or perhaps doom, our whole effort. We spent hours reviewing the debt of subsidiaries in places like Russia, Colombia, and Thailand to determine whether funding their needs would violate the *Washington Post* test. Meanwhile, Ron focused on reassuring the Canadians; Matt and Harry on reviewing the legal strategy and documents to guard against last-minute snafus; David on an eleventh-hour brouhaha with a group of hedge funds that had bought bonds issued by GM Nova Scotia; Sadiq on providing numbers and analysis to everyone. Harry's final work frenzy was so intense that when Feldman gathered the team late in the day to make sure all the preparations were on track, Harry dialed into the meeting from the conference room next door — he didn't want to waste the seconds it would take to walk ten feet and exchange pleasantries as the meeting began.

The closing crunch was particularly unnerving for supporting players who hadn't been through the Chrysler bankruptcy. Just as GM was putting the final touches on its bankruptcy petition, a senior attorney at the Treasury Department, Laurie Schaffer, objected to the whole idea of our forming Shiny New GM. She argued that this would make the new GM an arm — an "instrumentality" — of the federal government, which would mean that the government would be responsible for any GM liability, including any lawsuit brought against it. Matt had reviewed our approach repeatedly with Treasury officials during the month of preparations, and everyone was comfortable that it did not present the "instrumentality" risk. Everyone except Laurie Schaffer, who now suggested that we have the VEBA form the new company. It was a ridiculous idea. Matt tried, not very patiently, to convince her otherwise. When that failed, he called Tim's deputy, Neal Wolin, and got her overruled.

Sunday afternoon, Ron, Harry, and I returned to Washington, where we rejoined Deese and again gathered that evening in the Oval Office to stand by as President Obama made another set of outreach calls to politicians. Just two months had passed since the first session of calls we had witnessed, when Obama had paused to watch Tiger Woods on TV. By now I had spent more time in the Oval Office than do many officials of far higher rank in the course of an entire administration. I never imagined a presidential meeting could feel so routine. Exhaustion was part of it — everyone on Team Auto felt a little numb after months of doing battle with some of America's biggest economic dragons.

The next morning, Ron and I took our appointed places as potted plants on the steps in the Grand Foyer of the White House as President Obama announced the reorganization of General Motors. I couldn't see beyond the lights, but I knew that across the large room, somewhere behind the banks of cameras and reporters, was the rest of the team.

Witnessing the President talk about our work was one of the few perks we could offer our extraordinarily talented and dedicated colleagues.

"Our goal," President Obama was saying, "is to get GM back on its feet, take a hands-off approach, and get out quickly." I relished hearing him deliver a few sentences I had helped craft: "Many experts said that a quick, surgical bankruptcy was impossible. They were wrong. Others predicted that Chrysler's decision to enter bankruptcy would lead to an immediate collapse in consumer confidence that would send car sales over a cliff. They were wrong, as well."

Unbeknownst to me, a small drama was unfolding downstairs. Like everyone on our team in New York, David Markowitz had gotten almost no sleep during the final frenzy of preparation. They'd all come to the White House for this occasion, but as he walked to the Grand Foyer, David felt dizzy and sick. Sadiq tried to steady him, but David could go no further. Hearing of David's dizziness, several White House aides appeared out of their warrens to offer chocolates, presumably to cure a sugar low. David and Sadiq turned back, and someone pointed them to the White House infirmary — two small offices used by the President's physicians. A doctor checked David over, fed him fluids, and asked him to sit and rest. Sadiq was disappointed on David's behalf but didn't want to miss the President's statement, so he hurried back upstairs.

Twenty minutes later, sitting groggily in his trousers and undershirt, David heard a commotion at the door. In came President Obama, who had just finished his speech and was in search of a couple of Tylenols. Our young Team Auto colleague found himself shaking hands with the man on whose behalf he had been working around the clock for three months.

12

DEALER NATION

As I sat bleary-eyed in my Washington condo on the morning of June 1, the newspaper headlines were jarring reminders that we were playing for historic stakes. "G.M. Heads to Bankruptcy Protection as Government Steps In: Obama Makes a Bet That the Carmaker Can Recover," proclaimed the *New York Times* in a banner spanning the top of the front page. Below was an analysis — a "Q-hed," in *Times* parlance — that evoked the consequences of the moment: "After Many Stumbles, the Fall of an American Giant."

Throughout the spring, I had been surprised by the relative quiet that greeted Team Auto's surgery, but suddenly we seemed to have struck a nationwide nerve. GM's announcement that seventeen factories and parts centers would be shuttered by the end of 2011 drew a powerful reaction from Barney Frank, the volatile Massachusetts Democrat who chaired the House Financial Services Committee. GM did not build cars in his state, and the only thing that Frank's district was slated to lose was a parts depot near Boston employing a grand total of about eighty workers. But that didn't stop Frank from blasting a GM lobbyist in a profanity-laced phone call. Fritz Henderson was so unnerved by the congressman's reaction that he visited Frank while in Washington a couple of days later, and took a thrashing in person. By the end of that meeting, he had agreed to delay the closing by fourteen months. I was dismayed; we had consistently tried to avoid politicizing the process by insisting that GM alone should decide which facilities it would keep or close.

"How did that happen?" I asked Fritz when I tracked him down.

"I didn't think I had much of a choice when I had the chairman of the House Financial Services Committee yelling at me," he replied.

The *Wall Street Journal* quickly weighed in with an editorial, "Barney Frank, Car Czar," darkly predicting that this would be only the beginning of congressional interference. I feared the editorial might be right. But happily, although we fielded many calls from other elected officials, keeping the Massachusetts depot open was the only change that GM was forced to make to its facility-closing plan.

I was not surprised by reactions such as Barney Frank's to the fate of individual facilities. Although he was way out of bounds to browbeat Fritz over eighty jobs, a large employer like an auto plant can be the lifeblood of a community, as Rahm Emanuel had recognized back in March when he reeled off the names of the legislators in whose districts the major Chrysler plants were located. I was more surprised at the lack of reaction to the overall magnitude of the job cuts. At the end of 2008, GM employed 90,650 people in the U.S. In the final restructuring plan, that number was projected to be slashed to approximately 63,000. It was no better for Chrysler: from 36,500 down to 30,250.

To be sure, we had ended up including vitality commitments — promises to maintain U.S. production as part of our investments in both automakers. Even so, the job cuts were draconian, especially in an industry where, as recently as late 2008, laid-off workers received nearly full pay. Now there would be wholesale eliminations without any obligatory payments whatsoever. So where were the protests? Why weren't autoworkers marching in the streets? Perhaps the reason for the relative calm was that the job cuts weren't instantaneous but would be phased in over a number of years. Perhaps it was that the companies were offering buyouts to workers to encourage voluntary departures. Perhaps many of those affected had been stunned into apathy by the economic disasters their communities had already suffered. In the end, I concluded that the most likely explanation was the magnitude of the auto crisis. Workers and those who sympathized with them understood that only through amputation could these companies be saved.

Car dealers were another story. Even though auto companies don't pay their dealers anything directly, every industry expert agreed that having fewer, more productive dealers results in higher total sales and lower marketing expenses for an automaker than having large numbers of small, inefficient ones. This was fine in theory, until the letters went out identifying specific stores to close. In mid-May, GM notified 1,124 dealers that their franchises would not be renewed. They were offered the chance to be wound down over an eighteen-month period. Scrappy, tough Chrysler waited until it was halfway through bankruptcy to send out terse letters to 789 dealers, instructing them to take down their Chrysler signs by June 9.

Senator Kay Bailey Hutchison, a Republican from Texas, was among the first politicians to react. She threatened to hold up a war-funding bill because of the dealer closings in her state. Many other legislators who had insisted that we keep our hands off the auto companies started attacking us for doing exactly that. Then the National Automobile Dealers Association—NADA—came out against us, denouncing the dealer-reduction programs in full-page ads. "Cutting dealers at this time would do absolutely nothing to make either GM or Chrysler more viable," read the text over the signature of the association's chairman, John McEleney. "The idea that dealer numbers should be rapidly and drastically reduced apparently comes from Wall Street advisers." I was mystified. Most NADA members would be keeping their franchises and would benefit from the elimination of the marginal stores—not to mention the fact that, absent our intervention, they all would have gone out of business.

The Senate Commerce Committee quickly summoned Henderson and Chrysler's sales and marketing chief, Jim Press, to testify on Capitol Hill. Sitting before the committee on June 3, they were castigated before they could say a word. Committee chairman John D. Rockefeller IV, a West Virginia Democrat, called the closings "a nationwide tragedy that a lot of us feel strongly about." Jim DeMint, a South Carolina Republican, said he was getting to know what "government-managed economies feel like."

We were deluged with calls from national, state, and local officials pleading for individual dealers. As tempting as it felt, it didn't strike me as a great idea for Team Auto to blow off these requests. Instead we painstakingly responded to each one, often by consulting GM or Chrysler for background on why a particular store was being closed. Invariably, we would conclude that the decision was appropriate and try to convey that gently to the aggrieved official. This sometimes took two or three tries, and we didn't always succeed. But we never asked either company to reverse a decision.

Meanwhile, GM started a dialogue with NADA aimed at winning its support. In early June, the trade association agreed to stand down after the automaker made relatively minor changes in the wind-down contracts. But when NADA officials tried to avoid publicly announcing this course reversal, GM — with typical passivity — was prepared to let them. We felt otherwise. After checking with me, David Markowitz, who was closest to the negotiation, insisted that NADA put out a press release saying that while it would not endorse the new agreement, "the revised document addresses the majority of dealer concerns."

But almost immediately, the statement mysteriously disappeared from the NADA website, which NADA attributed to "technical problems." The trade group resumed its carpet-bombing. On June 11, McEleney published an op-ed in *USA Today* proclaiming, "Dealers Aren't to Blame." NADA reminded me of the Newspaper Guild, another organization I'd seen try to protect underperformers at the expense of those who delivered.

With our last big announcement behind us, we decided to meet with the editorial boards of major newspapers and CNBC to defend the Obama administration's handling of Chrysler and GM. Notwithstanding our regular conversations with editorial writers, we'd been frustrated by the continued second-guessing of our actions. Had we tilted in favor of labor and against capital, particularly in the case of Chrysler? Had we overspent? Should the government have intervened at all, as opposed to leaving GM and Chrysler to the mercy of market forces? The questioning at our visits to the *Wall Street Journal* and the *New York Times* was predictable.

The *Washington Post* editorial page, under Fred Hiatt, was not the reflexively liberal voice that most would have assumed. It had opposed the notion of government bailouts. And now, over sandwiches in a windowless conference room at the *Post*'s headquarters, Chuck Lane, its lead writer on auto issues, took us on. Coincidentally, my former employer, the New York Times Company, had just asked news personnel at its *Boston Globe* subsidiary to take substantial wage cuts as part of reducing operating losses. Why, Lane asked in his thoughtful but feisty manner, shouldn't workers at GM be asked to take outright reductions in pay? I repeated my mantra about needing workers to make cars and the impracticality of replacing UAW members with a non-union labor force. And I noted that with new workers coming in at much lower pay, wages paid by the Detroit Three would soon reach those of the transplants. Lane, who got increasingly agitated, almost to the point of tears, was not satisfied, and understandably so. Even if the complex projections of future labor costs proved accurate, the UAW had sold out new hires — who would be paid far less than workers at the Japanese transplants — in order to protect the wages of existing UAW members.

We were determined to use GM's time in bankruptcy to jump-start changes in the company's culture — to my mind, the critical unfinished step in the overhaul. When the Treasury press department got a request from Micheline Maynard, a senior reporter who had written a well-regarded book called *The End of Detroit,* in connection with a long article she was planning on GM, I readily agreed to an interview.

The urgency of my concern about GM's culture jibed with her knowledge of the company's long-standing weaknesses, and the resulting front-page story declared: ". . . It will be up to the federal government, which will own a majority of General Motors when it emerges from bankruptcy, to tackle what is perhaps the most difficult challenge in Detroit: transforming GM's insular culture — at times as bureaucratic as the government's — to make the company more competitive. If the effort fails, the Treasury may never recoup the $50 billion it has provided GM."

What the story didn't mention was the fact, very much on my mind, that this was Team Auto's last chance to influence events. The administration was going to adhere to its explicit commitment that once GM emerged from bankruptcy, it would manage its own affairs, for better or worse. It wouldn't be our baby anymore.

Ed Whitacre, with his reputation for toughness and intolerance of bull, was an important symbol of what we were trying to achieve. Announcing his appointment as chairman on June 9, I had left nothing to chance. I asked the executive-search firm Spencer Stuart to run a background check to make sure there were no skeletons in his closet. I even had Haley research his political contributions. I was delighted to hear that Ed had served as campaign finance chair for Kay Bailey Hutchison. I was equally pleased to learn that he had contributed to the campaigns of other Republicans, such as John McCain, as well as a handful of Democrats, including Rahm Emanuel. While the White House had never tried to influence our management or board choices, I knew that Obama's critics would look for any way to impute partisan motives. (Indeed, I later learned that the *Wall Street Journal* ordered up a story on the "real" reason Ed was selected, but as there was no "real" reason, the story never ran.)

We believed, and had told the world, that GM's bankruptcy would take longer than Chrysler's — between sixty and ninety days — because of GM's vastly larger scale and global operations. But Harry and Matt decided to try to do better. In the fine print of the $33.3 billion of debtor-in-possession financing that we'd extended to the company, they set a deadline of July 10. At the end of that time — a scant forty days! — either the Treasury would have to extend its financing or GM would be forced to liquidate. This was the financial equivalent of putting a gun to the heads of the bankruptcy judge, GM's stakeholders, and of course Team Auto itself.

The success of the gamble depended in no small part on Chrysler. If it could clear the bankruptcy court quickly, then a precedent would be set for GM. But while President Obama had declared victory in the Chrysler bankruptcy as part of his June 1 address, that deal hadn't actually closed. The early weeks of June were nerve-racking for us, thanks to Tom Lauria, the renegade lawyer who helped short-circuit the potential eleventh-hour creditors' settlement. Because of a suit he'd filed, Chrysler's sale of its operating assets to the new Chrysler had gotten hung up.

Lauria was now representing a group of Indiana pension funds that held less than 1 percent of Chrysler debt. The funds were scavengers; they'd paid 43 cents on the dollar for some $42.5 million of debt and were holding out for 100 cents on the dollar. Judge Arthur Gonzalez of the bankruptcy court had overruled their claim, but Lauria appealed, first to the federal circuit court in Manhattan and then, after being summarily turned down there, to the U.S. Supreme Court.

We thought this was ludicrous — no judge had so much as tipped his hat to the objectors' case — and expected a quick rebuff from the "Supremes." But one day passed, then another, without a decision. I began to feel as though we were watching the Vatican to see if white smoke or black smoke emerged. I refused to give Lauria the satisfaction of getting nervous. But we wondered: What could the delay mean? What if the justices took months to rule? What if they decided we had overstepped the limits of the bankruptcy code? Larry finally called Elena Kagan, his ex-colleague from Harvard who was then Obama's solicitor general, the official who represents the U.S. government before the Supreme Court. She reassured him not to read anything into the delay. At last, on June 9, the justices released a terse, two-page decision in which they found that the Indiana funds "have not carried [the] burden" of demonstrating the need for the Supreme Court to intervene. The Chrysler deal was free to close. We never learned the reason for the justices' delay.

Ed Whitacre was ready for his first trip to GM headquarters the following week. Having had no experience as a corporate executive, I was eager to observe a top-notch one at work. Fritz and I had developed an agenda for him that included, at Ed's request, one-on-one meetings with each of the senior executives at GM. For all of his reputation as a tough guy, I was fascinated to see him take the time to get to know the individuals as people. By the end of the day, he could talk knowledgeably about each executive's background, personality, and aspirations.

High on my agenda for that visit was to persuade Fritz to overcome his protectiveness and replace GM's poorest performers with executives who could spark change. Ray Young was at the top of my list. The CFO had not improved in all the time we'd worked with him. He was still making mistakes that were causing us nightmares. The day after GM filed for bankruptcy, for example, he told reporters that as a private company, the automaker was "not going to disclose information except to the shareholders." Could he possibly have said that? It should have been obvious to him that if anything, as a business that was now 61 percent taxpayer-owned, GM would be making more robust public disclosures than before the bankruptcy.

While Ray had been CFO for only fifteen months, he had spent virtually his entire career within the orbit of GM's treasury. The fact that GM had no one more qualified to be its chief financial officer spoke volumes about the quality of the company's talent pool.

To push Fritz, I had lined up an interim CFO: John Alchin, a retired CFO of Comcast, which had been a client of mine for two decades.

John was capable and available and had an easygoing, warm personality. If Fritz would view any newcomer as nonthreatening, I figured, it would be him. I persuaded Fritz to at least let me invite John to spend a day with us in Detroit. Everyone who met him that day found him professional and collegial. But Fritz dug in his heels, arguing that we were at too critical a moment to bring in a new CFO. This was precisely why Harry and I wanted one! But the best we could do was to get Fritz to promise that he would seek a permanent replacement for Ray as soon as the bankruptcy was behind us.

We encountered many other questionable personnel situations, such as one involving Katy Barclay, GM's head of human resources. I did not know her well, but Fritz had correctly determined that she should be replaced. Then we learned that GM did not intend to leave her contract behind in Motors Liquidation Company, which would have saved Shiny New GM as much as $2.5 million. When David and I called Fritz to ask about this, he said he needed her for the next month or two. "What HR person on earth is worth a million dollars a month?" David stormed. Despite our protests, GM honored her contract.

Another underperformer was GM's chief lobbyist in Washington, Ken Cole. We'd found him utterly ineffective, most recently in critical negotiations with Congress about the dealers. Yet when we complained to Fritz, he replied that Cole's relationships were with Republicans, implying that such strengths would be invisible to us Obamaites. To double-check, we made inquiries among Republicans and got the same reaction to Cole as among Democrats. (Among the first personnel decisions that Whitacre made when he became CEO was to replace Cole.)

My frustration with Fritz was still on my mind a day later, back in Washington, when Ron and I broke bread with Carlos Ghosn, the Renault and Nissan CEO. Carlos had first sought us out a month earlier, for reasons that remained mysterious. He'd been out of the mix in Detroit since the previous summer, when he'd backed away from bringing Chrysler into the global alliance of Renault and Nissan. Steve Girsky, the former Wall Street analyst whom I'd tried to recruit for Team Auto, was the one who now put us in touch.

My first meeting with Ghosn had been for dinner at my apartment in New York, and my impression of him from that evening was still vivid:

the fifty-five-year-old was intense—almost like a coiled spring—earnest, and precise, all wrapped in a compact package of determination and drive. He had been jetting around the globe running his worldwide empire for almost a decade and showed no sign of fatigue. I quickly discovered that he was not big on small talk. Neither am I, yet we had an amiable three hours of conversation, almost entirely about business, particularly how he managed two auto companies that were half a world away from each other.

But I couldn't figure out why Ghosn had been so eager to meet. So when the second dinner—in a private room at the Four Seasons Hotel, paid for out of my pocket—began with the same fascinating but general business talk, I asked in my direct fashion why he had made a special trip to Washington to see us.

"I would like GM to be part of our alliance," he replied.

Ron (who was part of both dinners) and I asked a lot of questions about how that would work. Unlike Nissan and Renault, which had almost no geographic overlap, GM sold cars in many of the same places as Ghosn's two automakers.

Perhaps I lacked imagination, but I could not see how even extraordinary leadership could overcome the redundancy. I had also concluded that the success of Renault-Nissan was a function of Ghosn's personality and drive; it was not clear that the alliance would survive his eventual retirement. So after discussing it for a while, I politely deflected the idea. Later I would learn that Ghosn's interest reflected his fear that GM would form an alliance with one of his global competitors. He was maneuvering to forestall that.

Because I was in the midst of worrying about the management situation at GM, I did not let the dinner end without putting the question directly to Ghosn: "Would you be interested in becoming CEO of GM?" I knew it was a long shot and was not surprised when he deftly demurred.

Fritz's refusal to move fast on the hiring front was doubly worrisome because I knew capable executives would be hard to recruit. Among other things, money was going to pose a major challenge. Just a few doors down the basement hallway from me, Ken Feinberg, President

Obama's newly installed "pay czar," was making it clear that compensation, or, more accurately, overcompensation, was something the administration was closely monitoring. A long-faced, nearly bald sixty-three-year-old mediator from working-class Brockton, Massachusetts, Feinberg had earned national prominence as the "special master" administering the September 11th Victim Compensation Fund. He'd done similar service in Agent Orange and asbestos cases and would go on to handle compensation for the BP Gulf of Mexico oil spill. His mission at this time was to regulate top executives' pay in the companies that had received TARP bailouts — in particular seven that the White House deemed to have received "exceptional" help. Four of those seven were General Motors, GMAC, Chrysler, and Chrysler Financial.

In response to public outrage over Wall Street's excesses and the financial panic, Congress and the Obama administration had each instituted rules regarding pay for top executives at companies receiving TARP funds. The administration's carefully thought-out approach was designed to regulate pay without hamstringing the firms' ability to attract and reward the best people. It provided for maximum cash salaries of $500,000, but put no limit on total salaries or bonuses, although anything above $500,000 had to be paid in restricted stock or the like.

Congress, meanwhile, could not be deterred from imposing harsher, less practical restrictions. Chris Dodd, the chairman of the Senate Banking Committee, pushed into law a requirement that bonuses could not be more than 50 percent of salary. This limitation, and a related ban on stock options, struck me as silly: bonuses and options are an important way to align the interests of executives with those of the shareholders in the companies they are running. Dodd's logic was that incentive compensation had driven many Wall Street firms to take imprudent risks. I understood his thinking but still disagreed.

The big problem was that the Obama order and the Dodd limit were essentially in conflict. If an executive couldn't receive a salary of more than $500,000 (the Obama rule) or a bonus of more than 50 percent of that (the Dodd rule), then his or her total income couldn't be more than $750,000 a year. While this was high pay compared to the income of a senior public servant, it was woefully short of what employers spend to attract and retain top talent. Enforcing such rules was clearly going to be difficult, divisive, and emotional, so the administration had come up with a clever way to get the monkey off its back: by appointing Ken Feinberg as pay czar.

My first meeting with Ken, in mid-June, went smoothly enough. I was struck by his affability and gregariousness. What brought me to his door was Al de Molina's desire for clarification on pay for himself and his lieutenants at GMAC. Al wasn't shy. He told Feinberg that he had gone without a bonus in 2008 and hoped to be treated "fairly" from now on. He'd brought along a schedule of what he and his team had in mind. It proposed that Al be paid around $12 million a year to run the giant finance company, with his executives scaling down from there.

"This won't be a problem," Feinberg said in his heavy Boston accent. "I've got people looking to be paid $100 million!" (He was referring, we later learned, to Andrew Hall, a hugely successful energy trader at Citigroup. In part because of controversy over Hall's pay, Citi ended up unloading its valuable trading unit at a fire-sale price — not a happy outcome for taxpayers, who would end up owning 34 percent of the bank.)

But in subsequent meetings, as public sentiment toward executive pay became ever uglier, the pay czar began to backpedal. Slowly and steadily, he ratcheted down the amount of "total comp" that he was willing to approve while ratcheting up the percentage of remuneration that could only be paid in stock. By the fall, he would effectively decree that no CEO could earn more than $9.5 million (thereby conspicuously ruling out compensation in eight figures).

I was disappointed that Feinberg was not more resistant to political influence. While I understood the sensitivity about compensation at companies saved by TARP, virtually none of these businesses were run by the same executives who had gotten them in trouble, and it was penny wise and pound foolish not to hire the very best. In the auto companies alone, the Treasury had invested more than $80 billion. Why should we jeopardize that? I wished Feinberg had been willing to speak up forcefully about the dangers of succumbing to mob psychology.

As this headache began to develop, GM's head of accounting, Nick Cyprus, won himself a place among the executives who weren't pushing GM forward fast enough. In mid-May, Harry had told Ray Young that we would want the 363 sale to close as soon as the court approved the plan. Based on guidance from Cyprus, Young said that because of the complexity of GM's bookkeeping, there was no way the company could do this other than at the end of a calendar quarter — in this case, September 30.

Harry went ballistic. "How much revenue do you think you miss every day you're in bankruptcy?" he thundered, knowing that the answer was $100 million. "There isn't a problem in this company that can't be solved by the billion-plus dollars you'll lose if you don't move more quickly!" He demanded a list of all the obstacles to closing on the day of the judge's decision. When he and Matt received it, they worked through them one by one to eliminate them as reasons.

Meanwhile, Fritz was taking a different approach with Cyprus, trying to walk him back gradually from his fixation on September 30, all the while making him believe it was his idea. Over several days, Fritz persuaded Nick that the deal didn't have to be at a quarter's end — maybe a month's end would do, maybe August 31. Next he persuaded him that it didn't need to be August 31, but maybe July 31. In due course, Nick agreed that with a bit of cooperation from the SEC (which was forthcoming), the July 10 date Harry and Matt had set was achievable. Watching this cajolery, I concluded that Fritz and Harry were both right. Fritz understood GM's culture and the need to approach Cyprus delicately. But Harry was also right that this kind of horse-whispering to get things done shouldn't be needed at a world-class company.

I made much faster progress with Ed as we teamed up to recast the General Motors board. Back on March 30, our announcements had included the fact that GM would be asked to replace a majority of its directors. I had no magic in picking that formulation; I had cribbed it from an earlier decision to "request" that Citi replace a majority of its board. After providing seats for Ed, the Canadian representative, and the UAW's nominee, we still had four slots to fill.

Ed and I are both strong-willed, yet we sorted through the candidates in a spirit of collegiality. He mainly wanted ex-CEOs with whom he'd had enough personal experience to be confident of their strengths; I wanted to bring the discipline of private equity to GM and had my favorites from that world. We made a list of candidates and split up the calls. With only one exception, a CEO who had just taken a competing board assignment, all of our targets agreed. It was clear from the conversations that these people, like Ed, viewed accepting a GM board appointment as a form of public service. I became confident that as Team Auto stepped back, the new directors would step up.

From the corporate world we chose Robert Krebs, the former chairman and CEO of Burlington Northern Santa Fe, a giant railroad on whose board Ed had served. When I met Krebs, he struck me as a lot like Ed: a laconic, no-nonsense clear thinker. Some months later, Warren Buffett bought the company that he had helped build. Also from the corporate world came Patricia Russo. She'd had a rollercoaster tenure as CEO of Alcatel-Lucent, but AT&T had been a major customer and Ed knew her well.

We recruited Dan Akerson, a managing director of the Carlyle Group, one of the biggest private equity shops. Dan had attended Annapolis and was still Navy-tough. Ed and I had each gotten to know him a bit because he had alternated stints in private equity with work as a top executive in the telecommunications industry. Dan was also direct and honest. Rounding out the foursome was David Bonderman, a friend of mine for more than twenty years. A lawyer turned investor, David had helped manage the fortune of Texas oil scion Robert Bass before cofounding TPG, now one of the world's largest and most successful private equity firms. He was razor-smart and one of the best investors in the world. Neither he nor Akerson suffered fools lightly — a big plus, I thought, for incoming directors of GM.

I knew nothing about Canada's choice, a business school dean named Carol Stephenson, but was delighted when the autoworkers chose Steve Girsky. This was a nice consolation for my having been unable to enlist him for Team Auto. Steve had lived and breathed the car industry for decades and was ecstatic to be asked to serve. When Gettelfinger put Steve on the board, his instructions to him were clear: "You are to worry about the stock price," on which a large proportion of the autoworkers' future health benefits would now depend. Our efforts to align the workers' interests with the company's by having the VEBA hold common stock had paid off.

The federal bankruptcy court in Manhattan was strictly off-limits to us while the case was pending. Under the law, anyone who showed up was eligible to be called to the witness stand. To make our case, we sent flocks of Treasury Department, General Motors, and outside lawyers, and just two witnesses: Harry and Fritz. The rest of us were relegated to tracking the proceedings via phone calls during breaks and terse text messages from the lawyers.

Not surprisingly for such an enormous case, opposition to GM's bankruptcy plan was legion. It included a handful of renegade bond-holders protesting the sale of assets to Shiny New GM, product liability and asbestos claimants whose suits were being relegated to Motors Liquidation Company, disenfranchised dealers, splinter unions, and scores of other parties who thought themselves aggrieved. About two dozen law firms came out of the woodwork to file some 850 objections.

The case had fallen to Judge Robert Gerber, who had built a formidable reputation in the small, intense world of the bankruptcy bar. He was been chosen by lot for this assignment, as was the custom, and yet he seemed born to handle GM. Judge Gerber thrived on big cases and tight deadlines, and was known for his willingness to run important hearings late into the night to make sure all sides had their say, and then to deliver a balanced, well-written opinion the very next day.

Fritz and Harry prepped intensively for their testimony, but that didn't cramp Harry's style. A cardinal rule in giving a pretrial deposition is never to get into a debate with the opposition lawyer; the risk of stumbling or saying something wrong is too high. Harry, being Harry, not only violated that principle but even turned the tables, questioning the questioner. A Cadwalader lawyer on hand couldn't believe what he was hearing. "Harry is scary," he texted us.

Harry's court appearance, on July 1, was only slightly more restrained. The e-mails from the courtroom came fast and furious:

> 9:48 A.M.: "Harry is the toughest witness I've ever seen. It's scary.
>   I would not want to cross him."
> 9:49 A.M.: "Harry is an animal on the stand."
> 10:08 A.M.: "He's continuing to do well. The judge seems to like him
>   and is listening attentively."
> 10:59 A.M.: "First tort guys are done. They didn't lay a glove on Harry."
> 12:12 P.M.: "Splinters are done . . . we're really rolling."
> 12:28 P.M.: "Harry has been one of the most phenomenal witnesses
>   I've ever seen. I feel very comfortable about the overall sale."

True to his reputation, Judge Gerber wrapped up the hearing before July 4. Hoping for a positive outcome, we prepared to close. But hiccups occurred, some typical of complex transactions and others emanating from GM's lack of rigor. For example, GM projected that it would need $1.5 billion to make up for lost sources of dealer financing outside the United States. To arrive at that figure, GM simply assumed it would lose a certain percentage of its funding sources in those locations. The company had made no effort to check its assumptions, had not so much as called its offices in those countries. Our finance company guru Brian Stern checked with various financing sources and concluded that only $200 million of funding would be lost.

A more important example of the lack of financial rigor surrounded the decision of how much financing to provide GM as it exited bankruptcy. On Sunday, June 28, Brian Osias (who had joined the GM team to help with the burdensome workload) and Sadiq Malik met with their counterparts in New York to try to resolve how much capital GM would need. A month earlier, before the bankruptcy petition was filed, GM had estimated that its total peak capital need would be $59 billion. However, over the ensuing four weeks, GM's cash flows had been better than expected, in part because again, as with Chrysler, consumers showed more loyalty than we had budgeted. Nonetheless, GM kept its need at $59 billion by assuming that whatever outperformance it had achieved over the previous few weeks would be offset by underperformance later in 2009.

Harry was unyielding. Over the July Fourth weekend, lawyers for Treasury and GM got into a tussle over a small but important aspect of how the new loan agreement would be structured. To an e-mail list of sixty-four participants, most of them lawyers, Soo-Jin Shim, a Weil Gotshal attorney representing GM, said that the closing would have to be delayed while the issue was resolved. Harry didn't hold back. "Soo-Jin, I am stunned that you would so offhandedly threaten the closing for which we are all working so hard," he wrote at 8:24 P.M. on July 4, while most Americans were concentrating on barbeques and fireworks. "To be clear, this will not delay [the] closing. Nor will anything else." He went on in the same vein for several paragraphs, also pointing out that he had been trying to reach "GM people" all afternoon to discuss the matter, with no success. To Harry, it was indicative of GM's problems: he and hundreds of others were working around the clock to save the company, yet most of the management team had turned off their cell phones at a critical juncture in the deal.

Judge Gerber not only worked on his opinion over the weekend, he delivered his ruling on July 5 — a Sunday. It gave us a complete victory, clearing the way for Shiny New GM to emerge from the carcass of Motors Liquidation Company by July 10, the seemingly impossible deadline we'd set.

That forty-day limit set by Harry and Matt turned out to have been a deciding factor, the judge's two written opinions in the matter made clear. The primary objection from the bondholders had been that the sale of GM's best-performing assets to a new entity gave them a raw deal. They wanted GM to go through a conventional Chapter 11 restructuring under the supervision of the court, which they thought offered creditors a fuller, fairer recovery and could be completed almost as quickly as a 363 sale. With powerful eloquence, Judge Gerber rejected this argument and reminded the creditors that they were only bit players in a game of enormous stakes:

> This case involves not just the ability of GM creditors to recover on their claims . . . it involves the interests of 225,000 employees (91,000 in the U.S. alone); an estimated 500,000 retirees; 6,000 dealers and 11,500 suppliers. If GM were to have to liquidate, the injury to the public would be staggering. This case likewise raises the specter of systemic failure throughout the North American auto industry, and grievous damage to all of the communities in which GM operates. If GM goes under, the number of supplier bankruptcies which we already have . . . is likely to multiply exponentially. If employees lose their paychecks or their healthcare benefits, they will suffer great hardship. And states and municipalities would lose the tax revenues they get from GM and the people employed by GM, and the Government would be paying out more in unemployment insurance and other hardship benefits. Under these circumstances, I find it hardly surprising that the U.S., Canadian, and Ontario governments would not stand idly by and allow those consequences to happen.

Addressing the urgency of the case, the judge agreed with Harry and the Treasury legal team:

> Anyone with a knowledge of Chapter 11 cases . . . can well understand why none of Harry Wilson's advisors thought that GM could survive a normal plan confirmation process . . . The court fully understands the unwillingness of the Government to keep funding GM indefinitely — especially to await the resolution of disputes among creditors trying to maximize their recoveries . . . The problem is that if the 363 Transaction got off track . . . customer confidence would plummet; and that the U.S. Treasury would have to keep funding GM while bondholders (and, then, perhaps others) jousted to maximize their individual incremental recoveries. The Court fully takes Harry Wilson at his word.

July 5 was my birthday, as it happened, but Harry and Matt certainly had reason to celebrate too.

The ink on Judge Gerber's signature had barely dried when Congress started undercutting the deal. On July 7, the House Appropriations Committee passed a spending bill that included an amendment by Ohio Republican Steve LaTourette that would reinstate dealer franchises canceled during the GM and Chrysler bankruptcies. Brian Deese and the legislative affairs people at Treasury believed the bill was headed inexorably toward passage into law.

Deese's summer had been remarkably successful up to that point. While the rest of Team Auto had been consumed with GM and Chrysler, he'd virtually single-handedly taken on Cash for Clunkers, the sales incentive program that we'd added to our charter almost accidentally in March. He faced a difficult set of negotiations, navigating among environmentalists who wanted the program to favor small cars, Detroit boosters who wanted the Big Three to be the principal beneficiaries, and the executive branch, which wanted to be sure that no international trade rules were violated by having legislation that blatantly favored Detroit.

By mid-May, Brian had succeeded in getting the House and Senate to add $1 billion for the program, now officially known as the Car

Allowance Rebate System, onto a supplemental appropriations bill for the Iraq and Afghanistan wars. A month later, the President signed it into law. In the end, Deese had maneuvered the new law to emphasize the scrapping of SUVs and trucks, a win for Detroit, because most were American brands, likely to be replaced with American brands, and a win for environmentalists, because SUVs and trucks had the highest emissions.

He next pushed the Department of Transportation to develop the necessary implementation policies and procedures. What, for example, would be the steps for making sure the clunkers were truly junked? Using the Team Auto approach of daily early-morning conference calls, in just over three weeks — a nanosecond by bureaucratic standards — Cash for Clunkers was up and running. It was an extraordinary success, far beyond anything we had imagined. The first $1 billion was exhausted in less than a week, and the White House scrambled to persuade Congress to appropriate more. Cash for Clunkers became an all too rare example of what can happen when a smart and energetic staffer develops a good idea and runs with it.

In the midst of pushing through the historic GM bankruptcy, Matt and Harry remained attentive to Delphi — including midnight phone updates during which Harry would occasionally fall asleep — and managed to put the parts company onto a glide path toward successful resolution. On the same day that GM filed for bankruptcy, Delphi announced an agreement with GM under which the automaker would buy four key factories from Delphi, along with Delphi's global steering business. This would give GM access to the critical parts that had allowed Delphi essentially to extort billions of dollars of financing from GM over the years. The rest of Delphi would be bought by a private equity firm, Platinum Equity, that had made a specialty of troubled investments.

Under bankruptcy rules, the agreement among GM, Platinum, and Delphi was subject to higher bids from others, including the existing debtor-in-possession lenders, who had been negotiating toward a separate, but ultimately unsuccessful, agreement in May. In late July, the existing lenders decided to trump the agreement by credit bidding — basically, turning in their claims for the equity in Delphi. While the DIP lenders tried to portray this as a victory over GM and the government, in truth we didn't care who got Delphi as long as GM could extricate itself from the continual drain on its finances and assure itself of a reliable supply of parts; we had actually proposed a very similar deal to the lenders way back in April. The successful bid by the DIP lenders allowed GM to accomplish these objectives. And the transaction ended up being profitable for all the buyers, including GM. For an investment of $2.3 billion in the new Delphi, it had — as of May 2010 — a stake with a value estimated by JPMorgan at $4 billion.

Still, there was no way for Deese, or anybody else, to contain the politicians' anger over dealer closings. It simmered all summer, erupting periodically like a geyser fed by a vast underground reservoir of superheated water. Hapless members of Team Auto would be summoned to Capitol Hill at such times to get browbeaten by legislators or their staffs. In early July, it was House Majority Leader Steny Hoyer's moment to vent. A tall, jowly, gravel-voiced Democrat who represented an area of Maryland just south of D.C., Hoyer had been among the most persistent critics of the dealer-reduction plans. Among his constituents were two particularly visible and unhappy dealers who each operated both GM and Chrysler stores, Tammy Darvish and Jack Fitzgerald. When we asked GM and Chrysler to fill us in, we learned that the franchises more than deserved to be closed. Fitzgerald, for example, had sold only around three new Chryslers in 2008.

I was mystified that the House majority leader chose to devote so much time to this. The nation was plagued by economic and financial crises; why would the second most important member of the House after Speaker Pelosi think that two car dealerships merited his personal attention?

Deese and other colleagues worked patiently with Hoyer's staff to explain the need for reductions and the logic behind these particular ones. Brian came away from those conversations believing that he had convinced Hoyer's staff that the automakers were acting appropriately. Nonetheless, Hoyer was not satisfied and called me to say so. Then he ordered a summit meeting of several senior congressmen and representatives of the car companies and Team Auto. We wanted the leaders of NADA to join us but, true to form, the trade association found an excuse not to attend. On July 8, we gathered in Hoyer's small meeting room in the maze of the Capitol. Like the other principals, I was accompanied by a clutch of aides (Deese, Markowitz, and Calhoon). We felt as if we were entering the O.K. Corral.

I did not wish to get on the bad side of important lawmakers, so I vowed to make myself as inconspicuous as possible. I mentally staked out a chair for myself set back from the main table, where lesser aides generally sat. But as soon as Hoyer arrived and took his seat in the center of the rectangular table, he pulled out the chair next to him and said, "Steve, come and sit here."

Hoyer made a generic opening statement: "We're proud of all the work everyone is doing. We know you're working hard. We just want to make sure everyone is treated fairly." Then he turned to me, expecting a response. I was exceedingly uncomfortable. "We are just here to facilitate the conversation," I said as neutrally as I could. "We didn't have anything to do with what dealers were chosen and this entire process was decided by the companies. Therefore, the companies are here to talk with you. We hope we can get something resolved quickly."

Neither I nor anyone else from Team Auto said another word after that. Hoyer and the other House members took turns hammering the GM and Chrysler executives. Like us, they had no interest in antagonizing Congress, but the questioning was intense. Each legislator had a pet dealer and kept insisting the dealer was effective, profitable, and meritorious. Representative Gabrielle Giffords of Arizona was especially adamant about a Chrysler dealer and repeated her talking points over and over. The conversation went in circles, mercifully ending after an hour or so. But the legislators left unsatisfied and determined to move forward with bills to block the much-needed reduction in stores.

Even my friend Bob Corker, who had railed against government meddling with the car companies, did some meddling himself with the dealers. Back in 2008, Corker had complained about Detroit's bloated dealer networks and expressed frustration that dealers couldn't be eliminated efficiently outside a bankruptcy. (Indeed, he had said that GM should have only 1,500 dealers, versus the 3,600 that we settled on.) But now he introduced the Automobile Dealers Assistance Act, which would have provided much more generous terms to superfluous dealers than common sense would dictate. His proposal was a long way from the notion—so strongly endorsed by him just a few months earlier—of shared sacrifice.

I was back in Detroit with Ed Whitacre on July 9. Shiny New GM was about to debut, and I went mainly to accompany Ed as he continued to immerse himself in the giant enterprise he was about to chair. We spent the morning at RenCen headquarters, in presentations designed to explain to him what went on at the world's second-largest automaker.

Ed wasted no time picking out what he saw as a grave flaw in the management structure: too many executives reporting directly to the CEO. It appalled him to hear that Rick had had more than twenty, and he "encouraged" Fritz to slim down the number. After lunch, he gathered the company's dozen or so top executives in the Chairman's Conference Room, where Team Auto had held many of its meetings. The men and women listened intently as Ed explained in his measured Texas drawl that he had no interest in presiding over a second-rate company. He praised the people. He stressed the need to make decisions. He emphasized his personal belief in the power of marketing. Then, looking straight into the eyes of one attendee after another, he said, "I'm used to winning and have no intention of seeing that change at GM." The GM executives, unused to this sort of bluntness, were impressed, and so was I. It was superlative leadership as I had always imagined it.

Fritz Henderson himself gave the final talk, which started with a PowerPoint slide that read: "A realignment of the operating model and culture with the strategy of the new GM is necessary." Ed and I were pleased. Unlike Rick Wagoner, who seemed to believe that GM's practices were automatically the world's best, Fritz was at least outwardly on the program that we had laid out for him in March.

The next morning, Ron and I went to visit Sergio and his team at Chrysler. This was the first time I'd made the trek to Auburn Hills, the company's headquarters outside Detroit. Lee Iacocca had built the vast 5.3-million-square-foot complex as a monument to himself at a cost of $1.6 billion. At one end of the facility stood a fifteen-story office tower with imposing horizontal bands of black and silver glass and a gigantic Chrysler pentagon on the roof. It looked like the Death Star. Sergio had taken one look at the capacious executive suite on the top floor of the tower and immediately decamped to a modest office on the fourth floor of the central building, where many of his direct reports worked.

Never mind that Ed Whitacre was pushing Fritz to cut back on direct reports — Sergio was doing exactly the opposite, flattening Chrysler's organization so that he directly supervised twenty-five executives, not including his Fiat reports. (I later learned that Alan Mulally had a similarly flat structure at Ford.) This difference in philosophies fascinated me; ultimately I concluded that either approach could work with the right CEO and the right team. Sergio, perhaps the most extreme workaholic I have ever encountered, wanted to be involved in innumerable decisions without being slowed by bureaucratic layers. Ed, by contrast, had no interest in working Sergio's hours and preferred to empower the people under him to make as many decisions as possible.

Chrysler headquarters was so large that Sergio used a golf cart to get around. He tried to give us a tour but got lost in the honeycomb of underground passageways, and we had to stop repeatedly to ask for directions. Eventually, we settled down in a large conference room near Sergio's office for a briefing by his top executives. Sergio, Ron, Clay Calhoon, Brian Osias, and I faced a projection screen at the far end of the U-shaped arrangement of tables. It had been just over a month since Chrysler had emerged from bankruptcy. While the new Chrysler's plans were still very much in formation, we were eager for an update and a chance to meet the new team. As slides flashed by on the screen, we fired questions at the executives. Some of the material was also new to Sergio, who made no effort to pretend that he knew it all.

When the presentation turned to Jeep, Michael Manley, the British head of the Jeep brand, said that the company would continue to manufacture both the Liberty and the Patriot, mediocre vehicles that were similar in design. "Why do we have two?" Sergio interjected. "In the future, we're not going to have both of these. We're going to consolidate." He had the same reaction upon hearing that both the Dodge and the Chrysler minivans (essentially the same design) were still being built. "There is only going to be one minivan," he declared. This was decisionmaking Sergio-style: quick, instinctive, and sure-footed.

I flew back to Washington that afternoon feeling that we had left both GM and Chrysler in very capable hands, with every opportunity to succeed. The headlines that day were full of GM's emergence from

bankruptcy, and the front page of the *Wall Street Journal* acknowledged Team Auto's work: "The quicker-than-expected reorganization
could represent a major accomplishment for the Obama administration, which committed $50 billion to GM as part of its bailout of the
U.S. auto industry."

Meanwhile, since its eruption in mid-April, the pay-to-play controversy in which I was embroiled had shown no signs of going away.
Instead it was intensifying, as New York Attorney General Andrew
Cuomo decided to dig more deeply and other jurisdictions began their
own examinations. At the same time, with the emergence of both companies from bankruptcy, it was time to take our hands off. Almost immediately, my workload dropped precipitously. After feeling as if I had
several full-time jobs crammed into one, I found myself with idle hours.
I contemplated other assignments within Treasury or the broader administration, and I talked with friends, including Mark Patterson, Tim's
chief of staff, about what to do next. After reflecting on these conversations, however, I concluded that trying to undertake another government role at that point would be too complicated for both me and the
administration.

We had just finished building a house on Martha's Vineyard, where
I had vacationed for more than thirty years, and I had twin sons entering college in September. The prospect of a month on the Vineyard
with them was tantalizing. Shortly after my return from Detroit, I talked
with Mark again and told him that I had decided to leave Treasury at
the end of July. In the press statement announcing my departure, Tim
was incredibly gracious, as he had been throughout my time under his
command. "We are extremely grateful to Steve for his efforts in helping
to strengthen GM and Chrysler, recapitalize GMAC, and support the
American auto industry," Tim said in the news release. "I hope that he
takes another opportunity to bring his unique skills to government service in the future."

I had made a point of taking Team Auto out for a celebratory dinner after each of the President's national addresses, which represented our
three major milestones. On July 21, we convened for the fourth and last
time, at the same Rosa Mexicano restaurant, in Washington's newly
renovated Penn Quarter, where Bob Corker and I had dined exactly

four weeks earlier. Safely sequestered in a private room, we let loose, aware that our adventure together was nearing an end. The liquor flowed freely, cell-phone cameras flashed. In due course, I stood up and tried to pay tribute to the work we had done.

Such celebrations, I reminded my colleagues, are standard on Wall Street at the successful close of a deal. But in those victories, the objective is private gain. This victory was different. I choked up as I spoke about our commitment to quality. "I've worked with a lot of talented people in my life but never with a group smarter or more dedicated than Team Auto," I said. And I thanked my colleagues for the enormous sacrifices that each had made. "In this deal, in this incarnation," I said, "you have epitomized what it means to serve your country."

Fortunately, after I spoke, Ron Bloom was there to lighten the mood. "I did this all for the unions!" he jokingly declared.

Everyone laughed and the war stories began to fly. Cell-phone images from later that night reveal that as the celebration went on, the rowdiness quotient rose. One set of pictures shows an impromptu contest to see how easy it would be to power-lift a supine Sadiq. "Leave the little guy alone," he kept protesting. I left after eleven, well past my normal early bedtime, but the party went on. Harry managed to fall asleep standing upright against a pillar during after-dinner revelry at the open-air roof bar of the W Hotel across from Treasury.

The next night, another muggy July evening just two days before my departure, I walked out of Treasury through the south doorway, the opposite end of the long building from where I had first tried to enter many months earlier. A tourist who had stopped to take a picture of the statue of Alexander Hamilton, the founding secretary of the Treasury, recognized me. "You guys did good work," she said. "He would have been proud of you."

13

THE CHIEF EXECUTIVE SHUFFLE

HARRY WILSON HATED the idea of letting go of GM. All spring he had pressed me, higher-ups in the administration, and even GM executives about the possibility of an ongoing federal involvement — "so they won't fuck up what we did," as he put it. His proposals ranged from a senior-level consulting assignment for himself inside the company to his being part of a government monitoring group that would be on hand for monthly board meetings and quarterly gatherings of senior management. The group would also help with the search for a new CFO and with decisions on supplier relations, Asian joint ventures, and more.

Ron Bloom found all this highly amusing — dealing with GM had turned Harry, the fiercest laissez-faire capitalist on our team, into an outright government interventionist. Harry argued he was just carrying out our mandate to safeguard the taxpayers' investment. But by late July, mostly because of the administration's hands-off policy, it became clear there would be no long-term role for him or any task force member inside GM. Harry was boxed between Ed Whitacre, who at the outset had elicited from me a commitment that the board would be free to run the company, and Larry, who was unyielding in his view that continued intervention would bring more risk than reward. Bowing to the inevitable, Harry proposed a sort of formal handoff: a briefing of the incoming board by Team Auto. Whitacre liked the idea, and a date was set for Monday, August 3, the day before the first formal meeting of the new GM board.

"We have been living and breathing GM for months, and we want to be very honest with you," Harry began. He was seated at the head of a long rectangular table, flanked by Ron and other members of the team, in a conference room at the GM Tech Center. Next to Sadiq, across from Harry, was Ed Whitacre, and around the table were the other directors of Shiny New GM, assembled in person for the first time. Only two of the thirteen were absent: David Bonderman, because of a long-standing prior commitment, and Fritz, who as head of current management had been excused from the briefing.

The potential for division among the new board was not lost on the attendees. Around the table, they had mostly segregated themselves into two groups — five who had been members of the board that had allowed GM to career off a cliff and six new members who had been chosen in part because of their reputation for toughness.

Harry launched the presentation with a thirty-three-page report, which the team intentionally did not hand out in hopes of avoiding leaks about the Treasury's withering views of GM. It was organized in three main sections — GM's past successes, a recap of the bankruptcy, and GM's challenges — whose page counts alone reflected the team's mindset. GM's triumphs got three pages, including a cover page — very different from the glass-half-full presentations to which the old GM board had been accustomed. The bankruptcy recap got ten pages. And the bulk of the report dealt with GM's challenges.

Harry began the third section by laying out our scathing opinion of GM's culture in bullet points that pretty much spoke for themselves. "Insularity," which Harry called "The GM Way," came first. Then "lack of accountability," followed by "[lack of a] sense of urgency," "need for more change agents," and a "culture of losing." "If you really think about GM and where they are coming from," Harry said as he pointed to a line about consistent market-share losses for thirty-three years, "they've mostly lost. Most of these managers have never won." He also knocked the company for bad supplier relations, for GMAC's misadventures in subprime mortgages, and for the lack of "green" cars on the road.

The room was quiet. Some old board members were shifting in their seats. Kent Kresa and a few others nodded when Harry lambasted GM's bureaucracy and inability to make fast decisions. Whitacre, rarely one to speak much, occasionally murmured, "That's right."

To highlight GM's weaknesses in finance, Harry went back to one of his favorite criticisms: poor cash management. Kathryn Marinello, an information services executive who had joined the board in 2007 just as the company entered its death spiral, spoke up. "We knew something like this was going on. We were asking for that kind of information. But GM wouldn't give it to us." (Her comments struck some board members as ironic, because she had earned a reputation for talking too much at board meetings and saying too little of interest.)

David Markowitz, who felt no director of the Wagoner era should have been allowed back, glared.

Harry also harped on the need for change agents at GM, people from inside or outside who would shake the place up.

"I get it. The top management is not good," interrupted Patricia Russo, the ex-CEO of Alcatel-Lucent, who was new to the board. "But do you see that spark somewhere?"

Harry paused for a long time and volunteered a name: "Bob Lutz."

"I don't think he's that good," objected Steve Girsky, the former Morgan Stanley analyst who now occupied the UAW seat on the board.

"We like that he actually knows product," said Harry. "But we need more like him that are younger."

I would have agreed with Girsky. Lutz's swashbuckling personality stood out at fusty GM but I'd never been overwhelmed by the substance of what he had to say. And I'd been somewhat dismayed that Fritz's idea of change was to let the seventy-seven-year-old Lutz "unretire." But in truth none of us on Team Auto was a management expert.

The atmosphere seemed to become more tense as Markowitz took the floor to highlight problems related to vehicles, brands, and consumer perceptions. Old board members who had been nodding in agreement began to grow defensive. Team Auto named a few executives whom we thought were lacking, which some of the old board thought unseemly and harsh. Meanwhile, new board members muttered and shook their heads. When David reminded them about the market share loss, Whitacre offered one of his few unsolicited comments. "That has got to stop. Just can't have that," he said. From his first moment at GM, Whitacre had made clear his view that continuing loss of market share was a recipe for another failure.

The session, which was supposed to run for an hour, pushed closer to two. Finally the focus turned to Fritz — whom, after all, the task force had chosen as CEO.

"Does he have a chance at success?" Whitacre asked Harry point-blank. Another director echoed, "How positive are you that Fritz can bring about all that change that is needed?"

Harry told the board that at first he'd assumed GM would need a CEO from outside. "But eventually I realized that Fritz gets it. He has shown a capacity for change." He related the anecdote of Fritz's struggle in March to answer a question about GM's culture, and how finally he'd said, "It's the only culture I know." To Harry, this showed Fritz could recognize and be honest about his shortcomings, even in a big group setting.

Neville Isdell, a former Coca-Cola CEO who had been the last to join the old board, asked what were Fritz's odds. Bloom volunteered that Team Auto saw him as a 60–40 proposition, with some thinking he had a 60 percent chance of success and others putting it at 40 percent. Harry tried to soften things by putting his own odds of Fritz's survival at 60 percent. Even so, the directors seemed stunned. On their first day on the job they were being told they would as likely as not have to fire the CEO.

As the meeting ended and the board rose to leave, Whitacre quietly asked Sadiq for a copy of the presentation. Meanwhile, Isdell came around the table and told Harry, "You guys did a great job." In the coming weeks, many directors would tell me that they both appreciated the candor of the briefing and were dismayed by much of what they heard. None took issue with the core message.

It was not lost on Fritz that the new board was hearing from Team Auto before it heard from GM, but that had been Whitacre's wish. The next day, the board assembled at the Milford Proving Ground, northwest of Detroit, for a chance to see GM's vehicles and drive them on the test track. This helped lighten the mood. Recent models had been winning good reviews, and old board members got a kick out of hearing new members make comments like, "Wow, I didn't know Buick made a car like this."

"See, I told you it wasn't all bad," Kent Kresa told a newcomer. "There are some good things here."

Fritz had sent Whitacre an agenda for the board meeting. It would be a milestone of sorts as the first board meeting under Ed Whitacre and the first of the new GM. At the top of the agenda Fritz had put "Chairman's Review," figuring that Ed would welcome the opportunity to note the occasion and say a few words about his expectations and the state of the company. Then the board would turn its attention to the issues at hand.

But as the meeting began, Whitacre had no remarks. He just looked at Fritz and asked, "You want to make some introductory comments?"

The CEO froze, saying nothing for several seconds. Finally he said, "Welcome to the new GM." Then he simply got the meeting started, telling the board, "We have a lot of things to cover," and turning over the floor to — of all people — Ray Young.

As discussion unfolded, Fritz was kicking himself. He'd let slip an opportunity to lay out his vision and strategy for GM. He could always provide that vision in later meetings and speeches, but never again would there be a chance to set the course of the company at the start of the first meeting of the new GM board of directors.

By mid-afternoon, the agenda was finished and Fritz stepped out so the board could continue in executive session, a routine good-governance procedure. It quickly emerged that while older board members like Kresa hadn't been looking for an opening speech, new members had been. Dan Akerson said that when his firm, Carlyle, bought a company, it expected the CEO to set out his goals and vision and also impose a plan setting benchmarks for the first hundred days. The comments resonated with other directors, current and former chief executives to whom Fritz had come across as more a chief operating officer than a CEO.

Fritz's misgivings were confirmed after the meeting adjourned. Isdell pulled him aside and said, "You missed your moment." A little later, Whitacre sat down with him privately to discuss the board's initial determinations. He told Fritz the board would give him 120 to 150 days, then assess his performance as CEO. Fritz pointed out that that wasn't a lot of time. And what exactly, he asked, would he be graded on?

"Change," said Whitacre.

"How will you measure change?" Fritz asked.

Whitacre's answer seemed vague.

"I'm cooked," Fritz thought. He was disappointed but not totally surprised. He'd been wondering if Whitacre had become interested in the CEO's job for himself—he wouldn't be the first CEO to retire only to realize after a few years of golf that retirement wasn't for him. Fritz recalled how in their first meeting back in June, Whitacre had remarked, "I've never been a nonexecutive chairman. I don't know if I will be good at it."

Fritz's suspicions were understandable, but if he'd asked my advice, I'd have disagreed. I'd had too tough a time recruiting Whitacre to believe that he came into the job with any aspirations beyond seeing Fritz and GM succeed. Subsequent events would prove me correct.

While Whitacre and Fritz struggled to forge a working relationship, the chairman hit it off right away with Steve Girsky. The two couldn't have been more different: one a tall, taciturn Texan with a George Bush–like affection for his ranch, and the other a chatty New Yorker, a former star automotive analyst who'd spent years as one of the best interviews an auto journalist could have. This unlikely duo shared the view that GM's biggest enemy was itself. And they had complementary strengths. Whitacre had decades of experience managing people and running organizations. Girsky knew the industry cold and was willing to share his knowledge with Whitacre. Before long, people were calling him "Whitacre's automotive brain."

Twenty-nine miles to the northwest, at Chrysler headquarters, Sergio was unambiguously in command. He'd swept into Auburn Hills with his black sweaters, his iPod, and his packs of Muratti Ambassador cigarettes, and even while Chrysler was still in bankruptcy, he had begun interviewing top executives to figure out who would stay and who would go.

Chrysler's downward spiral had left its veterans cynical and embittered; many top managers had reported to six CEOs or presidents over the past decade. But Sergio turned out to be more laid back and less rah-rah than they'd expected. He showed none of the bad temper we'd witnessed, and instead talked quietly about who he was, his work ethic, and what he had done to fix Fiat. He was open to questions.

And he surprised the executives by letting many keep their jobs. For the most part, Chrysler people remained in charge of Chrysler operations, although power-train design and manufacturing was taken over by Italian experts, as were finance and communications. Sergio also imported Fiat people to teach his vaunted "World-Class Manufacturing" program.

On June 10, the day Chrysler emerged from bankruptcy, Sergio gave a speech to some three thousand salaried workers at headquarters. He knew it was a pretty disheartened group. As a senior manager put it, "Four months of Leno jokes wears you down." The consensus among many employees, and not resisted by Sergio's team, was that Cerberus had treated the automaker as a poor sibling to the potentially more lucrative Chrysler Financial.

Sergio told the workers he knew they'd been through a "sometimes embarrassing and difficult process" and "a great deal of hardship and uncertainty." Then he added, "It's not often in business or in life that you receive a second chance."

After laying out the challenges facing Chrysler, offset with soaring words about how the Fiat alliance would enable both companies to prosper, he pivoted abruptly at the end of his ten-page speech to introduce the African concept of *ubuntu*. A philosophy made globally famous by Archbishop Desmond Tutu, *ubuntu* roughly translates as "a person is a person because of other people."

Sergio told the employees, "When you function in such an environment, your identity, what you are as a person, is based on the fact that you are seen and acknowledged by others as a person. It is reflected in the way in which people greet each other. The equivalent to 'hello' is the expression *sawubona,* which literally means 'I see you.' The response is *sikhona,* 'I am here.' The sequence of the exchange is important: until you are seen, you do not exist."

He then told his new workforce, "From my end, as your leader, I can simply tell you that: I see you. I am glad you are here."

Early on, Sergio made two bold moves. First he gave Chrysler managers $700 million and three months to attack the quality problems and cheap interiors of the current product line. An internal study had shown that customers rated thirty-two of Chrysler's cars or trucks as "mediocre to bad." Complaints ranged from rattles, stiff brakes, and sloppy steering to the dreaded condemnation "it feels cheap." A Boston Consulting Group study showed that only 11 percent of consumers would even consider buying a Chrysler. The Dodge brand of trucks scored a little better, but still far behind rivals like Ford.

Sergio's aim was to eke out a couple more years of life from Chrysler's aging product lines, until 2012 and 2013 when new car and truck designs, many using Fiat platforms, would arrive. Those hundreds of millions of dollars bought a lot of improvements. *Consumer Reports* had singled out Chrysler and Dodge minivans for an inability to handle well in an emergency, hardly an appealing attribute in a suburban kid-mover. The minivans got newly designed suspensions. The Chrysler 300 and Dodge Stratus — sedans so bad they'd been lampooned on *Saturday Night Live* — got new V6 engines with a six-speed transmission option, plus new suspensions and tires to improve the ride. Nor was all Sergio's spending on products. He pumped tens of millions into fixing up cafeterias and restrooms in Chrysler plants as well as doing other long-deferred maintenance and repairs, all of which helped boost morale.

His second bold decision was to let retail sales fall to a "natural" level by slashing the incentives to which Chrysler had become addicted. "Buy a Chrysler — get a check" had been the joke for years. By early 2009, the company was slapping $4,400 or more in incentives on every car or truck it sold, compared with about $1,600 on average for Honda and Toyota.

Cutting incentives was a gutsy move that reflected Sergio's instinctive management style. No amount of analysis could predict how fast or how far sales would fall before they stabilized. Yet month after month he notched the incentives down. Despite the $3 billion of Cash for Clunkers money that flowed into consumers' hands, stimulating sales for most automakers, Chrysler's numbers plunged.

By November, when Sergio and his managers held a seven-hour briefing for several hundred dealers, journalists, and Wall Street analysts to present Chrysler's five-year plan, sales were down a scary 39 percent from their depressed 2008 levels. "The new Chrysler is parsimonious — cheap," Sergio said, explaining why he'd sworn off the incentives game. Behind his bravado he was probably nervous, yet he believed brand reputation was everything — he often pointed to Apple as the ideal. Years of discounting had cheapened all of Chrysler's brands, and he thought that incentives, unless checked, would ultimately destroy the company.

Watching from Washington, Ron Bloom had become increasingly uneasy. We had told Larry that the $8 billion of new money would carry Chrysler for at least eighteen months, and possibly forever. But sales were now bumping up against our worst-case scenarios, and we all knew how fast cash can disappear when an automaker's sales fall. Ron stepped up his pace of calls and e-mails to Sergio. Finally Sergio's response was direct: "What can I tell you? It will be a shitty year." This was his way of asking Ron to be patient while Chrysler kicked the incentives habit.

That did not reassure Ron. What did calm him was the company's third-quarter results. Sergio wasn't kidding about being cheap: the company had $5.7 billion in cash at the end of the third quarter of 2009, $1.7 billion more than it had at the start of the year. Despite the sales collapse, Sergio had imposed cost-cutting measures that enabled Chrysler to build up its cash. That surprised all of us. If nothing else, we had believed that Cerberus and Nardelli had been brutally focused on costs. Yet, even as he was pumping money into fixing the product, Sergio had found places to cut.

And unlike the first months of Shiny New GM, Sergio's board was happy with him from the start. We had appointed Bob Kidder, a former CEO of both Duracell and Borden, as chairman. Kidder had attended the University of Michigan and lived in Columbus, Ohio; for him, helping save a major industrial company was a labor of love. He was as undemonstrative as Sergio was flamboyant, a combination that clicked, even though Kidder spent several days a week in Auburn Hills, up in the old executive offices on the fifteenth floor of the tower.

GM's numbers were far better than Chrysler's. In its first quarter of existence, Shiny New GM sold $28 billion worth of vehicles, $4.5 billion ahead of our forecast. Top management worked fast to implement the streamlining and cost-cutting called for in our plans. The company's cash position was better than predicted too, so much so that when the White House wanted some money back to improve its political standing, GM proudly announced it would start repaying its U.S. and Canadian loans.

Yet that fall, with each passing day, the board grew less patient with Fritz. One early source of trouble was the sale of money-losing Opel. The buyer that had won the favor of the German government after tortuous, months-long bidding was Magna International, a Canada-based auto-parts maker with about $24 billion in annual sales. Sberbank, Russia's largest bank, which was 60 percent government-owned, was to be a significant equity investor.

"Sale" was something of a misnomer. Magna was essentially proposing to take the $34-billion-a-year Opel off GM's hands with the help of $6 billion in German government financing. GM would retain a minority stake, while the rest of the equity would be split among Sberbank, Magna, and Opel's employees.

GM would have preferred another bidder, the private equity firm Ripplewood, in large part because the deal would have included an option to buy Opel back — many at the company were concerned about the loss of a European presence and the lack of a midsize-car-design capability. But the German government, which had a long-standing antipathy toward private equity, insisted on Magna. Chancellor Angela Merkel, in the midst of her reelection campaign, believed the Magna deal would save jobs.

Fritz, not wanting to further prolong the ordeal, convened the board via conference call in mid-August, asking them to approve the preliminary terms. The docile board of the old GM would have blessed the deal instantly. The new board, however, resisted.

Bonderman and Akerson, the private equity duo, argued against the proposal. As professional deal guys, they hated the terms, which had been framed back in the spring when business was at its nadir. To them, a deal is not a deal until a binding agreement is signed. They felt GM should renegotiate, and if that was impossible, maybe GM should hold on to Opel and sell it in two years and get more for it as the global economy improved. Girsky was also against the sale, for strategic reasons. He argued that for GM to be a global automaker it needed a presence in Europe. And he was certain that GM needed Opel to develop midsize cars for the United States and elsewhere.

It would not be the last time that Bonderman, Akerson, and Girsky teamed up to challenge a management proposal. GM executives came to nickname them "the three amigos." But almost all the directors were skittish about the Magna deal. Kresa said that GM should consider keeping Opel now that the U.S. economy was improving. Isdell agreed that a global company needed a large European operation. Another member of the old guard, Phil Laskawy, mostly kept silent, willing to go with whatever the majority decided, but chimed in that it was a poor deal for GM. The consensus was that this was too important a decision to make via conference call.

Fritz was forced to wait until the September board meeting. There, Opel was high on the agenda, and after more discussion, he won the directors' reluctant approval for the preliminary terms. But it was clear to everyone that this was far from a done deal. The European autoworkers had yet to agree, for one thing, and the European Union also had to approve.

The rest of the meeting did not go any better for Fritz. As the directors worked their way through the day's agenda, they came upon a request to finance the development of a new engine called the Ecotec. To GM, this highly efficient four-cylinder design represented a critical improvement. It was slated to become the largest-volume engine in GM's lineup, to be used in small cars, midsize sedans like the Malibu, and crossover vehicles like the Chevy Equinox. Every GM brand except for Cadillac would feature it, and it would occupy three or four engine plants employing thousands of workers. Fritz and his team saw the proposal as routine; at $1.2 billion, in the old days it barely would have qualified for board-level attention. It occupied a single page deep inside the board book, $650 million for Phase I and $550 million for Phase II, with a resolution of approval attached.

Team Auto, of course, had bounced back many such requests for lack of substance and analysis, but the lesson had not sunk in. "What would you do if you got this at Carlyle?" Bonderman asked Akerson, who snorted in response. Other new directors were also perplexed. It didn't help management's cause that John Smith, the stubborn, imperious group vice president, was overseeing both the Ecotec and the troubled Opel deal. Smith bristled when one of the board's newcomers suggested that the proposal should include an analysis showing critical metrics such as return on investment. Car companies need new engines to boost fuel economy and meet U.S. standards, he answered impatiently. They don't calculate what they will get from the investment, another executive added.

This didn't sit well with Bonderman. "Back where I come from, we first have to justify why we need a new engine," he shot back. "Then you would give us a series of materials justifying how much it would cost and why. Let's make it easy. Assume you need an engine. What's the rate of return?"

The executives were now baffled and upset. In their minds, cars need engines, and when an automaker develops a new one like the Ecotec, no one knows for sure which vehicles it will go into. They also did not believe — with some justification — that a rate of return on a single element of a car can be accurately calculated.

They were more baffled when a new board member asked why an engine couldn't just be purchased from somewhere else. Automakers see engines as the core of their business and are very reluctant to farm them out, especially engines expected to be as widely used as this one. Both the executives and the old directors felt that the newcomers had a lot to learn. The new directors viewed exchanges of this sort as further confirmation that Harry and his colleagues had spoken the truth in their August 3 presentation. And the more they got to know GM executives like Smith, the more they thought that a personnel housecleaning was in order.

Fritz eventually tabled the discussion. He told his team to proceed with the design and engineering of the Ecotec while the financial staff developed the analysis the board wanted. In part because of the unusual nature of the request and in part because of GM's hidebound accounting systems, the analysis would take two months and untold manhours. Bonderman rejected the first version, forcing the work to be redone before the board finally voted to approve the Ecotec.

The confrontation left a bad taste on both sides. Word of friction between management and board began to leak into the press, with anonymous executives accusing the board of wasting time and getting too involved in the nitty-gritty at GM.

Whitacre stayed out of such debates, but the uncertainty in the boardroom about Fritz's status inadvertently seeped into public consciousness when he, and not Fritz, suddenly emerged as GM's TV pitchman. A sixty-second commercial that debuted on September 13 featured the GM chairman wearing a dark suit and a red tie and striding through a brightly lit automotive design studio in a campaign called "May the Best Car Win."

"Before I started this job, I admit I had some doubts—probably a lot like you," he tells the viewer in his soft Texas drawl. "But I like what I found. I think you will too."

He then launches his pitch. "Car for car, when compared to the competition, we win. It is as simple as that . . . We're putting our money where our mouth is . . . Put us to the test," Whitacre says, offering a sixty-day, money-back guarantee. "Put us up against anyone, and may the best car win."

The commercial was reminiscent of Lee Iacocca's iconic Chrysler ads thirty years earlier, challenging America, "If you can find a better car, buy it." It left industry watchers wondering what was going on inside GM. Some saw it as a signal of Whitacre's interest in being more than a nonexecutive chairman. Others speculated that Fritz had put Whitacre up to it in hopes of ingratiating himself.

In fact, the decision to put Whitacre on the air was made by the GM marketing department. Marketing was among Whitacre's passions, as he'd made clear to me during our first trip together to Detroit. He hammered constantly at the staff, complaining that GM did a poor job of selling people on its cars. He liked the "May the Best Car Win" concept, and wanted somehow to acknowledge taxpayers for the help they'd given GM. The challenge, of course, was to make the message ring true—the bailout was immensely unpopular, and taxpayers didn't like to be reminded of it. Whitacre resisted being in the commercial at first, but then told the marketers, "If you test the crap out of it, I will do it." In market testing he came across as credible. Someone with his folksy drawl obviously wasn't part of the team that had driven GM to ruin.

The commercial ran for barely a week, but with constant replay on cable TV news and on the Internet, it created an impression that Whitacre was now in charge—or soon would be.

For Fritz, the Opel deal was a nightmare. Negotiations dragged on into the fall. Germany's 1.5 billion euro bridge loan was keeping the company solvent, but ironically, it removed any real urgency to close the deal. The European autoworkers still hadn't fully agreed to terms. Magna founder Frank Stronach, a crusty and notoriously tight-fisted Austrian-born entrepreneur, seized every opportunity to haggle. This gave even Ron Bloom misgivings; he called Fritz repeatedly to complain that Magna was continually recutting the deal to squeeze GM.

Then the European Union completed its review, only to kick the problem right back into Fritz's lap. Worried about the impact of Germany's loans on Opel's commitment to other European countries, it requested a formal reevaluation by the GM board. All of this was just as I had told President Obama in regard to Chrysler back in March: a deal that looks iffy at the start typically only gets worse. With so many governments involved, Opel was beyond typical. In fact, GM was on its way to creating an international incident.

By November 3, as the directors assembled for the monthly board meeting, their sentiment had clearly swung toward keeping the European unit. Pat Russo, for example, noted that other automakers make money there, so perhaps it was just a question of improving Opel's management. She also observed that Opel was strategically positioned to take advantage of the growing central European market.

Fritz, who'd run GM Europe and Opel, doubted that the business could ever generate a profit. He believed that GM should finish the deal it had started. Wasn't jettisoning money-losing operations the kind of tough decision the new GM should embrace? Europe was a mature auto market where competition was as ruthless as in the United States, or more so. And tough restructuring moves were harder to make in the heavily regulated EU. The board's resistance started to feel to Fritz like a pretext to run him out of his job.

Kresa and others, meanwhile, were surprised that Fritz didn't respond to the board's increasing skepticism of the Opel deal. The world was different now, and GM actually had cash and no longer needed a fire sale. What the board wanted were options. But all Fritz offered was the Magna transaction.

No one in Detroit appeared concerned, or perhaps even to be aware, that Chancellor Merkel was in Washington that day, where she was to address Congress. This was her first visit to the United States since her reelection in September. Perhaps mindful of that, the Opel union announced that morning it had agreed to concessions that would have saved 265 million euros a year if GM proceeded with the deal, thus removing one of the final obstacles. But none of this seemed of consequence to the GM board, which now voted to back out. Just hours after the union announcement, GM declared that it had decided not to sell Opel, and that it would restructure the company instead.

Merkel was completely blindsided, much to the Obama administration's chagrin. Fritz called her aides to convey the news just before she was to board her plane home. By all accounts, she was furious. She made no public statement, but by the next morning her ministers blasted GM, and one of her aides called for the company to repay the bridge loan. The autoworkers threatened mass demonstrations. Other European leaders, as well as Russian Prime Minister Vladimir Putin, chimed in. And Treasury spokesperson Meg Reilly said in a statement, "The Administration was not involved with this decision, which was made by GM's board of directors."

After that November board meeting adjourned, Fritz and Ed sat down to strategize. Fritz told Ed it "would be hell" in Europe following this decision, but volunteered to cancel a planned trip to Brazil to go to Europe "and take all the bullets on this thing."

It was hard for Fritz not to believe that the unraveling of the deal might cost him his job. So he asked Whitacre point-blank, "If you're going to get rid of me, let me know now because I've got better things to do with my life."

Ed reassured Fritz he was not being fired and should fly to Europe. All the same, rumors continued to swirl, even after Whitacre publicly expressed support for Henderson a week later, telling Bloomberg News, "The Board is fully behind Fritz; he's working hard."

In reality, opposition to Henderson was mounting, especially among the new directors who had always been skeptics. Bonderman and Akerson were thoroughly disenchanted. Girsky was unhappy with what he saw as disarray in GM's sales and marketing. Carol Stephenson, the Ontario business school dean who occupied the Canadian board seat, had arrived under the influence of officials who had negotiated her nation's share of the bailout. The GMers had struck the Canadians as highhanded and dismissive of outside ideas. While generally quiet in board meetings, Stephenson expressed concerns that GM wasn't giving the board the data and details it needed to make informed decisions.

Change — or lack of it — had become a major sticking point. Many directors felt that GM's presentations remained too optimistic, just as the task force had warned. And even though Wagoner was gone, board members saw some of the old arrogance, including a resurgence of the view that GM's bankruptcy was not its fault but rather was due to the financial collapse and economic downturn. Patricia Russo was so put off that she suggested to Fritz that he tell his executives to quit talking as though GM were such a top-notch company; it still had a long way to go.

Some members of the old board, including Laskawy and Kresa, were inclined to give Fritz more time. Compared to Wagoner, he was a believer in change. During his brief tenure as interim chairman, Kresa had coached Fritz about the need to bring in new blood. Fritz had duly read up on other companies and cultures. But recruiting outsiders for top posts wasn't his strength; he remained doggedly loyal to GM people and ways. Ray Young was still CFO. His decision to bring back Bob Lutz left many on the board scratching their heads. And when Katy Barclay, the head of human resources, finally resigned, Fritz proposed a GM manufacturing executive to take her post.

Whitacre and the board had asked Fritz to reduce the number of his direct reports, in part by naming a chief of GM North America, a position Fritz had eliminated when GM emerged from bankruptcy. But Fritz resisted. In one tart exchange, he told Whitacre that people would simply go around the North American head to the CEO to get their way. Whitacre replied that it was the CEO's job not to let that happen.

Throughout the fall, board members discussed among themselves what to do. I talked periodically to a number of the directors and sensed growing and widespread unhappiness with Fritz. But Whitacre put off all talk of replacements; he had promised Henderson at least 120 days — until early December — to show what he could do, and meant to honor that commitment.

By the time of the discussion in the executive session after the November board meeting, it was clear to all that Fritz would be asked to leave in a month's time. The problem was whom to replace him with. For reasons much like our decision to replace Rick with Fritz, no one believed that GM could be left rudderless while a search was conducted. Nor, of course, were there any potential successors within the executive team.

So the board looked in its own midst for at least an interim solution. Girsky wanted the job, but while he was well liked and highly respected, no one thought he was ready to be CEO of General Motors. Akerson, a former CEO, declined to be considered, citing his obligations to Carlyle and lack of enthusiasm for living in Detroit. Directors began to wonder whether Whitacre could be pressed into service.

Fritz could sense rumblings, but he was in the dark. On November 30, the day before the December board meeting, he decided to end the suspense. His calendar called for him to leave right after the meeting to be the keynote speaker at the Los Angeles auto show; he asked Whitacre whether he ought to keep to his travel plan. The chairman told him to hang back. Although the board had not yet made a formal decision, Whitacre knew with virtual certainty what would occur the next day. About the same time, he phoned Ron Bloom to give him a heads-up that the board was likely to fire Fritz. This didn't surprise Ron — he'd been in the camp that had rated Fritz's chances of success at 40 percent.

The next morning, the board plowed through its regular agenda. Afterward, in an executive session that lasted less than five minutes, the directors voted unanimously to relieve Fritz. Then the board turned to Whitacre, securing his assent to become interim CEO while a search for a permanent replacement was conducted.

When Whitacre delivered the news to him a few minutes later, Fritz had two reactions. He told Whitacre he didn't want to stay on if the board didn't want him. And he asked, "Could I have done anything differently?"

For some reason, Whitacre answered "No."

A little later, Whitacre pulled Girsky aside. "You with me on this?" he asked. He offered the former auto analyst a full-time job as a top adviser, with the title of vice chairman. Girsky was elated, but since his responsibility on the board was to represent the UAW, he said that Whitacre should call Gettelfinger to get his approval.

Whitacre reached the UAW leader, who asked, "When are you doing this?"

"In about thirty minutes," Whitacre replied.

"Nothing gets done at GM in thirty minutes," Gettelfinger said, laughing. But he readily agreed. It couldn't hurt to have the UAW board designee doubling as consigliere to GM's CEO.

Before the public announcement, Whitacre assembled many of Fritz's direct reports in a thirty-eighth-floor conference room — executives such as Ray Young, the global head of manufacturing and labor relations Tim Lee, and GM's new head of human resources Mary Barra.

"Fritz Henderson has decided to step aside and the board has accepted that decision," he told them. "I will step in as interim CEO."

There were few happy or relieved faces; mostly the executives responded with a mix of anger and sorrow. "I was handpicked by Fritz, so if you had a problem with him, then you probably have a problem with me," Lee said and offered to step down on the spot.

"Hey, hey, I am not taking anyone's resignation tonight," said Whitacre. "Fritz is the least surprised person right now. This is the way it has to be. We all have to stand together." The last thing he wanted was a mass exodus, which would look really bad in the media. A little later, in a hastily arranged press conference, the company released the news to the world. Fritz Henderson, the first CEO of the new General Motors, was gone. It had been 247 days since I had asked Rick Wagoner to step aside and Fritz Henderson to take his place.

Fritz's ouster drew headlines. "GM CEO Fritz Henderson Abruptly Sent Packing," declared *USA Today*. But for the most part, bigger issues like health care reform and stepping up the war in Afghanistan had long since eclipsed the bailout on the front page.

The company retained Spencer Stuart to search for a permanent CEO, determined to secure a superstar like Mulally. But the target list was small, because the board wanted only candidates who had already served as chief executives, which of course Mulally had not before joining Ford. Living in Detroit was another turnoff for candidates, as was the prospect of facing the government's pay czar. Not a single candidate had been interviewed when Whitacre did an about-face and told the board, "Hell, I'll do it." But he refused to make the two-year commitment that the board requested, promising instead to stay long enough to carry the company through an initial public offering. To the outside world, the announcement in January 2010 that the GM board voted to remove the "interim" from Whitacre's title confirmed the impression that Ed had, indeed, flunked retirement.

Whitacre's impact as CEO was dramatic. Within days of taking command, he reorganized the company's sprawling sales and marketing operation and announced Mark Reuss as president of GM North America, the position that Fritz had resisted creating. Soon afterward, Ray Young was gone as chief of finance, replaced by a surprise recruit from the tech world, Chris Liddell, the former CFO of Microsoft. Liddell was appalled at what he found, from GM's inability to assess its cash position to its habit of delivering data without insight — he told his three thousand staffers worldwide that such data were useless. He ordered an immediate and sweeping overhaul of the company's financial systems.

The changes at the top accelerated, and by the time he had been in place ninety days, Whitacre had eased out four top-level executives, reassigned twenty more, and brought in seven outsiders to fill top jobs. Vice chairman Lutz announced his re-retirement on March 3 and Whitacre cut back on direct reports. GM's executive committee now consisted of twelve people, nearly all of whom were either new to their jobs or auto industry rookies, like Ed Whitacre himself.

The shakeup caused growing consternation inside GM, to the point where Whitacre felt it necessary to send a calming message to the troops. "I want to reassure you that the major leadership changes are behind us," he wrote in an e-mail in late March, after reorganizing the marketing department for a second time. "The team we have in place today is the team that will take us forward."

Now that he was a full-time auto executive, Whitacre got an apartment in downtown Detroit, in the same complex where Steve Girsky lived. He used a hefty chunk of his new compensation package of $9 million a year to charter private jets to fly up to the city from San Antonio on Sunday night and back on Friday afternoon or evening, a cost of government oversight that irked him no end. As he revamped the leadership, Whitacre made it a point to mingle with rank-and-file employees. He would show up in the RenCen's food court to eat a fast-food lunch among GM middle managers, and used the same elevators as they did, often greeting a fellow rider with, "Hi, I'm Ed. Who're you?" In May, he showed up unannounced at the Detroit-Hamtramck Assembly Plant wearing jeans and a sweatshirt and with no corporate ID. After waiting in the lobby for twenty minutes while someone tracked down the plant manager, he was let in to wander around and chat with workers. Getting out to meet employees, he told his lieutenants, enabled him to ask if their bosses were delivering on promises they had made. He was equally down-to-earth in his interactions with Gettelfinger, having breakfast with him at Gettelfinger's favorite diner.

Simplicity was Whitacre's favorite message. He crusaded to eliminate meetings, streamline reports, and drive down decisionmaking to lower levels of management. At a "future product design" meeting, a quasi-ritual assembly of senior design directors traditionally attended by the CEO, he abruptly stood up and said, "You are all smart guys, right? You know what to do," and left the room. Whitacre liked to remind people that the CEO did not have to be involved in every single issue. His job was to set long-term strategy — like whether GM should create an in-house finance company now that it was no longer tied to GMAC — and to offer inspiration and guidance. After that, if he was smart, he would get out of the way.

Board meetings changed too. They ran hours shorter, wrapping up by 11:30 A.M. so directors could catch planes home in the early afternoon — very much as Whitacre had described to me over dinner in Washington back in May. He seemed to know what information the board wanted to see, and they seemed to agree with the majority of his decisions. Whitacre also made it clear he wasn't looking for or encouraging much oversight, even from Bonderman and Akerson, who'd been such thorns in Fritz's side. Some directors, recalling the confrontations with Fritz, laughed privately that the board was now almost as deferential to Ed Whitacre as the prebankruptcy board had been to Rick Wagoner. In the minds of the directors, they didn't have much choice: Whitacre was the only man to do the job, and he was only going to do the job on his terms.

The simplicity mantra didn't always go over well with battle-scarred GM veterans, however. Just before he was named CEO, Whitacre attended a town-hall-style meeting at the Tech Center in Warren. He told the engineers that the job of GM was "to sell more cars and more trucks for more money. Period." This sounded simplistic to the engineers, and they bombarded him with questions on process and protocol, which he batted away. By the time he addressed another gathering of engineers a few months later, he had sharpened his pitch: "If your bosses are asking you to do something that is not about selling more vehicles or fixing quality, question what they are doing." The engineers were pleased; *this* was the sort of simplicity mandate they could relate to.

From the perspective of selling cars, Whitacre's timing could hardly have been better. Not only did the recession seem to be ending, but on January 21, four days before his CEO status was made permanent, Toyota found itself in the largest product safety scandal in its seventy-seven-year history. It recalled millions of vehicles and suspended sales and production on more than half its U.S. models, including its best-selling Camry, because of faulty accelerator pedals that could stick, causing uncontrollable acceleration.

The problems marred the sterling reputation of the world's largest automaker. By February, Toyota executives were facing congressional hearings and grand jury inquiries as consumers came forward with heart-wrenching tales of vehicles accelerating out of control and killing loved ones. All three Detroit carmakers benefited from Toyota's crisis: Ford sales jumped 43 percent in February, and GM's rose 12 percent. Chrysler's also rose, just 0.47 percent, but its first monthly increase since 2007. More importantly, the Detroit automakers continued to pull back on rebates and low-interest offers — narrowing, at least slightly, the incentive gap with Toyota.

Two problems that had beset his predecessors remained intractable for Whitacre. Opel was still losing money — $500 million in the first quarter of 2010 alone — leaving unanswered the question of whether the board had been right to keep the European operation. Not only was GM obliged to pay back the bridge loan Germany had provided, but also the German government declared it would offer no longer-term support. This meant GM was now on its own to face restructuring costs estimated at 3.3 billion euros. Whitacre believed that the new labor agreement in Germany would cut the losses in half, and if the German government continued to play hardball, production could be moved to places like Poland to further reduce costs.

Dealers posed a more difficult problem. Their proponents and lobbyists on Capitol Hill had drowned out the automakers' arguments as well as a firm declaration from the White House: "The Administration strongly opposes the language in the bill that attempts to restore prior Chrysler and General Motors franchise agreements," it began. In December, as part of a $1.1 trillion spending bill for 2010, the House and the Senate tucked in a provision guaranteeing to every dealer closed as a result of the bailout the right to seek reinstatement through arbitration—laborious and distracting for the companies. Sergio immediately threatened to sue, though the new law would have a far smaller impact on Chrysler, which had cut off unwanted dealers so quickly and brutally that it would end up having to reinstate only a handful.

General Motors, however, was paying the price for having been considerate. It had given franchisees eighteen months to wind down, so almost all of the 2,000 dealers slated to be closed were still in business. Whitacre had no choice but to relent. In March, GM said it would retain some 660 dealers it had initially planned to shut down. By August, another 65 had gotten a reprieve.

This left the domestic dealer network at 4,500, well north of the 3,600 that GM and Team Auto had concluded, a year earlier, made sense. Officially, Whitacre maintained that a bigger network would be good for business: more dealers should equal more sales, especially in rural and suburban areas. I wasn't so sure. If more dealers were better than fewer, then why weren't the transplants seeking to add more dealerships? I had heard many industry experts emphasize the need to reduce the number of stores. And in our conversations, Fritz had agreed.

Any criticism of Whitacre's management shakeup or of GM's ongoing problems was muted by the company's better-than-expected performance. It posted its first quarterly profit in almost three years in the first quarter of 2010, exceeding Team Auto's projections handily. Its net income of $865 million wildly outpaced a first-quarter 2009 loss of nearly $6 billion. Revenue jumped 40 percent globally, despite the elimination of the Saturn, Hummer, and Pontiac nameplates.

Business had turned around so demonstrably that by spring Whitacre was having regular conversations with Ron Bloom about a public offering. The goal of many in the Obama administration, including Larry Summers, had long been for a stock sale in late 2010—not coincidentally around the time of the midterm elections. Now Whitacre embraced the idea. He felt an offering that got the government back some more of its money and reduced its ownership stake would ease animosity among the car-buying public toward "Government Motors." This animosity wasn't just in GM's imagination: Ford had reams of data showing that consumers were considering its Focuses and Explorers because Ford was the sole Detroit automaker that hadn't taken a handout.

Looking toward a November IPO, the U.S. Treasury issued a public request on May 10 seeking a bank to serve as GM's underwriter. This was a plum opportunity in the wake of the financial crash. Not only did GM have a shot at becoming the largest IPO in history, but in the future it would also need lines of credit, revolving loans, and other services. All the top banks threw their hats in the ring, each dispatching to Washington on May 19 a team of no more than five people and a pitch book of no more than twenty pages, as the Treasury had carefully specified.

Ordinary sales teams these were not: Bank of America and Morgan Stanley brought their CEOs, Goldman Sachs brought its president, and Citi had its CEO, Vikram Pandit, call in. Each presentation had an unabashedly patriotic tenor, emphasizing what a great advertisement for America it would be to cap a fast, successful government bailout with a triumphant return to the public markets.

As might have been expected, Jimmy Lee's pitch took the cake. A year earlier, during the Chrysler talks, he had angrily declared that he would steer clear of doing business with the government and that JPMorgan was "making a list" of industries, like autos, that it would avoid in the future because of government interference. But a brightening economy, an uptick in car sales, and an auto industry newly freed of leverage and legacy costs had prompted Jimmy to reconsider. To underscore the importance of the deal to JPMorgan, he'd brought his CEO, Jamie Dimon, down with him on the Acela.

GM's IPO would be "a historic day for America," Jimmy told the assembled Treasury and GM officials. The bank's pitch book, its cover emblazoned with "The Best Car Wins," included a copy of an old *Wall Street Journal* article about JPMorgan's funding of a GM deal in 1920. Jimmy also volunteered that the bank would be willing to take its fees in GM equity. And to anyone who was interested, he showed pictures on his BlackBerry of his new $110,000 cobalt blue ZR1, a top-of-the-line Corvette. He'd bought it to demonstrate his commitment to the product.

Bloom did not miss the opportunity to tease. "Oh, you like us now," he said to Jimmy. Others asked if Jimmy would like to visit the old rooms at Treasury where he and I had butted heads.

In the end, GM picked JPMorgan and Morgan Stanley as co-lead managers. The Treasury drove a hard bargain on fees. On a mega-IPO, the banks would typically keep 2 to 3 percentage points of the "gross spread"—the difference between the public offering price and the price per share paid by the underwriter. But Bloom and his team argued that the chance to be part of this once-in-a-lifetime deal warranted a big discount. The two banks agreed to a 0.75 percent gross spread after another bank, Goldman Sachs, offered to work for that low fee.

On August 12, just days before an expected filing of an initial public offering prospectus, GM threw its throng of observers and stakeholders a curve. In the middle of a second-quarter earnings call, whose good news had been thoroughly previewed by Whitacre the previous week, the chief executive suddenly announced that he would be stepping down on September 1 and that director Dan Akerson would replace him. The analysts and reporters were stunned. Wild rumors circulated—had the government pushed out the tall Texan just as it had Rick Wagoner?

The board had been just as surprised a few days earlier when Whitacre had informed them in the executive session portion of its regular monthly meeting that he was quitting. The only clue the board had received was in the advance agenda: extra time had been allotted for the executive session. The directors were far from thrilled. Whitacre wasn't perfect—he hated detail work and wasn't regarded as a genius—but his decisiveness and emphasis on speed had been just what GM needed. A brief effort was made to talk Ed out of his decision, but Ed was not a man who changed his mind.

Several directors felt left in the lurch. Just as when they had asked Fritz to leave in late 2009, GM had no internal candidates (this was one of many management problems that remained to be addressed). With the IPO looming, there was no time to organize and conduct a search.

Once again, the board would have to look among its members for a chief executive.

Three potential candidates — Akerson, Russo, and Girsky — were asked to step out of the room while the others deliberated. ("We should ask everyone" if they want to be considered, Kathy Marinello said, in one of her usual half-baked comments, annoying the other directors.) They narrowed the list quickly. Girsky was not seen as a plausible replacement — no real management experience. And while Russo had done well as GM's lead director, her past performances as a chief executive had been rocky. That left Akerson.

In my view, he was the right choice. Akerson and Whitacre possess the same kind of toughness and decisiveness. Akerson, younger and more energetic, will likely have even less patience for the old GM ways than Whitacre did. Once he became so impatient with doctors who were treating his gallbladder in a German hospital that he removed the tubes from his arm, checked out, and flew back to the U.S. On top of that determination, he brings the private equity sensibility I value highly.

My former Team Auto colleagues David Markowitz and Sadiq Malik had been Akerson fans since he told them at their first meeting how much he had hated losing a golf game the day before on the eighteenth hole. "He was more passionate about a round of eighteen than most of the employees at GM were about their company," David remarked to Sadiq after the meeting.

His sole potential disadvantage is age. At sixty-one, Akerson may wish to serve only for a few years, which would necessitate yet another change at the top. Despite this, he might well have gotten the job even if the board had conducted a full-blown outside search. His name, after all, had been floated twice before, when Fritz was fired and again at the beginning of the abortive search to replace Whitacre when he was still interim CEO. On both occasions Akerson had declined to be considered. But by spring, he was kicking himself for letting the opportunity slip. He had come to realize that he'd much preferred his years as a chief executive at General Instrument and other companies to being a private equity guy. A former naval officer, he also saw becoming CEO of General Motors at this crucial point in history as an opportunity for public service.

Choosing GM over Carlyle entailed a major financial and personal sacrifice for Dan. It meant walking away from a massive amount of Carlyle equity for lonely, grueling workweeks in Detroit, with weekend commutes home to Virginia at his own expense. Though Dan took the job without knowing how much he would be paid, the compensation was sure to be low by CEO standards. Whitacre's compensation had been limited to $9 million a year, mostly in the form of stock, placing him in the bottom 25 percent of comparable CEOs, and the same government strictures on executive pay would apply to Dan.

As glad as I was to see Akerson step up, I shared the board's disappointment with Whitacre. He had promised to see GM through its initial public offering, which the directors took to mean that he would stay until at least mid-2011. (A company can't market an IPO if it knows of impending management changes, and in any event, the board would want to mount an orderly search for a more permanent chief.) Instead he forced GM to scramble to appoint its fourth CEO in less than eighteen months. If anyone had asked Jack Welch, I'm sure he would have advised against this rapid shuffling of CEOs.

I was also disappointed when I heard that Akerson would become chairman as well as CEO on December 1. Nothing has occurred to change my view that "best practices" in corporate governance means separating the chairman and chief executive roles. And if ever a company needed to hew firmly to best practices in corporate governance, it is the one that owes its existence to the support and goodwill of the American taxpayer: shiny new General Motors.

EPILOGUE

SHINY NEW GM celebrated its first birthday on July 10, 2010, a month after the first anniversary of the reconstituted Chrysler. As hard-nosed realists, all of us on Team Auto have been, for the most part, reassured and relieved by the generally good news from Detroit since those important anniversaries. General Motors and Chrysler continue to pay their workers and are gradually adding shifts as they sell more cars. The unemployment rates in Michigan, Indiana, and Ohio, while still painfully high, have begun to edge down. We remain proud of the work that got us to this point, a mission that was not designed to further a particular economic theory, serve anyone's ideology or political party, or make anyone a buck (beyond the companies and their workers). So devastating were the possible consequences of this crisis that we were impelled to push ourselves, to question and requestion, to look at each decision from every possible angle and perspective. We were scared enough to stay focused on one and only one objective: getting it right.

To be able, on August 18, 2010, to pick up General Motors's newly filed 734-page IPO prospectus was for me an emotional moment. This thick legal document symbolized, like no other development thus far, the transformation of so-called Government Motors back into General Motors. Page after page of figures told the story of a remarkable turnaround. The decision to move forward with this public offering was the strongest and most telling indication that the U.S. Treasury will recover most if not all of the $82 billion the American taxpayer staked on overhauling Detroit.

Let's pause to run the numbers. Here's where the $82 billion went:

Reason	Company/Program	Amount Invested (billions)
Emergency funding before restructuring	GM	$19.4
Funding at behest of Team Auto for reorganization under bankruptcy	GM	$30.1
Emergency funding before restructuring	Chrysler	$4.0
Funding at behest of Team Auto for reorganization under bankruptcy	Chrysler	$8.1
Emergency funding in January 2009 to allow Chrysler to continue making auto loans	Chrysler Financial	$1.5
Emergency funding in December 2008	GMAC	$5.9[1]
Funding at behest of Team Auto to recapitalize the bank	GMAC	$11.8[2]
To maintain consumer confidence as GM and Chrysler reorganized under bankruptcy	Warranty Program	$0.6
To strengthen supply chain as GM and Chrysler reorganized under bankruptcy	Supplier Support Program	$0.4[3]
TOTAL		**$81.8**

1. Includes $0.9 billion loan to GM for GMAC rights offering on January 16, 2009.
2. Includes $0.5 billion loan to Chrysler for GMAC loss share agreement.
3. Actual size of the Supplier Support Program was $5 billion. Given the general success of the program, a much lower amount was needed to stabilize the supplier base.

Assessing what the taxpayer has gotten in return is more complicated. GM's value won't become clear until after the IPO, when the stock will be publicly traded and the market sets the price. As of August 2010, the best proxy is the trading level of old GM bonds, to which we grudgingly allocated 10 percent of the equity of Shiny New GM (along with some warrants). By that measure, the value of Treasury's 60.8 percent ownership of GM is approximately $31 billion. Adding to that the $6.7 billion of debt that GM has already repaid, and $2.1 billion of GM preferred stock, brings the total to nearly $40 billion.

This is $10 billion more than the $30 billion the United States injected into GM at the time of its bankruptcy filing as a result of Team

Auto's work. But it's roughly $10 billion short if you also count the emergency $19.4 billion spent by the Bush and Obama administrations to prop up GM before Team Auto came on the scene. I view that $19.4 billion as lost money — a cost of the delays due to the presidential election, the transition, and the doctrine of "one President at a time."

Question marks remain regarding the smaller but still significant commitments of taxpayer dollars to Chrysler and GMAC. I've described the heated debates in the West Wing and at Treasury about Chrysler; Team Auto always knew that asking the Treasury to infuse another $8 billion into this hollowed-out, North-America-only player was a risky call. I was delighted when Chrysler notched two successive quarterly operating profits in the first half of 2010. But until we see sales results from new products due to appear in dealers' showrooms in late 2010 and beyond, we cannot know whether our surgery saved the patient.

Meanwhile, the auto loan portfolio belonging to GMAC (which had changed its name to Ally) performed well throughout, just as we had assured the FDIC it would, even as the company continued to unwind its terrible mortgage portfolio. The trading levels for Ally bonds indicated that the market viewed the company as solvent, although not without risks. Nonetheless, the value of the $11.3 billion of TARP equity was still not clear.

So predicting with any accuracy how much of the $82 billion of bailout money will ultimately be recovered is a difficult exercise. If the return of the government money were managed as it would be in the private sector, I believe the government would have a very good chance of getting back all of its money, including the early bridge financing. But with the White House justifiably eager to be out of the auto business, premature exits may occur. If we ultimately lose $10 billion or $20 billion on the auto rescues, that seems a small price to pay for averting a major economic calamity in the industrial Midwest and helping keep the national economy from spiraling from deep recession into outright depression.

President Obama was well justified during the summer of 2010 to take a series of victory laps, visiting plants belonging to each of the Big Three as well as smaller facilities working toward next-generation vehicles. "We are moving in the right direction," he said on a July 30 visit to Detroit. "The trend lines are good." Indeed, in the time since GM and Chrysler completed their restructurings, the auto industry added 76,000 jobs, a remarkable turnaround from the 460,000 that had been lost in the year before their bankruptcies. Summer shutdowns were canceled for some plants and shifts were added at others. I thought of the faces of the rank-and-file workers whom we saw on our trip to Detroit, and felt proud of the improved job prospects that we had provided them.

I could not help but be struck by the change in mood from the dark winter days of 2009 when I despaired over the seemingly impossible task before us. Respected publications like the *Economist* heralded the outcome. "Rising from the Ashes in Detroit," was the headline of one story in August 2010. The subheading read, "General Motors' return to the stock market heralds a remarkable turnaround for America's carmakers." If anyone had predicted at the start of our work that by the summer of 2010 the auto bailout would be one of the clearest successes of tough presidential decisionmaking, they would have been derided.

Even so, the auto rescue effort continued to take flak. Senator John McCain, for example, said in November 2009: "I don't think we ever should have bailed out Chrysler and General Motors. We should have let them go into bankruptcy, emerge, and become viable corporations again."

This is the kind of posturing that makes me reluctant to want to return to Washington. McCain, a bright and experienced man, had to have understood the enormity of the crisis the automakers faced at that dangerous juncture in our history. But he turned the debate political with a sound bite that served not to educate anyone but only to encourage narrow-minded listeners in the kind of misunderstanding that will ultimately do no one any good. Had he learned nothing from the debates of spring 2009 about bankruptcy or the state of the financing markets? We were lucky to have been given the opportunity to find the right course of action for Detroit and then follow it.

More aggravating than McCain's wild ruminations was the second-guessing from people who should have known better. For example, in July 2010, the special inspector general for TARP released a report arguing that Team Auto had erred in pushing GM and Chrysler to accelerate the pace of dealer closings. Dealers again!

The report was ludicrous. Every responsible auto industry expert agreed that the dealer networks needed to be shrunk, the quicker the better. Not only did we never get involved with which dealers to close, but also we never dictated the *number* of dealers to shutter. What we did do was try to inject a note of urgency and intellectual rigor into the companies' analysis, particularly that of GM.

While I remain proud of how many decisions we got right, especially in light of the need for instantaneous action, I do have a few second thoughts (what on Wall Street we call buyer's remorse). I wonder in particular whether we achieved enough of the shared sacrifice that President Obama called for from the auto industry stakeholders. More sacrifice, of course, would have benefited the government, yielding greater confidence in recovering all of its $82 billion, perhaps even a well-deserved profit.

For all the Chrysler lenders' theatrics about the boot of government on their throats, the $2 billion that we ended up paying for their $6.9 billion claim was probably double what they would have extracted from a liquidation. Similarly, I wish we had avoided the crazy math that led us to give 10 percent of the new GM (plus warrants) to the old GM bondholders. They now stand to recover 35 cents on the dollar from claims that should have been worthless.

And I brooded about the UAW, struggling with the good questions posed by Chuck Lane of the *Washington Post* at our editorial board meeting there: Why didn't we ask active UAW workers at GM and Chrysler to take a pay cut? Why didn't we modify both companies' overly generous pension plans?

Several reasons, I ultimately concluded. First, we had met the specific test of the Bush loan agreements, that total compensation to UAW workers be competitive with the transplants, even though we had allowed the UAW to maintain its policy of protecting the existing workers at a huge cost to the $14-an-hour new hires. Second, as in every negotiation, we could succeed only if the parties met somewhere in the middle. If we'd pushed too hard—for example, by taking on the much-needed reform of both companies' pension plans—the UAW might well have walked off the job. Third, we were pressed for time. And fourth, while having the power and the money of the government behind us was an enormous advantage, it also probably led to a somewhat kinder outcome than a purely private restructuring would have done. Restructurings in the take-no-prisoners world of Wall Street are bloody fights over the wreckage of insolvent companies; taking it all the way with GM and Chrysler could have involved trying to break the UAW and crushing the creditors into the minimal recoveries that they deserved—steps that we believed unimaginable for the Obama administration.

I spent many hours revisiting our toughest decision, to save Chrysler. The company was moribund; under almost any other economic circumstances, I would have been among those arguing to let it go. Diana Farrell was surely right that government should not be in the business of saving losers. Austan Goolsbee was equally correct in his assessment that the long-term consequences of a Chrysler liquidation would be relatively minor. And Harry Wilson was spot-on in his calculation of how much Chrysler's demise would have boosted GM and Ford. But I believed then, and feel even more strongly now, that Chrysler has a very good chance of succeeding, particularly with Sergio Marchionne at the helm. In that context, at the critical moment, when we all felt as if we were looking down a bottomless black hole, the President surely made the right call.

The auto rescue succeeded in no small part because we did not have to deal with Congress. Before taking up my post, I didn't realize how important this would be. I went to Washington thinking I understood the strengths and weaknesses of our legislative branch. Either I'd been hopelessly naive when I'd covered Congress as a reporter or it had changed for the worse. I was stunned to realize that if the task force had not been able to operate under the aegis of TARP, we would have been subject to endless congressional posturing, deliberating, bickering, and micromanagement, in the midst of which one or more of the troubled companies under our care would have gone bankrupt. Congress yields authority only under the direst of circumstances, as the example of TARP shows.

As Rahm had presciently urged his team at the outset, "Never let a crisis go to waste." Congress had been bludgeoned into passing TARP by Hank Paulson and the Bush administration in the midst of the near panic caused by the collapse of Lehman Brothers. At Paulson's insistence, TARP granted the White House and the Treasury unprecedented discretion over the use of $700 billion, bypassing Congress's customary role in approving individual appropriations.

Almost immediately, Congress tried to walk back the cat. The Democratic leadership appointed an oversight panel, led by Elizabeth Warren, a professor at Harvard Law School, that seemed to spend most of its time second-guessing tough calls that the administration had made (including those on autos). Meanwhile, Republicans — particularly those running for reelection — stepped up their attacks on it.

When Congress did try to intervene, as with auto dealer closures, the result was an enormous, pointless distraction for the two companies at a critical time. Its interference left me wondering what in the auto rescue Congress might like to micromanage next — choosing factory locations or deciding which executives and workers stayed and which had to go?

The fact was that like the auto rescues, the TARP as a whole had been a huge success at little or no cost to taxpayers. It saved our nation's financial system and, as a consequence, our economy. If, instead of being able to inject $250 billion into struggling banks on Columbus Day 2008, Hank Paulson had had to subject himself to congressional appropriations hearings, the result would have been an economic Chernobyl.

In January 2010, I spent a day at the North American International Auto Show, at Cobo Center in Detroit. Outside, it was cold and snowy, but inside, the mood was celebratory. "What a difference a year makes!" exclaimed Michigan Senator Debbie Stabenow, who had questioned my qualifications, before dignitaries assembled for lunch in a sterile third-floor meeting room. Congressman Steny Hoyer, who had wasted so much time browbeating the task force about a couple of Maryland car dealers, was there, basking in the excitement.

Afterward, I mischievously approached Hoyer, curious to see what kind of reception I would get.

"Nice to see you, Steve," he exclaimed in his best politician's voice. "You did a fabulous job on the autos, except for the dealers. You should have closed dealers the way that Ford did."

With that, he was gone, leaving me to wonder what he was talking about. Ford's dealer-closing program had closely resembled those of

GM and Chrysler in prebankruptcy — culling a relatively small number of stores, one by one, over several years. (Months later, I was gratified to see that the principal dealer about whom Hoyer had harassed us lost the arbitration to have his four Chrysler stores reopened. The arbitrator ruled: "I found little evidence that the dealer had a well thought out and sound business plan for fitting within the Chrysler business plan, which I considered as itself well thought out and sound, having been developed by experts in the field.")

I could not imagine that this sort of congressional behavior was what the founding fathers had in mind. We know from our high school history lessons that the framers of the Constitution created a powerful presidency only reluctantly, after the loosely structured government of the Articles of Confederation proved dysfunctional. In their fear of overly strong executives (such as, say, King George III), they took care to empower the legislative branch as a strong check on the President. Looking back two centuries later, some of our founding fathers' views seem quaint. James Madison envisioned the Senate as a "firm, wise, and impartial body" that would give stability to the "General Government." And the architects of the Constitution believed that serving in Congress would be more an avocation than a vocation. Congressmen would serve a couple of terms and then go on to something else. The founders would have been shocked at a Senate whose members today have an *average* tenure of thirteen years and an *average* age of sixty-three.

One day, stewing about our partisan, posturing, gridlocked Senate, I was struck by a thought about the layout of Washington. As we all know, the Capitol is built on top of a hill, a lofty perch from which the legislature is meant to look down on the White House and surrounding executive buildings. It's a sad irony to think how low the institution has actually sunk.

TARP and autos were hardly the only examples of Congress worrying more about its prerogatives than the good of the country. The same dysfunction was evident in the battle to pass financial regulatory reform. After the meltdown of 2008, who could doubt the need for an overhaul of our regulatory apparatus? And yet, after nearly coming up empty, what we got was disappointing.

Virtually nothing was done to bring order to the hodgepodge of regulators that oversaw banks and other financial institutions. What might have been logical seventy-five years ago, when much of the current regulatory apparatus was put in place, made little or no sense in the twenty-first century. But Congress blocked the way. For example, the Securities and Exchange Commission and the Commodities Futures Trading Commission had jurisdiction over increasingly overlapping trading activities, particularly of derivatives. The sensible thing would have been to merge the two agencies. However, the SEC was supervised by the banking committees and the CFTC by the agriculture committees. Neither set of committees was prepared to give up its authority, so the agencies remain separate.

In the short tenure of the Obama administration, I was interested to see the public's opinion of Congress catch up to my own. When I joined the administration, Congress had an approval rating of 31 percent. By July 2010, its approval rating had dropped to 11 percent, the lowest since the 1970s and well below ratings for banks and "big business." A stunning 32 percent of Americans rated the current Congress as one of the worst ever.

Either Congress needs to get its act together or we should explore alternatives. When I lived in London, I was impressed by the parliamentary system. Britain's prime minister stays in office only as long as Parliament approves his or her proposals. Since the members of the majority party of the House of Commons understand that rejecting an important piece of legislation will force a national election, they think seriously before voting against their leader. Thus, in 2010, when the new government of David Cameron proposed tough austerity measures to deal with gaping budget deficits, many were enacted almost immediately.

If our country wants government to do a better job of solving its problems, it needs to find a way to let talented government officials operate more like they would be able to in the private sector. Deese was struck by how often people in the White House or at Treasury talked about Team Auto in wistful tones, wondering how we were able to cut through the government bureaucracy, make decisions, and move forward so effectively. Had our model been used to address other problems — anything from small business to housing to allocating stimulus dollars — the outcomes would surely have been better for the nation.

I had seen this vividly demonstrated in New York City in recent years. New York has a city council, but the city's charter also provides the mayor with strong executive powers, much like what my Washington colleagues longed for. With someone like Mike Bloomberg as mayor, the result is government at its best — efficient, disciplined, and effective. Had Bloomberg fallen short, the voters could have ejected him, as they have done with subpar mayors in the past. In contrast, New York's state government, based in Albany, is saddled with a very powerful legislature that is even more dysfunctional than the U.S. Senate. In the summer of 2010, it was mired in stalemate over the state's massive fiscal crisis and about to face its fourth governor in four years.

Of course, as someone who came of age during the Nixon era, I understand why the public mood shifted toward more checks on executive power, not just by Congress but through watchdog innovations like inspectors general, such as the one who issued the silly report about dealer closings. Actions like the serious overreach by the Bush administration on national security matters present legitimate concerns. However, if we don't find a way to make our government more effective, we will be much the worse for it as a country. In February 2010, a CNN/Opinion Research Corp. poll found that 86 percent of Americans felt that government is broken, up 8 percentage points from 2006.

My sojourn in autoland gave me an uncomfortably clear vantage from which to observe the negative consequences of globalization for U.S. manufacturing. I knew the broad outlines from the business press: our manufacturing base was being threatened by increasingly high-quality output from countries with much lower wages. China was, of course, a prime rival, but so were lots of other countries in Asia as well as in eastern Europe. Not surprisingly, the potential solutions are less clear. To oversimplify, the left believes the remedy lies in limiting free trade; the right puts its hopes in pro-business, anti-union policies.

As a product of Brown University's classical economics department, I was a signed-up, paid-up free-trader. I had studied Adam Smith as well as David Ricardo's theory of comparative advantage and enthusiastically accepted the superiority of open markets. Consumers have benefited greatly from the availability of lower-cost imported goods. Those iPhones and iPads and iPods that Americans are snapping up would cost a lot more if they were being made in America instead of in China — as would the clothes, shoes, and other basic goods that make up a typical family's budget.

And yet those invisible benefits of globalization are often overshadowed by its ugly and painful costs — high unemployment and stagnant real wages for too many Americans. Based on Census Bureau data, the wages of middle-class Americans have declined by 0.2 percent a year for the past decade, after adjustment for inflation.

The challenges of manufacturing in America hit home for me on a March afternoon early in my tenure on the auto task force. We were in a routine meeting with the parts producer Delphi. Delphi looked and smelled like a quintessential American company, with its Troy, Michigan, headquarters and its management team of mostly plainspoken midwesterners. The executives had come in that day to plead their case for a supplier rescue program.

As they went through their pitch, a question suddenly popped into my head: "How many people do you employ?" I asked.

They told me they had 146,600 workers.

"How many of them are in the U.S.?" I asked, suspecting that the number was low.

The quick answer — 18,900 — exceeded my pessimistic expectations. Most of Delphi's labor force, it turned out, was in Mexico, Brazil, and China.

"There's nothing we can do for you," I announced. Delphi flunked my *Washington Post* test: How could we use taxpayer money to help a company 87 percent of whose employees were outside the United States?

The bigger question posed by Delphi hasn't gone away. Here was a red-blooded American company with roots going back a hundred years that had, for all practical purposes, become no more American than all the manufacturers that had sprung up throughout Asia in recent decades.

While I have always been an ardent supporter of NAFTA, a casual conversation one day with Fritz Henderson after he became GM's CEO gave me pause. The company had three assembly plants in Mexico, at which it paid its workers a little over $7 per hour.

"How is the productivity in Mexico?" I asked Fritz.

"At least as good as in the U.S., maybe better," he replied. With American workers receiving $55 per hour, even after the changes to the UAW contract, it's not hard to see that downward pressure on wages could continue, notwithstanding the greater costs of importing the products. (In China GM pays workers about $4.50 per hour, and in India a bit more than $1 per hour. In both countries, as well as in Mexico, GM is considered a high-paying employer.)

Of course, history sides with free trade. Countries, states, and regions had all seen it help their economies successfully evolve. When I lived in Britain thirty years ago, coal and steel were major industries. Today they are essentially gone, and yet Britain is far more prosperous now than it was then.

This process of "creative destruction," famously articulated by Joseph Schumpeter, has also been, in fact, the engine of economic development for the older parts of the Northeast, where I've lived nearly all my life. Take Long Island City, a section of Queens just across the East River from Manhattan. Well into the twentieth century, the area was a center of American manufacturing, home to industrial businesses that made chewing gum, pianos, batteries, glass, chemicals, and many other products. There were even oil refineries and a Packard auto assembly plant.

I had a personal connection to this forgotten bit of history: my family's paint business there was one of a dozen similar ones within a short distance of each other. Today every one of those companies is gone, and yet, after a somnolent period, Long Island City is vibrant with new housing, restaurants, and service businesses, including the world headquarters of the discount airline JetBlue.

Manhattan itself has been through an equally dramatic evolution. When I was a boy, from my father's factory I could see across the river the gleaming United Nations buildings in Manhattan, built on the site of cattle yards and slaughterhouses. Those enterprises, and the jobs that went with them, moved west long ago. Farther up the East Side, a large structure housing several big-box retailers such as Target and Costco recently opened for business on the site of Washburn Wire, the last true industrial business in all of Manhattan.

Trumpeting creative destruction is easy until your own business or community gets in the way of it. The evolutionary process that worked so well for New York City has to date been a formula for extinction for Detroit and Buffalo and many other hard-hit cities. But as Diana Farrell said in the context of rescuing Chrysler, we need to be careful about how many "old jobs" we try to preserve if global competitive dynamics have overtaken them. Or as Larry Summers put it in one of his colorful metaphors, "It's like a hotel that tries to raise its occupancy by not letting people check out."

We also must be mindful that the declining employment rate in manufacturing is, perversely, due in part to success in becoming more efficient. As in farming, productivity has been growing faster in manufacturing than in service businesses, and is likely to continue to do so, meaning that, in any scenario, manufacturing will continue to shrink as a percentage of the U.S. employment pie.

We need to be hardheaded about what kinds of new jobs can be successfully nurtured. An advanced industrial economy competes best in jobs that involve high levels of skill and intellectual content, like technology and financial services. We simply cannot win with prosaic, commoditylike products that require large numbers of low-skilled workers. As tough as recent decades have been for Detroit's Big Three, the car industry is better positioned to compete than many other U.S. manufacturing businesses because labor is a relatively small part of the cost of building a car — only about 7 or 8 percent.

Our current economic problems — and the massive doses of government stimulus spending in response to them — have brought back occasional mentions of an almost forgotten phrase, industrial policy. When the American economy was floundering in the late 1970s, Japanese-style intervention in the industrial sector was all the rage. Advocates mistakenly assumed that experts and policymakers had the sagacity to spot winners and losers among businesses and to allocate government support accordingly.

We've veered dangerously close to that discredited approach again. In our well-intentioned effort to jump-start the economy, tens of billions of dollars in stimulus funds have been disbursed without anything like the rigor that private equity or venture capital investors apply. When the dust settles, we will be disappointed by how little lasting benefit we get for those dollars.

Energy technology has been a particular beneficiary of federal largess. In summer 2010, eager to claim credit for ending America's recession and to bolster his flagging standings in public opinion polls, President Obama visited projects around the country that owed their existence to dollars from D.C.

Advanced car-related facilities, like battery plants, were high on his list. But mixed in with the evidence of progress were telltale signs of waste. While there's a healthy debate about the future prospects of the industry, the *Wall Street Journal* quoted one expert, Menahem Anderman of Total Battery Consulting, as estimating that the capacity to produce batteries for electric cars just from stimulus-funded U.S. plants will be three times greater than global demand by 2014.

On a trip to Michigan in July 2010, the President roughly duplicated the trip Team Auto had made back in March 2009. He visited a traditional Chrysler assembly plant, and he drove GM's Volt—about ten feet. While the Secret Service dictated the short distance, it nonetheless symbolized for me the limitations of the Volt. There is no scenario under which the Volt, estimable as it may be, will make any material contribution to GM's fortunes for many years. "Green" jobs may be the fad of the moment, but in supporting them we need to forgo irrational exuberance.

When we succeed in making a manufacturing enterprise competitive again, as I believe we've done with the Detroit auto companies, we have to be vigilant about not allowing that accomplishment to be diminished. It was dispiriting to watch what happened at Ford in November 2009. The company had asked the UAW to adjust its contracts to match the improvements won by GM and Chrysler. Ron Gettelfinger and his leadership team agreed; it was only fair. But when the proposition was put to all of the Ford UAW workers, they voted it down.

A few months later, Gettelfinger's successor, Bob King, delivered his first formal address, getting a standing ovation for his call to "win back the concessions and sacrifices we made and win more than that." While I can understand why King felt a need to start from a hard-line rhetorical stance, the Detroit Three cannot possibly reinstate old wage rates or labor practices and remain competitive.

In talking with Ron Bloom as he plunged into his new assignment as the administration's "manufacturing czar," I found that, as with so many issues, Ron saw the picture clearly. Manufacturing jobs as a percentage of total jobs were inevitably going to decline; the more reasonable objective — still tough — should be to try to maintain and, ideally, to expand the absolute number of these jobs.

In Ron's mind, this means concentrating on high-productivity work, with a lot of intellectual and physical capital, meaning that labor is a relatively small part of the total cost of the item — like a car! Germany, for example, has remained a very successful exporter of manufactured goods by concentrating on high-end products like sophisticated machine tools.

Ron has searched for ways that government can help — for example, by providing tax incentives for investment. With other countries providing such incentives, particularly for the "renewable economy," Ron believes that we need to do more to be competitive. But so far, progress has been slow.

We can't blame the problems of American manufacturing entirely on the cost of labor. Management matters too. Even at a very large company, individuals can make an incalculable difference. In April 1981, not long before I arrived on Wall Street, Jack Welch became CEO of General Electric. At that time, GE and Westinghouse were archrivals. While GE's revenues of about $27 billion were substantially larger than Westinghouse's, both companies made light bulbs, appliances, turbines, and nuclear equipment and owned television stations and credit companies. The two corporations could not have been more similar if their founders had set out to accomplish that goal.

Yet, two decades later, Westinghouse was gone and GE was regularly listed among the most admired and most valuable companies. In the fourteen years before Westinghouse sold its industrial businesses, its stock rose 126 percent (mostly in the year of the divestitures) and GE's rose 931 percent. What was the difference? GE had Welch, and Westinghouse had a series of mediocre CEOs. In years of occasionally interacting with GE, I never failed to be amazed by the difference that one man made.

Disney's is a similar story. In 1984, it looked much like GM two decades later: foundering with an inadequate CEO and under attack from activist shareholders. To achieve peace, Disney brought in the Bass brothers as investors, who recruited Michael Eisner and Frank Wells to the top jobs. I had just joined Morgan Stanley, which was representing the company, and none of us would have bought Disney stock on a bet. We saw no way that it could be rejuvenated. Boy, were we wrong. Over the following ten years, Disney stock rose by nearly 30 percent per annum.

For those inclined to accept Rick Wagoner's explanation that everyone and everything was to blame for GM's problems except its CEO, consider Ford. The number two U.S. automaker faced an identical set of challenges: the same Japanese transplants, the same cost of oil, the same UAW. Indeed, by many measures Ford was in worse shape than GM in 2006, when SUV sales plunged.

But the company was lucky to have Bill Ford as chairman and CEO. As market conditions worsened and Ford's results deteriorated in 2006, he realized that he was not the man to run his company. That was extraordinary by any measure, let alone Detroit's. But Bill Ford is an unusual guy. "We're an insular company in an insular industry in an insular town," he had told an interviewer in early 2006 when the company was just beginning to show signs of financial trouble. Bill Ford's humility extended to recognizing the risks that his company faced and making the decision to pledge all its assets to borrow the $23.5 billion that arrived three months after Alan Mulally became CEO.

"I thought that I would have been absolutely the wrong person to lead a major restructuring," Ford told me as we sat at a small conference table in his Dearborn office on a warm May day. "I needed to do two things. One was to go out and find that person, and the other was to raise the money so that he would be able to restructure the place."

As a result, Ford not only weathered the crisis without bankruptcy, but as the market began to turn in early 2010, the company became solidly profitable. In fact, in the second quarter, Ford reported net income of $2.6 billion, while GM — notwithstanding its larger size and the bankruptcy scrubbing of $65 billion of liabilities — earned $1.3 billion. Clearly, GM's new CEO and his team had some catching up to do.

A key component of management failures like GM's is almost always the board of directors, historically the weakest link in American corporate governance. Ironically, GM was once considered an exemplar of board practices. In the early 1990s, after one of the company's periodic near-death experiences, the board fired the CEO, appointed a nonexecutive chairman, and developed twenty-eight structural guidelines for ensuring board independence. *BusinessWeek* hailed the plan as a "Magna Carta for directors." But the board's assertiveness and vigilance soon lapsed. In 2003, it made Rick Wagoner chairman as well as CEO, a fateful step backward.

Wagoner proved more adept at manipulating the board than at running the company. In early 2006, after many quarters of disastrous earnings, board members began to grumble about Rick. Though he enjoyed the staunch support of his lead outside director, George Fisher, the dissidents took advantage of a meeting that Fisher missed and agreed to hold an executive session in which to discuss the CEO.

Wagoner got wind of this before it happened, and used an earlier, Sunday afternoon session to head it off. On that call, he issued an ultimatum. Either the board must put out a statement of support for him or he would resign immediately. Every director except Phil Laskawy, a former chairman and CEO of the accounting firm Ernst & Young, instantly fell into line. The next day, GM issued a statement by Fisher: "While there is still much work to be done, the GM board has great confidence in Rick Wagoner, his management team and the plan they are implementing to restore the company to profitability." For all the grief that President Obama has taken for how Rick came to step aside — which I sincerely regret — I have no doubt that without a new CEO, GM would be in a far worse place than it is today.

In contrast with GM's boardroom laxity, Mulally insisted when he was hired that Bill Ford remain as executive chairman. Mulally fully expects Ford and the board to judge his performance independently and to fire him if he doesn't produce results. As I left Ford headquarters after spending a couple of hours with Bill Ford and Alan Mulally, I could not help but compare my impressions from this first visit to Dearborn with my first meeting with Rick Wagoner and Ray Young. Management matters.

• • •

We came to Team Auto as strangers and we left as friends. We were fourteen men and women who had shared an experience that would be indelibly seared in our memories. For Deese, Team Auto was reminiscent of the movie *Ocean's Eleven:* a team of professionals who come together to do a job, execute it seamlessly, and then just as quickly go their separate ways. While we would also go our separate ways, we would always be connected by our time together and the knowledge that we had made a significant contribution to President Obama's determined struggle to lift the economy out of recession. While I had tried to show (like the night at Rosa Mexicano) how grateful I was to my colleagues for their extraordinary effort and dedication, I decided on one final, tangible symbol of thanks. On Wall Street, when a large transaction is consummated, it is traditional to give "deal toys" to those who worked on them. With the help of a firm in New York that specialized in such commemorations, I designed a trophy: a wooden plaque with a Plexiglas windshield and brushed aluminum steering wheel mounted on it. On the steering wheel were the words "Team Auto 2009." Each person's name was etched on a small metal plaque at the bottom. And on the Plexiglas windshield, I had had the following words inscribed:

> RARELY HAVE SUCH DEDICATED PROFESSIONALS HAD
> THE OPPORTUNITY TO RENDER INVALUABLE SERVICE
> TO THEIR COUNTRY AT A TIME OF CRISIS.

Some of our team members had come to Washington intending to put in several years of government service. In addition to overseeing the government's investment in the auto companies, Ron bravely took on the tough new assignment of trying to help American manufacturing — and Haley Stevens stayed on to help him. Diana Farrell continued as part of Larry's National Economic Council and played a key role in the passage of financial regulatory reform. Brian Deese also remained at his little desk outside Larry's office, pitching in on one economic policy challenge after another.

After considering a variety of options, Harry Wilson decided to run for the office of New York State comptroller, where he would help to salvage the state's disastrous finances. Although he ran as a Republican, I could think of no one who would be a better addition to our state's leadership than Harry. Matt Feldman elected to return to Willkie Farr & Gallagher as a senior partner, with a role in the firm's leadership.

Brian Stern went back to Wall Street and financial services investing by joining Blackrock. His capable helper, Rob Fraser, resumed his position at his private equity firm and then matriculated at Harvard

Business School. David Markowitz moved to Cleveland and founded a hedge fund, and Brian Osias decided to saddle up with him. Sadiq Malik planned to join them too, but happily for me agreed first to spend six months helping with this book. My former Quadrangle colleagues Paul Nathanson and Clay Calhoon also continued the upward march of their careers. After a short stint in the Treasury general counsel's office, Paul joined the U.S. attorney's office in the eastern district of Virginia, while Clay began at Stanford Business School.

As for me, after taking time to recover from an operation to repair a detached retina, I turned my attention to this book and to working through the Quadrangle legal mess. During my thirty-five years in the working world, I had never been accused of so much as jaywalking, so it was painful for me and my family to have my honesty and integrity impugned, often by innuendo.

For example, back in April, one thoroughly irresponsible reporter, William Cohan (who had flunked out of investment banking), had written that one of my Quadrangle-related holdings presented a conflict with my auto responsibilities. He had been fed this misinformation by a disgruntled former colleague of mine, and nothing would dissuade him from publishing the allegations, including Jenni Engebretsen's unequivocal statement that I had fully complied with Treasury's rules.

I understood that having held a position of public trust, I was fair game. But just as I found journalists' treatment of my financial disclosure form disproportionate to its relevance, so too did I find the media's treatment of the investigation sensationalistic. As of August 2010, my onetime employer, the *New York Times,* had put my travails on the front page five times (and not once for anything related to Team Auto).

All told, I found that serving in government was a tougher and more thankless role than I imagined, even after years of having my nose pressed to the glass. Certainly the actions of anyone who serves as a government official can and should be examined. But as I've tried to convey, the pettiness and misplaced priorities of some of the scrutiny is debilitating to those who serve, whether it's the incessant barrage of self-serving or ignorant requests from Capitol Hill or the newspaper stories that inevitably accentuate the negative and minimize the positive. Not to mention, of course, the blogosphere, which has put irresponsible "journalism" through an enlarger. It's tough stuff even for battle-hardened veterans to deal with; I can't imagine how Tim and Larry have endured so many years under such a distorted lens.

Yet for someone like myself who believes in public service, an assignment like Team Auto can be a dream come true — the chance to make a meaningful difference on a huge issue that requires only minimal interaction with Congress. As for the tribulations of public life, working in the world's largest bureaucracy brings an offsetting advantage — when you call saying that you are from the U.S. Treasury, it is astonishing how quickly people respond and react! For all the sacrifices that my family and I made so that I could serve, I would do it again, and without the fear and second thoughts. Unfortunately, there aren't many assignments like Team Auto. Most jobs involve trying to inch some initiative through an executive branch review and then through Congress, which can easily become a Sisyphean task. Taking on one of those would be a much tougher decision.

Three years to the day after my chance encounter with candidate Barack Obama at the Vineyard Golf Club in 2007, I saw him there again. My extraordinary friend Mike Bloomberg was on Martha's Vineyard to play golf with the President and invited me to join him beforehand to hit some balls and catch up. When the President arrived at the driving range, he greeted me with a smile so big it seemed to make his prominent ears protrude even more.

"I was just telling Mike that I was bragging about you," he said, and described a recent meeting in which he'd gotten *New York Times* columnist David Brooks to admit that his March 2009 column criticizing Obama's intervention in the auto crisis had been wrong. We exchanged laughs about how Brooks, whose pieces are generally exceptional, had been far off target in this case. After a few more pleasantries, the President stepped into position on the range and began hitting. As I struggled with my shots a few yards away, I felt that a fulfilling coda had just been attached to my government service. I had helped a man whom I greatly admire achieve an important success of his young administration.

Note on Sources

This book is primarily derived from my experiences and recollections. However, as a former journalist who always wanted to write a book but never found the subject matter or the stamina, I was intrigued by the opportunity to go beyond my memory and opinions. Among other things, I was curious to know the story of the auto crisis during the Bush period—I had no time while I was in the Obama administration to find out. I also thought this book would benefit from having the story continue through to the truly monumental event of GM's filing of its initial public offering prospectus.

The result was more than 150 interviews, mostly conducted by me but some by my able colleagues Jeffrey McCracken, Peter Petre, and Sadiq Malik. In addition to the formal interviews, there were countless — I'm sure hundreds of — shorter conversations or e-mails to try to nail down every detail. To protect the anonymity of those who wished to speak confidentially, I have chosen not to list any of my interviewees. But I was gratified that nearly every player of consequence in this drama was willing to share his or her recollections, in some cases on multiple occasions. I am deeply grateful to all who helped us; I am certain the book is better for their collective contributions.

Like other works of its genre, this account includes direct, contemporaneous quotations from participants in the many meetings and conversations. While some of these come from my memory, I have attempted to verify all quotations with as many participants as possible. (The handful of descriptions of other people's thoughts are based on later interviews with those people.) Having said that, I've now learned from direct experience that no book of this sort can honestly warrant that every quotation is precisely accurate in every detail.

Finally, Sadiq — a worker of Harry Wilson intensity and stamina — attempted to verify every single fact in these pages. If any errors remain, the fault is mine alone.

Acknowledgments

First and foremost, I want to extend my deepest appreciation to the dedicated members of Team Auto, whose names are listed in the front of the book. They deserve the thanks of the entire nation for their selfless dedication to a seemingly impossible task. Working with such a talented and collegial group of extraordinary individuals has been the high point of my career.

Second, I am grateful to my bosses, Tim Geithner and Larry Summers, for having the confidence in me to ask me to take on this important role. Throughout our many months of work, they were available, supportive, and decisive. They are public servants of the highest order and integrity.

During my time in Washington, I was fortunate to interact with many other government employees. Contrary to what some Americans may think, the Treasury is blessed with a large array of talented and dedicated staff members, both those who came as part of the Obama administration and those who have made it their careers to serve their country. In particular, I would like to thank Mark Patterson, Lee Sachs, Matt Kabaker, Michael Tae, Duane Morse, Mara McNeill, Lindsay Simmons, Alan Krueger, Stephanie Cutter, Jenni Engebretsen LeCompte, Meg Reilly, Jake Siewert, Herb Allison, Jim Lambright, Bernie Knight, Shira Minton, Ken Feinberg, and Gene Sperling.

Throughout this tumultuous period of my life, I was fortified by the friendship and support of many. I pay particular tribute to Mayor Michael R. Bloomberg, who truly knows the meaning of loyalty and standing up for people you believe in. But there are many others to whom I am equally grateful:

Ali Wambold, Margaret Carlson, Henry Hubschman, Michi Kakutani, Richard Cohen, David Westin, Louise Grunwald, Diana Taylor, Richard Holbrooke, Kim Fennebresque, Marc Nathanson, Ron Rappaport, Barry Diller, Paul Goldberger, Vernon Jordan, Tom Lee, Jes Staley, Amos Hostetter, Michael Kramer, Orin Kramer, Leon Black, Chuck Schumer, Josh Gotbaum, David Rubenstein, Harvey Weinstein, Warren Spector, Patti Harris, Glenn

Dubin, John White, Judy Miller, Richard Haass, Jerry Speyer, Alice Ruth, Tim White, Mort Zuckerman, John Hess, Susan Rattner, Steve Shepard, Jeff Greenberg, David Bonderman, Eliot Spitzer, Paula Kerger, Tina Brown, Arthur Segel, Mitch Driesman, Ken Jacobs, Bob Rubin, Mickey Drexler, Bill Clinton, Henry Kravis, Charlie Rose, Dick DeScherer, Matt Mallow, Jamie Dimon, Bob Pittman, Susan McCaw, Charles Kaiser, Brian Roberts, Meryl Tisch, Jeff Nordhaus, David Stockman, David Ignatius, Mark Gallogly, Barbara Walters, Adam Miller, Walter Shapiro, Dan Lewis, Richard Plepler, Gordon Holmes, Roger Altman, Dan Rosensweig, Jim Tisch, Chris White, Joel Klein, Dick Fuld, Bill and Pat White, Sherrie Westin, Mark White, Norm Pearlstine, Tom White, Arthur Sulzberger Jr., Steve Weisman, Lynn Povich, Craig McCaw, Mort Janklow, Blair Effron, Nicole Seligman, Fred Wilpon, Skip Gates, Walter Isaacson, Ken Auletta, Francesca Stanfill, Greg Feldman, and Andrew Ross Sorkin.

At Houghton Mifflin Harcourt, I was the fortunate beneficiary of superb editing by George Hodgman, whose enthusiasm, dedication, and gentle lash kept me going when I flagged. I also appreciate the great attention and professionalism that I received from Gary Gentel, Bruce Nichols, Andrea Schulz, Laurie Brown, Bridget Marmion, Lori Glazer, Taryn Roeder, Becky Saikia-Wilson, Larry Cooper, Michaela Sullivan, and Melissa Lotfy.

My agent, Amanda "Binky" Urban, has been a close friend for more than twenty years, and I now understand why she has been so successful in her profession.

I've enjoyed working as part of teams for the past twenty-seven years of my career, so just as we had Team Auto, we had Team Book. At the forefront was Peter Petre, a distinguished former *Fortune* editor and experienced book hand. Peter was my patient guide through this new land, offering expert editing, great instruction in developing the narrative, and the all-important positive reinforcement. Sadiq Malik, a devoted member of Team Auto, generously signed up for Team Book and worked countless hours helping to re-create this complex story. I am also grateful to Jeff McCracken, a crackerjack financial journalist, who took time between jobs to bring to bear his reporting, financial, and auto expertise. Last, we had a terrific supporting cast of Maris Kreizman, Catherine Talese, Julie Sloane, Cynthia Colonna, and Hajera Dehqanzada. I am amazed at how much work it takes to produce a book!

My children — Rebecca, Daniel, David, and Izzy — have suffered through a father who spent six months perpetually preoccupied and with his study door closed as he tried to wrestle this tome to the ground. I hope that from this book—as well as from watching their parents try to do good in addition to doing well—they will take to heart the importance of giving back.

Most of all, I could not have gotten through the past eighteen months without the steadfast love and support of my wife, Maureen. She is truly my best friend and partner until death us do part.

West Tisbury, Massachusetts
August 2010

Index